Conspiracy and Romance

Cambridge Studies in American Literature and Culture

Editor
Albert Gelpi, Stanford University

Advisory board
Nina Baym, University of Illinois, Champaign-Urbana
Sacvan Bercovich, Harvard University
Richard Bridgman, University of California, Berkeley
David Levin, University of Virginia
Joel Porte, Harvard University
Eric Sundquist, University of California, Berkeley
Mike Weaver, Oxford University

Conspiracy and Romance

Studies in Brockden Brown, Cooper, Hawthorne, and Melville

ROBERT S. LEVINE

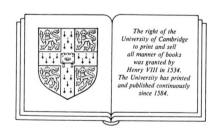

The right of the
University of Cambridge
to print and sell
all manner of books
was granted by
Henry VIII in 1534.
The University has printed
and published continuously
since 1584.

CAMBRIDGE UNIVERSITY PRESS

Cambridge
New York   New Rochelle   Melbourne   Sydney

Published by the Press Syndicate of the University of Cambridge
The Pitt Building, Trumpington Street, Cambridge CB2 1RP
32 East 57th Street, New York, NY 10022, USA
10 Stamford Road, Oakleigh, Melbourne 3166, Australia

© Cambridge University Press 1989

First published 1989

Printed in the United States of America

Library of Congress Cataloging-in-Publication Data
Levine, Robert S.
Conspiracy and romance: studies in Brockden Brown, Cooper,
Hawthorne, and Melville / Robert S. Levine.
p.   cm. – (Cambridge studies in American literature and culture)
ISBN 0-521-36654-2
1. American fiction – 19th century – History and criticism.
2. Conspiracies in literature.   3. Romanticism – United States.
4. Brown, Charles Brockden, 1771–1810. Ormond.   5. Cooper,
James Fenimore, 1789–1851. Bravo.   6. Hawthorne, Nathaniel,
1804–1864. Blithedale Romance.   7. Melville, Herman, 1819–1891.
Benito Cereno.
I. Title.   II. Series.
PS374.C594L4 1989
813'.2'09 – dc 19   88-27448
                                                                     CIP

British Library Cataloguing in Publication Data
Levine, Robert S.
Conspiracy and romance: studies in
Brockden Brown, Cooper, Hawthorne, and
Melville. – (Cambridge studies in American
literature and culture).
1. Fiction in English. American Writers.
1789–1900 – Critical studies
I. Title
813'.009

ISBN 0-521-36654-2

For my parents,
Joan and Harold Levine

Contents

Acknowledgments

From the very earliest stages of this project, George Dekker and Jay Fliegelman have offered their unflagging encouragement and support. Their scholarly and personal examples have taught me much more than how to organize and support an argument, though I will always be grateful for their attention, over too many drafts, to such mundane matters. For their generous and helpful readings of various sections of the manuscript, I am also grateful to Wyn Kelley and my colleagues Jonathan Auerbach, Maurice Bennett, John McWilliams, and Richard Vitzthum. Peter Carafiol's no-holds-barred reading of the manuscript helped me to see that the "final draft" was a penultimate draft; I am indebted to him for his brutally amicable honesty. For advice on final revisions, I am also indebted to Cambridge's two anonymous readers.

Several research grants facilitated the writing and helped to renew my energy. I wish to thank the University of Maryland for a Summer Research Award and a Special Research Assignment, and Stanford University's English Department for a Postdoctoral Teaching and Research Fellowship. A portion of Chapter 1, in somewhat different form, first appeared in *Early American Literature*. My thanks to the editor for the early forum and permission to reprint.

I am pleased to acknowledge my indebtedness to Albert Gelpi, whose editorial acumen and enthusiasm made the review process an almost enjoyable experience. For their editorial assistance at Cambridge University Press, I want also to thank Elizabeth Maguire and Mary Nevader.

My greatest debt is to my wife, Ivy Goodman, whose love sustained me through the project. She read the drafts, entertained my mutterings, and tried her best to convince me (though never subversively) that there is life beyond conspiracy.

Introduction

Eternal vigilance is the price of liberty.

Wendell Phillips, *Public Opinion*

I

In a prefatory note to *Edgar Huntly* (1799), Brockden Brown issued a manifesto on the American-ness of American literature. His novel was in every possible sense "a new performance," he proclaimed, for the new nation "opened new views" not only to "the naturalist and politician" but also to "the moral painter," who necessarily should explore "new springs of action, and new motives to curiosity." And because America offered the promise of new views, actions, and motives, it followed that the "field[s] of investigation" opened to its emerging writers "should differ essentially from those which exist in Europe." Thus, Brown insisted, the American writer needed to relinquish such unsuitable European "materials" as "Gothic castles" and to embrace instead such "suitable" American materials as "incidents of Indian hostility, and the perils of the western wilderness." This engagement with the distinctively American would lead to the production of a new and powerful literary art "calling forth the passions and engaging the sympathy of the reader, by means hitherto unemployed by preceding authors."[1]

Though Brown's reference to "the perils of the western wilderness" exuberantly directed attention to the presence of Indians, a specific social source for his fiction, it was more often the case that when nineteenth-century writers assessed the early national and antebellum scene they noted various absences.[2] According to Henry James, who declared in his study of Hawthorne (1879) that "one might enumerate the items of high civilisation, as it exists in other countries, which are absent from the

1

texture of American life, until it should become a wonder to know what was left," these absences in effect defined the provincial art of the American romance. It is an art, he believed, that in its youthful innocence was invariably "disconnected" from what he wryly called the "way things happen." As he asserted in the preface to the New York edition of *The American* (1907), romance deals with "experience liberated, so to speak; experience disengaged, disembroiled, disencumbered, exempt from the conditions that we usually know to attach to it." Concerned that *The American* betrayed his own provinciality, he retrospectively remarked that in this early work he had deliberately "cut the cable" linking "imagination" to "experience." Labeling *The American* a "romance," he sent it floating skyward like a child's wayward balloon.[3]

James's pronouncements on absence and disconnection came to inform a number of influential twentieth-century statements on American romance, most notably Richard Chase's *The American Novel and Its Tradition* (1957). But as opposed to James, Chase celebrated absence and disconnection as virtues, establishing a great tradition of American romancers who skillfully exploited the "ancient and honorable, if easily degraded, form" of melodrama. Chase explained: "In a romance, 'experience' has less to do with human beings as 'social creatures' than as individuals. Heroes, villains, victims, legendary types, confronting other individuals or confronting mysterious or otherwise dire forces – this is what we meet in romances." The unfettered romance, according to Chase and his many followers, liberated the American writer from the demands of the traditional novel – the delineation of the manners and morals of a society steeped in a historical past, metonymically represented by its castles – and accordingly served precisely the needs of writers like Brown who were exhilarated by an American newness. Freed from the novelistic imperative of addressing particularized matters of history and culture, so the argument usually goes, the American romancer could boldly explore "ultimates and absolutes" amidst archetypal settings located worlds apart from what in the English novel would be a delimiting and defining – a *conditioning* – social community.[4]

It is a guiding assumption of this study that antebellum fictional narratives are "conditioned" by the social world from which they emerged and are necessarily engaged with and informed by the discursive energies, conflicts, desires, and anxieties of that world. As Mikhail Bakhtin observes on the inherent intertextuality of novelistic discourse: "Each word tastes of the context and contexts in which it has lived its socially charged life; all words and forms are populated by intentions. Contextual overtones (generic, tendentious, individualistic) are inevitable in the word."[5] These "overtones" may be "inevitable," and yet, even though the past fifteen years or so have seen a renewal in the critical effort to rehistoricize American literature, it remains quite difficult to locate history in the American romance. Typically, America's classic romancers seem intent on denying their relation to contemporaneous systems and forces by employing rhetorical and formal strategies that preserve in their texts an aura of New World disconnectedness.[6] Additionally complicating the effort to rehistoricize American romance is the possibility that there may not even be an "American romance." William Spengemann has argued that, all nationalistic mystifications aside, American literature is best viewed in relation to the tradition of literature in English; and Nina Baym has shown that among nineteenth-century reviewers the terms "romance" and "novel" were often used interchangeably.[7] Though I readily concede that Americanists can often be parochial in their pursuit of American traditions and continuities, and though I am wary of insisting on generic distinctions between novel and romance, and will myself often use the terms interchangeably, I nevertheless believe that there are compelling reasons, literary and historical, for continuing to talk about the American-ness and the "romance" of antebellum fictional narratives.

In a recent revisionary study, Evan Carton proposes that we view American romance as "a specific and urgent kind of rhetorical performance, a self-consciously dialectical enactment of critical and philosophical concerns about the relationship of words to things and the nature of the self," that "convert[s] limitation into power, or at least into potential."[8] The urgency of the American romancer's performative art, I would add, has its sources not only in critical and philosophical concerns but in social ones as well; for it is precisely the need to convert limitation into power – and the accompanying concern about the experimental provisionality of creation – that links romance to America. Like Brockden Brown's ideal romance, America was an invention, a "new performance," a nation "differing essentially from those which exist in Europe"; and like Henry James's ideal romance, the creation of America was informed by a utopian desire to attain "the dream of an intenser experience."[9] But an inevitable concomitant of the American newness and utopian dream was an anxiety that the performance lacked power and concealed mere limitation. Viewed darkly, especially during times of social crisis, the relationship between words – "America," "Union" – and things – the vast continent, its multifarious peoples – seemed tenuous at best. Was the American self merely a fictional self lacking an absolute foundation?

From this perspective we may view George Washington's Farewell Address of 1796, a text sacred to nineteenth-century Americans, as an exemplary American romance. Impelled by a "solicitude for your welfare," Washington bestowed a blessing upon the republican citizenry that "the happiness of the people of these states, under the auspices of liberty, may be more complete." Yet the nation's newness, its fragility and vulnerability, made him fear for its future; everywhere he looked he saw perils. He thus conjured a somewhat melodramatic picture that would alert Americans to their precarious situation:

> The Unity of Government is a main Pillar in the Edifice of your real independence, the support of your tranquility at home; your peace abroad. . . . But as it is easy to foresee, that from different causes and from different quarters, much pains will be taken, many artifices employed, to weaken in your minds the conviction of this truth; as this is the point in your political fortress against which the batteries of internal and external enemies will be most constantly and actively (though often covertly and insidiously) directed, it is of infinite moment, that you should properly estimate the immense value of your national Union to your collective and individual happiness; . . . accustoming yourselves to think and speak of it as the Palladium of your political safety and prosperity.[10]

Washington's vague presentation of ubiquitous danger situated Americans in a disencumbered social field in which nameless plotters were conspiring to undermine not actual political institutions but an abstraction: the "Unity of Government." At the center of this passage, then, and at the center of the overall address, was an uneasy tension between the desire, in Carton's terms, to imagine "a supreme reality," the glories of Union and the anxiety that the Union was imaginary and metaphorical, "merely linguistic."[11] A romancer of sorts, Washington responded to this tension by offering an urgent rhetorical performance that sought to relate words to things: In a new nation wherein castles were notably absent, he created a castle out of words, a national Palladium, which, in the manner of Troy's citadel, would provide a safeguard against the covert and insidious plottings of antirepublican subversives. As a linguistic creation, as an imaginary and metaphorical safeguard, the Palladium would remain quite vulnerable. Lacking an absolute or even mere physical foundation, its existence would depend upon a consensual desire to "imagine the highest reality" and will it into being; in effect, Washington called on citizens to participate in his American romance if they wished to help him perpetuate it.

The impulse toward romance, then, was a form of countersubversion; the hopeful implication of Washington's address was that if America's "free people" put their faith in the Union's Palladium, if they converted limitation into power by imaginatively transforming an absence into a presence, they would fend off their "baneful foes." Infused with dangers, romance provided a fortification against dangers; romance indeed was dialectical.[12]

It was also, in Northrop Frye's terms, archetypal. Warning "against the baneful effects of the Spirit of Party, generally," and against "the insidious wiles of foreign influence," generally, Washington bequeathed to his readers a "wish-fulfillment dream" in which the virtuous would triumph over the "insidious."[13] At the same time, however, the address sought to provide, as Fredric Jameson argues all romances seek to provide, "a symbolic resolution to a concrete historical situation." Romance, according to Jameson, performs specific cultural work at precise historical moments: Immanent in the apparently "'pure' narrative" of dream-expressive romance, he argues, is a "deep-rooted ideology which has only too clearly the function of drawing the boundaries of a given social order and providing a powerful internal deterrent against deviancy or subversion."[14] Following Jameson, I would argue that Washington's address was at its most ideological in its insistence, during a time of factional dispute and increasing immigration, on American *sameness*. "With slight shades of difference," Washington instructed his American readers, "you have the same Religion, Manners, Habits and political Principles."[15] Central to the wishes and desires informing Washington's romance was that this sameness existed and would remain. Two years after the address, Washington's Federalist Party forcefully attempted to legislate sameness through the enactment of the Alien and Sedition Laws, "a powerful internal deterrent against deviancy or subversion" – Washington's ideal romance made actual.

My intention here is not to demonize Washington's idealistic plea for communal consensus. Rather, I want simply to call attention to the ways in which the classic formulas and tropes of "ahistorical" romance found their ways into a romance-like text that was historically situated, ideological, and interested – a text that attempted to re-create community by calling attention to conspiratorial threats against it. During the early national and antebellum period, various conspiratorial fears – of the Illuminati, the Free Masons, and the Catholic church, for example – generated countersubversive discourse that contributed to the making of the new republic's culture and its fictions. A consideration of the interactions, exchanges, and negotiations between the discourse of conspiracy and the discourse of romance – the main focus of this study – thus promises to provide a way of making visibly present some of the "absent" historical engagements and concerns of American romance. And if, as historian David Brion Davis suggests, "the imagery of countersubversion may give symbolic expression to the deepest fears and needs of a people," an investigation of this imagery in American romances also promises to provide a revised understanding of the romance's "symbolic" participation in the boundary drawing and social expedients sustaining Americans' "wish-fulfillment dream."[16]

II

The fear of conspiracy – the fear, to paraphrase the *O.E.D.*, of two or more persons uniting in common cause to carry out an unlawful or reprehensible plot against a social community and its privileged ideals – is, of course, not distinctively American. From the sixteenth through the twentieth century, tensions between social classes and fears of revolutionary disturbances to established forms of order generated conspiratorial anxieties throughout Europe, especially among elites of England, France, Germany, and Italy. More generally, it has long been the case that the fear of a deviously plotting competitor state has helped to strengthen nationalistic allegiances, particularly at moments of crisis. Although it is not so surprising, then, that America's colonists and, later, republican citizenry should have demonstrated a regular need to detect and redetect conspirators, we may nevertheless ask how "normal" or "crazy" the need and its expressions were. Richard Hofstadter argued in an influential essay that America's countersubversives from the 1790s to the 1950s shared a decidedly alarmist outlook that took expression in a "paranoid style." "The distinguishing thing about the paranoid style," he concluded, "is not that its exponents see conspiracies or plots here and there in history, but that they regard a 'vast' or 'gigantic' conspiracy as *the motive force* in historical events."[17] Now, while Hofstadter usefully directed attention to recurrences of conspiratorial thinking in American cultural debate, I believe that the post-McCarthy context of his study led him to err in presenting all of the nation's countersubversives as hysterical, resolutely mean-spirited, and, in a sense, clinically unhinged. As we shall see, conspiratorial fears during the pre- and post-Revolutionary period were expressed not only by "paranoiacs" on the fringe but also by America's most influential religious and political leaders. Their fears were grounded in relatively "sane" perceptions of reality and served a variety of sociopolitical purposes.

During the seventeenth century, conspiratorial fears helped the Pilgrim and Puritan colonists to create and define their communities. Conceiving of themselves as the New Israelites in New Canaan and convinced of the imminent fulfillment of Revelation's apocalyptic prophecies, they believed they were God's agents engaged in a terrifying struggle against satanic forces for control of the universe. The peculiar tensions informing their millennialist world view and fear of conspiracy can be discerned in the opening of William Bradford's *Of Plymouth Plantation*:

> It is well knowne unto the godly and judicious, how ever since the first breaking out of the lighte of the gospell in our Honourable Nation of England, (which was the first of nations whom the Lord adorned ther

> with, affter the grosse darknes of popery which had covered & over-
> spred the Christian worled), what warrs & opposissions ever since,
> Satan hath raised, maintained, and continued against the Saincts, from
> time to time, in one sorte or other.[18]

Central to Bradford's conception of the Pilgrims' holy task was the
struggle itself, the "warrs and opposissions" between the "Saincts" and
Satan. The afflictions confronting the Pilgrims – from the wilderness,
from the Indians, from the "popery" of the likes of Thomas Morton –
could therefore be taken as signs of Satan's antagonistic response to the
threat posed to his reign by the purifying settlers. But because they
believed, like the Puritans, that Satan's evil was subsumed under God's
divine sovereignty, their millennialism gave rise to a seeming paradox:
The worse things looked for them – the more afflictions, the more
plotters – the clearer it was that God took an interest in their affairs and
was confident of their eventual success. A typological reading of New
World history virtually demanded that there be conspirators to combat
and overcome.

The need for conspirators ineluctably bred fears. As a result, Richard
Slotkin suggests, an "atmosphere of apocalyptic crisis, the prevalent
sense that immanent horror lurked behind the façade of commonday
existence," contributed to the crueler manifestations of the New England
colonists' regenerative project.[19] From the Puritans' perspective, Indians
could be killed because they were demonic plotters; Quakers and witches
could be tried and executed because they were satanic infiltrators. As
Cotton Mather explained in *The Wonders of the Invisible World* (1692),
Salem was especially vulnerable to witchcraft because

> the *New-Englanders* are a People of God settled in those, which were
> once the *Devil's* territories; and it may easily be supposed that the *Devil*
> was exceedingly disturbed, when he perceived such a People here ac-
> complishing the Promise of old made unto our Blessed Jesus, *That He
> should have the Utmost parts of the Earth for his Possession.* . . . The Devil
> thus Irritated, immediately try'd all sorts of Methods to overturn this
> poor Plantation. . . . I believe that never were more *Satanical Devices*
> used for the Unsettling of any People under the Sun, than what have
> been Employ'd for the Extirpation of the *Vine* which God has here
> *Planted.*

Dispossessing Satan, the Puritans called down the wrath of Satan; the
existence of plotting witches testified both to Satan's desperate need to
subvert the holy People and to God's faith in His People. Mather thus
indulged in a bit of braggadoccio when he proclaimed, "I believe, there
was never a poor Plantation, more pursued by the *wrath* of the *Devil,*
than our poor *New-England.*" And yet his confident boasting masked a

deeper dread. When he announced, in apocalyptic rhetoric anticipating the alarmism of later countersubversive texts, that he feared "*an Horrible PLOT against the Country by* WITCHCRAFT . . . *which if it were not seasonably discovered, would probably Blow up, and pull down all the Churches in the Country*," he also voiced genuine concerns about the ability of "*the churches*" to withstand the secularizing pressures that were transforming the Puritans into Yankees. A display of the Puritans' power and a confession of their anxiety, the witchcraft crisis served to redefine boundaries between the holy and the unholy, thereby reviving, however temporarily, the Puritans' commitment to their redemptive "Citty upon a Hill."[20]

The Puritans' civil millennialism would continue to inform religious and political rhetoric of the eighteenth and nineteenth centuries: The image of America as the promised Kingdom of God undergirded consensual idealizations of the nation's redemptive mission and, relatedly, consensual fears of the conspiratorial threats posed by "satanic" subversives to the fulfillment of that mission.[21] Yet by the eighteenth century the scientific bases of Enlightenment rationalism came to diminish the prominence given to typological conceptions of conspiracy. Under the impact of Isaac Newton's *Philosophiae naturalis principia mathematica* (1687), there arose throughout the West a widely shared belief that social, economic, and political phenomena could best be explained, not providentially, but through the mechanistic paradigm of cause and effect. Contributing to this reorientation were two revolutionary developments of the fifteenth and sixteenth centuries: the invention of modern printing, which figured significantly in the Protestant reformers' "countersubversive" demystification of the Roman Catholic church, and the emergence of the "placeless" market, which brought with it new concerns about the possible duplicity and misrepresentation attending the exchange of commodities for currency. In large part, then, human plots came to replace divine plots, contributing to the rise of the novel, the popularity of satire and masquerade, and a renewed interest in the "science" of politics. Human affairs, according to the most respected political theorists of the day, represented the visible effects of concealed human designs; necessarily, such a belief fueled desires to detect human conspiratorial designs.[22] During the 1750s and early 1760s, then, the French and Indian War, which was generally perceived by the colonists as a millennial struggle against a satanic plot, was also regarded as a bloody struggle against a French imperialistic plot. The fear of conspiring (and demonic) European imperialists would continue to alarm and mobilize Americans long after the Peace of 1763.[23]

As Bernard Bailyn has shown, the belief that a conspiratorial plot lay behind England's imperial relations with the colonies pervaded the colonists' political writings of the 1760s and 1770s. The ideological sources of this conspiratorial mode of explanation lay in the Puritans' lingering and still highly influential civil millennialism and in the Enlightenment interest in discovering the natural cause behind the effect. More specifically, it had its principal sources in the radical "Country Party" Whiggism of eighteenth-century England, an outgrowth of the civic humanism of Renaissance Florence as adapted in England by the Commonwealth republicans. The "Country" republican mistrust of centralized "Courtly" power informed the Whigs' attacks on George III and his putatively self-interested and plotting ministerial counselors. When the colonists adopted this interpretive framework during the 1760s, such measures as the Stamp Act and the Townshend Duties provided "evidence of nothing less than a deliberate assault launched surreptitiously by plotters against liberty both in England and in America." Convinced of the need to defend their liberty and virtue against "a design to reduce them under absolute despotism," the colonists could justify taking up arms against a hopelessly corrupt and enslaving England, a conspiratorial other.[24]

Detecting a conspiracy against their political liberty, the patriots heroically created a new nation; intent on asserting their own commitment to liberty and virtue, subsequent generations aligned themselves with the Revolutionary generation through ritual reenactments of the nation-creating battle against conspirators.[25] During the period from 1780 to 1815, however, the persistence of conspiratorial fears probably had more to do with concerns about America's fragile newness than with any psychological compulsion to reenact the Revolution. While a Whiggish mistrust of centralized power had contributed to the political configuration established by the Articles of Confederation, for many Americans Shays's Rebellion of 1786 signaled the grave dangers posed to republican liberty by anarchic mobs and ineffective state legislatures. Even after the creation of a new federal republic, America's political leaders anticipated several more decades of instability. As Jefferson cautioned in a 1790 letter to Lafayette, "We are not to expect to be translated from despotism to liberty in a feather bed." Though Americans confronted and survived a series of crises during the period from 1790 to 1815, uncertainty about the nation's perpetuity, which was exacerbated by sectional tensions, increasing immigration, and other social, political, and economic pressures, persisted at least to the end of the Civil War.[26]

As a result of such nagging uncertainty, there remained a powerful need to confirm and reconfirm the national identity; like the Puritans, the citizenry of the new nation needed to conceive of itself in opposition to threatening and villainous communities. Kai Erikson writes, "One of the surest ways to confirm an identity, for communities as well as for individuals, is to find some way of measuring what one is *not*."[27] To the vast majority of the new republic's first several generations it remained clear, as it was clear to the colonists, that Americans were *not* a Roman Catholic, "savage," satanic, aristocratic, or despotic people. And it also remained clear that Americans really were threatened by numerous conspiratorial enemies. As historian Robert Wiebe observes, widely shared concerns "about hidden corruptions and conspiratorial intentions affected enough people of diverse temperaments and persuasions to qualify as cultural norms. . . . No decade stood apart from another in either the range or the intensity of these conspiratorial alarms, and almost no legislation or election of any consequence escaped their influence."[28] Detecting and opposing conspirators helped Americans to create, define, modify, and sustain their new "republic."

Republican ideology and discourse, in fact, played a crucial role in perpetuating the fear of conspiracy in early national and antebellum culture. Though varying in precise meaning and function among different social groups, and no longer strictly classical, republicanism nevertheless offered many Americans a system of beliefs, a conceptual paradigm, for defining their ideal community and identifying conspiratorial threats to it.[29] At this point it would be useful to abstract several of the key lessons that republicanism, so central to the Revolution and the Constitution, continued to teach Americans about conspiracy.

The first lesson republican ideology taught was that the fate of a republic was uncertain, for traditionally republics were short-lived, subject to cyclical decline, and vulnerable to the plottings of internal and external enemies. It was feared that the new American republic would be especially vulnerable because its large geographical territory and "republican" mistrust of standing armies made foreign infiltration all too tempting and easy. Montesquieu in *The Spirit of the Laws* (1748) had argued that a republic could not long survive in a large territory because the overextension would dissipate national loyalties. Whereas Madison dissented from Montesquieu on this matter, arguing that the geographical immensity of the new nation would ensure a healthy competition among factional interests, Hamilton warned in *Federalist* no. 22, "One of the weak sides of republics, among their numerous advantages, is that they afford too easy an inlet to foreign corruption."[30] "Corruption" is the significant word here, for it was generally believed – and this brings us to a second lesson taught by republican ideology and a lesson both Hamilton and Madison agreed was a principal one – that whether geographically large or small, possessive of a standing army or not, republics held together only if their citizenry could resist the fall into luxury and self-interest. Republican ideology taught, then, that there was an acute need for, and indeed a symbiotic relationship between, private and public virtue. To be sure, by the early nineteenth century John Locke's and

Adam Smith's instrumentalist theories of laissez faire individualism came to dominate economic thinking and practice. But that does not mean Americans relinquished republican ideology; if anything, the pressures of marketplace competition spawned a host of anxieties that were calmed, not only by appeals to Smith's "invisible hand," but also by appeals to republican virtue. Ideally, virtuous republicans were civic-minded and honest – they disdained secrecy – though as a result, such was the darker implication of this republican desideratum, the citizenry would always be vulnerable to scheming aristocrats from above, riotous malcontents from below, and plotting confidence men from every direction.[31]

Thus a third lesson taught by republican ideology, and one that followed from the dangers adumbrated in the first two, was the paramount importance of maintaining a jealous awareness of threats to the republic's virtuous civic order. In short, republicanism taught of the ubiquity of corruption and conspiracy, and therefore demanded of its citizenry, in the words of Wendell Phillips, an "Eternal vigilance." Indeed, the imperative to maintain an "Eternal vigilance" or, as Washington counseled in his Farewell Address, a "jealous anxiety" generated what James H. Huston terms a "jealous strain in American politics," a distinctively American expression of national anxiety that persisted well into the nineteenth century. "Putting the imprimatur of republicanism upon it," Huston explains, "jealousy consummated its legitimization in America and decisively differentiated it from its status in Britain, where it remained an equivocal element and gradually lost its political significance."[32] In their dutiful commitment to preserving the health and stability of the republic, citizens needed to remain jealous of their liberty and vigilant about conspiracy. Situated within the national newness, ever on the lookout for subversion, they needed perpetually to be reading and interpreting a protean social landscape. Such was their republican romance.

III

Let us now reconsider a putatively ahistorical aspect of the putatively ahistorical American romance. Chase, we recall, argues that the romance generally "ignore[s] the spectacle of man in society," concerning itself instead with "the marvelous, the sensational, the legendary, and . . . the heightened effect." And he suggests that America's classic romancers found melodrama to be especially congenial to their explorations of moral and psychological absolutes. With its archetypal characters and extreme stylizations, melodrama allows for, and indeed encourages, a veering toward abstraction, and thus, he concludes, it is the mode most "suitable to writers who do not have a firm sense of living in a culture." Surely Chase is right about the centrality of melodrama to romance, and his seminal study, the frequent target of revisionary historicists, must be acknowledged as a necessary defense of the American melodramatic imagination. What Chase failed to see, however, is that melodrama was the mode most suitable to American writers – particularly romancers and countersubversives – who had a *firm* sense of living in a culture that was unsettled and unsettling. Conspiratorial discourse, an absolutely central expression of early national and antebellum culture, was a melodramatic discourse that presented oppositional conflicts between villainous plotters and virtuous Americans in the vaguely defined social space of the American republic.[33] As we noted with Washington's Farewell Address, the discourse of conspiracy was itself a version of "American romance." And it was a discourse regularly appropriated by America's romancers to portray the individual in society as spectacle.

A rhetoric of extremity, conspiratorial discourse more often than not manifests at its least flexible and most repressive a culture's dominant ideology – the network of beliefs, values, and, especially, fears and prejudices that help social groups to construct and make sense of their social identity and reality. America's greatest romancers, when appropriating conspiratorial discourse, generally placed its ideological assumptions and political program under an ironic and parodic challenge; ideology may be hegemonic but it is not necessarily imprisoning. And yet, however ironic the romancer's appropriations may seem, it is usually the case that the appropriation signaled a desire to engage shared cultural concerns, and not always from a critical distance. In a call for a "new American literary history" that takes such cultural engagement into account, Bercovitch writes:

> On some basic level, we will have to reconceive our so-called radical or subversive literary tradition as an insistent engagement with society, rather than a recurrent flight from it. In other words, we will have to re-historicize the ideal Americas projected in our major texts – those fabled frontier republics of the soul and worlds elsewhere of endless (because self-generating) ambiguity, those romance lands of moral antinomies (Old Serpent and New Adam, Innocence and Experience) – we will have to re-see these fictions historically, in dynamic relation to the culture: neither as mirrors of their time, nor as lamps of the creative imagination, but as works of *ideological* mimesis, at once implicated in the society they resist, capable of overcoming the forces that compel their complicity, and nourished by the culture they often seem to subvert.[34]

By examining the "ideal Americas" projected in romance together with the ideal Americas projected in the culture's conspiratorial discourse, and by attending to the romancer's simultaneously complicitous and subversive relationship to this discourse, I will suggest one possible way of achieving such a rehistoricization and revision of America's romance tradition.

This rehistoricizing revision, however, will have to remain a partial one, a reflection of both my distrust of totalizing interpretive models and my practical decision with respect to methodological procedure. Conspiratorial discourse, I believe, provides us less with a paradigm capable of instantly illuminating numerous romances than with a heuristic aid that presses us to pursue with some care the implications of what Bakhtin terms the "novel's special relationship with extraliterary genres, with the genres of everyday life and ideological genres."[35] Therefore, rather than try to "survey" the many early national and antebellum romances that depict conspiring villains and vulnerable Americans, I have chosen to focus on four texts that are at once highly representative and unusually powerful expressions of the melodramatic imagination. Brown's *Ormond* (1799) I will examine in relation to anti-Illuminati writings, Cooper's *The Bravo* (1831) to Antimasonic writings, Hawthorne's *The Blithedale Romance* (1852) to anti-Catholic and communitarian writings, and Melville's *Benito Cereno* (1855) to a range of writings on mutiny at sea and slave revolt on land. Each of the chapters will look closely at the relevant "extraliterary" conspiratorial discourse, will suggest ways of viewing the author's works in relation to the rhetorical form and ideological concerns of that discourse, and will offer an extended reading of the selected romance that pays especially close attention to its transactions with conspiracy.[36] At times the connections between conspiracy and romance will appear quite clear; at other times they may not, and analysis will proceed through the use of analogy and interpretive "guesswork." Clifford Geertz writes of the value of guesswork to anthropological study, "Cultural analysis is (or should be) guessings at meanings, assessing the guesses, not discovering the Continent of Meaning and mapping out its bodiless landscape."[37] In order to avoid the pitfall of similarly rendering our romancers "bodiless," it is essential that literary analysis assess their writings not only as meditations on "timeless" absolutes but also as mediated responses to their culture's discursive practices.

During a period in which much critical energy is being profitably channeled toward "reconstructing" American literature, it may appear retrogressive and exclusionary to focus on four white male authors. Yet it seems to me that accompanying the process of canon expansion and revision should be a reconsideration of the ways that we read the traditional. As one critic recently put it, "What is needed is a situating of authors, texts, genres . . . in a milieu capable of accommodating diverse, often radically disjointed, linguistic works and of generating new appreciations of what might emerge as 'American' about American writings."[38] In my effort to resituate American romance, I will examine canonical authors in relation to religious clerics, political pamphleteers, popular women novelists such as Rebecca Reed and Maria Monk, reformers, and various other cultural spokespersons. My readings will to some extent pull us back into the discursive world of the nineteenth century, for it is an underlying premise of this study that to understand the romance in its own time − to attempt to read, in effect, the new republic's romances and not our own romances − ultimately helps us to locate the romance's transhistorical artistry and thematics. That said, I concede the impossibility of achieving a full recovery of the nineteenth-century perspective − we can never really become nineteenth-century readers − and I am aware that the themes I will pursue, particularly the relationship of the discourses of romance to pre−Civil War discourses of power, reflect the post-Foucauldian perspective of a late-twentieth-century critic enmeshed in his own institutional discourses. The chapters that follow, then, should perhaps best be regarded as an attempt to entertain sometimes conflicting nineteenth- and twentieth-century perspectives on romances that speak with continued urgency on the desires, fears, risks, and abuses accompanying Americans' quest for unified community.[39]

1

"The Defencelessness of Her Condition"

Villainy and Vulnerability in Charles Brockden Brown's Ormond

We are frequently in most danger when we deem ourselves most safe, and our fortress is taken sometimes through a point, whose weakness nothing, it should seem, but the blindest stupidity, could overlook.

Brown, *Memoirs of Carwin*

Charles Brockden Brown's novels abound with mysterious villains who for a variety of reasons have fled Europe and emigrated to America. Wanderers in the shifting terrain of his fiction, they are for the most part enigmatic and fearsome, their rootlessness endowing them with an ominous conspiratorial aura. In *Wieland* (1798) two isolated families in the remote settlements of Pennsylvania are thrown into a state of alarm and confusion when the outsider Carwin begins to visit. Commenting on the native-born Carwin's conversion to Roman Catholicism while in Spain, Clara notes, "A suspicion was, sometimes, admitted, that his belief was counterfeited for some political purpose." Throughout *Ormond* (1799) those coming into contact with the mysterious European are brought to wonder about Ormond's identity, origins, and intentions, as the narrator repeatedly alludes to his veiled "political projects." A pivotal moment in *Edgar Huntly* (1799) occurs when Edgar reveals why he regards the Irish emigrant Clithero as the chief suspect in Waldegrave's murder: "The more I revolved the pensive and reserved deportment of this man, the ignorance in which we were placed respecting his former situation, his possible motives for abandoning his country . . . the stronger my suspicions became." The eponymous protagonist of *Arthur Mervyn* (1799–1800) expresses similar suspicions when he meets the fugitive Welbeck; not surprisingly, Mervyn's subsequent troubles owe a good deal to his willingness to trust a plotter whose face "was cast . . . in a foreign mold."[1]

"We are all emigrants, or the progeny of emigrants from Europe and Africa," Brown declared in a magazine article of 1800.[2] His elaborations on this proposition in his fiction hardly provide the assurances of, say, Crèvecoeur's idealized picture of America as asylum and melting pot. Rather, Brown's major romances depict America as a vulnerable new land threatened by an influx of aliens plotting, as is typical of melodramatically conceived villains, to advance their personal interests at the expense of the larger social community. To be sure, these villains are not alone in their failure to demonstrate an allegiance to the abstract claims of republican community. Several of Brown's novels portray Americans generally as self-promoting plotters seeking to take advantage of their competitors in the marketplace. Brown's villains, however, tend to be at an even greater remove from the community, far more skilled in the arts of duplicity, and acutely self-conscious about the philosophical, psychological, and political implications of their actions. In addition, his principal villains, even those born in America, seem more European than American: For the most part they are guided by a rationalism that Americans associated with the radical Enlightenment in Europe, or else are (allegedly) aligned with secretive political operatives based on the Continent. Rationalistic, artful, and un-American, Brown's villains raise dark questions indeed about the futurity of a republic wherein "emigrants" can theatrically fabricate identities as "Americans," all the while cloaking their origins, politics, and agendas. Villainy points to conspiracy.

According to many American ministers and moralists of the 1790s, an emergent villainous cadre trading on plot and duplicity was the newly popular legion of novelists and romancers, who appealed to the private imaginations and restless passions of their readers. Influenced by Hugh Blair's *Lectures on Rhetoric and Belles Lettres* (1783) and the writings of other Scottish Common Sense aestheticians, these moralists typecast writers of fiction as subversives posing a significant social threat. In this respect, it is tempting to view Brown's artfully duplicitous villains as allegorical representations of the romancer himself, and hence to conclude that in his characterizations of these men of "soaring passions and intellectual energy" Brown demonstrated an uncommon willingness to engage the provincial antifictionist biases of commonsensical Federalist America.[3] But while Brown surely was self-conscious about the duplicities inherent in his artistry, he was self-conscious as well about the duplicities inherent in conspiracy. I shall argue in this chapter not only that Brown's conception of villainy has less to do with the status of the American romancer than we usually suppose, but also that the distinctive power of his romances owes considerably to his willingness to engage the "provincial" conspiratorial fears of his time. All of Brown's major romances develop connections between social and narrative uncertainty, all express concerns about individual and social vulnerability, and all draw on themes and images of conspiracy. An examination of Brown's engagement with the Illuminati conspiratorial fear in particular will enable us to study both the uses to which he put his appropriations of countersubversive discourse and the ways this discourse helped to shape his fiction. The focus of the chapter is on the relationship of villainy to vulnerability, with the overall aim of reevaluating *Ormond,* and Brown's romances in general, from a perspective more thoroughly situated in the countersubversive mentality of post-Revolutionary America.

"The concubines of the Illuminati"

The preposterous Illuminati fear of 1798–9 arose in America during a time of heated political debate that was itself dominated by conspiratorial rhetoric. Federalists made nervous by the French Revolution and its aftermath insisted that the riotous enthusiasm greeting Genêt's audacious visit, the insurrectionary spirit of the Whiskey Rebellion, and the increasingly virulent opposition of the Jeffersonian Republicans were all secretly kindled and enflamed by Jacobin subversives. In contrast, Jeffersonian Republicans proclaimed that Federalist policies of economic centralization reflected the corruption of an oligarchical ministry deviously plotting to subvert the freedoms achieved by the American Revolution. "In sum," John R. Howe, Jr., reports, "American political life during much of the 1790s was gross and distorted, characterized by heated exaggeration and haunted by conspiratorial fantasy. Events were viewed in apocalyptic terms with the very survival of republican liberty riding in the balance."[4]

And in the late 1790s Americans had good reason to worry about their perpetuity: The outbreak of the "quasi war" with France, along with the humiliation of the XYZ affair, meant that the new republic was under attack and disdained by the most powerful military nation in Europe. Nevertheless, the XYZ incident was just what the Federalists needed to justify their Francophobia and to cast the Francophile Republicans as enemies of the nation. Thus they released key documents in April 1798, publicized the affair, and, taking advantage of their resurgent popularity, rushed the Alien and Sedition Laws through Congress. These laws, as Representative Robert Goodloe Harper declared during the debate on the Sedition Bill, were intended to stave off "a domestic – what . . . shall I call it? – a conspiracy, a faction leagued with a foreign power to effect a revolution or a subjugation of this country."[5] In their campaign to overcome domestic and foreign subversives, the Federalists received their most vociferous support from the publishing clergy, especially Congregationalist ministers, who, like the Federalists, blamed Jacobin plotting for their diminishing prestige. Disturbed by the liberalizing tendencies giving rise to Unitarianism, a number of the clergy in their sermons of 1798 and 1799 attempted to renew cohesion within church and state by pointing to a threat even more alarming than Jacobinical violence and heresy. They argued that behind the turbulence in France and on the Continent, behind even the increasing political tensions in America, lurked a chief precipitating agent, the alien and seditious Order of the Bavarian Illuminati, a conspiratorial group of Enlightenment-spawned atheists seeking world domination.[6]

The Order was in fact a secret society founded at Bavaria's University of Ingolstadt by Adam Weishaupt, a member of the Faculty of Law. Its initial purpose was to offer resistance to the influential Society of Jesus, which in 1774 opposed the naming of the liberal Weishaupt to an honorary chair and eventually succeeded in withholding his salary when he obtained the appointment. Weishaupt therefore became convinced of the need to fight the Jesuits secretly and in 1776 instituted the Order of the Illuminati, a hierarchical organization modeled on the Jesuits, with an initial membership of five. One historian describes Weishaupt at this point in his career as "a familiar hazard of academic and collegiate life: the clever, cantankerous, self-absorbed and self-deceiving bore."[7] But Weishaupt was also a committed progressive thinker, a utopianist of Enlightenment rationalism, and a shrewd politician. His small and seemingly insignificant group soon managed to align itself with Masonic societies and, with the help of the promotional skills of a key Mason, one Baron Adolf Knigge, spread its influence during the early 1780s into Germany, Austria, and Italy, attracting such intellectuals as Goethe, Herder, and perhaps the poet Wieland, eventually claiming more than two thousand members. Its self-proclaimed revolutionary goal, James Billington writes, was to lead "all humanity to a new moral perfection, freed from all established religious and political authority." Not surprisingly, the group's anticlericism and antinationalism alarmed social conservatives throughout the German-speaking world, and in 1784 Carl Theodore, Duke of Bavaria, moved to crush the group. Over the next several years documents discrediting the Illuminati were seized and published by the government, and Weishaupt and his order soon faded into obscurity.[8]

But the specter of the Illuminati remained, and with revolutionary upheaval persisting throughout Europe during the 1790s, confused political theorists found in the defunct Illuminati a first cause, a way of explaining the unexplainable. A significant early reference to Illuminati agency in the French Revolution was a footnote in Edmund Burke's

Reflections on the Revolution in France (1790). But the crucial text in Europe was Abbé de Barruel's four-volume *Mémoires pour servir à l'histoire du Jacobinism* (1797–8), "the bible of the secret society mythology and the indispensable foundation of future anti-masonic writing."[9] The first two volumes blamed the philosophes and Free Masons for inciting revolutionary insurgency; the final two volumes proposed the larger conspiratorial theory that behind even the philosophes and Free Masons stood the Order of the Bavarian Illuminati. The quickly translated opus, *Memoirs Illustrating the History of Jacobinism* (1799), had some impact in England and America, but the most influential Anglo-American text was John Robison's *Proofs of a Conspiracy* (1797), a dazzling and relatively concise polemic that set forth the same theory as Barruel while exculpating from blame the still reputable English Free Masons. An Edinburgh theologian of some distinction – in 1783 he was elected general secretary to the Royal Society of Edinburgh and in 1790 he was awarded an LL.D. by Princeton – Robison warned that the Illuminati were secretly engaged in "ROOTING OUT ALL THE RELIGIOUS ESTABLISHMENTS, AND OVERTURNING ALL THE EXISTING GOVERNMENTS OF EUROPE."[10] Having fulfilled their aims in Europe by directing the course of the destabilizing French Revolution, the conspiratorial Illuminati, according to Robison and Barruel, now set their sights on overturning government and religion in America.

When the high Federalist-Congregationalist minister Jedidiah Morse delivered his May 1798 Fast Day sermon at the New North Church in Boston, he became the first American clergyman to alert the country to the plottings of the Illuminati. Drawing on Robison's *Proofs of a Conspiracy* (and 2 Kings 19:3), Morse addressed the crisis facing the new nation: "The present may be considered as a day of *trouble*, of *reviling*, and blasphemy." Beneath the eyes of "the unsuspecting American people," he contended, "THE ILLUMINATED," the group chiefly responsible for the French Revolution, had infiltrated the vulnerable republic to foment an equally crippling political and theological chaos in America. These secretive and omnipresent conspirators, he asserted, scorned the claims of family and nation, calling "patriotism and loyalty narrow-minded prejudices." Even worse, such was their single-minded dedication to the group's subversive quest for power that they advocated a villainous expediency, holding "it proper to employ for a good purpose, the means which the wicked employ for bad purposes."[11] According to Barruel, Robison, Morse, and virtually every other commentator on the Illuminati, villainous expediency, the miserable but inevitable result of Enlightenment rationalism, was the trait that made monsters out of men. And yet monstrous and powerful as these conspirators appeared, Morse declared that if Americans offered their allegiances to the Federalist administration and the Congregationalist churches – that is to say, if they practiced a Protestant republican virtue – the Illuminati could be defeated. From Morse's millennial (and rather sentimental) perspective, an infidel community was simply no match for a saintly community.

Morse's warnings of Illuminati conspiracy were promptly disseminated by the leading ministers of the time. David Tappan relayed news of the threat in *Discourse Delivered in the Chapel of Harvard College;* Samuel McCorkle of North Carolina warned of Illuminati plotting in *Work of God for the French Revolution.* Timothy Dwight, the distinguished president of Yale College, found in Robison confirmation of all his fears concerning the Triumph of Infidelity, and in his millennial *The Duty of Americans, at the Present Crisis,* delivered on the Fourth of July, 1798, provided an especially vivid picture of Illuminati villainy. Fearing that Americans were vulnerable, as predicted in Revelation, to *"men in a professed and unusual opposition to God,"* specifically to the conspiratorial Illuminati, Dwight, like Morse, took it upon himself to enumerate those key Illuminati tenets "which strike at the root of all human happiness and virtue." Unregenerate atheists, members of the Illuminati mocked the idea of marriage and family, declared "CHASTITY and natural affection . . . to be nothing more than groundless prejudices," detested all national governments, and deemed "authority a mere usurpation." While Dwight welcomed the Illuminati's subversion of Roman Catholic authority in France, he feared that these expedient conspirators were attempting to subvert Federalist and Congregationalist authority in America by infiltrating "every place of power and trust, and . . . every literary, political and friendly society." Given the precarious situation, Dwight offered emphatic guidance. Americans should cultivate "personal piety, righteousness, and temperance"; they should beware the seductions of the Illuminati's "wretched doctrines"; and they should swear an undivided, allegiance to the national government under John Adams: "Adherence ought to be unequivocally manifested." He thus echoed many of the themes of Washington's Farewell Address, which had similarly called for a renewed commitment to the national government through a reverencing of Union and a renunciation of "all combinations and associations." Like Washington, Dwight appealed for an enforced neutrality, "an entire separation from our enemies"; and with his vivid depiction of Illuminati villainy, he virtually constrained his auditors and readers to pay more vigilant attention to those aliens within their midst whom they had previously ignored.[12]

The Farewell Address, we recall, expressed Washington's paternal concern that Americans were vulnerable to the ingress of "foreign influence and corruption." Imaging America as a frail youth in need of further maturation, he counseled the nation to "steer clear of permanent Alliances, with any portion of the foreign world," and to adopt for the time being a policy of isolationism and neutrality. Using melodramatic rhetoric to convey his sense of danger, he warned of "the insidious wiles of foreign influence" and concluded that Americans needed to beware the "arts of seduction" of those unprincipled foreign nations that appear to be courting America as an ally but are in fact plotting to make America a conquest.[13] Though Hamilton's Federalism most explicitly informed the address – Hamilton had written the crucial early draft – its alarmist imagery of seduction also reflected the "Federalism" implicit in America's popular seduction novels of the period. In Susanna Rowson's *Charlotte Temple* (1791), for example, a virtuous young American woman finds herself deceived and eventually brought to ruin by the artful seductions of villainous French and British plotters. The narrator moralizes on Charlotte's credulity: "The mind of youth eagerly catches at promised pleasure: pure and innocent by nature, it thinks not of the dangers lurking beneath those pleasures till too late to avoid them." Only on her deathbed does Charlotte realize, as Washington wanted "innocent" Americans to realize, that she should have been more skeptical of the foreigners' "arts of seduction" and more protective of her inviolate neutrality. Similar lessons on the need for vigilance and neutrality inform William Hill Brown's *The Power of Sympathy* (1789) and Hannah Foster's *The Coquette* (1797).[14]

In the melodramatic mode of Washington's Farewell Address and contemporaneous seduction novels, the apocalyptic anti-Illuminati sermons of Morse, Dwight, and other Congregationalist ministers focused on the struggle between good and evil, envisioning the victory – a victory Washington and the seduction novelists could not so confidently envision – that would always be achieved by the morally righteous. To be sure, America's clerical countersubversives shared many of the fears of European countersubversives, who warned of the dangers posed to property and class by "republican" revolutionaries. But in the Americanized versions of anti-Illuminati texts, these concerns were subordinated to an archetypal and melodramatically conceived portrayal of the Manichean confrontation between (European) villainy and (American) vulnerability. More in the spirit of Susanna Rowson than Washington, anti-Illuminati writers projected their fears about the vulnerability of the youthful American republic onto an emblematic chaste maiden surrounded by plotting seducers who would stop at nothing to corrupt her sacred virtue. Morse spoke of the Illuminati's advocation of "a promiscuous intercourse among the sexes"; Tappan warned that Illuminati conspirators were "outraging female modesty, prostrating the venerable rites of marriage"; Dwight prophesized "that we may see our wives and daughters the victims of legal prostitution, soberly dishonoured; speciously polluted; the outcasts of delicacy and virtue." Speaking for all of the Congregationalist sentimentalists, he asked rhetorically, "Shall our . . . daughters [become] the concubines of the Illuminati?"[15] Portrayed in such bold and awful (and familiar) colors, the image of the expedient conspiratorial seducer temporarily took hold: Whether Jacobin or Illuminati, the secretly plotting antirepublican villain eager to besmirch American "CHASTITY" remained part of the popular vocabulary of the late 1790s.

As historian Richard Buel notes, by mid-1798 " 'Illuminati' became a household word in America."[16] Though the special province of Congregationalist ministers, the Illuminati conspiratorial fear expressed in extreme pervasive concerns about the ability of a new republic to maintain its sovereignty during a time of revolutionary upheaval – characterized in France by a universalist political millennialism – and increasingly hostile foreign entanglements. By focusing attention on threatening, self-interested aliens, anti-Illuminati discourse also served to displace Americans' uneasiness about their own self-interested pursuit of money and power; the Illuminati fear thus helped to reaffirm an ideal of virtuous republican community even as factionalism and conflict appeared to be the new order of the day.[17] Yet by the spring of 1799 the specific fear of the Bavarian Illuminati began to wane, in part because not one member of the Illuminati had ever been discovered in America.[18] Furthermore, Americans alert to European fashion soon learned that Robison had been discredited in his own country. And as the fear of the plotting Illuminati diminished, so did the fear of the plotting Jacobin (and Jeffersonian Republican). To many Americans, especially those swayed by the assertion of states' rights in the Virginia and Kentucky Resolutions, the Federalists' repressively countersubversive Alien and Sedition Laws seemed to be the most threatening signs of political self-interest on the domestic scene. After the election of Jefferson, the Federalists, with no popular ideology to speak of, rapidly lost their ability to influence public events.

But an important question still remains: Did Americans at the height of the Illuminati scare really believe that foreign subversives threatened the nation? Fifteen years after Morse first announced the existence of the Illuminati conspiracy as a way of supporting Adams's claims of French conspiracy, Adams, in a letter to Jefferson, reaffirmed his belief in the appropriateness of the Alien and Sedition Laws as countersubversive measures:

> We were then at War with France: French Spies then swarmed in our Cities and in the Country. Some of them were, intollerably, [sic] turbulent, impudent and seditious. To check these was the design of this law. Was there ever a Government, which had not Authority to defend itself against Spies in its own Bosom? Spies of an Ennemy [sic] at War?

Two weeks later, however, in a follow-up letter to Jefferson, he remarked that the "real terrors of both parties have allways [sic] been, and now are, the fear that they shall lose the Elections and consequently the Loaves and Fishes; and that their antagonists will obtain them."[19] I would suggest that Adams's double perspective of 1813 mirrored his perspective of the 1790s and that he was not alone during the 1798–1800 period in alternately experiencing anxiety and skepticism about the possibility of conspiracy. Surely there were a number of Americans, however anxious about "Spies in its own Bosom," who suspected that cries of conspiracy helped politicians to gain votes and religious leaders to gain congregants. But in Brockden Brown's home city of Philadelphia, the city of choice for the political refugees of the 1790s, the end result of the repeated declarations of French, Illuminati, Federalist-aristocratic, and even Irish conspiracy was a near panic situation.[20]

Because Philadelphia was a factionally divided political center – few cities offered such polemical newspapers as William Cobbett's Federalist *Porcupine Gazette* and William Duane's Jeffersonian *Aurora* – no populace was more exposed to alarmist rhetoric. The conspiracy of the Bavarian Illuminati was widely reported in Philadelphia newspapers and broadsides of 1798 and 1799, as was a related conspiracy: that of the New England Illuminati. Seeking to defuse the political impact of the Federalists' anti-Illuminati and anti-"alien" crusade, Duane in January 1799 began to publish regularly in the *Aurora* the countersubversive essays of John C. Ogden, an Episcopal clergyman temporarily imprisoned under the Sedition Law, who became convinced that the New England Congregationalists in fact *were* the Illuminati! As Ogden asserted in a major statement on the matter, *A View of the New-England Illuminati* (1799), New England's Congregationalist clergy, early supporters of the French Revolution, "bear too near an affinity to the Illuminati Societies of Europe, not be viewed part of the same: at least if Professor *Robeson* [sic] and Abbé *Barruel* are to be believed, they must be *sister societies*." Though these Congregationalist subversives championed themselves as republican countersubversives, Ogden maintained that, if Americans paid close attention to anti-Illuminati tracts, particularly to *The Duty of Americans*, penned by the "head of the Illuminati, Doctor *Dwight*" (whom Ogden held personally responsible for his failure to obtain a clerical position in New England), they would obtain "a perfect picture of the Illuminati of Connecticut, under [Dwight's] control." Like the Congregationalists, Ogden warned his readers that the Illuminati threatened "our families, religion, and country," and like Washington he called on Americans to exercise "[d]iligent attention." Such was the citizenry's attentiveness to the Illuminati, Bavarian and New England, that the conspiratorial fear played a major role in determining the results of Philadelphia's election of 1800.[21] Even in "enlightened" Philadelphia, concerns about the Illuminati informed debate on political power, republican identity, and civic and national vulnerability.

"It was only a voice"

In *Letters on Various Interesting and Important Subjects* (1799), a collection of satirical essays that first appeared in the *Aurora*, Philip Freneau, through the persona of the credulous Robert Slender, provides a striking picture of the havoc the alarmism of the late 1790s could wreak on the patriotic Philadelphian's fragile constitution. Suspicious of even a friendly visit from his neighbor, Slender seems fast approaching a nervous breakdown: "Constantly on the watch – ever on the wing – Why Hercules could not stand it – and how then can I – Frightened by plots, astonished with wonders, made jealous and mistrustful by conspiracies and combinations, robbed of my natural rest by insurrections, terrified to death by whipping, pummelling, choking, nose-bumping, eye-bruising, and cow-skinning." Slender describes his hysterical response to plots ranging from William Cobbett's announcement of the United Irishmen conspiracy to the Federalist alert of French conspiracy, until he finally apprehends an expedient "voice":

> I quaking at every limb, believed every word as firmly as if it had been a revelation, barred my gates, double locked all my doors, and if a mouse but scratched on the wall I was ready to hide behind the curtains. But in a short time Cobbett grew quiet, and all our experience from that to this has proved that *it was only a voice*. Next our city was to be burned – I trembled very much, and I believe so did a great many more. I every night had a sharp eye about me, praised the carefulness of the friends of good government, and wetting out all the fires in the house *myself*, went quaking to bed – and this proved *a voice only*. I was much perplexed about the affair of X. Y. and Z.; dreamt every night of a French invasion – dreaded terribly that the negroes would rebel – prayed all my friends to strive with all their might to increase our *navy* – wished heartily for a league offensive and defensive with our mother England – and thought our Envoys, the President, the King of England, and the Grand Signior, the greatest men upon earth. Think, only think of my disappointment, when this, by the plain tale of Mr. Gerry, was shown to be like the rest, *for some special purpose,* only a voice. . . . But think how I felt confounded when I got my eyes opened, and saw the whole plan of the United Irishmen, burning the city, and the clue of conspiracy, were only to prepare the way for the Alien and Sedition bills.[22]

With his presentation of Slender's eye-opening recognitions, Freneau dramatically calls attention to the pursuit of power underlying the Federalists' promulgation of conspiratorial fears. But for Freneau, a partisan Jeffersonian Republican, more is at stake than simply exposing the relationship of countersubversion to power. He also wants to show that countersubversion is a form of subversion. Like Ogden, then, he promotes a conspiratorial fear of his own by depicting the Federalists as self-interested plotters craftily manipulating Americans at a time when, so Freneau implies, all is otherwise well with the republic. A text that at least on one level intends to unmask conspiracy – "*it was only a voice*" – thus further entangles the reader in a web of plot and deceit.

Brockden Brown, I will argue, shared Freneau's skepticism of conspiracy and his prescience about the expedient uses to which alarmist calls could be put. But that does not mean that he, any more than Freneau, was able to transcend the fears and uncertainties of the 1790s. Nor should we underrate Brown's preoccupation with social concerns. Alan Axelrod's schematic portrayal of Brown as divided "between the light mood of society and the dark one of literary composition" fails to attend to the realities of post-Revolutionary America and Brown's involvement with them.[23] His "dark" literary works emerge from and address the tensions of a not so "light" contemporary moment.

As William Hedges observes, Brown was torn, as his world was torn, "by conflicts between rationalism and religion, radicalism and reaction." Though he enthusiastically read the major figures of the radical Enlightenment – Godwin, Paine, Volney, Wollstonecraft, and many others – he wavered considerably in his work, at times uncritically allowing his most progressive characters to champion radical ideas, at other moments pointedly suggesting the possibly dangerous consequences of their politics. His responsiveness to a range of texts and positions makes it relatively difficult to pin down his political identity or his attitude toward conspiracy; Brown of the 1790s eludes political classification as Freneau of the 1790s does not. To be sure, by the early 1800s Brown would seem most at ease with Federalist mercantile policies, and thus as a way of explaining his interest in the Illuminati it is tempting to view him in the late 1790s, particularly in his association with the conservative members of New York's Friendly Society, as a Federalist in the making. But the extant biographical evidence suggests that throughout his career he maintained a distance from party. To pigeonhole him as a Federalist or Republican, and consequently to reduce his writings to a series of political statements, would finally only crudely distort his literary intentions and methods. At least through the 1790s, Brown's commitment to exploring and testing a range of ideas far outweighed his limited interest in party politics.[24] His texts reflect less a political line than a sensibility – inquiring, capacious, and anxious.

In *Alcuin* (1798), for example, a novelistic dialogue on women's rights, one character, Mrs. Carter, boldly develops the feminist arguments of Wollstonecraft's *A Vindication of the Rights of Women* (1792), while another, Alcuin, laments in the Congregationalist mode the "licentiousness and profligacy" of a world in which "marriages can be dissolved and contracted at pleasure." As if to emphasize the irrelevance of political affiliation to the debate, Brown has the initially obtuse Alcuin pose as his first question to Mrs. Carter: "Pray, Madam, are you a Federalist?"[25] For Mrs. Carter, political disenfranchisement and not affiliation is the crucial issue, and it is noteworthy that the dialogue rapidly veers away from considerations of party, and this at a time of especially heightened factionalism in the political arena. By the end of the text, Alcuin's early determination to tie the conversation on women's rights to party politics stands retrospectively as an effort to contain the play of ideas. Unmoored, *Alcuin* becomes a troubling text, a dialogue without a center that generates conflicting ideas on such issues as marriage, sexuality, and the division of labor. Cathy N. Davidson perceptively notes, "The dialogue form itself virtually precludes our seeking in *Alcuin* Brown's own theories."[26] To take Davidson's argument one step further, I would suggest that Brown's literary career writ large constitutes a dialogue without an authoritative center in which various positions at different times move into prominence. Responsive to a range of cultural discourses and typically decentering his narrative authority so that we are never quite sure of his "own theories," Brown stands, in Bakhtin's terms, as one of the most aggressively "dialogical" of America's early national writers.

Following the passage of the coercive Alien and Sedition Laws, Brown's dialogical stance necessitated aggression. Shuttling between New York and Philadelphia in 1798, Brown, like all literate citizens of the period, was assailed by alarmist political writings in newspapers, journals, and pamphlets. In addition to reading about "Jacobin" Republicans and "oligarchical" Federalists, in July of that year, while residing at the New York quarters of his close friend Elihu Hubbard Smith, he read Robison's *Proofs of a Conspiracy* and, in all probability, Dwight's *Duty of Americans;* Smith's diary records his own reading of Robison and two (unspecified) Dwight sermons during Brown's extended visit. Over the next year or so, as evidenced by reviews in his *Monthly Magazine and American Review*, Brown familiarized himself with additional countersubversive sermons by Dwight and also with the anti-Illuminati writings of Morse, William Brown, and Barruel.[27] Certainly of the numerous prevalent conspiratorial fears, that of the Illuminati most captured his imagination; and we may posit for the moment that his dialogical mode or sensibility helps to explain his interest in texts enacting melodramas of oppositional conflict on issues of vital social concern. Anti-Illuminati texts, one-sided and alarmist as they may have been, emerged from and addressed central conflicts between proponents and opponents of the radical Enlightenment; they participated as well in America's dialogue on the new nation's ideological foundations and revolutionary heritage. As such, they spoke to Brown's own conflicting responses to the possibilities of the Enlightenment, his own attractions and reactions as they developed during the final years of Adams's administration.

In September 1798, shortly after Brown completed *Wieland,* William Dunlap noted in his diary: "Afternoon read C. B. Browns [*sic*] beginning for the life of Carwin – as far as he has gone he has done well: he has taken up the schemes of the Illuminati."[28] There are indications that Brown had also contemplated taking up the Illuminati's schemes in his first published novel, for hints abound in *Wieland* that the mysterious Carwin may be a political subversive with ties to a conspiratorial organization. Pleyel first met the peripatetic Carwin in Spain three years before the present of the action, and at that time, for entirely unexplained reasons, the supposed Pennsylvanian's "garb, aspect, and deportment, were wholly Spanish. A residence of three years in the country, indefatigable attention to the language, and a studious conformity with the customs of the people, had made him indistinguishable from a native, when he chose to assume that character." Even more disturbing information about Carwin's predilection for studied "transformation" is provided by Ludloe, a stranger whose credibility is never really at issue in *Wieland* (as it will be in *Memoirs of Carwin,* where he is revealed to be the leader of a conspiratorial Illuminati-like group). Ludloe places an announcement in the local newspaper warning that Carwin, putatively a convicted murderer in flight from an Irish prison, plots with others for highly suspect purposes. As Pleyel informs Clara, Ludloe's announcement, which offers a reward for Carwin's apprehension,

> describes him in general terms, as the most incomprehensible and formidable among men; as engaged in schemes, reasonably suspected to be, in the highest degree, criminal, but such as no human intelligence is able to unravel: that his ends are pursued by means which leave it in doubt whether he be not in league with some infernal spirit: that his crimes have hitherto been perpetrated with the aid of some unknown but desperate accomplices: that he wages a perpetual war against the happiness of mankind, and sets his engines of destruction at work against every object that presents itself.[29]

Reflective of the fear of aliens and obsession with surveillance contributing to the enactment of the Naturalization Law in June 1798 (and informing such countersubversive writings as William Cobbett's *Detection of a Conspiracy, Formed by the United Irishmen* [1798]), Pleyel's secondhand account of Carwin's crimes and "schemes" begs the question, central to all of Brown's fiction, of how to establish the authority of information and construe the shape of plot.

Yet to a large extent the problem of whether to view Carwin as a political conspirator is beside the point, for it becomes increasingly clear that the society at the summerhouse-temple bequeathed by the paranoid elder Wieland is in such precarious balance that Carwin's possible affiliation with subversives has no bearing at all on his destructive power as originator of voices. Instead, Carwin's villainy is shown to be interrelated with and perhaps principally dependent on his victims' psychological vulnerability, a vulnerability powerfully dramatized through the uncertainties and confusions of Clara, the first-person narrator. After learning of her brother's homicidal madness, for instance, she reveals that the implications of Wieland's actions are by no means lost on her: "Now was I stupified [sic] with tenfold wonder in contemplating myself. Was I not likewise transformed from rational and human into a creature of nameless and fearful attributes? Was I not transported to the brink of the same abyss? Ere a new day should come, my hands might be embrued with blood, and my remaining life be consigned to a dungeon and chains." Imagining herself as a bloodthirsty savage, a maniacal other, she feels enormously vulnerable: "What was my security against influences equally terrific and equally irresistible [sic]?" Her realization, however, that internal influences are perhaps as lethal as external ones is too much to bear, and so she fends off her intuitions and rediscovers an enemy: "In this paroxysm of distress, my attention fastened on him [Carwin] as the grand deceiver; the author of this black conspiracy; the intelligence that governed in this storm."[30] In her desire to avoid the conundrum of disintegrative psychological pressures – epitomized by her father's and brother's religious fanaticism and her own incestuous dreams – she displaces all onto the voice of a villainous outsider. Whereas Freneau's *Letters* builds to a somewhat anticlimactic "*it was only a voice,*" Brown shows, in effect, how a voice can be everything, and why, sometimes, for those who insist on and desperately need a first cause, a voice *must* be everything. Clara's "discovery" of Carwin's ventriloquial plotting and her happy marriage to Pleyel enable her to shut her eyes to the intimation of irruptive forces within. But the reader is left with the disturbing sense that fearsome villains, perhaps for their very existence, more often than not require fearsome "victims."

Brown's etiological emphasis on the psychosocial pressures giving rise to conspiratorial fears distinguishes *Wieland* from popular political-allegorical sentimental novels and alarmist countersubversive tracts. His treatment of the tension between innate and external influences – his exploration from a postrevolutionary Gothic perspective of the dark recesses of the civilized psyche – thus poses a fundamental challenge to the Lockean sensationalist epistemology centrally informing the novel of seduction.[31] Yet, though more ironic and philosophically probing than a work like *Charlotte Temple,* the novel does suggest a connection, as literary and clerical sentimentalists again and again suggested a connection, between the onset of plotting and the failure of vigilance. Like Charlotte's "Temple," *Wieland*'s innocent temple community is imaged as a synecdochic model of the American community. Socially isolated and idyllically happy at the summerhouse-temple, reveling in their "present enjoyment" while bestowing "no thought . . . on the future," the Wielands and Pleyels, naïve Lockean utopianists, become especially vulnerable to outsiders and even tempt the machinations of a seductive plotter whose rumored association with conspirators implies a political allegory of seduction.[32]

Although Carwin begins his confessional testimony to Clara with the declaration, "Deem me not capable of the iniquity of seduction," he proceeds to reveal how soon after meeting her he resolved to put her celebrated virtuous independence to the test. Clara is actually quite vulnerable to the perils of seduction because she, like Clarissa and Charlotte Temple, is strongly attracted to the plotter and is all too credulous. Attraction and danger are conjoined at Carwin's initial appearance, as Clara muses on his appealingly radiant face and mellifluous voice while simultaneously, and unaccountably, imagining the downfall of her bucolic community: "Something whispered that the happiness we at present enjoyed was set on mutable foundations." According to sentimentalists of republican virtue, the foundation of the American community rests on the pure maiden's ability to preserve her chastity; in *Wieland* (and there are some ambiguities about this) that particular foundation survives intact, though to the very end the possibility of rape remains a real one because Carwin, in the manner of both Lovelace and the Congregationalists' Illuminati seducer (and anticipating the expedient Ormond), scoffs at its demonization: "Even if I execute my purpose, what injury is done? Your prejudices will call it by that name, but it merits it not." Nevertheless, while likewise scoffing at the idealization of chastity, he assures her, "Be this chimera still worshipped; I will do nothing to pollute it." But he does put the "chimera" to a test; and though Clara apparently maintains an inviolate virtue, the community itself proves to be vulnerable to Carwin's machinations. Accordingly, it is Carwin the testing plotter – he who knows best – who audaciously instructs his victims on their several key failures. Washington-like, he abjures Clara: "Upright and sincere, you used no watchfulness and practiced no precautions." And he explains that Wieland's murders and Pleyel's (short-lived) loss of faith in her virtue reveal "the evils of credulity on the one hand, and of imposture on the other."[33] Though Brown's canonical status as Father of the American Romance encourages the modern reader to take such admonitions as ironical, the fact is that Carwin's morals are consistent with the informing melodramatic structure of the novel.

Viewed in terms of its political allegory of seduction, *Wieland,* it can be argued, gives expression to Brown's "Federalist" concerns about the threat posed by expedient seducers to credulous Americans lacking self-knowledge, self-control, and a tradition of self-government, Americans, in Clara's words, "every where equally defenceless."[34] Yet his plotting villain, the outsider Carwin, "the author of this black conspiracy" (and a surrogate for the author of the "black" *Wieland*), unlike the typical villain of Federalist sentimental fictions, remains rather sympathetically inclined toward his unintended victims, dupes of internal and external voices. Moreover, the prefatory presentation of the summerhouse-temple's unstable past suggests that the later identification and fear of a polluting alien may well have been an inevitable concomitant of the tightly bonded community's need to quell its foundational anxieties and assert its faith in the fiction of its naturalized status. In this respect the novel can be read as an ironic critique of the foundationalism implicit in the Naturalization Law, in the Alien and Sedition Laws, and, by extension, in the idea of America as reified national entity. On the matter of plot and conspiracy, as on other matters, Brown offers conflicting perspectives suggestive of anxiety and irony; and in his weaving together of a sentimental dread of seduction with a Gothic interest in psychological extremity and a political theorist's interest in the nation's troubled claims to ontological authority, he achieves in *Wieland* a dialogical relation to his thematics of villainy and vulnerability that, as with *Alcuin*'s literal dialogue, makes it difficult to determine his own theories.

In the dialogical novel, Bakhtin remarks, the author entertains various cultural discourses and perspectives while concealing his own theories. That does not mean, however, that the author must remain disengaged and noncommital in his appropriations and refashionings. Bakhtin explains:

> The author is not to be found in the language of the narrator, not in the normal literary language to which the story opposes itself (although a given story may be closer to a given language) – but rather, the author utilizes now one language, now another, in order to avoid giving himself up wholly to either of them; he makes use of this verbal give-and-take, this dialogue of languages at every point in his work, in order that he himself might remain as it were neutral with regard to language, a third party in a quarrel between two people (although he might be a *biased* third party).[35]

Brown's "biases" in *Wieland*, I would argue, lie in the direction of social anxiety. Despite the novel's many ironies, the prevalence of conspiratorial themes and melodramatic tropes, along with the several bloody climaxes, suggest Brown's fears, if not of the Illuminati, then of related, or analogous, subversive threats facing post-Revolutionary America – hence his insistence at the end of the novel on reiterating the dangers of credulity and the need for vigilance through the awkward device of having Clara narrate the story of the Stuarts and Maxwells. A redaction of the novel's melodramatic plot, the tale demonstrates once again how the "artifices of [a] seducer" can "subvert the happiness" of those not "gifted with ordinary equanimity or foresight."[36] Given *Wieland*'s dearth of characters possessing such perspicacity, Clara's concluding tale points chillingly to the inevitability of "seduction" and subversion in a world of self-seeking plotters.

In his second published novel, *Ormond; or the Secret Witness*, written in late 1798 at the height of the interest in the Illuminati conspiracy, Brown explicitly relates the possibility of social disintegration to the threat of conspiracy, and he does so by paying a more rigorous attention, like Freneau, to the uses and abuses of countersubversive discourse. Drawing on his reading of Robison and other anti-Illuminati writers, and abstracting from the political and literary rhetoric of the 1790s the compelling image of chaste America threatened by expedient plotters and a master seducer, Brown subjects the conspiratorial discourse of his time to a close scrutiny while betraying his own very real concerns about the authority, stability, and, in the largest possible sense, vulnerability of the new republic.

"A danger thus inscrutable and imminent"

Composed in approximately six weeks and consisting of a series of seemingly disconnected episodes and characters, *Ormond* on first reading would appear to be an impossible jumble. Almost apologetically, Brown's sympathetically inclined critics and biographers tend to remind us that during the two-year period before *Ormond*'s publication he wrote three novels, six fragments of novels, and numerous short stories, reviews, essays, and dialogues. Moreover, in September 1798, just one month before Brown began writing the novel, his friend Elihu Hubbard Smith died in New York after contracting yellow fever. Given how thinly he spread himself among his many literary endeavors, and given the lingering impact of Smith's death, it could only be expected, so it is usually averred, that the "improvisatory" *Ormond* would be a deeply flawed work.[37] The appeal to circumstances, however, is ultimately condescending, and it has served over the years to diminish our appreciation of what I believe to be Brown's most challenging novel, and certainly his most thoroughgoing effort to engage and work transformations on his culture's normative conspiratorial discourse. Though hardly a "well wrought urn," *Ormond* is powerfully coherent in its narrative representation of vulnerability and brilliantly ironic. And yet in significant ways the novel is also a highly conventional literary performance, and it is with the conventional that I want to begin.

The novel opens with a skillful set piece that immediately teaches the reader the more or less familiar lesson of just how easily confidence men may take advantage of an unsuspicious American family. Stephen Dudley, educated in Europe as a painter but eventually forced by financial pressures to assume management of his father's New York apothecary house, is one day approached by a youthful stranger of "modest and ingenuous aspect."[38] The stranger, who goes by the name of Thomas Craig, declares that he has recently come to America from Wakefield, in Yorkshire, and has virtually no money to his name. Because his story was "consistent, and his veracity appeared liable to no doubt" (8), Dudley takes Craig on as his apprentice and welcomes him into his family. Craig's assistance allows a grateful Dudley to devote more time to his painting; equally grateful is Craig's "mother," who writes from England to thank Dudley for hiring her son.

Three years pass, and Craig is made a partner in the firm. Two more years elapse, and the benevolent Dudley offers to help Craig's "brother" get into business as well. But Craig unaccountably refuses to contact his brother, and the perplexed Dudley soon after secretly opens a letter to Craig from one Mary Mansfield of New Hampshire, who, it turns out, is Craig's unhappily deserted mother. Even after reading the letter Dudley refuses to believe that Craig is other than he seems, but Craig's recent puzzling activities and the letter from Mrs. Mansfield eventually alter Dudley's trusting disposition: "He was now as prone to suspect, as he was formerly disposed to confidence" (15). Unfortunately, this change occurs too late: Craig flees with a friend to Jamaica, and Dudley subsequently discovers that over the past five years he has been the victim of a series of embezzlements and credit ruses. Infiltrated and now bankrupt, the devastated Dudleys must move from New York to Philadelphia, where they experience consecutive catastrophes: Dudley's wife dies, and the grief-stricken Dudley goes blind. Abruptly the weight of the family falls on Constantia, Dudley's sixteen-year-old daughter, who "yielded nothing to caprice or passion" (21).

This opening sad vignette works with a master theme of novelistic/romance literature, "the deceitfulness of appearances" (210), and, as appropriate to the social thematics of the novel, makes the chief culprit not the overactive imagination but a manipulative plotter. It also establishes the metaphorical appropriateness of Dudley's reaction to his wife's death: In a world of selfish hypocrites, the trusting individual suffers from a kind of blindness. Relatedly, the vignette dramatizes the republican family's vulnerability to the commercial duplicities threatening to dissolve the boundaries between the private and the public realm. That an economic marketplace governed by laissez-faire individualism should become a proving ground for hoaxes, frauds, and counterfeitings of identity and currency is an important working premise of much early American fiction and, more generally, Anglo-American literature from the sixteenth century on.[39] As represented in the fiction of Brown, Cooper, Hawthorne, Melville, and many other antebellum writers, concerns about the adequacy of the family, the dynamism of marketplace forces, and the schemes of plotters are interrelated concerns, suggestive of just how tenuous is the republican ideal of virtuous community in a "liberal" age of economic self-interest.

According to the narrator of *Ormond*, however, a narrator who throughout the novel moralizes on each discrete episode of the Dudley saga, there is an especially pressing lesson to be learned from Dudley's naïve tendering of confidence in a "subtle imposter" (16). The opening episode, the narrator makes clear, exemplifies the importance of maintaining a heightened vigilance against plotting outsiders, even when threats are not so readily apparent. Those lulled into placing their confidence in the "disinterested exertions" (9) of strangers, while "discard-[ing] all apprehensions respecting futurity" (11), risk economic and social disasters. As the narrator puts it, "Thus in a moment was this man thrown from the summit of affluence to the lowest indigence. He had been habituated to independence and ease. This reverse, therefore, was the harder to bear. . . . It was imbittered by the consciousness of his own imprudence, and by recollecting that the serpent which had stung him, was nurtured in his own bosom" (18). Warning of the dangers posed by malevolent infiltrators to those incautiously luxuriating in a fragile independence, the language is strikingly similar to the admonitory political rhetoric of the 1790s, especially Washington's Farewell Address. Who is Brockden Brown's Washington redux?

The narrator is Sophia Courtland, née Sophia Westwyn, Constantia's friend from childhood who recently journeyed to Europe with her frail mother, an alcoholic and former prostitute. She relates the Dudleys' story to the forever offstage German, I. E. Rosenberg, perhaps a suitor of Constantia's who wants to know more about the tainted past of his beloved, a murderess. As a narrator who figures only marginally in the action she describes, Sophia musters a third-person narrative that seeks, through its authoritative presence, to compensate for her absence. Identifying herself as "a faithful biographer" (3), the narrator attempts to lull the reader into confidence by seemingly offering simply the facts: "Stephen Dudley was a native of New York. He was educated to the profession of a painter. His father's trade was that of an apothecary" (5). But as a concerned narrator who throughout the narrative will make numerous bold assertions about the significance of "events upon the character and the happiness of individuals in America" (3), Sophia in effect adopts the stance not only of a biographer but also of a political alarmist. Like the sermonizers, moralists, and politicians of the late 1790s, she remains ever alert to the lessons provided by misfortune, perceiving in the local troubles of the Dudleys signs and signals relevant to all Americans. Her alarmist perspective governs the structure and development of the novel, organizing events, as is characteristic of Brown's romances, through "successive and cumulative analogy."[40]

A novel that begins with an alarming instance of economic infiltration subsequently moves by analogy to an alarming instance of biological infiltration: the yellow fever epidemic in Philadelphia of 1793. Like the Dudley household of the opening chapters, the capital city appears to be a secure environment immune to infiltration and upheaval; thus, Sophia explains, the onset of the fever amazes Constantia:

> Contagious diseases, she well knew, periodically visited and laid waste the Greek and Egyptian cities. It constituted no small part of that mass of evil, political and physical, by which that portion of the world has been so long afflicted. That a pest equally malignant had assailed the metropolis of her own country, a town famous for the salubrity of its airs and the perfection of its police, had something in it so wild and uncouth that she could not reconcile herself to the possibility of such an event. (35)

Somewhat curious here is Sophia's linking of the physical "evil" of fever to political evils and her linking of both to foreign locales. Yet Sophia's conception of fever actually is conventional, for during the 1790s the fever was regularly portrayed as a duplicitous form of foreign infiltration and subversion. In a letter to his brother James, Brown described his own encounter with the fever: "Plague operates by invisible agents, and we know not in what quarter it is about to attack us." Brown's anthropomorphic imaging of fever as a martial corps of stealthy saboteurs conveys a social anxiety similar to that of numerous contemporaneous countersubversive texts, particularly Federalist texts warning Americans to beware "the foul contagion of French principles." The linkage of fever to revolutionary subversion is also central to Barruel's anti-Illuminati *Memoirs of Jacobinism,* which warned its readers that "as the plague flies on the wings of the wind, so do [the Illuminati's] conspiring legions infect America."[41]

Barruel wanted his readers to realize that subversion, like the fever, infects the body politic gradually and invisibly; Sophia similarly wants her readers to realize that beneath any façade of seeming good health may lurk invisibly infecting agents. "The air was bright and pure, and apparently salubrious," Sophia remarks on Philadelphia's atmosphere. "Security and silence seemed to hover over the scene" (44). But citizens reposing in their apparent security soon succumb in large numbers to the disintegrative fever: The Dudleys' landlord dies, as does their neighbor, who attempts to flee the city rather than help his dying family. Concerned about her neighbors and subsisting on Joel Barlow's ennobled hasty pudding, Constantia among the panic-stricken and greedy emerges as a singular exemplar of republican virtue.[42] But even while applauding Constantia's conduct as a model of beneficence, Sophia underscores the importance of keeping one's distance from the diseased. Accordingly, given the implied connection between fever and foreign infiltration, she promotes a xenophobic ideal of virtuous neutrality: "To seclude herself as much as possible from others, was the best means of avoiding infection" (57). Even after the fever passes, Sophia insists on the importance of maintaining a prudent vigilance. Depicting Philadelphians indulging in a postfever "general festivity" (73), she invites her readers to discern the dangers of complacency: "The return of health was hailed with rapture by all ranks of people. The streets were once more busy and frequented. The sensation of present security seemed to shut out from all hearts the memory of recent disasters" (72). The two opening episodes of the novel have shown, on the contrary, that disasters precipitated by infiltrating "invisible agents" remain ever imminent.

Embedded in Sophia's alarmist presentation of the havoc wrought by invisible germs, however, is an account of one Baxter that portrays infiltration fears as a form of local hysteria. Employed as a night watchman to guard abandoned homes from plunderers, Baxter regularly spies on his new neighbors, the "French" emigrant Monrose (Roselli) and a young woman presumed to be his daughter (Martinette), fearing that if the French, to his mind a nation of supermen immune to fever, are actually diseased, then all is over for his own family. And so when he observes the "daughter" secretly burying her septuagenarian "father," who may well have died a natural death, he soon after dies from a self-induced malignant terror. The narrator remarks: "His case may be quoted as an example of the force of imagination. He had probably already received, through the medium of the air, or by contact of which he was not conscious, the seeds of this disease. They might perhaps have lain dormant, had not this panic occurred to endow them with activity" (71).

But though it is Sophia as narrator who paraphrases Mrs. Baxter's tale of her husband's demise, the guiding intelligence behind the "enlightened" moral seems very different from the conventional narrator's. The presence of a less conventional perspective within Sophia's apparently monological narrative can be discerned early on in the sympathetic (and ironic) portrayal of Dudley's relinquishing of his "attraction to the pencil" (6) for "nothing but gain" (6). In addition to the antibusiness tone and art allegory of the opening, wholly inappropriate to Sophia's narration, there are also several rhetorical attacks on lawyers that clearly speak to Brown's personal loathing for the profession he renounced as a young man. As for Baxter's story, Brown published an early version of the chapter in a magazine series, "The Man at Home" (1798), and in incorporating it into *Ormond* made little effort to accommodate its moral and style to Sophia's.[43] Inserted into the novel, Mrs. Baxter's story serves in effect as a competing narrative, a dialogical intrusion, that challenges Sophia's alarmist presentation of fever by suggesting that rational benevolence, rather than spectatorial terror, is the more sensitive response to the infected. As the novel develops, Sophia's conventional alarmist perspective and an ironic and more capacious one will remain in dialogical competition, though at times they will be surprisingly complementary.

The opening episodes of the novel call attention to the perils of independence by dramatizing the dangers of vulnerability. Constantia's early encounters with false suitors further develop this theme, for marriage from Sophia's alarmist outlook is a form of familial and sexual infiltration posing considerable dangers to vulnerable young women. As with the presentation of fever, and as in *Alcuin, Ormond* offers competing views on marriage. Sophia presents a sentimentalized political allegory on the need to retain one's independence from self-interested seducers until the potential marriage partner's intentions and character are well known; marriage then becomes a bedrock in a threatening world. But for readers of Godwin and Wollstonecraft, marriage would not be regarded as a mere political alliance vouchsafing a superficial security. From a competing perspective, Brown shapes the marriage plot in *Ormond* to suggest that a marriage between intellectual equals forged in the spirit of love and friendship is the best possible marriage.[44] But as different as are these positions, both pivot on an equation between vulnerable Constantia and vulnerable America, and together buttress the informing political alarmism of the novel.

Constantia's first suitor, a young man "amply recommended by the circumstances of family and fortune" (21), is introduced soon after the onset of Dudley's blindness. Though her noncoercive parents want her to marry into an economically stable situation, Constantia refrains from making a commitment and subsequently is abandoned by her suitor when he learns of her father's financial misfortunes. Two lessons emerge from this first marriage prospect: the potential unhappiness that would have resulted from the union of a man and woman who care nothing for one another and the need to beware selfish courters. The former lesson, adumbrating the enlightened theme of the need for equality in marriage, has an important place in the novel; but the latter and more alarmist lesson on selfish betrayal will come to predominate. Like Charlotte Temple, and like Washington's America in both the Neutrality Proclamation and the Farewell Address, Constantia at age sixteen is a vulnerable youth in need of further maturation and, hence, continued isolation. Accordingly, Sophia reports that Constantia's first experience with courtship prompts her to assert her own Neutrality Proclamation: "She had no design of entering into marriage, in less than seven years from this period" (23). The wisdom of her proclamation is borne out by every marriage situation in the book.

A foreshadowing of Constantia's most pressing marriage problem – how to repay a personal debt to her benefactor Ormond – occurs soon after the return of calm to postfever Philadelphia, when Balfour, a Scottish merchant, rescues her from the advances of two leering men and, within a few weeks, proposes marriage. Though Balfour seems deserving enough of a good wife, Constantia resists his entreaties for several well-considered reasons. Not only does she feel no genuine affection for him, but in the merchant's "poverty of . . . discourse and ideas, she quickly found reasons for determining her conduct" (83). Nevertheless, there remains the moral problem of gratitude: "Difficulties . . . arose from the consideration of what was due to the man who had already benefited her, and who, in this act, intended to confer upon her further benefit" (85–6). Like those Federalists who felt grateful to the French for their assistance during the Revolutionary War and yet resistant to any permanent alliance, Constantia finally rejects the proposals of her benefactor and then discovers how right she was to do so. Feeling cheated, Balfour exacts repayment by permitting his sister to spread ugly rumors damaging to Constantia's reputation; the savior turns out to be a monster.[45] Constantia's experiences with her first two suitors resoundingly confirm an important alarmist theme of the narrative: the need for the independent to maintain their independence, even from those, like Ormond, who exude a seductive charm.

That Ormond possesses the ability to charm is clear from the moment he enters the world of the novel. This is true even though no one knows the identity or origins of the wealthy European alien, even though he first appears as a possible accomplice (or, Constantia fears, potential victim) of the recently surfaced Craig, and even though his peculiarly late introduction, about a third of the way into the narrative, suggests that he embodies by analogy in this novel of analogy the subversive potential of Craig, yellow fever, and false suitors. But instead of fulfilling these dire expectations, the appealing Ormond threatens only to disrupt Sophia's orderly and admonitory "biographical sketch." Initially more benevolent than subversive, he early on claims the reader's sympathies through a delightful virtuoso performance that, in contrast to Craig's duplicities, seems positively saintly: After Craig passes off a counterfeit bill to Constantia, which nearly lands Dudley in jail, Ormond audaciously disguises himself as a black chimney sweep and delivers some much needed cash to the Dudleys. A wit and a benefactor, who, like Carwin, has "a remarkable facility in imitating the voice . . . of others" (115), Ormond cannot but gain admirers at this juncture of the novel.

Ormond is also admirably enlightened on the issue of women's education, and his attraction to Constantia's mind, his ability to perceive the special worth of the novel's heroine, emerges as a strong early recommendation for his character. Though he keeps as his mistress the pampered and sensual Helena Cleves, he is well aware that "Helena's intellectual deficiencies could not be concealed" (128). Unlike Constantia, Helena knows nothing of history and science; she is simply "an object charming to the senses" (120). Constantia, in contrast, has "an ardent thirst of knowledge" (29) and knows her Tacitus and Milton, her Newton and Hartley. She embodies for Ormond the intellectual woman he most desires and always believed a patriarchal society could not produce. And just as Clara in *Wieland* is beguiled by the fascinating outsider Carwin, so Constantia is enchanted by Ormond: "The image of Ormond occupied the chief place in her fancy, and was endowed with attractive and venerable qualities" (157).

Because the unconventional Ormond initially appears "attractive and venerable," it can be assumed that the somewhat unconventional Brown identified in part with such an "artistic" performer.[46] Nevertheless, Brown's narrator seems intent on portraying Ormond, like the fever, as a "pest." Thus though we may want to applaud Ormond's theatrical offering of funds to the Dudleys, Sophia asserts that this early instance of Ormond's deceptiveness points to the moral problems inherent in duplicity and concealment. He may have charitably aided the Dudleys, but in his hierarchy of values, according to Sophia, curiosity and the performance itself rise above benevolence; his practice of "gaining access to families, and marking them in unguarded attitudes" (133–4) links observation to power and anticipates his later malicious abuses of such secret witnessing.[47] Further, Ormond's painless transmogrification of self "from the highest to the lowest rank in society" (134), a recapitulation of the descent Dudley made not as a theatrical gesture but in the realities of the marketplace, strikes Sophia as nothing but glib. Ormond's wealth permits him the luxury of playacting an economic fall without experiencing its attendant social and psychological hardships. As she remarks on his avowedly democratic dispensing with the polite forms of address: "It was easier for him to reduce his notions of equality to practice than for most others. To level himself with others was an act of condescension" (114). His "feminism" too is undercut, for Sophia maintains that it cloaks a rationalism so extreme as to reduce both Helena and Constantia to mere figures in an algebraic equation: Ormond desires, so she insists, a woman "whose character was squared, with a mathematical exactness, to his situation" (128). This may be true, but compared with the other suitors of the novel, Ormond stands honorably alone in his desire to link himself with an energetic and intelligent woman. Despite Sophia's negative assessments, the pest does seem impressive.

I am arguing, then, that while Brown appears to grant Sophia a totalizing narrative authority, his ironic and interpolated intrusions work to suggest competing views that challenge her conventional moralizations. In this respect the seemingly monological *Ormond* resembles the generically dialogical *Alcuin,* for both texts involve the reader in the act of evaluating radically divergent positions. With the introduction of Ormond, the novel's dialogical structure becomes even more apparent, as Ormond, the unconventional Enlightenment progressive, and Sophia, the vigilant and moralistic conservative, are each provided with a forum for voicing their respective views. But ultimately within the novel's fictive world it is Sophia the sermonic narrator who remains in control of the "dialogue," and it will become increasingly difficult to wrest Ormond from her shaping discourse. Soon after Ormond's introduction the tenor of the novel dramatically changes: What was formerly an alarmist sentimental narrative, one that, under the challenge of a competing sensibility, can seem rather provincial and limited – Brown's parodic recasting of normative discourse – abruptly becomes more explicitly a narrative of conspiracy. Accordingly, the novel becomes a narrative about the discourse of conspiracy, a novel simultaneously ironic (and parodic) in its representation of Sophia's secretive witnessing and genuinely countersubversive in its sustained portrayal of villainy and vulnerability.

Initiating the move to conspiracy is an odd narrative digression that hints at Ormond's secretive ties to an Illuminati-like organization whose "political projects are likely to possess an extensive influence on the future condition of this western world" (111–12). A countersubversive in the mode of Timothy Dwight, Sophia announces a disinterested desire to fulfill her Duty to Americans by sharing alarming information: "My knowledge is far from being absolute, but I am conscious of a kind of duty, first to my friend, and secondly to mankind, to impart the knowledge I possess" (111). But whereas her account of Craig, the fever, and false suitors, however conventional, carried the impressive weight of a "biographer's" authority, in this first extended consideration of Ormond's enigmatic background she is rather tentative and hypothetical. For example, after asserting as fact that Ormond belongs to a conspiratorial group, she qualifies the accusation and then declares she will pursue the matter no longer: "A mind of uncommon energy like Ormond's, which had occupied a wide sphere of action, and which could not fail of confederating its efforts with those of minds like itself, must have given birth to innumerable incidents, not unworthy to be exhibited by the most eloquent historian. It is not my business to relate any of these" (116). Yet immediately after abdicating the "business" of counter-subversion, she ominously warns that Ormond's "instruments and coadjutors were culled from a field, whose bounds were those of the civilized world . . . . [and] his intents were too assiduously shrowded from profane inspection, for them to scan" (116–17).

The self-consciousness and imprecision of Sophia's digressive counter-subversive warning call attention to the problem of her narrative authori-ty in ways that her admonitory account of earlier incidents did not. Granted, she prefaces her warning with the concession that her "knowl-edge is far from absolute." But exactly what sort of knowledge of Or-mond does she possess, and how obtained? Her knowledge of Con-stantia's travails, we are told early on, derives from "an uninterrupted correspondence . . . [which] confided a circumstantial and copious rela-tion of all these particulars" (27). But she tells us nothing about how she knows so much about Ormond, and so we can only wonder about the reliability of information whose sources remain concealed. In the novel's epistolary preface, Sophia allows that her portrayal of Ormond may meet with some skeptical resistance, but she defends her use of conceal-ment even as she acknowledges that her narrative is imperfect: "It was not prudent to unfold *all* the means by which I gained a knowledge of his actions; but these means, though singularly fortunate and accurate, could not be unerring and compleat" (3). When she later first suggests that Ormond belongs to a conspiratorial group, she again insists upon her right to keep secret her corroborating evidence, though this time without apology: "I shall omit to mention the means by which I became ac-quainted with his character, nor shall I enter, at this time, into every part of it. . . . I do not conceive myself authorized to communicate a knowl-edge of his schemes, which I gained, in some sort, surreptitiously, or, at least, by means of which he was not apprized" (111–12).

Sophia's cunning appeals to secrecy resemble Robison's in *Proofs of a Conspiracy*. There, the text opens with the claim that "the obligation of secrecy respecting the important matters which are the very subjects of debate, prevents the author from giving the full information that is re-quired from an historian."[48] Sophia's insistence on concealment, iron-ically, links countersubversive to subversive, for both depend upon se-crecy and surveillance as prime sources of their power. At times Sophia can seem as ominously and secretively informed about the hidden moti-vations of others, as much a suspicious "secret witness," as Ormond, her designated "secret witness," appears to be. Accordingly, we begin to wonder about the relationship of her own pursuit of power to her nar-rative of conspiracy.

In Brown's other major romances a first-person narrator intimately involved in the action tells the story, and the reader soon realizes that participation makes the tale teller somewhat suspect. As Clara observes in *Wieland*, "What but ambiguities, abruptnesses, and dark transitions, can be expected from the historian who is, at the same time, the sufferer of these disasters?"[49] By having Clara reflect on her limited perspective, Brown impels the reader to create a supplemental narrative that takes note of her attraction to Carwin, her complicated psychological relationship with her brother, and even her possible complicity with Carwin in precipitating Wieland's fall. In the same way, readers of *Arthur Mervyn* and *Edgar Huntly* are encouraged by Brown's first-person strategies to supplement, and even challenge as lies, the efforts by Arthur and Edgar to tell their version of events. Though Sophia has virtually no role as a corporeal presence in the events she describes, her self-conscious use of surveillance and concealment, along with the possessive guardianship inherent in her conventionally alarmist narrative, encourages a similar suspicion of her conspiratorial vision and a similar desire to construct a supplemental, more "truthful" narrative. This is especially the case as details accrue, some comically perverse – such as the narrator's description of Constantia's obsessive loving devotion to Sophia's portrait – suggestive of Sophia's desire to portray the object of her obsessive love as mutually loving.[50] Increasingly aware that the seemingly disinterested Sophia is in fact locked in a battle with Ormond for possession of her beloved Constantia, the reader is tempted to dismiss her alarmist narrative, particularly the countersubversive attacks on Ormond, as the concoction of a mean-spirited paranoiac jealous of the man who attracts her friend's attention.

The skeptical perspective that Brown encourages us to adopt toward Sophia's alarmism therefore provokes us to reflect on the relationship between her construction of a countersubversive narrative and her anxiety about being relegated to the margins; relatedly, it provokes us to reflect on the similar anxiety and compensatory will to power informing political alarmism as a discourse.[51] It seems likely, then, that Brown structured Sophia's narrative to convey his own distrust of the Federalists' countersubversive tactics during a time when, under the duress of the Alien and Sedition Laws, a more direct attack would have left him vulnerable to the charge of high misdemeanor. *Ormond*'s apparent lack of structure – its picaresque account of Constantia's various encounters with subversive forces – would have allowed Brown, as Davidson remarks generally on the political uses of the picaresque in early American fiction, to "evade both censure and censorship through . . . indeterminacy," because the picaresque "did not require an author to take a 'position' on any of the various issues adumbrated within the text." Brown himself commented in the *Monthly Magazine and American Review* on an additional danger facing the writer who voices his politics unambiguously: "If he should open his mouth to utter a political sentiment, however moderately and discreetly it might be delivered, he would not fail to offend one half his readers."[52] Wary of Federalist policing and the volatile temper of his democratic reading public, Brown, it can be argued, like the ironically indirect Melville of the 1850s, conveys his social-critical themes by encouraging readers sensitive to his ironies to become more self-conscious about the relationship between cultural discourses and the particularized interests of their sponsors.

And yet while Brown's act of appropriating conspiratorial discourse for a romance subverts the countersubversive impulse by insisting, however quietly and ironically, on the problematical nature of interpretation, we should not dismiss the possibility that he is interested less in undercutting the authority of Sophia's narrative than in utilizing her narrative to express his own less alarmist concerns about Enlightenment rationalism, foreign infiltration, "artistic" and marketplace duplicities, and American vulnerability. Although Sophia's countersubversive narrative comes under challenge from the competing narrative that Brown prompts us to construct as we take note of her will to power and manipulative "secret witnessing" (and as we sense Brown's delight in the resourcefulness of his artist-villain), the reader can nevertheless glean from the "dialogue" between the two narratives converging emphases which suggest that Sophia's assessment of Ormond's character and threat may well reflect some of Brown's own "biases."

Certainly the initial discussion of Ormond and his perpetually off-stage "intimate associates" (131) conveys a nervousness about duplicitous infiltrators and, a recurrent theme in Brown and his counter-subversive contemporaries, a distrust of the hyperrational mind.[53] With the aid of his alarmist narrator, Brown deemphasizes the group's idealistic utopianism and chooses instead to accent their antirepublican pursuit of power. As Ormond explains their philosophy (in Sophia's paraphrase), because social and political institutions are inherently corrupt, all attempts to do good necessarily become absorbed by the "social machine" (112) and are "sure of answering a contrary purpose" (112). Given this highly determined social reality (and here Brown uses Sophia's attack on Ormond to express his own hesitations about the "perfectibilitarian" utopianism of Godwin's *Political Justice* [1793]), the individual's pursuit of happiness, according to Ormond, must take precedence over any larger communal commitment: "A man may reasonably hope to accomplish his end, when he proposes nothing but his own good: Any other point is inaccessible" (113). Governed by an ideologically sanctioned hedonism, Ormond abruptly terminates his relationship with the helpless Helena, thereby precipitating his mistress's suicide. Intellectually underpinning his selfish behavior, so Sophia asserts, is an amoralism derived from Enlightenment sciences: "The universe was to him, a series of events, connected by an undesigning and inscrutable necessity, and an assemblage of forms, to which no beginning or end can be conceived" (180). Possessing the mentality perfectly suited to the mechanistic world he envisages, he stands over Helena's corpse and icily remarks, "Thou has done my work for me. . . . Thou has acted as seemed to thee best, and I am satisfied" (171).[54] Driven by an egomaniacal passion for mastery, by the desire to "exercise absolute power over the conduct of others, not by constraining their limbs, or by exacting obedience to his authority, but in a way of which his subjects should be scarcely conscious" (177), Sophia's Ormond looks forward to Hawthorne's gallery of rationalistic mesmerists. And by the end of the novel this quasi-mesmerical utopianist revolutionary would appear to stand as hollowly exposed as Westervelt; for as events transpire and the Constantia–Ormond relationship develops, Ormond's will to "absolute power" soon centers on but one object: achieving complete domination over the mind and body of Constantia.

Let us pursue just a while longer, then, a more or less unironic reading of Sophia's conventional representation of Ormond's pursuit of power, as the novel builds to a climax that apparently vindicates her alarmist account. She tells of how Constantia surprisingly inherits from Helena not only Dudley's former property, which somehow had revolved into Helena's possession, but also the extensive funds and property bestowed upon her by Ormond. Clearly the reader is meant to realize that Constantia's economic descent and unsettling confrontation with harsh social realities have provided her with an enriching education now literalized into riches. Similarly, Dudley's fall into poverty has provided him with a more acute vision into the hazards of democracy and the shallowness of "luxurious indulgences" (174), soon literalized into restored vision: Ormond employs a surgeon, one of his "numerous agents and dependants [sic]" (175), who performs a cataract operation that triumphantly restores Dudley's sight.[55] Dudley's revolution in circumstances and Constantia's revolution in economic fortunes bring into renewed focus the politically charged issues of gratitude and "marriage," as Ormond tries to barter his kindness toward Dudley for an alliance with Constantia by appealing, like Balfour, to her sense that "gratitude was no perverse or ignoble principle" (176). Subsequently he discloses to Constantia the broad outlines of his "schemes of an arduous and elevated nature" (177) in an attempt to pique her curiosity, "regulate her condition" (177), and eventually convert her to the cause. Sophia pithily sums up her friend's situation: "Constantia's peril was imminent" (179).

Equally convinced of her peril, now that he can once again see, is

Constantia's father, who plans secretly to abscond with his daughter to Italy. But when he is abruptly "assailed by the great subverter of human schemes" (214) – he has been murdered! – Sophia, ever the self-satisfied sermonizer, comments rather lyrically on Constantia's situation: "Thou sawest nothing in futurity but an eternal variation and succession of delights. Thou wast hastening to forget dangers and sorrows which thou fondly imaginedst were never to return. This day was to be the outset of a new career; existence was henceforth to be embellished with enjoyments, hitherto scarcely within the reach of hope" (214). In terms of the narrator's "Federalist" sentimentalism, Constantia's credulous receptivity to Ormond's seductive influences exemplifies an absolute failure of vigilance, which threatens her with an absolute fall. And now, like America as imaged in Washington's Farewell Address, the innocent and frail Constantia stands alone, exposed and vulnerable in a world of imminent danger.

Actually, Constantia is not entirely alone, for soon after Dudley's death Sophia makes a late entrance into the action of the novel, as if to substitute for the father. Her presence becomes a new obstacle in the way of Ormond's pursuit of Constantia – or does Ormond stand as the final obstacle in the way of Sophia's pursuit of her beloved Constantia? As my question suggests, Sophia's emergence as a participating character necessarily brings to surface the personal desires and anxieties underpinning her countersubversive narrative, and it brings to surface the political anxieties underpinning it as well. Having witnessed the upheaval of the French Revolution, "a scene of horrors, of which the history of former wars, furnish us with few examples" (232), Sophia claims special knowledge of what lies behind the mask of Enlightenment progressivism. She asserts, for example, that "pillage and murder are engrafted, on systems of all-embracing and self-oblivious benevolence, and the good of mankind is professed to be pursued with bonds of association and covenants of secrecy" (253). Thus she suspects the secretive associationist Ormond: "I had seen too much of innovation and imposture, in France and Italy, not to regard a man like this with aversion and fear. The mind of my friend was wavering and unsuspicious" (252). Appropriately, after having touched on the French Revolution, Enlightenment rationalism, and Constantia's credulity, Sophia makes the Federalist-Congregationalist leap to conspiracy and has Ormond speak with relative candor on his background and intentions.

In an account of his political activity, Ormond, whose favorite pastime is chess, portrays the Continent as a gameboard of revolutionary activity over which he stands as a grand master. He boasts to Constantia:

> That he had embraced, when almost a child, the trade of arms: That he had found service and promotion in the armies of Potemkin and Ro-

manzow: That he had executed secret and diplomatic functions, at Constantinople and Berlin: That, in the latter city, he had met with schemers and reasoners, who aimed at the new-modelling of the world, and the subversion of all that has hitherto been conceived elementary and fundamental, in the constitution of man and of government: That some of those reformers had secretly united, to break down the military and monarchical fabric of German policy: That others, more wisely, had devoted their secret efforts, not to overturn, but to build: That, for this end, they embraced an exploring and colonizing project: That he had allied himself to these, and, for the promotion of their projects, had spent six years of his life, in journeys by sea and land, in tracts unfrequented, till then, by any European. (252)

The picture of "schemers and reasoners" plotting to "break down" traditional forms of government throughout Europe evokes the threat of the Illuminati. Like the conspirators of Barruel, Robison, and the Congregationalists, Ormond and his associates are Enlightenment rationalists who seek to impose their moral and political views on peoples throughout the world. Evincing no respect for national boundaries and identities, they are international utopianists who want to bring the many into unity through "the subversion of all that has hitherto been conceived elementary and fundamental, in the constitution of man and of government." Because of the youthful and relatively untested nature of its "constitution," America would be especially vulnerable to such subversives. And so the alarmist Sophia teasingly adds, "What were the moral or political maxims, which this adventurous and visionary sect had adopted, and what was the seat of their new-born empire, whether on the shore of an *Austral* continent, or in the heart of desert America, he carefully concealed" (252). In anti-Illuminati tracts of the period, it was the countersubversive's *undocumented* assertion of the Illuminati's presence in America that made their threat loom so ominously.[56] Sophia's preserving of mystery, her heightening of suspense, and her possible use, like the subversive Ormond attempting to convert Constantia, of "fictional embellishments . . . adapted . . . to [her] purpose" (178) – all work to make the conspiring Ormond, almost completely defined now by her countersubversive discourse, both frightening and appalling.

Defined by Sophia's discourse, however, he is familiarly appalling. When Ormond perceives that he has failed to convince Constantia to join his "schemers," he tosses aside his mask of Enlightenment utopianist to reveal himself as the archetypal villain of popular fictions and countersubversive rhetoric: the expedient satanic seducer who wants nothing more than to defame and deflower America's chaste women, emblems (as the Congregationalists would have it) of America's Protestant republican purity. Arriving to contest Constantia's decision to travel with Sophia to England, he threatens her, albeit vaguely, with an impending rape, "one more disaster" (259), that, perversely, he believes will educate her on the shallowness of her moral values. And though Ormond's use of language had earlier been comic and audacious, somewhat "artistic," he now wields language as an intimidating weapon that obscures the immorality of rape and, so his wordplay suggests – "The moment we inspect it nearly, it vanishes" (259) – mocks Constantia's chastity. As secret witness seemingly present – "Henceforth, the stream of our existence was to mix; we were to act and think in common: Casual witnesses and written testimony should become superfluous" (251) – Sophia underscores in heightened melodramatic prose the urgency of the impending crisis: "What reliance should she place upon prophetic incoherencies, thus wild? What precautions should she take, against a danger thus inscrutable and imminent?" (261).

The final scene addresses these questions and brings to focus the anxieties, political and moral, informing the novel of seduction and the fear of conspiracy in Federalist America. The orphaned Constantia retreats to her father's house in New Jersey, like the temple in *Wieland* a metaphorical construct for America's precarious position in a world of dead or soon to be dead fathers. Sophia writes: "Every thing in this scene had been created and modelled by the genius of her father. It was a kind of fane, sanctified by his imaginary presence" (266). In this chaste and simple but vulnerable sanctuary, Constantia at last learns a principal lesson of the political rhetoric of the 1790s, a lesson that Sophia has stressed repeatedly in the novel's many analogous presentations of invisible infiltration: Although American domestic life does not appear to be under any great threat, beneath the calm lurk awful subversive forces. "She had hitherto indulged an habitual indifference to danger," Sophia remarks as Constantia views Ormond approaching the house. "Now the presence of Ormond, the unknown purpose that led him hither, and the defencelessness of her condition, inspired her with apprehensions to which she had hitherto been a stranger" (271). It is night, the climactic scene takes place in a disorienting darkness, and Constantia is alone in her second-floor study, "a kind of closet" (268). Horrors ensue: Constantia steps over a dead body, Ormond enters the house and traps her in a hallway, and a dreadful revelation of his villainous expediency is at last achieved. The dead man is Craig, who had murdered Constantia's father at Ormond's behest. The master rationalizer chivalrously justifies his actions: "My happiness and your's [sic], depended on your concurrence with my wishes. Your father's life was an obstacle to your concurrence. For killing him, therefore, I may claim your gratitude" (281). And now, with no apparent obstacle standing between him and Constantia, the expedient villain prepares to make his final assault upon American "CHASTITY."

"Gratification of personal desires or passions, especially the sex urge, is the main wellspring of evil in Brown's arch-villains," one critic writes.[57] The sex urge is also analogous to all other forms of infiltration we have encountered in the narrative: Like Craig, marketplace forces, fever, and Ormond himself, its "gradual and invisible approaches" (26) pose a disintegrative threat to self and community. Ormond earlier commented on the subversive nature of sexuality: "Sexual sensations associating themselves, in a certain way, with our ideas, beget a disease, which has, indeed, found no place in the catalogue, but is a case of more entire subversion and confusion of mind than any other" (160). Now infected with this disorienting "disease," Ormond abandons his political idealism for an immediate gratification that signifies his ultimate debasement from utopianist to rapist. He places Constantia in the position of submitting in life or else in death (necrophilia to Ormond is better than nothing at all), and only when the threat achieves such clear definition can Constantia finally act: With her penknife she slays the baneful foe. Having finally been aroused to self-defense, having finally properly perceived her enemy, Constantia discovers that her virtue endows her with a force capable of warding off demons. Similarly, Congregationalist sermons counseled that, in Dwight's words, "personal piety, righteousness, and temperance" (along with proper political and religious affiliations) would suffice to ward off even so portentous a threat as the Illuminati, thus ensuring, as Washington had prayed, "that the free constitution, which is the work of your hands, may be sacredly maintained." The threat of rape literalizes the notion of constitution, which is preserved through the work of Constantia's hands. Dwight remarked in *The Duty of Americans,* "No one can conjecture how many will be made safer, and happier, by the virtue of one."[58] Constantia's virtuous constancy is saving and, ideally, representative.

Creating a narrator who employs the melodramatic rhetorical strategies of the Federalist-Congregationalist persuasion, Brown permits an alarmist vision of American vulnerability to dominate the novel. It is an alarmism reflective of the narrator's self-avowed political and social anxiety and, I think we are meant to realize, of her desire to bring the reader's anxiety to such a pitch that we are prepared to condone, or even applaud, the violence that purges her narratized world of its prime subversive threat. There is something frightening about the way in which Sophia uses melodrama to implicate the reader in the sort of "dragon-killing" that Frye identifies as the central "wish-fulfillment" of archetypal romance.[59] Whereas Freneau links Federalist countersubversion to the political will to dominate opposing others, Brown more disturbingly links Sophia's "Federalism" to the political will to eliminate opposing others.

According to Washington, however, the best defense for Americans under seige from plotters is not brute force (or imprisonment and deportation, as set in place by the Alien and Sedition Laws), but an imaginary Palladium willed into being by a consensual desire for virtuous independence. In her account of Constantia's self-defensive violence, Sophia rhetorically fashions her own version of Washington's "American romance." Like Washington, Sophia emphasizes American vulnerability by noting, shortly after Constantia realizes she is imperiled, the new republic's absence of protective edifices: "There was no fortress, guarded by barriers of stone and iron, and watched by centinels that never slept, to which she might retire from his strategems" (264). But though lacking the refuge of an actual fortress, Constantia possesses something far more impregnable. Describing Constantia's seemingly hopeless situation in her father's "fane," Sophia uses the words "conspiracy" and "conspired" for the first and only time in the narrative. In doing so, given that she is describing a one-on-one encounter, she points to the political-allegorical significance of the confrontation. Constantia wants to flee Ormond's presence but, Sophia relates, "this impulse was followed by the recollection, that her liberty was taken away: That egress from the hall was denied her, and that this restriction might be part of some conspiracy of Ormond, against her life" (282). On the verge of being raped by a plotter synecdochically (and allegorically) representing anti-republican conspirators, Constantia, according to Sophia, has two options: "strategem or force" (282). But as Sophia goes on to explain, "For the contrivance and execution of frauds, all the habits of her life and all the maxims of her education, had conspired to unfit her. Her force of muscles would avail her nothing, against the superior energy of Ormond" (282). Confronted by a powerful conspirator, the republican heroine transcends power and conspiracy, her violence sentimentalized by Sophia as passive and seemingly providential, enabled, in effect, by her Palladium of virtue. Constantia's might signifies right; such is Sophia's American romance. The murder, remarkably, is not dramatized by our "secret witness," who has Constantia absolved by a legal panel before taking her to England, a country of "security and repose" (292). For Sophia, repose may be attained simply by returning to a prerevolutionary moment, a moment that, on the evidence of *Ormond,* has forever disappeared. Before herself disappearing, Sophia concludes her text with an appropriate final word to the reader: "Farewell" (294). As in Washington's Farewell Address, her own farewell bequeathes to the reader the responsibilities of vigilance and, as post-Farewell Federalists understood the address, the prerogative of force.

I have suggested that *Ormond* consists of competing perspectives – Sophia's sentimentalized alarmism and a submerged "Enlightenment" irony that encourages us to distrust her moralizations. A sense of competition between the two perspectives informs the final melodramatic scene; for while Sophia conventionalizes the confrontation between Ormond and Constantia as a battle between villainy and vulnerability, the development of feminist themes throughout the novel encourages us to view Constantia's vanquishing of Ormond as an expression as well of her "vindication of the rights of women." Ormond's extreme insistence on imposing power elicits an extreme response, one that is presaged in *Alcuin* by Mrs. Carter's passionate declaration on the utter necessity of free choice in marriage: "Offer me any alternative, condemn me to the workshop of an Egyptian task-master, imprison me in chains of toil and stripes and contumelies, but allow me, I beseech you, the liberty, at least, of conjugal choice."[60] Ormond offers Constantia no choice at all, and he pays the price that he did not have to pay when dealing with the pliant Helena. Sophia develops a sentimental political allegory of Constantia's triumph over villainy; a competing discourse asks us to consider Constantia's violence in the larger context of her antipatriarchal quest for liberty.

On the one hand, Brown uses Sophia's narrative to suggest that the preservation of liberty may require a "reactionary" power; on the other hand, he develops a competing perspective to demystify countersubversive power. But though at odds and competing, the novel's two perspectives (or narratives) are also complementary and often congruent with each other, yielding a relatively coherent picture of Ormond as a socially irresponsible and immoral villain who is anything but "a tribute to the Enlightenment."[61] Moreover, Sophia's alarmist narrative responds to a world that her creator too suggests is provisional and threatening. No matter how dismissive we might be of Sophia's conventionalizations, we cannot ignore the fact of Brown's complicitous involvement in emphasizing the unstable, shifting, indeterminate qualities of Sophia and Constantia's America. Sophia's narrative, however simple-mindedly, seeks to order a disorderly social landscape that both she and Brown, the plotter behind the narrator, view with some apprehension.

From the outset of the novel, social and economic interactions in republican America are characterized by self-interest and duplicity. Craig forges letters and counterfeits identity, undermining the familial order of the Dudleys, who counterfeit a new name of their own, Acworth, that serves as a protective mask permitting a submergence in the democratic stream: The Dudley–Acworth plunge looks forward to the Fauntleroy–Moodie plunge in *The Blithedale Romance*. *Ormond*, like *Blithedale*, dramatizes the difficulty of achieving stability in a democratic nation in which everyone, not just stigmatized villains, "affect[s] to conceal nothing" (114) while in fact concealing all. Helena is not married to Ormond and her name is not Mrs. Eden; Monrose is not Monrose, and Ursula Monrose is not Ursula Monrose or "Monrose"'s daughter. Lacking Sophia's ability to manufacture explanatory melodramatic narratives that, as Peter Brooks comments generally on melodrama, "allay the threat of moral chaos," the defenseless American quite naturally could succumb to the self-consuming paranoia of a Baxter.[62]

Recurring images of psychological instability further convey an unsettling sense of the postrevolutionary moment that is at least as disturbing as Sophia's topographical alarmism. To return to the problem of Constantia's violence, what is obviously evasive about Sophia's narrative is its failure to address the problem of human psychology. In the interpolated portrait of the fearful Baxter working himself into a frenzy, Brown deftly shows how citizens of the new nation could create their own subversive demons. But because Sophia refuses to consider the possibility that Constantia has herself suffered a mental disintegration, she can very easily tidy up a novel that builds to her pure maiden's homicidal act.

Brown generates the more complex psychological themes of the text by obliquely suggesting that submerged in the psyche of Sophia's idealized heroine is a repressed other self that is potentially murderous. The other self is exemplified by the seemingly peripheral Martinette, an ardent revolutionary and Ormond's long-lost sister. From the moment Constantia first views "Ursula Monrose" (Martinette) in a music store, she is fascinated by the foreigner's face. According to Sophia, Constantia has a "sixth sense" (77) that responds tellingly to physiognomy, but Sophia remarks that the real reason for Constantia's engaged response to the stranger is that "if we substitute a nobler stature, and a complexion less uniform and delicate, it is suited, with the utmost accuracy, to herself" (78). Sophia asserts that Constantia "was probably unconscious of this resemblance" (77); but surely it is Sophia who retreats from exploring the significance of Constantia's attraction to her double. Ormond, who we eventually learn is Martinette's brother, asks Constantia during one of their earlier conversations, "Is there no part of me in which you discover your own likeness?" (167). Martinette is that part of Ormond in which she discovers that likeness and confronts it.

The essential likeness, Constantia supposes for quite some time, is that both she and Martinette are long-suffering daughters valiantly caring for their enfeebled fathers. Thus when she finally converses with Martinette, more than two-thirds of the way into the novel, she is surprised to learn that the woman who seemingly had been frightened off by Baxter when her "father" died, in fact, as an emigrant in a city of emigrants, had found immediate refuge with her compatriots, "fugitives from Marat and from St. Domingo" (209), who somewhat threateningly form a secretive subcommunity within Philadelphia. As it turns out, the ide-alized virtuous daughter is an antipatriarchal foreign revolutionary whose universalist political vision, like Ormond's, poses a distinct chal-lenge to the very idea of *American* nationality. The daughter of a Greek and a Ragusan, orphaned in youth, and educated in several countries, Martinette lacks the roots of a "frail Mimosa" (192–3) and soon develops sympathies that are transnational and revolutionary. While in Verona she studies with Father Bartoli, a philosophe and a thoroughly corrupt se-ducer. "I panted after liberty" (196), Martinette tells Constantia; and her desire to free herself from the lecherous Bartoli stands as her first anti-patriarchal revolutionary act (and one that Brown's Protestant reading public would have readily applauded). As a natural outgrowth of her initial revolutionism, Martinette marries a political enthusiast and travels with him to fight in America's glorious Revolutionary War.

But as Martinette continues to relate her life story she seems in-creasingly monstrous, an itinerant revolutionary whose character is de-termined and shaped almost entirely by the unloosed revolutionary ener-gies of the age. Hardly pausing to mourn the death of her husband before journeying to France to participate in that country's revolution, Mar-tinette asserts that she participates in violent military actions as part of her impassioned quest for universal political liberty: "I am an adorer of liberty, and liberty without peril can never exist" (206). It would appear, however, that in the course of her pursuit of "liberty" the political progressive has become a revolutionary savage and that her transforma-tion has everything to do with the cycles of violence characterizing the French Revolution. As her name suggests, Martinette during the French Revolution becomes a stalwart revolutionary and a victim as well, both a martinet and Marie Antoinette. Forced to return to America to escape the fury of her former associates' Reign of Terror, she speaks of her delight in the fall of Robespierre, while the "blood, which it occasioned to flow was mentioned without any symptoms of disgust or horror" (206). She asks Constantia, "What are bleeding wounds and mangled corpses, when accustomed to the daily sight of them for years? Am I not a lover of liberty . . . ?" (206). So enthusiastic is her revolutionism that she can justify killing two former lovers, again in the name of "liberty": "My hand never faultered when liberty demanded the victim" (206). She even contemplates committing suicide for the revolutionary cause. "What could lead to such an outrage?" Constantia asks (207), prompting the predictable response: "The love of liberty" (207). Though Brown had indeed suggested in *Alcuin* that women properly trained could serve as soldiers, his portrait of Martinette's bloody soldiery appears calculated to shock the reader and express his own, not just Sophia's, distrust of the revolutionary personality in the late eighteenth century. With her blood passion looming above all political, personal, and national loyalties, Martinette is in spirit as well as in flesh the sister of Ormond, who, we learn a few chapters later, had once taken five Turkish heads in vengeful sport.[63]

Martinette's narrative offers Constantia a direct encounter with the revolutionary impulses of the age that threaten to collapse the dichotomy between the civilized self and the savage other. After listening to Martinette's recital of murders serving the cause of "liberty," Constantia recoils in disgust from her implied double. The narrator remarks, "She felt that antipathy was preparing to displace love" (207). But though Constantia in effect expels Martinette, she cannot rid her world or herself of a violent potentiality. Her subsequent engagement in a "spectacle of death" (290) expresses a side to her character that Sophia needs to ignore. As Sophia calmly instructs the reader, the murder "was surely not a deed to be thought upon with lasting horror, or to be allowed to generate remorse" (291). In her narrative of conspiracy, all disorder and violence can be projected onto the expedient seducer Ormond; intent on preserving the dichotomy between Jacobin–Illuminati and American, she takes refuge in melodramatic plot.

Viewed ironically and dialogically, however – viewed, that is to say, as *Brown's* narrative of Sophia's narrative – the text leaves wide open the problem of the subversion of self in the postrevolutionary age. The use of doubles throughout the novel suggests that Constantia's final confrontation with Ormond, sentimentalized as is Sophia's account, enacts not simply the vanquishing of an expedient villain but also a transformative coming to life, off stage, of Constantia's murderous other self, a coming to life of what Clara Wieland called in herself a "creature of nameless and fearful attributes." Constantia can thus be seen as an American seeking refuge from those revolutionary energies that, like Ormond's sexuality or Martinette's "love of liberty," threaten to subvert not only self-possession and self-control but also, given America's own revolutionary origins, the political and social order of the new republic. Alone in her father's chaste mansion, post-Edenic America, Constantia seeks shelter from the current "tendency to revolution and war which seemed to actuate all the nations of Europe" (267), in a country "by no means exempt from similar tendencies" (267). And when she has to resort to a self-defensive murder to stave off the "diseased" revolutionary, she seems to intuit that she too, by virtue of her own descent into an anti-patriarchal revolutionary savagery, is "by no means exempt from similar tendencies." From Sophia's point of view, the murder represents a triumphant moral victory, a national exorcism of sorts that, for the time being anyway, maintains the boundary between chaste America and "vileness and pollution" (291). But as Constantia bewails herself as "the lost Constantia" (289) – "her eyes wildly fixed upon the cieling [*sic*] and streaming with tears and her hair unbound and falling confusedly over her bosom and neck" (289) – the virtuous heroine has never appeared more vulnerable.

With their dual emphases on vulnerability, Sophia's countersubversive narrative and the postrevolutionary/Enlightenment narrative complement one another in presenting a dark picture of America's political and social precariousness during the years immediately following the stabilizing intent of the Constitution and the destabilizing impact of the French Revolution. *Ormond*'s complex historicism thus derives in large part from Brown's suggestion of a competing perspective that does not mock but rather deepens an understanding of the drive toward narrative (and national) coherence informing Sophia's alarmist presentation, and for that matter informing alarmist writings of the 1790s in general. Brown understands full well the melodramatic symbolic universe of the countersubversive. In *Ormond* what separates him from his narrator Sophia, among other things, is that he possesses a reflective and ironic sense of the relationship between villainy and vulnerability that can guide the reader to perceive at one and the same time the expedient uses of, and anxious needs for, a conspiring other. And yet, appealing as is the presentation of the engagingly unconventional Ormond, and acute as is the demystifying challenge to Sophia's alarmist discourse, Brown nevertheless conveys a "bias" in more than partial sympathy with Sophia's conception of Ormond's villainy and Constantia's vulnerability by emphasizing the dangers attending political, social, economic, and "artistic" concealment, by linking Ormond to Martinette, the political revolutionary gone out of control, and by linking both to Constantia. The image of a vulnerable post-Revolutionary America populated by "creature[s] of nameless and fearful attributes" emerges as the dominating and lingering image of the novel.

"A world of revolutions and perils"

Six months after the publication of *Ormond*, Brown reflected in his *Monthly Magazine and American Review* on the American publication of Augustine Barruel's *Memoirs of Jacobinism*. Declaring that "Barruel was an honest and zealous man," he informed his readers of the plottings, as described by Barruel, "of certain confraternities who called themselves 'The Illuminated'": They have the aim "of destroying the present domestic, political, and religious systems, not partially or locally, but completely and universally; of annihilating every tie of kindred, and every claim of property; of reducing mankind to the state of brutes, and the world to nakedness and desolation." And they seek to do this "not only in Germany and France but throughout the earth." In rehearsing Barruel's charges in such detail, Brown begs the question of whether Illuminati plotting is fantastical or terrifying, but to the very end archly avoids offering his own interpretation: "The validity of Mr. B's conclusions we shall leave to the reader's consideration." Although evasive in his final summation, however, he does pose an ironic challenge to Barruel's conspiratorial theory. In passing, he notes that as an abbé in the Roman Catholic church, Barruel would have wanted to believe that insidious conspirators were responsible for the French Revolution's "reign of impiety and terror." Barruel, for the wholly understandable reason that he felt vulnerable and confused, therefore resorted to a causal explanatory paradigm enabling him to view all dire events as "*foreseen and intended.*"[64] Undermining the authority of Barruel's countersubversive narrative by reminding his readers of its origin and function, Brown suggests, as he suggests in *Wieland* and *Ormond,* that there is an intimate relationship between the villainy of purported subversives and the vulnerability of countersubversives.

Though they do not directly appropriate the flamboyant rhetoric and imagery of the conspiratorial writings of 1798–9, Brown's other major romances also pivot on the relationship of villainy to vulnerability. But whereas the narrators of *Wieland* and *Ormond* insist on preserving a dichotomy between the virtuous American self and the villainous other, in *Edgar Huntly* and *Arthur Mervyn* the dichotomy collapses into dualism: A conspiratorial poetics yields to a postrevolutionary poetics in which inversion is the frightening reality. In *Edgar Huntly,* Huntly does not simply learn that the savagery lurking without also lurks within; he experiences the discovery as a completely unforeseen event – as a "French Revolutionary" irruption – that nearly shatters him. Lost in a mazy wilderness, impelled by impulses and energies he can neither control nor understand, he descends into an unconscious frenzy that eventually leads him to kill several Indians and, "Indianized" himself, attack his "civilized" white pursuers. Contemplating his murderous actions and desires, he confesses to an utter astonishment at his inability to pull himself apart from a guiding bloody "spirit": "All my education and the habits of my life tended to unfit me for a contest and a scene like this. But I was not governed by the soul which usually regulates my conduct. I had imbibed from the unparalleled events which had lately happened a spirit vengeful, unrelenting, and ferocious." Although he eventually returns to the bounds of civilization, the dichotomy between civilized self and savage other is never restored; in this novel, unlike *Wieland* and *Ormond,* conspiratorial theories do not save. We leave Huntly in a state of disintegration and confusion, for he can cull from his experience only a dreadful insight into human fragility: "How little cognizance have men over the actions and motives of each other! How total is our blindness with regard to our own performances!"[65]

While *Arthur Mervyn* presents an alarming vision of the urban American surrounded by a circulating multitude with a multitude of hidden motives, Brown emphasizes in this novel too the collapse of social and psychological boundaries. Guided by "blind and foreign impulses," Mervyn, like Huntly (and Caleb Williams), is throughout the novel both persecuted and persecutory. Professing an inability to gain control over the impulses that seem to guide his actions, Mervyn emerges as a sort of storehouse and generator of free-floating revolutionary energies, repeatedly affecting upheavals in the lives of the unsuspecting. Alarmed and appalled by the many horrible scenes he encounters and affects, he asks himself, "Is every man, who leaves his cottage and the impressions of his infancy behind him, ushered into such a world of revolutions and perils as have trammelled my steps?"[66] In the postrevolutionary moment, the answer, it would appear, is yes. The sum of Mervyn's experiences with various irruptions of disordering phenomena finally prompts him to declare his love for his "Mama" Achsa Fielding and secure a bedrock in marriage. Like Clara and Constantia, he subsequently decides to transplant himself to England, which he nostalgically views as a refuge from the constitutional infirmities of a nation infected by revolutionary fevers.

In the fragment *Memoirs of Carwin the Biloquist* (1803–5), most likely drafted in 1798, shortly after the completion of *Wieland,* Brown explores another side of Americans' fascination with conspiracy, an aspect that was touched on in *Ormond* and would later engage Hawthorne and Melville: the potential attractiveness of a fraternal association that promises to provide the individual with a stable "familial" refuge from the anomie and jolts of the democratic marketplace. In *Ormond,* Constantia is especially susceptible to Ormond's efforts at recruitment precisely because her family's misfortunes have left her so vulnerable. Sophia explains, "To have found her friendless and indigent, accorded, with the most fortunate exactness, with his views." Similarly, in *Memoirs of Carwin* the arch conspirator Ludloe chooses to recruit Carwin, the victim of a tyrannical father, when he is impoverished. Tempted by the harmonious order of Ludloe's secretive utopianist organization, Carwin prepares to throw in his lot with a group that treats him like "a member of [a] family." Brown, however, ultimately seeks community with his republican and predominantly Protestant readers by developing an analogy between Ludloe's Illuminati-like utopianist group and America's traditionally detested antirepublican enemy, the Roman Catholic church. Drawing on Robison's portrayal of Illuminati initiation as a form of "auricular confession," Brown, like Robison, arouses reader anxiety by dramatizing the dangers inherent in priestcraft. Ironically, the Enlightenment rationalist Ludloe emerges as a type of crafty priest, a frightening confessor who bestows privilege only after attaining total mastery: To join the secretive order Carwin "must determine to disclose every fact in his story, and every secret of his heart." By the end of the fragment, Carwin faces his "judicial inquisitor" with the diminishing hope of keeping secret what it would appear Ludloe knows full – that he commands biloquial powers. "To confide the secret to one," Carwin confesses to his reader, "was to put an end to my privilege."[67] A text that begins as a sympathetic portrayal of Carwin's search for community concludes with the fearful image of inquisitorial Ludloe lording it over an American on the verge of having to surrender all privilege.

After the election of Jefferson a political conservatism would come to dominate Brown's work. The preface to his *American Review and Literary Journal for the Year 1801* straightforwardly announces his journalistic aspirations at that time: "*Morality* and *Religion,* the pillars which uphold the fabrics of society and government, we feel it is our duty, on this and on every other occasion, to strengthen and maintain to the best of our ability." His final two novels, the more conventionally sentimental *Clara Howard* (1801) and *Jane Talbot* (1801), are in large part efforts by the "Sophia" side of his authorial self to "uphold the fabrics of society and government" during a time of "revolutions and perils." In *Clara Howard,* Edward Hartley is prompted by his beloved Clara to act on his promise to marry Miss Wilmot; he achieves "terrestrial felicity" only after he takes to heart Clara's belief "that the welfare of another may demand self denial . . . and that in bestowing benefits on others, there is a purer delight than in gratifications merely selfish and exclusive." Similarly, in *Jane Talbot* Henry Colden, "a man without religion," obtains the hand of his beloved Jane only after he perceives the limitations of his skepticism. He declares, "I have awakened from my dreams of doubt and misery, not to the cold and vague belief, but to the living and delightful consciousness of every tie that can bind man to his divine parent and judge." In both of these epistolary novels the courter is brought under social control, not by a melodramatic vanquishing, but by a sentimental conversion: In response to the entreaties of various letter writers, Hartley and Colden eventually renounce their former ways to become Christian "Federalists." Whereas the villain of *Ormond* is violently purged, the not so very villainous suitors of *Clara Howard* and *Jane Talbot* are "treated." Brown's fiction in the early 1800s becomes therapeutic.[68]

His political writings of the period likewise reflect a more pronounced Sophia-like concern about "the defencelessness of her condition" – a concern that the new nation loomed as an especially seductive temptation to expedient foreign plotters. This prominent and ironically presented motif of his major novels found relatively sober expression in his widely read anonymous pamphlet *An Address to the Government of the United States, on the Cession of Louisiana to the French* (1803). In this decidedly countersubversive text, Brown sought to alert Americans to the dangerous situation brought about by the Spanish cession of the Western territories to the French. Claiming to have intercepted the French first consul's secret letter to his government, Brown prints for the reader's edification the message itself, a first-person narrative recommending that France exploit the fact that "the states are vulnerable in every way and in every point" to pursue nothing less than total conquest. As the consul proclaims: "To contract our empire is not the end of my councils. On the contrary, my heart beats high with the hope of adding to it, not an island, but a *world*." Brown's narrative performance builds to the consul's revelation of plot:

> We shall find, in the Indian tribes, an army permanently cantoned in the most convenient stations; endowed with skill and temper best adapted to the nature and the scene of war, and armed and impelled with far less trouble and expense than an equal number of our own troops. . . . We shall find, in the bowels of the States, a mischief that only wants the touch of a well-directed spark to involve in its explosion, the utter ruin of half their nation. *Such will be the powers we shall derive from a military station and a growing colony on the Mississippi.*[69]

Never more the political alarmist than during the years of Jefferson's administration, Brown in the *Address* touches upon a deeply engrained republican tenet contributing to the Louisiana Purchase and, a few years later, to the outcry over Burr's alleged Western Conspiracy: the fear that a republic inhabiting a large geographical territory remains particularly vulnerable to "the insidious wiles of foreign influence." Whereas his major novels of the late 1790s ironically portray attempts to preserve the moral boundary between the virtuous American self and the villainous European other, the *Address* dramatically points to the need literally to shore up and extend America's geographical boundaries in order to preserve the national self. This is Brown's "transformation." Yet because Brown as pamphleteer-fictionist must work upon his reader's imagination through "the insidious wiles of foreign influence," he appears to relish not only the role of concerned citizen unmasking conspiracy but also the opportunity of imagining himself into the role of such a bold and energetic subversive. Even at his most politically concerned, Brown, a connoisseur of conspiracy, cannot relinquish the pleasures afforded by his masterminding villains.

2

"Soulless Corporation"

Oligarchy and the Countersubversive Presence in James Fenimore Cooper's The Bravo

Here are no aristocratical families, no courts, no kings, no bishops, no ecclesiastical dominion, no invisible power giving to a few a very visible one.

Crèvecoeur, *Letters from an American Farmer*

It appears to be the melancholy lot of humanity, that every institution which ingenuity can devise shall be perverted to an end different from the legitimate. . . . So it is with life; in politics, religion, arms, arts and letters, yes, even the republic of letters, as it is called, is the prey of schemers and parasites, and things *in fact,* are very different from things *as they seem to be.*

Cooper, *Gleanings in Europe: France*

Although Fenimore Cooper expressed his admiration for Brockden Brown's fiction in *Notions of the Americans* (1828), he differed from Brown in celebrating the openness of the trustful American republic, "the only civilized country, I believe, into which a stranger can enter without being liable to intrusion on his privacy by agents of the police."[1] But despite his avowed lack of concern over the permeability of America's borders, that same year, in private letters to friends, he began to express his own fears of the republic's vulnerability to imperialistic intrigue. Seeking to account for the tense sectional debates on the tariff and Nullification, Cooper came to believe that England was conspiring to divide the Union so as to regain control over its former colony (and in significant ways he anticipated the British government's policies during the American Civil War). Writing to Luther Bradish in 1828, for example, he speculated on England's subversive intentions: "That England

58

will, if she does not now, make powerful efforts in secret to divide the States, I think no man who calmly regards the question, and remembers her uniform course of policy can doubt." Two years later, in a letter to Peter Augustus Jay, he concluded that British plotting "to divide the states" figured as the principal cause of the Nullification crisis: "I am fully persuaded that England is, at this moment, intriguing in the Southern States in order to separate the Union. It is a common topic in all English society, and they scarcely affect to conceal their hopes." Not only had the British engineered the crisis, but, as he confided to William Branford Shubrick, Britain's infiltrators continued to exacerbate sectional tensions: "I am perfectly persuaded that England has her Agents to fan the flames." In *Gleanings in Europe: England* (1837), Cooper went public with his suspicions of England's subversive "project of attempting recolonization," noting that the government's imperial design was a matter of local gossip in English towns: "It would be folly for an American to shut his eyes to the confidence with which even the women, here, speak of the dismemberment of the Union. This is the point to which our enemies will be certain to direct their machinations." And in 1840 he wrote directly to President Martin Van Buren to warn that "British Agents" were recruiting Indians to "fight the Americans."[2] Whereas Brown in the 1790s challenged the authority of the countersubversive by adopting an ironic stance toward narrative, Cooper by the 1830s moved confidently from indications of antirepublican subversion to authoritative pronouncements of conspiracy.

The responses of the two authors to the Illuminati further reveal their differing attitudes toward conspiracy. In Brockden Brown's review of Augustine Barruel, we observed that although Brown may have shared some of the abbé's concerns, he ultimately responded with skepticism by interpreting the fear of Illuminati conspiracy as a desperate effort by Barruel and others to shore up their diminishing prestige. Commenting on the Illuminati in *England,* Cooper similarly viewed the promulgation of this fear as a self-defensive reaction, but one so well organized as to comprise its own sort of conspiracy:

> Little accustomed to think for ourselves, and with a corrupt and interested press, we have lent greedy ears to *ex-parte* testimony, and, ready enough to oppose the principles of the Age of Reason and of the Illuminati, we have overlooked the essential circumstances that they are merely the reaction of extreme abuses, and that the root of the evil lies deeper than the disgusting excesses which have been so zealously paraded before our eyes.

According to Cooper, the extremes of the French Revolution and the dissemination of countersubversive texts warning of Illuminati conspiracy constituted "deeper" organized efforts on the part of British and French aristocrats both to discredit desires for reform and to promote reactionary counterrevolutionary measures. As evidence for his theory of the plot behind the plot, Cooper offered an account of a discussion he had with Lafayette:

> We were conversing on the subject of the probable agency of the monarchs and aristocrats of Europe, in bringing about the excesses of the revolution. "Count N_____ was in England during the peace of Amiens," said our venerable friend [Lafayette], "and he dined with Lord G_____, one of Mr. Pitt's cabinet. They were standing together at a window of the drawing-room, when Lord G_____ pointed to a window of a house at a little distance, and said, 'that is the window of the room in which F_____ lodged, when in England.' 'F_____,' exclaimed Count N_____, 'what can you know, my Lord, of such a man as F_____!' The English minister smiled significantly, and replied, 'why, *we sent him to France.*'" By substituting for "Count N_____" the name of a Frenchman who has been a minister under nearly every government in France for the last forty years, and whose private and public character is one of the best of that country; for that of Lord G_____, a well known English statesmen; and that of F_____, one of the greatest monsters to which the Reign of Terror gave birth, you will have the story almost in the words in which it was related to me by General Lafayette, who told me he had it from Count N_____ himself.[3]

Inclined to suspect villainous Englishmen, Cooper was willing publicly to imply, on the basis of an informal conversation two hands removed, that conspiratorial intrigue among British aristocrats "gave birth" to the violent extremes of the French Revolution.

As these several passages indicate, Cooper was more prone to suspicion than Brown, and certainly more insistent on his authority to unmask and unveil the truths behind hidden goings-on. His faith in his acumen as countersubversive would affect his art considerably. Whereas Brown's skeptical undermining of narrative authority informed romances that in the main are characterized by ambiguity and dialogical play, Cooper generally (and, fortunately, not always successfully) endeavored to contain the play of language, especially in his romances of the 1830s and 1840s on sociopolitical themes, by employing an authoritative omniscient narrator, or a first-person narrator very much like Cooper, who knows all and reveals all. In this respect Cooper's sense of his authorial self was markedly different than Brown's. At least until the election of Jefferson, Brown remained on the political margins, an outsider who implicitly challenged praxis by raising disturbing questions about the limits of human authority and self-knowledge. In contrast, Cooper, by 1830 or so, conceived of himself as a guardian of republican liberty who, with a prescience shared by few others, detected a conspiracy of the "aristocrats of Europe" to subvert and control the world's republics.

Concerned that America too could fall victim to a conspiracy of antirepublican aristocrats, Cooper sought to warn Americans about the hidden dangers facing any seemingly healthy and prosperous republican community. Significantly, he warned of the threat posed by plotting aristocrats at a time when many Americans similarly feared their insidious subversive influence. This chapter studies the relationship of the conspiratorial fears and discourse of the American 1820s and 1830s, particularly the fear of conspiring aristocrats, to Cooper's parallel concerns as expressed in his nonfictional writings and romances. Cooper's emergence in *The Bravo* (1831) as a republican Jeremiah warning, as the Antimasons and Jacksonians warned, of oligarchical-corporate subversion is my central focus.

"The efficacy of perfect organization"

The American 1820s, a postheroic moment during which Cooper rose to international prominence as the nation's leading novelist, consisted of a "light" and a "dark": It was a culture of masks. Celebrations of America's republican virtue and burgeoning economy masked concerns about the ingress of "European" corruption and luxury; millennial assertions of the republic's future glory and redemptive mission masked intimations of cyclical decline and uneasiness over the slaughter of the Indians; faith in the sacred bonds of Union, as espoused in Clay's American System and embodied in internal improvements, masked the sectional strains of the Missouri Compromise and, later, the Nullification and tariff debates.[4] To be sure, America of the 1820s was far more secure, far more an established historical fact, than America of the late eighteenth century.[5] But in attempting to understand the reemergence of widely shared conspiratorial fears in the 1820s, we may return to the 1790s for instructive parallels. Like the mid-1790s, the mid-1820s saw an idealized political consensus shattered by party politics when Quincy Adams obtained electoral support from the Clay camp to win the election of 1824. What especially disturbed Jacksonian partisans about the "corrupt bargain" was that it all happened behind the scenes. Though Jackson was the choice of the electorate, plain Old World deal making determined the result of a purportedly democratic election. Like the Jeffersonians, Jacksonians turned to republican rhetoric for a compelling polarity: Those in power were corrupt aristocrats; those excluded from power were virtuous republicans. Michael Rogin explains, "Jackson located republican simplicity in the countryside; pomp, intrigue, hidden motives, and conspiracy dominated Washington."[6] By the late 1820s politicians on all sides found it useful to champion themselves as democratic representatives of "the people" doing heroic battle against conspiring aristocrats and their secretive organizations.

Perhaps the most revealing indication of the resurgent countersubversive temper was the rise of Antimasonry, an extreme expression of pervasive doubts about America's ability to retain its virtuous republican character during a time of growth and prosperity. The story has become a familiar one. In the summer of 1826, William Morgan, a stonemason and former Mason from Batavia, New York, announced his plans to publish an exposé of the secretive Free Masons. Shortly thereafter he was arrested on a dubious debt claim, kidnapped from jail, and, apparently, drowned in the Niagara River, presumably by angry Masons. With an apparently complicitous (because silent) press and police, people began to suspect a conspiracy; these suspicions seemed borne out when Morgan's accused murderers at the 1827 trial were either released or given short jail terms by Masonic jurors. As a result of the trial and the posthumous publication of Morgan's *Illustrations of Masonry* (1826), the interstate Antimasonic Party took shape. Dedicated to the quashing of what it alleged was an aristocratic organization threatening to corrupt the character of the republic, the Antimasonic Party demonstrated considerable political strength through the early 1830s.[7]

Although somewhat bizarre, the Antimasonic response to the events of 1826–7 should not be dismissed as mere hysteria. Because modern Masonry had its origins in London's Grand Lodge of 1717, there is a sense in which the countersubversive campaign against Masons re-enacted the Revolutionary campaign against George's subversive court, thereby fulfilling, we may hypothesize, a postheroic generation's need to lay equal claim to the creation and shaping of the new republic. Antimasonry also expressed a typically American hostility toward secretive societies, which were generally perceived as antirepublican, antidemocratic, and antinationalistic. In this respect the popular outcry against the Society of the Cincinnati, the Federalists' suspicion of the Democratic Clubs, the Jeffersonians' suspicion of Hamilton's Bank of the United States, and the fear of plotting Jacobins and conspiratorial Illuminati were all important cultural antecedents to the rise of Antimasonic activity. It is not surprising, then, that the second plank of the "Antimasonic National Platform of 1832" (1831) should have harked back to the 1790s and reasserted an apocalyptic warning from the Farewell Address of "the Illustrious Washington": " 'That all combinations and associations, under whatever plausible character, with the real design to direct, control, counteract, or awe the regular deliberation and action of the constituted authorities, are destructive of the fundamental principle of liberty, and of fatal tendency.' "[8]

Apocalyptic as it could be, Antimasonry of the 1820s and 1830s, considered in its more immediate social context, was a relatively down-to-earth political and religious movement that attracted followers, most notably New York's "burned-over district" farmers, who were suffering through a period of severe economic hardship. Antimasonry offered these participants a forum for venting their frustrations with the increasing centralization, urban orientation, and seeming mystification of economic institutions: Those who failed to achieve the successes promised by the economic expansion and egalitarian myths of the 1820s could place the blame on an occult fraternal organization that appeared to gain its power by separating wealthy insiders from struggling outsiders.[9] And the fear of Masons was not even so naïve. By 1825 there were approximately 450 Masonic chapters in America, with more than 20,000 members. To nonmembers this affluent association, which could execute a dissenter like Morgan with near impunity, was for good reason perceived as a daunting threat. For Antimasons the full extent of Masonic hegemony was made clear by a prominent Mason, W. F. Brainard, whose (probably apocryphal) peroration to an 1825 speech delivered before his union lodge was often cited in Antimasonic tracts:

> What is Masonry now? IT IS POWERFUL. It comprises men of RANK, wealth, office and talent, in power and out of power; and that in almost every place where POWER IS OF ANY IMPORTANCE. . . . They are distributed too, with the means of knowing one another, and the means of keeping secret, and the means of co-operating, in the DESK – in the LEGISLATIVE HALL – on the BENCH – in every GATHERING OF BUSINESS – in every PARTY OF PLEASURE – IN EVERY ENTERPRISE OF GOVERNMENT – in every DOMESTIC CIRCLE – in PEACE and in WAR – among ENEMIES AND FRIENDS – in ONE PLACE as well as in ANOTHER! SO POWERFUL indeed, is it at this time, (June 24th, 1825) [sic] that it fears nothing from VIOLENCE, either PUBLIC or PRIVATE; FOR IT HAS EVERY MEANS, TO LEARN IT IN SEASON TO COUNTERACT, DEFEAT AND PUNISH IT![10]

According to Antimasons, Brainard's boasting exemplified, in the words of David Bernard's widely read *Light on Masonry* (1829), the "unchastened ambition of Free Masonry."[11] Deviously sponsoring an unholy alliance between private and public enterprise, penetrating "almost every place where POWER IS OF ANY IMPORTANCE," and achieving an omniscient control over even the inviolate sanctum of the "DOMESTIC CIRCLE," covertly plotting Masons were believed to possess unlimited power.

The Illuminati similarly were depicted as omniscient subversives who secured power, as Timothy Dwight warned, by secretly penetrating American society and corrupting the family. But though rhetorical representations of the Free Masons bore striking resemblances to representations of the Illuminati, Antimasons, drawing on the sure-fire effectiveness of Jacksonian egalitarian rhetoric, placed a special emphasis on the conspirators' ability to infiltrate and control economic institutions. As a result, Antimasonic rhetoric tended to pivot on the melodramatic opposition between insidious aristocrats and vulnerable democrats. Portraying the contention for power allegedly consuming the nation, William Henry Seward, in "Address of the Minority of the Members of the [New York] legislature of 1831," offered a Manichean picture of the two opposing camps that was altogether typical:

> On the one side is an aristocratic nobility, composed of men bound together by the most terrific oaths, which conflict with the administration of justice, with private rights, and with the public security; a privileged order, claiming and securing to its members unequal advantages over their fellow-citizens, veiling its proceedings from scrutiny by pledges of secrecy, collecting funds to unknown amounts and for unknown purposes, and operating through our extended country at any time and on any subject, with all the efficacy of perfect organization, controlled and directed by unseen and unknown hands.
>
> On the other side, a portion of your fellow-citizens ask for equal rights and equal privileges among the freemen of this country. They say it is in vain that this equality of rights and privileges is secured in theory by our constitution and laws, if by a combination to subvert it, it is in fact no longer enjoyed. They point you to masonic oaths, and to the effects of those dreadful obligations upon our elections, upon witnesses in courts of justice, and upon jurors. They show you one of your citizens murdered upon their influence, and the offenders escaping with impunity. They exhibit to you the power of your courts defied, and the administration of justice defeated, through the instrumentality of these obligations. . . . They say to you that no man can tell who will be the next victim of masonic vengeance, or of masonic perjury.[12]

The *Dartmouth College* case of 1819 had recently endowed the corporation in America with a new status and power; and we note in Seward's "Address" that Masonic conspirators, unlike the personalized infiltrating Illuminati, were portrayed as an essentially faceless network of internal plotters invisibly undermining the economic opportunities of "the freemen of this country." The corporate "perfect organization" of the Free Masons, repeatedly emphasized in hostile rhetoric, thus made a mockery of democratic opportunity, for by secretly directing the courts, the law enforcement agencies, and the government, Masons would always possess "unfair advantages" over unaffiliated outsiders. In a supposedly egalitarian marketplace, this fraternal society enjoyed the benefits of an "aristocratic nobility." Given the "efficacy" of Masons, then, it seemed nearly impossible to overcome their influence, especially since these omniscient and expedient villains would commit perjury or even murder to preserve their power. But like the Congregationalists who told Americans that the Illuminati could be defeated through a virtuous voting for Federalists, Seward betrayed his own pursuit of power when, in the conclusion to his "Address," he called upon Americans to act: "Use the *only* effective weapon in your power; a weapon yet preserved to you, your own free and independent ballot."[13] Even in a world under Masonic control, a proper vote for the Antimasons could vanquish the arch conspirators.

The fear of Masonic conspiracy in the 1820s, as opposed to the fear of Illuminati conspiracy in the 1790s, centered more on native than on foreign subversives; but despite the shift in emphasis, key elements from anti-Illuminati texts retained their importance. Thus in his "Report on the Progress of the Antimasonic Cause" (1829), Thurlow Weed urged Americans to return to their Barruel and Robison and to study these anti-Illuminati writers with care;[14] for the anti-American conspirator, whether foreign-backed Enlightenment atheist or native-born aristocrat, continued to be conceptualized in terms of the nation's self-defining republican ideology. Formisano and Kutolowski explain: "Republicanism provided the vocabulary of protest; it conditioned the fear that equality before the law – a central tenet of republicanism – was threatened by a secret society's ability to cover up dark deeds and to thwart justice. From that sprang the belief that Masonry's behavior grossly contradicted republican virtue."[15] According to Antimasons, oath-taking Masons, like the Illuminati, indulged in perverse group rituals and sexually deviant behavior and, in their quest for privilege through the exclusiveness of organization, were obliged to renounce national and familial commitments. The threat posed to the nation by antirepublican Masons was therefore both economic and moral. As Antimason David Bernard warned, the large goal of the Masons, "like that of the *Illuminati,* [is] to abolish government and social order and extinguish Christianity."[16] By engaging in a melodramatically conceived battle against Masons, Antimasons could demonstrate their Christian piety, publicly renounce their own desire for economic success in the expanding free market, and reaffirm their commitment to the republic's communitarian ideals.

In this light Antimasonry, I want to emphasize, should be viewed not as an aberrant or local movement but as a particularly revealing indication of the postheroic republican mentality of the 1820s and 1830s. That an economically prospering nation should become especially vulnerable to the machinations of corrupt aristocrats was, of course, a tenet central to classical republican ideology. As theorists from Machiavelli to Madison warned, luxury undermined the citizenry's vigilance and virtue, thereby threatening the republican state with a sudden and silent downfall directed by the forces of oligarchy. It was precisely this sort of downfall that concerned the Jacksonians; and it is therefore ironic (or perhaps the inevitable result of Jackson's own Masonic affiliation) that Antimasonic activity should have contributed to the rise of the Northern Whig Party. Despite Weed's and Seward's demagogic insistence on their solidarity with the working classes, it was generally the case that those of the Jacksonian persuasion, not the Whigs, shared more genuinely in the "Antimasonic" fear of aristocratic monopoly and privilege. Like the Antimasons, Jacksonians believed that "a web of economic and political influence . . . . held invisible powers over the life of the community"; like the Antimasons, Jacksonians blamed a subversive "corporate" organization, the Second Bank of the United States, for "transgressions committed . . . against the political, social, and economic values of the Old Republic"; and like the Antimasons, Jacksonians repeatedly invoked "the great, essential opposition of the people and the aristocracy."[17] Whether Antimasonic, Jacksonian, or even Whiggish, countersubversives of the 1820s and 1830s found in the discourse of republicanism a vivid conceptual reminder of the heightened potential for internal subversion during a time of national prosperity and, for many Americans, seemingly unlimited opportunity. As we shall see, this expressive and anxious discourse would speak quite powerfully to Fenimore Cooper and through his literary art. In its responsiveness to cultural tensions and discourse, his art is not as programmatic as we normally suppose.

"There is at this moment a deep conspiracy, among the higher classes"

Throughout his career, and at a considerable cost to his contemporary and posthumous reputation, Cooper took pride in being a writer of principle. Whereas Hawthorne's prefaces speak of "phantasmagorical antics," Cooper's primarily address the moral and political issues that are the putative subjects of his fiction.[18] To be sure, the "mythopoeic" novels of the Leatherstocking series have managed to break free from Cooper's constricting avowals of thematic intention; but a number of his other novels remain bound to the prefaces, which have preserved the non-Leatherstocking Cooper for posterity as a didactic moralist whose art generally served to express his principled republicanism.[19] But surely there is a fundamental difference between writing a political tract and composing a five-hundred-page novel. At the risk of indulging in a romantic idealism, I would suggest that, in the course of the sustained creative and imaginative engagement giving rise to a novel, professed political ideas (much to the discomfort of the writer of principle) may find their foundations undermined or complicated as the work begins to take on a life of its own. Though hardly a "dialogical" author in the mode of Brockden Brown, Cooper nonetheless tended to test and discover ideas during the fictionalizing process, and I believe that this was especially true for his novels of the 1820s.[20] As a result, these seemingly controlled and celebratory novels often moved toward unintended discoveries or betrayed submerged concerns. His is an enactive and complicating fiction that, in the course of ten years, and reflective of a similar trajectory in the manifestly celebratory republican discourse of the American 1820s, moved from intimations of decline to formulations of conspiracy.

We must be wary, then, of Cooper's explicit statements of thematic intention. For example, though the preface to *The Spy* (1821) proclaims a desire to embrace "the patriotic ardour of the country,"[21] the novel presents a world that calls into question the worth and wisdom of "patriotic ardour." Central to *The Spy*'s celebration of disinterested patriotism, for instance, are the several scenes evocative of the André affair. During the Revolutionary War Washington had ordered the British spy André shot for his espionage activities, despite the patriotic motives prompting him to do for England what any equally daring American patriot would have done for America. In *Notions of the Americans,* Cooper's Cadwallader defends what in some quarters was an unpopular action:

> It was necessary to show the world that he who dared to assail the rights of the infant and struggling republic, incurred a penalty as fearful as he who worked his treason against the majesty of a king. The calmness, the humanity, the moderation, and the inflexible firmness, with which this serious duty was performed [by Washington], are worthy of all praise.[22]

Yet in *The Spy* all situations analogous to the André case present moral difficulties. When the British sympathizer Henry Wharton finds himself condemned to an André-like fate, the reader is brought to feel that the execution would constitute a vindictive act of injustice. The Americans' attempts to capture and condemn Harvey Birch also reveal their inability to read the signs of treason with any assurance. In fact, the novel's sole execution has the marauding Cow-Boys murdering a deserter before Birch's (and the reader's) horrified eyes. If Washington-Harper is the only character capable of decisive and correct action, and if the possibility of an absolutist patriotic justice is seen to be untenable in a world of selfish Skinners and Cow-Boys, what hope remains for the new republic?

Cooper's other avowedly celebratory novels of the period similarly raise dark questions about the new republic's origins and character. He begins *Lionel Lincoln* (1825) by lauding the rebellion against Britain's "impolitic restrictions on the port of Boston"; but in the course of portraying the Revolutionary cause the novel anticipates Hawthorne's "My Kinsman, Major Molineux" in delineating the unhinging and potentially lunatic aspects of revolutionism. In *The Pilot* (1823) Cooper wants to present John Paul Jones as a disinterested hero rivaling Harvey Birch, and yet the restless isolato Jones, like the shady and deceptive proto-Revolutionaries of *The Red Rover* (1828) and *The Water-Witch* (1830), bears little resemblance to the bold Roman profiles of America's Revolutionary heroes.[23] *The Pioneers* (1823) opens with a loving description of an ideal republican community of the 1820s that the reader is meant to view as the fruition of the late-eighteenth-century settlement at Templeton. The portrayal of the community in 1793, however, brings to life a host of seemingly insurmountable problems; the deus ex machina does little to balance Cooper's disturbing account of the centrality of self-interest and mobbism to America's social evolution.

The dark and chaotic social landscape of Cooper's early historical fiction owes a good deal, of course, to his appropriation of Sir Walter Scott's trope of the Neutral Ground, "the most lawless and morally equivocal place of all."[24] Central to Scott's representation of the Neutral Ground in such works as *Waverley* (1814), *Rob Roy* (1818), and *The Heart of Mid-Lothian* (1818) are epochal conflicts between opposed historical forces – conflicts set in motion by Jacobite conspiracies. Conflict, and to a certain extent conspiracy, have an equally important place in Cooper's representations of America's "Neutral Grounds." Throughout *The Spy* the Revolutionary conflict is staged in the "lawless and morally equivocal place" of Westchester County, a scene of relentless plotting between New York's loyalists and patriots. Similar conflicts and plottings inform all of the Revolutionary novels, and in *Lionel Lincoln* Cooper anticipates twentieth-century theories of the ideological origins of the Revolution by suggesting a causal connection between the colonists' conspiratorial fears of ministerial plotting and their eventual mobilization. As he explains, among the colonists "it was the characteristic of the times to attach importance to trifling incidents, and to suspect a concealed policy in movements which emanated only in inclination." Oppositional conflict between Judge Temple and Natty, along with the various plottings of Doolittle, Jones, and Riddel, nearly undoes the emergent community at Templeton; and in *The Last of the Mohicans* the imperial contention between the English and French, coupled with the overarching contention between white man and red man, culminates in the horrifying massacre at Fort William Henry, an eruption of absolute chaos in the Neutral

Ground of America's wilderness. Similarly, in *The Wept of Wish-ton-Wish* (1829), the reader enters a world of intractable racial conflict and plotting – the world of the massacre – and this in a novel, like *The Pioneers*, intended to disclose the origins of America's "present state of security and abundance."[25]

With their presentation of chaos and conflict, Cooper's early novels express an implicit pessimism about America's prospects that he would not address openly and deliberately until after 1833. Instead, and especially during his European residence of 1826–33, he conceived of himself as a spokesman for the glorious possibilities of American republicanism, offering his European readers in particular, in *Notions of the Americans*, a portrait of America as model republic. Similarly, in his fiction of the period, as William P. Kelly observes, he sought to demonstrate that such was the strength of America's republicanism that the young nation could "escape the determining power of the past."[26] Thus in *The Prairie* (1827), set in 1805 in the newly acquired territories of the Louisiana Purchase, Cooper seems altogether unconcerned, unlike Brockden Brown in his pre-Purchase *Address*, about the republic's vulnerability to infiltrating foreign imperialists. He remarks, "It soon became apparent, to the meanest capacity, that, while nature had placed a barrier of desert to the extension of our population in the west, the [Louisiana Purchase] had made us the masters of a belt of fertile country, which, in the revolutions of the day, might have become the property of a rival nation." But "revolutions" is a key word here, for though Americans are presented in the novel as free from the threat of revolutionary disturbances emanating from Europe, they are not exempt after all from the historical possibility of cyclical revolution, the possibility of republican decline, as revealed in the continent's landscape. Clearly the American analogue of Volney's Egyptian and Syrian deserts, the prairies are imaged as a titanic blanket covering the ruins of a former civilization. The novel's bloody events, oppositional conflicts, and numerous plottings – even with the concluding ideal marriage of Protestant gentleman to Catholic lady – affirm the symbolic truth etched into the desolate prairies: It will be difficult indeed for Americans to escape the fate of their predecessor empire(s). And so when Natty releases Middleton and Hover from their Indian captors and declares, "I dare say you thought it only needful to cut the thongs, to leave you masters of the ground," he voices Cooper's insight, and an insight shared by other "patriotic" Americans of the 1820s, that the mere cutting of "thongs" does not ensure everlasting liberty: America is bound, as Europe is bound, to cyclical patterns of history that point to an inevitable, if far-distant, fall.[27]

Cooper completed *The Prairie* after arriving in Europe in 1826. Additional influences on its presentation of cyclical decline would have been his firsthand observations of Europe's ancient ruins, and perhaps even his firsthand observations of what he patriotically regarded as the decadence of some contemporary European societies. He was particularly struck by imperial England's potential for decline. "From all that I saw and heard, in the fortnight I passed in England," he wrote his sister in 1826, "I have no doubt that Country is at the summit of her prosperity – How soon or how rapid may be her downfall it is impossible to say, but the destruction of great Nations is generally dreadful."[28] By 1828 Cooper concluded that England had indeed fallen from its former glory, for, so he posited as republican theorist, its very prosperity had left the nation vulnerable, as the Antimasons and Jacksonians argued America was vulnerable, to the silent subversive machinations of a secretive, plotting, and entrenched oligarchy that exploited the wealth of the nation for its own selfish ends. Even worse, in an age of revolution and reform that, according to Cooper, promised to spread republicanism throughout the world, these oligarchs were conspiring to subvert republican aspirations in nearby nations and in its former colony as well. The fear that Americans could fall victim to oligarchical conspirators, from within and without, may well stand behind *The Prairie*'s evocative imagery of decline, though in this particular novel conspiracy remains buried beneath the landscape's surface. Cooper's increasing concerns about subversive oligarchs, by 1831 a concern central to his politics, would lead to an eventual surfacing of conspiracy as a principal motif of his fiction.

In his novels of the 1820s, Cooper for the most part tenders the ideal and then reveals (or discovers) the real, exposing the reader to a deceptive social landscape expressive of his, and his culture's, conflicting views on American history and possibility. He celebrates the ideal, he explores the real, but he is not so cynical as to suggest that the real irrevocably cancels out the possibility of attaining a semblance of the ideal. Nor is he so coercive in his thematizing as to deny the reader the prerogative of interpretation. In the 1826 preface to *The Last of the Mohicans* he declares that "it is a very unsafe experiment either for a writer or a projector to trust to the inventive powers of any one but himself. Therefore nothing which can well be explained, should be left a mystery." But his comments here apply more to plot than to theme; and it should be noted that, despite his frequent use of an omniscient moralizing narrative voice in the early novels, the "explaining" is often accomplished through satire, irony, and dramatic action, or else through the words of the characters themselves. For example, in *Mohicans* the historical themes emerge in large part from the dramatic action; and the text's final moralizing remarks, "The pale-faces are masters of the earth, and the time of the redmen has not yet come again," are spoken by Tamenund.[29] Similarly, in *The Prairie* Cooper often uses Natty as his spokesman, though it is never entirely clear whether we should regard Natty's musings on American society and cyclical decline as the unqualified opinions of the author. Cooper's satirical passages in *The Pioneers,* on the other hand, certainly reflect his suspicion of Jones and Doolittle and help to shape our attitudes toward these pompous democrats. Nevertheless, the overall narrative leaves relatively wide open the problem of evaluating the social and political consequences of Judge Temple's trial of Natty. In that novel, as in the majority of the novels of his first decade as a professional author, Cooper's sociopolitical themes develop through the unfolding of narratives that simultaneously proffer hope and despair, light and dark; these are novels of the hopeful and fearful republicanism of the American 1820s.

Cooper's post-1830s novels generally continue to follow the structural pattern of the earlier novels, of the ideal giving way to the real, though these later novels are not as hopeful. The ideal, Cooper will insist again and again, is but a seductive fiction that can be manipulated by those in power to serve the ends of power. Accordingly, the task facing the republican-spirited author is to unmask and expose the secretive plottings of manipulators who would selfishly subvert and corrupt the ideal. What this means for his fiction, as my analysis of *The Bravo* will show in some detail, is that the discourse will take on a more alarmist character and the narrator, urgently desirous of clearing up all mysteries, will assert his authority more firmly. The republican author emerges as a sort of countersubversive, whose presence intrudes into the world of his fiction and into the world of realpolitik.

From his vantage point in Europe during the late 1820s and early 1830s, Cooper became preoccupied with the need to maintain a vigilant watchfulness over the health of a number of republics, which he feared were threatened not only by the generalized vicious passions represented in *The Prairie* and other novels intended to depict America on its way to republican glory, but also by a specific conspiracy of self-aggrandizing aristocrats, British and otherwise. Good republican that he was, he believed the fate of all republics to be intertwined and precarious. As he reminded Americans in *Contributions for the Poles* (1831), "Remember that not a freeman falls, in the most remote quarter of the world, that you do not lose a brother who is enlisted in your own noble enterprise."[30] Perceiving the early 1830s as a time of historical crisis demanding an engaged personal response, he served as chairman of the American Polish Committee and championed the Polish revolution against the Czar. Another "noble enterprise" engaging his sympathies was the Belgian revolution against the Dutch.

Cooper's most active political commitment was to the republican cause in France, which he believed was imperiled by the machinations of subversive aristocrats. English aristocrats would secretly try to influence events in France, he explained to Peter Jay, because "the two great objects of England are to preserve its monopolies as a country, and to preserve the ascendancy of its aristocracy." Even after the July Revolution that deposed Charles X, Cooper's distrust of "aristocracy" left him hesitant about embracing the reign of Louis Philippe. His doubts about the republican posturings of Louis Philippe and the Doctrinaires were borne out in December 1830, when his friend Lafayette was summarily dismissed from his post as commander of the National Guard. Cooper wrote Charles Wilkes in April 1831: "That Lafayette has been out maneuvered by the [Doctrinaire] party which surrounds the King, I take to be beyond a doubt." And he announced in the same letter, "The tendency of the government, now, is certainly to aristocracy." One month later he informed William Shubrick: "The people in power, in France, have completely cheated the people out of their liberty, and are aiming now at an Aristocracy. They will keep a King as a cloak; but the English system is their aim."[31]

By mid-1831 he concluded that conspiring aristocrats had betrayed the revolutions not only in France but throughout Europe, and in a June 1831 letter to Benjamin Sillman he proclaimed, "There is a deep conspiracy of Aristocrats, who wish to take the place of the Kings they have been, effectually, deposing." He presented his overarching theory of conspiracy in a subsequent letter to Mrs. Peter Augustus Jay:

> There is at this moment a deep conspiracy, among the higher classes, to cheat the lower out of their natural rights. Public opinion requires that it should be done with great art, and I am thoroughly convinced that the whole secret of the present amity between England and France is owing to a settled plan between the aristocrats to support each other.

Convinced of the ubiquity of aristocratic conspiracy, Cooper came to view all seemingly progressive developments in Europe as masks cloaking oligarchical subversion in nations that were anything but republics.[32] And like the typical countersubversive (recall Morse, Dwight, and Brown's Sophia), he put full faith in his ability to see through those masks; he would expose the conspirators' "deep" "great art" with his own deep great art.

Though Cooper's fears of aristocratic conspiracy were certainly responsive to the European political context – and to a certain extent were on the mark – in significant ways his countersubversive explanations and discourse paralleled the countersubversive explanations and discourse promulgated in America during the same period, particularly by the

Antimasons. Both the Antimasons and Cooper, for example, feared the power of the "Monied Corporation" of conspiring aristocrats;[33] both warned that republics were especially vulnerable to oligarchical subversion; both saw republican forms as cloaks masking and hence permitting the undetectable plotting of what Seward termed "an aristocratic nobility." The similarities suggest that Antimasonic discourse, which Cooper knew of primarily through newspaper reports, may have influenced his thinking on the European revolutions and guided him toward simple explanations for rather more complex phenomena.[34] That said, it must be allowed that there is little documentary evidence of Cooper's immediate response to the debate on Free Masonry and that the few references to Masons in his fiction of the 1820s convey a lack of concern with their subversive threat. In *The Pioneers* he jokes about Richard Jones's Masonic connections; and in *The Red Rover* he has the Rover use the trope of Masonic fraternity to tease Wilder about his seaworthiness: "Are there no watchwords in the Masonry of your trade by which a brother is known? Such terms as 'stemming the waves with the taffrail,' for instance, or some of those knowing phrases we have lately heard?"[35]

But while there is every indication that Cooper distanced himself from the alarmism of Antimasonry – that he never swallowed Antimasonic propaganda whole – his conspiratorial theorizing of 1829–31 provides compelling evidence that Antimasonic discourse, and its Jacksonian revisions, had a considerable impact on his conception of the worldwide struggle between villainous aristocrats and vulnerable republicans. In *The Bravo,* the novel that most directly emerges from his political involvement with European republican revolutionism, we note a very clear link between his concerns about oligarchical conspiracy in Europe and the Antimasonic/Jacksonian concern with oligarchical conspiracy in America. The link is republican Venice.

In *The American Democrat* (1838), Cooper describes the "extraordinary" similarity between (alleged) Masonic plotting in America and oligarchical plotting in "republican" Venice:

> In Venice, such was the jealousy and tyranny of the state, that a secret council existed, with an authority that was almost despotick, while it was inquisitorial, and which was removed from the usual responsibility of opinion, by an expedient that was devised to protect its members from the ordinary liabilities of common censure. This council consisted of three nobles, who held their office for a limited period, and were appointed by drawing lots, each person concealing the fact of the lot's having fallen on himself, until he met his associates at an appointed place. It is an extraordinary fact, that the same expedient was devised to conceal the murderers, in the well known case of Morgan, who fell a victim to the exaggeration and weakness of some of the members of the Masonic fraternity.[36]

Although these reflections appeared seven years after the publication of *The Bravo,* his novel of eighteenth-century Venice, which builds to the revelation of a murder and cover-up ordered by the Council of Three, they are in keeping with his conspiratorial thinking of the early 1830s and with his habit of remaining informed about political events at home during the same period. And though Cooper, even in this passage, appears relatively unconcerned about an extensive Masonic conspiracy "operating," in Seward's words, "through our extended country," he clearly was concerned about the ways in which such a secretive fraternity could lend itself to all sorts of smaller cabals, such as in the Morgan affair. As one obvious model of conspiratorial organization, the Masons must have been on Cooper's mind during the late 1820s and early 1830s.

It is beyond conjecture that well before 1838 he knew of the centrality of Venetian history to republican theorists of the past several centuries and that he perceived republican Venice as a legitimate analogue of other European republics and of the American republic. For example, in *The Water-Witch,* the novel written immediately before *The Bravo,* the smuggler "Seadrift" responds to the heroine Alida's admiration of fine Venetian velvets by offering a pithy history lesson relevant to all republican readers:

> [The velvets] come of Venice, too; but the commerce is like the favor which attends the rich, and the queen of the Adriatic is already far on the decline. That which causes the increase of the husbandman occasion [*sic*] the downfall of a city. The lagunes are filling with fat soil, and the keel of the trader is less frequent there than of old. Ages hence, the plough may trace furrows where the Bucentaur has floated! . . . Nations might learn a moral, by studying the sleepy canals and instructive magnificence of the fallen town; but pride fattens on its own lazy recollections, to the last.[37]

In *The Bravo* Cooper would seek to challenge that lazy pride by offering a full picture of "the sleepy canals and instructive magnificence of the fallen town." In doing so, he placed himself in the tradition of classical republican theorists who regarded Venice as the epitome of a prospering republic brought to its ruin by the plottings of its selfish oligarchy.[38] Especially disturbing about the course of Venetian history was that "the fallen town" continued to call itself a republic. Thus theorists warned that the mere designation of a state as "republic" does not ensure that such is the case. Madison emphatically made this point in *Federalist* no. 39: "Holland, in which no particle of the supreme authority is derived from the people, has passed almost universally under the denomination of a republic. The same title has been bestowed on Venice, where absolute power over the great body of the people, is exercised in the most absolute manner, by a small body of hereditary nobles."[39] Was the

American republic too a masquerading "fallen town"? This is the fear implicit in the celebratory rhetoric of the American 1820s and Cooper's early fiction, the fear underlying Antimasonic, Jacksonian, and Whig countersubversive discourse, and the fear exacerbated by Cooper's participation in European revolutionary politics; and it is the fear centrally informing the historical romance of *The Bravo*.

Regarded by Yvor Winters as one of Cooper's "indispensable works," *The Bravo* is a novel of authentic power.[40] The novel gains its power through the urgency with which Cooper writes as a kind of "Anti-Venetian" countersubversive, convinced of the pressing need for his political warnings and utterly convinced, Jeremiah-like, of his narrative authority. To be sure, because *The Bravo* was written during the first year of the July Monarchy, the novel at first glance appears to be little more than an allegorical unmasking of Louis Philippe's sham republican government.[41] Cooper in fact encourages this view in the novel's Preface, a disquisition on republicanism and despotism. But as with Cooper's novels of the 1820s, we must resist the pull of his reductive and stabilizing claims of intention.[42] Tapping into the traditional republican fear of oligarchical conspiracy, which lies behind his conspiratorial theory of the failed revolutions in Europe, Cooper conveys his concerns about the dangers facing even the most healthy of republics by envisioning eighteenth-century Venice as a subverted republic similar not just to contemporary France (or England) but also to the nightmarish American republic of Antimasonic discourse. In no other novel does he more forcefully express his sense of the dark conspiratorial world hidden behind the mask of republican idealism.

"What a fearful state is Venice!"

Writing to Charles Wilkes in April 1831, Cooper remarked on his engaged response to Venice during a visit of the preceding year: "I have a book in press, to be called 'the Bravo' I think, but I am not decided – The scene is Venice, which seized my fancy last spring, in a manner not to be spoken of." In *Gleanings in Europe: Italy* (1838), he again reflected on Venice's appeal: "Certainly, no other place ever struck my imagination so forcibly; and never before did I experience so much pleasure, from novel objects, in so short a time." But in that later work he commented as well on a less attractive side of the small, watered-in "city afloat": Within two weeks, Venice "became monotonous and wearying."[43] The doubleness of this characteristic nineteenth-century response – wonder and claustrophobia – informs Cooper's representation of eighteenth-century Venice in *The Bravo*.

The novel's opening scene introduces the reader to Venice's carnivalesque masquerades. With the coming of night, the masked citizenry enters the Square of St. Mark "like water gushing through some strait aqueduct, into a broad and bubbling basin."[44] As the impressionistic description of the crowd suggests, the third–person narrator at this early point in the novel affects an objective distance from events, seemingly observing the scene, like a Hudson River school painter, from an elevated perspective. As a result, William Cullen Bryant admiringly noted, the novel is remarkably visual: "The magnificent city of Venice, in which the scene of the story is laid, stands continually before the imagination."[45] Certainly we see quite vividly the masquerade's "gushing" together of Venice's republican cavalcade: "Gallant cavalieri and grave cittadini; soldiers of Dalmatia, and seamen of the galleys; dames of the city, and females of lighter manners; jewellers of the Rialto, and traders from the Levant; Jew, Turk, and Christian; traveller, adventurer, podesta, valet, avvocato and gondolier" (1:9). And yet despite their "movement and bustle" (1:10), the revelers seem rather dissipated and lethargic. Temporarily abandoning the "objective" panoramic perspective, the narrator explains, "Men lived among [Venice's] islands in that state of incipient lethargy, which marks the progress of a downward course, whether the decline be of a moral or of a physical decay" (1:10). According to the narrator, speaking now as republican historian, Venice in the early eighteenth century is in its postheroic age, desperately clinging to memories of its former glories. But as one character warns, "The enjoyment of the past is like the pleasure of the fool who dreams of the wine he drank yesterday" (1:22). With their nightly festive gatherings, Venetians attain an oblivion that, the reader soon realizes, allows them to close their eyes to the reality of their situation: that these "republicans" are under the dominion of a designing oligarchical cabal.

It is entirely appropriate, therefore, that a historical novel on eighteenth-century oligarchical subversion should begin with a masquerade, for, as Gordon Wood remarks, "masquerades and hidden designs formed the grammar and vocabulary for much of the thought of the age."[46] A central constituent of this "grammar" was Venice itself, which in the eighteenth century emerged as Europe's leading tourist center, renowned for its nightly carnivals. In this opening scene, however, what the narrator emphasizes about the masquerade, above and beyond its status as "a centre of amusement" (1:9), is the suspect character of its participants; the festive occasion is not so festive after all. The revelers move with "measured step and jealous glance" (1:9) amidst government spies, police agents, and "cowls of monks" (1:9). Like the English masquerade of the eighteenth century, the Venetian masquerade would seem to function as "a kind of institutionalized disorder" that, as the image of the "broad and bubbling basin" suggests, takes place within carefully circumscribed limits.[47] The most disturbing aspect of this particular masquerade, therefore, is the way the "circumscribers" remain offstage and invisible. The masquerade, like Seward's America, appears to be "controlled and directed by unseen and unknown hands."

The identity of those in control is only hinted at in the opening. Instead, Cooper uses the masquerade primarily as an expressive backdrop against which to set in motion the plot of the novel. Don Camillo Monforte, Duke of Sant' Agata and a Neapolitan whose family has ancient claims to membership in the Venetian Senate, has recently returned to Venice to press the senators for his hereditary rights. While in Venice he saved from drowning Violetta Tiepelo, a wealthy ward of the state, and (true to convention) they have fallen in love. We learn all this indirectly through a conversation between Gino, Don Camillo's gondolier, and his friend Stefano, a Calabrian trader. Gino expresses his personal loathing for the senators, and offers the first of many images suggestive of the brute force of their power, by talking of how the gondola was capsized "by an Ancona man, who passed over the boat, as if it were a senator stepping on a fly" (1:14). The discussion of the gondola accident occasioning Don Camillo's heroism thus offers a skillful "backdoor" entrance onto both the love interest and power relationships of the novel.[48] Just as important, the conversation evokes the suspicion and paranoia typifying life in eighteenth-century Venice; for as Gino and Stefano converse they become increasingly nervous that both the onlooking Jewish moneylender Hosea and the onlooking bravo Jacopo Frontoni (putatively the state's assassin) may be monitoring their conversation for the senatorial Council of Three Hundred. By requiring the reader to "overhear" the conversation between Gino and Stefano to acquire basic plot information, Cooper uses a conventional aspect of the novel to make the reader, too, a spying eavesdropper. All are implicated in the ubiquitous paranoia attending even the most ordinary of social transactions during Venice's "masquerades."

The first sustained action of the novel, Gino's attempt to deliver his master Don Camillo's signet ring and secret message to the fearful bravo Jacopo, further reveals the extent to which suspicion and deception dominate life in Venice.[49] Terrified of making contact with an assassin, Gino borrows a boatman's cap and mask from Annina, who is both a spy for the state and, as daughter of a wine smuggler, a plotter against the state. After luring her onto Stefano's supposedly wine-laden boat, he winds his way through dark alleys and canals and at the doge's palace is himself lured into surrendering the signet ring to a masked stranger, who deposits it into the Lions' Mouths, "famous as the receptacles of secret accusations" (1:49). When he realizes his mistake, he rushes into the crowd and seeks "in vain to select the delinquent from among a thousand masks"

(1:50). Unsuccessful, he manages nevertheless to persuade Jacopo to take the packet without Don Camillo's identifying ring. The scene ends like this: "Gino gladly turned away, but he had not left the other many paces, before he saw a female form gliding behind the pedestal of one of the granite columns. Moving swiftly in a direction to uncover this seeming spy, he saw at once that Annina had been a witness of his interview with the Bravo" (1:56).

With this account of ceaseless machinations, Cooper propels the reader into the midst of the plotting world of the Venetian citizenry in which everyone seems both a spy and an object of spies. One critic writes, "Venice, like the Neutral Ground of the earlier work, is a complex and treacherous domain of fear, masks, and subterranean passageways, where the faces of the rulers are always concealed and where deception and disguise are the modes of survival."[50] As indicated by the central role of smuggling in the novel, urban-commercial Venice is also a dominion, as in Brockden Brown's major novels, of marketplace competition and self-interest, in which an unwavering vigilance is also a mode of survival. Accordingly, throughout the novel Cooper emphasizes the function of the self-protective eye. Annina's "jealous eye" (1:46) detects Gino's escape and helps her to track him down. The bravo is defined at first in terms of his eye, Byronic and watchful, "an eye, that was full of brilliancy, meaning, and passion" (1:18); later we are told he has a "searching eye" (1:52) and a "glaring eye" (1:239). Violetta, the heroine, has a "dark, eloquent eye" (1:59).[51] Though the bravo tends not to wear a mask, the emphasis on the eyes of others reminds us that frequently the eye is all that is revealed of the masked and suspicious Venetians; suspicion generates surveillance and surveillance generates suspicion. Perpetually on the alert, Venetians must resort to perverse forms of secrecy, "a sort of similar freemasonry," as Cooper puts it in The Heidenmauer (1832), characterizing social relations "under despotic and dangerous governments, and where the social habits are much tinctured with violence and treachery."[52]

Masks, therefore, are necessary appurtenances in the conspiratorial Neutral Ground of republican Venice. The doge explains: "A mask is sacred in Venice. It is the glory of our excellent and wise laws, that he who seeketh to dwell within the privacy of his own thoughts, and to keep aloof from curiosity by shading his features, rangeth our streets and canals, as if he dwelt in the security of his own abode" (1:130). The doge celebrates masks as one of "the high privileges of liberty" (1:130), but clearly masks serve as a survival mechanism, as a means of retaining one's individuality and one's secrets in a society under constant surveillance. The most frightening "mask" of the novel is the doge's luxurious palace, a towering edifice that seemingly watches over the citizenry while revealing nothing of its inner workings: "No light was shed from the windows; but the entire building presented a fit emblem of that mysterious power which was known to preside over the fortunes of Venice and her citizens" (1:47). Linked to the adjoining state prison by the Bridge of Sighs, the palace's architectural arrangement hints at, and eventually testifies to, the intimate relationship in this fallen state between surveillance and social discipline.

Amidst such ubiquitous masking and suspicion, the reader, like Venice's republican citizenry, feels somewhat disoriented, implicated in the uneasy task of reading and interpreting a shifting social landscape. To a certain extent, then, the narrative enacts its social themes. Yet *The Bravo* is meant to be educative and not confusing, and accordingly Cooper's narrative strategy in the overall novel is to "preside over the fortunes of Venice and her citizens" in ways similar to the towering and presiding palace of the doge. The Hudson River school perspective of the opening, a perspective that Cooper employs now and again throughout the novel, thus serves precisely the ends of a vigilant countersubversive opposition: The narrator's use of surveillance counters the oligarchs' use of surveillance, ensuring that the reader's perception of eighteenth-century Venice shall remain properly republican.

As the novel develops, Cooper's desire to demystify and oppose the "mysterious power" presiding over Venice leads him as well to explore interiors, especially repositories of state power. Seeking to offer a comprehensive and clear picture of republican decline and oligarchical subversion, he begins regularly to adopt, like Brockden Brown's Sophia, a countersubversive omniscience that permits him to reveal all to the reader. In his republican novel of disclosure, no interior space will escape the penetrating eye of this "secret witness."

Cooper initiates the novel's inner movement by disclosing the interiors of two contrasting Venetian residences. Within the first resides the heroine, Violetta Tiepelo, whose virtue is inscribed in her home's "domestic comfort" (1:59). Watched over by two state-appointed but kindly guardians – Donna Florinda and the Carmelite monk Anselmo – she seems nevertheless a captive of church and state, a forerunner of the virtuous republican maidens of America's popular convent novels of the later 1830s and 1840s.[53] Violetta, we recall, has fallen in love with the Neapolitan Don Camillo Monforte, who saved her from drowning. But as Anselmo now explains: "There is a law in Venice which commandeth that none claiming an interest in its affairs shall so bind himself [*sic!*] to the stranger, as to endanger the devotion all owe to the republic. Thus may not . . . the heiress of a name, great and valued as thine, be given in marriage to any of note, in a foreign state without counsel and consent from those who are appointed to watch over the interests of all" (1:61).

However, when Cooper next moves his gaze to Senator Allesandro

Gradenigo's residence, where we observe Violetta's senatorial guardian plotting to marry Violetta to his eldest son, it quickly becomes apparent that the senators' appeal to the interests of the commonwealth in fact cloaks their desire to increase their personal wealth. In the portrayal of Gradenigo's marriage plotting, Cooper works with the social reality of arranged marriages in eighteenth-century Venice. As historians of the period have observed, by the eighteenth century there remained but forty-two noble families in Venice, all of whom were obsessed with enlarging their wealth. Accordingly, they allowed only their eldest sons to marry, with the predictable results: The rich became richer as they consolidated and concentrated their wealth, and consequently two-thirds of noble Venetians remained unmarried, leading to the rise of professional courtesans, on the one hand, and the proliferation of convents, on the other.[54] As adopted by Cooper, the Venetian marriage situation serves several important functions in his representation of Venice's fall into oligarchy: With regard to Violetta, it raises the specter of convent captivity, thus linking the oligarchs to Catholic priests; and with regard to the larger social picture, it raises the specter of unfair consolidation of wealth and power, thus linking the oligarchs to the subversive oligarchs of Antimasonic and Jacksonian discourse. As Cooper later remarks, in a most Jacksonian intrusion, Gradenigo "stood in relation to the state as a director of a moneyed institution is proverbially placed in respect to his corporation; an agent of its collective measures, removed from the responsibilities of the man" (1:101).

Intent on exposing the monstrous implications of Gradenigo's monstrous bankery, Cooper as countersubversive keeps his narrative gaze fixed within the walls of a mansion bespeaking luxury, pride, and "more than common gloom" (1:68), a mansion that is "no bad type of the republic itself" (1:69), as petitioners one after the other beseech Gradenigo for favors. The petitioning scenes therefore initiate the reader's political education in "the republic itself." The first petitioner is Violetta, who speaks for her suitor Don Camillo Monforte's claims on the Senate. While dishonestly agreeing to champion Don Camillo, Gradenigo selfishly tries to foist on Violetta his dissolute son Giacomo (later revealed as the masked man who intercepted Monforte's signet ring). But it is in his response to the next petitioner that Gradenigo's most appalling selfishness is put on display. Gradenigo's elderly impoverished foster brother Antonio Vecchio, a fisherman who lost all his sons in the Turkish wars, pleads for the freedom of his recently conscripted grandson. Although the "naturally noble" (1:78) Antonio, reminiscent of the elderly and ennobled Natty of *The Prairie*, makes strong claims on the reader's sympathies, Gradenigo's commitment to the state as "moneyed institution" and "corporation" has blinded him to all other concerns: "Removed from the responsibilities of the man," he cannot empathize with

Antonio, even as a brother. Instead, he responds as a senator, excoriating the poor fisherman for presumptuously demanding to know why Gradenigo's son is exempt from the draft.

As the smug Gradenigo continues to rebuff his petitioners, the omniscient but hardly disinterested narrator becomes increasingly involved in the novel's action as a speaking narrative presence: Interwoven with Cooper's omniscience is an authoritative moralizing voice, different from the satirical, celebratory, or dispassionate republican voice of his early novels, that intrudes on occasion to instruct the reader on the full significance of particular scenes. And so when Gradenigo rejects Don Camillo's request to address the senate and then seeks to betray him by purchasing the stolen ring from Hosea, Cooper can no longer keep himself at a narrative distance. He concludes the petitioning scene with an extended summary analysis of Gradenigo's senatorial character:

> The reader will have gained some insight into the character of the individual who was the chief actor in the foregoing scenes. The Signor Gradenigo was born with all the sympathies and natural kindliness of other men, but accident, and an education which had received a strong bias from the institutions of the self-styled republic, had made him the creature of a conventional policy. To him Venice seemed a free state, because he partook so largely of the benefits of her social system. . . . In short, he was an aristocrat; and no man had more industriously or more successfully persuaded himself into the belief of all the dogmas that were favorable to his caste. . . . With a philosophy that seemed to satisfy himself, he contended that, as God had established orders throughout his own creation, in a descending chain from angels to men, it was safe to follow an example which emanated from a wisdom that was infinite. (1:101–2)

As Cooper makes clear, the aristocrat-senator Gradenigo is a product of "conventional policy," an all too human example of the way those in power tend uncritically to accept and celebrate the institutions that sustain their power. In this respect Gradenigo looks forward to Melville's Delano, who similarly displays a culturally derived and shaped, and not simply villainous, obtuse blindness. For Gradenigo (as for Delano), the authority of a culture's distribution of political power seems grounded in nature and sanctioned by God. Thus he rhapsodizes to the bravo Jacopo, "Justice administers to the wants of society, and checks the passions with a force as silent and dignified, as if her decrees came from a higher volition" (1:87). But for Cooper the republican commentator, Gradenigo's repeated teleological justifications reveal only the self-sustaining complacency of a corrupt ruling oligarch who may conceive of himself as a "furious republican" (1:102) but is in fact a "shrewd and practised" (1:101) despot, one of Venice's "many tyrants" (1:102).

The narrator's intrusive didactic commentary on Gradenigo's obvious class prejudices, similar to the authoritative posture we noted in Cooper's account of British conspirators, suggests that Cooper may distrust his dramatic powers or, more likely, that he may distrust the interpretive abilities of his readers. Sensing Cooper's implied distrust "of anyone but himself," as he put it in *Mohicans*'s Preface, we may feel tempted to recoil from Cooper the coercive moralist, especially because as post-Jamesians we are inclined to believe that when an author speaks with such univocal authority he diminishes the complexity of his fiction. But in an important defense of the narrative intrusion as an aspect of the novel, Bakhtin remarks, "When the novelist comes forward with his own unitary and fully affirming language (without any distancing, refraction or qualifications) he knows that such language is not self-evident and is not in itself incontestable, that it is uttered in a heteroglot environment, that such a language must be championed, purified, defended, motivated."[55] That Cooper "knows" the truths he speaks are not "self-evident" is a matter of some debate; but that his "fully affirming language" is offered in a political and discursive context that is "heteroglot" – varied and competing – is a central fact of the novel's ontogenesis. Cooper's political commitments of the early 1830s made him acutely aware of the deceptiveness of political languages and of contention among political ideologies; his awareness of contention (and his contentiousness) motivated him to speak in his fictional and nonfictional writings with a blunt lack of equivocation. Over the course of *The Bravo*, the intrusive voice comes to define the narrator as an engaged countersubversive presence whose very engagement charges the novel with an added urgency. The narrator intrudes when his frustration with Gradenigo builds; subsequently he retreats to allow for further development of plot. When needed, he will step forth again, like Hawthorne's Gray Champion, ominously and defiantly.

Unlike Brockden Brown's ironically deployed countersubversive narrator in *Ormond*, then, Cooper's countersubversive narrator in *The Bravo*, whether describing the physical setting, reporting dialogue, or offering political commentary, speaks engagedly and unironically for Cooper the republican countersubversive. The engaged narrator, like the "engaging narrator" of Harriet Beecher Stowe's *Uncle Tom's Cabin* as characterized by Robyn Warhol, is "seldom playful," principally because there is little to be playful about: The fate of eighteenth-century Venice provides lessons all too applicable to the precarious situation of nineteenth-century Europe and America. Cooper thus writes with the hope of inspiring actual readers to see that *The Bravo*, despite its use of fictional characters and a historically remote setting, speaks to "real world conditions for which the reader should take active responsibility after putting aside the book."[56] Because Cooper wants the reader to become aware of a republic's vulnerability to the subversive wiles of manipulative aristocrats, he refuses to remain silent as Gradenigo exploits republican rhetoric to justify his privileged social position. Like the anti-Illuminati writers (and Brown's Sophia), and like the Antimasons, who proclaimed in their National Platform of 1832 that "diffusing information on the subject of freemasonry . . . is the best method to ensure the entire destruction of the institution," Cooper as demystifying "anti-Venetian" countersubversive seeks to stimulate his reader's desire to overcome conspirators by unambiguously exhibiting their villainy.[57]

In his account of the next day's state regatta and celebration of Venice's marriage to the Adriatic, Cooper pointedly shows how the ruling oligarchs seek to sustain their control by socially enlarging the rhetorical manipulations we observed at Gradenigo's. The narrator describes the "festive" scene: "Here the improvisatore, secretly employed by a politic and mysterious government, recounted, with a rapid utterance, and in language suited to the popular ear . . . the ancient triumphs of the republic. . . . Shouts of approbation . . . were the reward of the agents of the police, whenever they most administered to the self-delusion and vanity of their audience" (1:117–18). The delineation of the masses' susceptibility to ritualistic invocations of a mythic past suggests that Venice's patriotic festivals, like the state's circumscribed nighttime masquerades, are meant to contain restless and potentially revolutionary energies through the promotion of a national blindness.

As in Hawthorne's revolutionary tales of the 1830s, however, this particular ceremonial occasion among the ruling "luxurious and affluent aristocracy" (1:118) and those under its dominion gives rise to an incipient democratic revolutionism. Initially there is but a single rebel, the elderly Antonio, who challenges protocol by boldly entreating the unresponsive doge for the release of his grandson. But when the mysterious bravo subsequently surrenders the regatta victory to the energetic old man, Antonio's fellow fishermen, who had initially mocked him for his participation, abruptly undergo "a violent revolution in their feelings" (1:159) and adopt his cause as their own. The fishermen's sudden willingness to defend the claims, not of the state, but of their station, in effect undoes the bonding work of the patriotic festival. Even after the doge at the awards ceremony once again refuses to honor Antonio's request for his grandson (and refuses the bravo's similar request), the fishermen continue to express their outrage at the state's intransigence. Taking note "in ominous and brooding silence" (1:160) of emergent revolutionary energies are the state's senators, skilled in the art of silent government, who offer a masking show of solidarity before withdrawing into the palace to discuss how to deal with "the hardy band of rioters" (1:160).

Cooper thus moves the novel's focus back to Venice's secretive interiors. In a scene looking forward to the catacomb adventures of *The Marble Faun*, Jacopo, according to plan, meets Antonio at night, when "the thoughtless and the designing, the conspirator and the agent of the police, once more met in privileged security" (1:162), and guides him through the state palace's winding passages so that he can plead directly with the senators for his grandson.[58] Penetrating the palace, Jacopo and Antonio literally penetrate to the core of the state, prompting Cooper the engaged narrator to reemerge. In an extended narrative intrusion that demands our close attention, he takes temporary leave of his characters and suspends the plot for several pages in order to speak directly to his reader on the political character of the subverted Venetian "republic."

The intrusion begins with a few words on the meaning of republicanism:

> It may be well to explain, here, to the reader, some of the peculiar machinery of the state . . . for the name of a republic, a word which, if it mean anything, strictly implies the representation and supremacy of the general interests, but which has so frequently been prostituted to the protection and monopolies of privileged classes, may have induced him to believe that there was, at least, a resemblance between the outlines of that government, and the more just, because more popular, institutions of his own country. (1:166)

Clearly Cooper speaks in this passage as an American to Americans, knowing that as he describes the corruption of republican Venice the reader will wonder about the term "republicanism" as it pertains to "his own country." He therefore assures his (American) reader that though both Venice and America are called "republics," a discrepancy between a political system's name and its actual practices is not so unusual. And yet, the reader may well wonder, if the term "republic" "has so frequently been prostituted to the protection of monopolies and of privileged classes," how can Americans confidently assume that their own country will remain untainted by this historical phenomenon? Actually, it would seem that Cooper wants the reader to entertain this question, for soon after insisting on the absolute difference between the two republics he suggests the applicability of Venetian history to relatively recent American history, observing that though Venice descended to oligarchy, the patricians founding the state were republican idealists. In addition, he comments on the difficulty of sustaining lofty political ideals given the individual's inveterate will to power (1:170); republican decline, it would appear, is a historical inevitability. Nevertheless, he refrains from explicitly linking Venice to America by challenging "the fallacy of a reasoning, which is so fond of predicting the downfall of our own liberal system" (1:171), and by pointing out that America, unlike Venice, is not a hereditary aristocracy.

But to assert difference in the context of reflections on the eternal truth of cyclical decline is to speak tortuously and problematically. Wishing to disclose the horrors of Venetian decline and to cast these horrors within a larger historical and philosophical framework, Cooper cannot unconditionally exempt America from his conspiratorial political vision. Instead, he offers in his lengthy digression on Venetian polity an account of republican subversion that, through its deployment of the economic images typifying countersubversive writings of the American 1820s and 1830s, suggests the relevance of eighteenth-century Venice to nineteenth-century America. In the earlier analysis of Senator Gradenigo, for example, Cooper compared him to a director of a bank or corporation. Now developing the similarities of Venice to a corporation, Cooper reflects on the selfishness inherent in oligarchical rule: "It partakes, and it always has partaken, though necessarily tempered by circumstances and the opinions of different ages, of the selfishness of all corporations, in which the responsibility of the individual, while his acts are professedly submitted to the temporizing expedients of a collective interest, is lost in the sub-division of numbers" (1:171). In short, Gradenigo and his fellow senators, like Jackson's loathed "monster bankers" and Weed's loathed Masons who "support the interests of their members, in preference to others of equal qualifications,"[59] are "prostituted to the protection and monopolies of privileged classes."

As the analysis continues, and as the descriptions of oligarchical Venetians increasingly parallel the descriptions of oligarchical Americans imaged in Antimasonic and Jacksonian conspiratorial discourse, Cooper steps forth as the republican countersubversive par excellence, unabashedly exploiting alarmist tactics to alert and engage his reader. For the American countersubversive writing in the melodramatic mode, conspirators typically posed dangers through their antirepublican secrecy, antidemocratic hierarchy, anti-Christian expediency, and extranational and -familial loyalties. These are exactly the traits characterizing the Venetian oligarchs. Like the Illuminati and Masons, the Venetian oligarchy, according to Cooper, is structured hierarchically; historical Venice lends itself well to his countersubversive presentation. At the broad base of the government is the Council of Three Hundred, a body of senators who partake of the country's wealth but exert only a small influence on governmental policy. From within this body is selected both a Council of Ten, which has greater powers to enact policy and a greater responsibility for surveillance – it watches over Venice with "aristocratical jealousy" (1:173) – and a Council of Three, an "authority, as irresponsible as it was absolute" (1:173), which most directly controls the destiny of the city-state (the doge, like Cooper's English king and Louis Philippe, is but a figurehead). The council is chosen by lot and the identity of its members is kept secret; as a result, "there existed, at all times, in the heart of Venice, a mysterious and despotic power . . . apparently surrounded by all the ordinary charities of life; but which, in truth, was influenced by a set of political maxims that were perhaps as ruthless, as tyrannic, and as selfish as ever were invented by the evil ingenuity of man" (1:173). The senators of "the Council of Three met in secret, ordinarily issued its decrees without communicating with any other body, and had them enforced with a fearfulness of mystery, and a suddenness of execution, that resembled the blows of fate" (1:174). And because their interests are strictly those of their class, they exhibit a selfishness and expediency incompatible with the principles of republicanism. Much like a Congregationalist minister of the 1790s, Cooper speaks directly and with an alarmist flourish on the villainy of expediency: "There is still in existence a long list of the state maxims which this secret tribunal recognized as its rule of conduct, and it is not saying too much to affirm that they set at defiance every other consideration but expediency, – all the recognized laws of God, and every principle of justice which is esteemed among men" (1:174).

Though Cooper begins his analysis of the Venetian government by emphasizing the differences between Venice and America, his impassioned rhetoric indicates that in the course of his lengthy digression he may well have discovered an equivalency between the image of oligarchically subverted Venice and contemporaneous images of oligarchically subverted America. The secret Council of Three, like the Venetian-Masonic "secret council" of *The American Democrat,* is an "expedient that was devised to protect its members from the ordinary liabilities of common censure." And like W. F. Brainard's Masonic order, the council "fears nothing from VIOLENCE, either PUBLIC or PRIVATE; FOR IT HAS EVERY MEANS TO LEARN IT IN SEASON, TO COUNTERACT, DEFEAT, AND PUNISH IT." Cooper thus concludes his analysis by equivocating on the initial assertion of difference between republican America and "republican" Venice: "The advances of the human intellect, supported by the means of publicity, may temper the exercise of a similar irresponsible power, in our own age, but in no country has this substitution, of a soulless corporation for an elective representation, been made, in which a system of rule has not been established, that sets at naught the laws of natural justice and the rights of the citizen" (1:174). The conditional "may" only calls attention to the subversive potential of a "soulless corporation" in even a prospering and apparently healthy republic. That is why Cooper writes with such urgency about the re-presented historical past and so readily adopts the countersubversive role as a legitimate narrative posture. Given the potential for subversion in all republics, not just in Venice, there is a need for a committed truth teller, a republican Jeremiah, who, unlike the possessive Sophia of *Ormond,* can disinterestedly alert republican readers to "fearful secrets" (1:240).

Earlier in the novel Gradenigo had informed Don Camillo Monforte that the senate's "august bodies are secret . . . exceeding human penetration" (1:94). But central to Cooper's countersubversive presence, I am arguing, is an omniscience that can peer through the antirepublican veils of the Venetian oligarchy so as to demystify the plottings of Senator Gradenigo and his ilk. In this regard, Cooper's narrative persona, in addition to resembling that of the political countersubversive, also resembles that of the Gothic and, as we shall see in the next chapter, antebellum anti-Catholic novelist, both of whom disclose the veiled interiors of church, convent, and monastery. When Cooper resumes his narrative with the entrance of Jacopo and Antonio into the Council of Three's antechamber, for instance, he presents the three masked members of the council as a "political inquisition" (1:173). As inquisitors, they in effect put body and soul of the trespassing petitioners on trial. Like the depraved priestly confessor of anti-Catholic fiction, and in a manner looking forward to Hawthorne's Chillingworth, one senator sadistically poses questions "with the wily design of unmasking the fisherman's entire soul" (1:191). All three senators remain utterly unresponsive to Jacopo's confession that he "pitied an old man who mourned for his offspring" (1:180). Within the dark confines of the chamber, Jacopo and Antonio stand accused of their humanity.

And yet, Cooper reveals, it is a humanity shared by others: Following the departure of Jacopo and Antonio, the senators of the Council of Three literally unmask to reveal "the grave visages of men in the decline of life, athwart which worldly cares and worldly passions had drawn those deep lines, which no subsequent ease or resignation can erase" (1:192). Cooper's willingness to humanize the senators makes what follows especially disturbing. They address the matters at hand, considering first the problem of Violetta's love for Don Camillo. As the reader knows, Gradenigo greedily seeks a marriage between his son and Violetta; and somehow the other two senators of the council know this too. Without betraying any knowledge of Gradenigo's scheme, they announce their plan to withdraw Violetta from his wardship and confine her to a secretive retreat. Exposed but not exposed, Gradenigo must offer his assent: "Teaching his features . . . to wear a smile as treacherous as that of his wily companion, he answered with seeming gratitude" (1:204). His vulnerability to governmental surveillance makes even this selfish aristocrat somewhat sympathetic.

The Council of Three concludes its meeting with a discussion of Antonio's appeal for his grandson. Though the council arrives at a decision, Cooper decides not to reveal it immediately. Instead he makes the reader's discovery of the decision participatory and dramatic by using the Carmelite Anselmo, Violetta's patriotic attendant, as a surrogate resisting reader. Summoned by the bravo to shrive Antonio in the "midnight loveliness" (1:225) of the Lagune, Anselmo urges Antonio to be more respectful toward the Venetian senators. But when the naïve Carmelite learns that Antonio's "disrespect" stems simply from his desire to free his grandson, he is taken aback, amazed that for exhibiting such familial love the state authorities should have branded him "criminal" (1:234) and "sinner" (1:235). Meanwhile, the onlooking bravo suspects that Antonio faces great dangers, and his fears are soon borne out: As he watches from a distance (and this is the perspective that the narrator too adopts), government agents approach Antonio's boat, take Anselmo onto their gondola, and leave Antonio alone in his. The bravo and Anselmo subsequently witness the grim proceedings: "The rubbing of a rope was audible, and the anchor of Antonio was lifted by a sudden jerk. A heavy plashing of the water followed" (1:238). The emphasis on the mechanics of the capsizing, coupled with our remote perspective on Antonio's "heavy plashing," convey the impersonal efficiency of the Venetian "soulless corporation." That impersonality, Cooper suggests through a bleak description of the bravo's futile efforts to rescue the drowning Antonio, extends to nature as well:

> The water gurgled; an arm was visible in the air, and it disappeared. The gondola drove upon the spot where the limb had just been visible, and a backward stroke, that caused the ashen blade to bend like a reed, laid the trembling boat motionless. The furious action threw the Lagune into ebullition, but, when the foam subsided, it lay calm as the blue and peaceful vault it reflected. (1:239)

The calm is an empty calm, conveying finality and despair.

Within the subverted republican state, Anselmo abruptly realizes, there is no political justice. Upon returning to Violetta and Don Camillo, he announces his new knowledge of social reality: "What a fearful state is Venice!" (2:4). The state's governing body is especially fearful, Don Camillo observes, voicing a concern crucial to republican countersubversives, because "it hath, of all other dangers the greatest, the curse of secrecy on its intentions, its acts, and its responsibilities!" (2:5). Thurlow Weed, referring to the alleged murder of William Morgan by the Free Masons, spoke of the dangers posed to a republic by a secretive aristocratic network: "It encourages the commission of crime, by affording to the guilty facilities of escape."[60] When Cooper in *The American Democrat* compared the Masons to the Venetians he focused precisely on their similar temptations to abuse secrecy in malignant ways in order to sustain their aristocratic power. That passage and the broad similarities between the murder by drowning of the historical Morgan, who challenged the authority of the Masons, and the murder by drowning of the fictional Antonio, who challenged the authority of the Venetian leaders, suggest that Masonic controversy in America exerted a significant influence not only on Cooper's conception of oligarchical republican Venice but also on *The Bravo*'s plot. It also may have influenced Cooper's conception of his engaged narration. Morgan, we recall, was allegedly killed by the Masons for threatening to commit the "crime" of authorship; his demystifying *Illustrations of Masonry* was a posthumous publication that, by spawning a mass political movement, attested to the power of the word. Though not an author, Antonio was "seditious," and his words had begun to carry some weight. When he is silenced at the midpoint of a novel about "real world conditions," we are convinced more than ever of the need for Cooper's countersubversive presence.

With his inside view of senatorial plotting and his outside portrayal of the mandated murder, Cooper responds to that need by starkly putting on display the oligarchs' villainous expediency. And just as America's early national and antebellum countersubversives typically offered both a dark revelation of villainous expediency and then a sentimentalized picture of the damnable moral consequences of such villainy, so too does Cooper. As we have seen, late-eighteenth-century countersubversives usually focused on the way in which the family, pictured as a nurturing ground for virtuous republicans, came under attack by expedient villains whose loyalties were always extra-national and extra-familial. Americans throughout the nineteenth century continued to idealize the republican family even as the family proved to be vulnerable to marketplace and democratizing pressures. George Forgie writes, "In a society that valued progress and equality, and in which authority of any kind, no matter how mild, was on the defensive, the family was one archaic, hierarchical institution compatible with modernity and democracy."[61] In countersubversive and sentimental discourse in particular, that which threatened the "DOMESTIC CIRCLE" threatened the republic. Working within this conventional framework, Cooper in *The Bravo*'s second volume, like Sophia in *Ormond,* seeks to show that the "undermining of the security of families," as Don Camillo remarks, "is to destroy society at its core!" (2:37).

Cooper is particularly concerned that oligarchical infiltration and surveillance could undermine familial trust. In Venice, the bravo sardonically declares to Don Camillo, "You may know what it is to have your own wife turning your secret thoughts into gold" (2:37). Although

Violetta clearly would never adopt such deceitful practices, her home nevertheless remains under the eye of secret agents and is even infiltrated by such agents. When Anselmo defies the state by officiating at the marriage of Violetta and Don Camillo, for example, he does so in the presence of the governmental spy Annina. And when the marriage party attempts to flee Violetta's mansion, the full extent of governmental surveillance and infiltration is abruptly, and somewhat comically, revealed:

> The foot of Donna Violetta had scarcely touched the pavement of the lower hall, when several menials glided down the flight, and quitted the palace, by its different outlets. Each sought those who engaged him in the service. One flew along the narrow streets of the islands, to the residence of the Signor Gradenigo; another sought his son; and one, ignorant of the person of him he served, actually searched an agent of Don Camillo, to impart a circumstance in which that noble was himself so conspicuous an actor. (2:20–1)

Though comic, the end result of such ubiquitous spying is that the wedded couple is divided: Betrayed by "one or more . . . agents" (2:24), Don Camillo unwittingly places Violetta on a state gondola, and she is taken into captivity.

Oligarchical selfishness and surveillance drive a (temporary) wedge between husband and wife. More insidiously, the forces of oligarchy sunder whole families, as we learn from the plight of the enigmatic bravo. Though mysterious, Jacopo has already revealed a good deal about himself in his sympathetic embracing of Antonio's cause. As becomes clear, he aided Antonio because he viewed him as a substitute father. He appealed to the doge on Antonio's behalf "that the father and son may be restored to each other" (1:157) (Antonio sought restoration of a grandson), and retrospectively we realize that he spoke of his own desire to be reunited with his father. Antonio's past friendship with Jacopo's father, an army companion now presumed dead, and his willingness to plot with Jacopo despite a chronic suspiciousness that he never completely overcomes, suggest that, where Jacopo saw a substitute father, Antonio saw a substitute (grand)son. That their reciprocal needs remain unfulfilled at Antonio's death stands as a tragedy of the novel.

Until we actually meet Jacopo's father, however, we have little understanding of the bravo's situation beyond our sensing that he lacks, and seeks, human connectedness. Jacopo's desolation following Antonio's death, and, in a larger sense, the desolation characterizing a world in which the claims of family and friends must be subordinated to the claims of the oligarchs' state, comes through in the narrator's description of Jacopo's refuge of choice, Venice's Hebrew and heretic burial ground, a sterile world elsewhere on the Lido di Palestrina: "This place of interment is without the relief of trees, at the present day it is uninclosed, and in the opinions of those who have set it apart for heretic and Jew, it is unblessed" (2:31). Following the kidnapping of his wife, Don Camillo similarly takes refuge on the burial ground's "barren sands" (2:31); and it should be noted that, although Cooper's stereotypical presentation of Hosea the Jewish moneylender occasionally reflects and seemingly endorses Venice's own conspiratorial fear of Jewish "monster bankers," the encounter between Jacopo and Don Camillo at the Jewish cemetery suggests that all of Venice's stigmatized "subversive" outcasts form a community of potentially countersubversive "Jews." Appropriately, it is at the burial grounds that these two "Jews" discover their fellowship, as Jacopo, prompted by what he calls a "glimpse of sympathy, to which I have long been a stranger" (2:39), tells his life history to the initially suspicious Don Camillo. As with the Council of Three's decision to murder Antonio, Cooper chooses to retain Jacopo's secrets while employing Don Camillo, like Anselmo, as an exemplary surrogate reader. Listening to the bravo's story, his mistrust dissolves into "an ungovernable expression of pity" (2:42).

Don Camillo's sympathetic response to Jacopo guides the reader toward a similar response; but desiring to have the reader learn about Jacopo's situation firsthand and in dramatic fashion, Cooper has Jacopo journey to yet another Venetian "burial ground": the state prison. The morally admirable characters found within, such as Jacopo's long-suffering father and the innocent jailkeeper Gelsomina, offer the Thoreauvian lesson, and the lesson too of *The Spy* and *The Pioneers,* that "the true place for a just man is also a prison."[62] The prison is located in the building adjoining the doge's palace; dungeons are also located in the basements of the palace itself, where Jacopo's father is presently interred. That "the palace of the doge himself was polluted by the presence of the dungeons" (2:61) reveals what is so fearful about the state's "mysterious power": It is a punishing power. In effect, the Venetian oligarchy is a Slave Power with "its foot," Jacobo remarks, "on the neck of the people" (2:67).

It is also quite literally a "masonic" power, for Venice's physical landscape consists almost entirely of stones and mortar. The state palace, for example, is described in this way:

> A massive rustic basement of marble was seated as solidly in the element, as if it grew from a living rock, while story was seemingly raised on story, in the wanton observance of the most capricious rules of meretricious architecture, until the pile reached an altitude that is little known, except in the dwellings of princes. Colonnades, medallions, and massive cornices, overhung the canal, as if the art of man had taken pride in loading the superstructure in a manner to mock the unstable element which concealed its base. (1:25–26)

Emblematic of the pride and luxury infecting Venice's oligarchical leaders, and the state itself, the palace's masonry testifies to the triumph of craft over "nature." And because the prison is located within the palace, the enclosing stonework, especially in the context of the novel's burial imagery, further links the Venetian oligarchs to crafty Masons. The Masons, after all, were regularly depicted as subversives who buried their enemies within the imprisoning masonwork of their dwellings. In Edgar Allan Poe's "The Cask of Amontillado" (1844), for example, the narrator sardonically declares a Masonic affiliation just before laying the "tier of masonry" that buries Fortunato alive. And in Melville's *Israel Potter* (1854), Potter feels so "masoned up" while hiding in a small secret room in Squire Woodcock's mansion that he suffers a vertiginous panic. Significantly, he recalls that the mansion formerly belonged to the Masonic order of the Templars and that this particular room, "a little closet, or rather cell," had been used by them as a prison cell.[63]

Enclosed within a closet-like basement cell, Jacopo's frail father similarly seems buried alive, the victim of the Venetians' unyielding masonry. Maddened by his ordeal, he believes his deceased wife and daughter are awaiting his release, he has no idea that Jacopo serves as a bravo, and he stares obsessively at a spider. It is not until the old man is on the verge of death that Jacopo realizes, in Natty Bumppo fashion (and with the considerable help of the narrator's countersubversive presence), why his father, innocent of all charges against him, was "buried" in such a fashion: "The natural strength of his mind had enabled him to understand, that a system, which on its face professed to be founded on the superior acquirements of a privileged few, would be the least likely to admit the fallacy of its theories, by confessing it could err" (2:160). The system, Jacopo concludes, cannot admit to its human bases. His insights are reinforced near the end of the novel, when the history of Jacopo's father is at last revealed. The elder Frontoni had been tricked by an associate, a duplicitous suitor of his daughter, who "laid a snare of deception which . . . drew the anger of the state on his too confiding friend" (2:221–2). Like Clifford in *The House of the Seven Gables,* he was falsely accused of a crime that appearances suggest he committed – in Jacopo's father's case stealing money from the customs. But because he was officially pronounced guilty by the government, there can be no backing down, no admission that the system can err, even after the plotter recanted on his deathbed. Falsely promised that his service as a government spy would help to mitigate his father's sentence, Jacopo thus adopted the guise of a bravo but not its murderous functions. Like all good citizens of Venice, he assumes a role that exacerbates paranoia and, ironically, helps to preserve the state's stability.

The state must preserve at least the appearance of stability, for beneath the paranoiac surface of day-to-day life, as the several accounts of the nighttime masquerades suggest, lies an incipient revolutionism. Cooper commented in his journal on Naple's nighttime masquerades: "Evening delightful, and the streets alive. Bad policy in a Government not to encourage domestic life, as it clearly has a tendency to make good citizens. This system of amusements is like a palliative for a disease, which aides the ravages of the malady while it soothes for a moment –."[64] In *The Bravo* the nighttime revelries, along with the extended account of the state festivities at the Adriatic, are presented as governmental efforts to offer "a palliative for a disease" that results from, among other things, the sundering of family. The "disease" is a revolutionism that so surged to the fore with Antonio's victory in the state regatta that the oligarchs felt compelled to murder. Violetta's decision to marry Don Camillo Monforte against the state's wishes also reveals a measure of rebelliousness, as does Jacopo's decision to betray the rulers for whom he supposedly works. After participating in the numerous plottings that finally allow Don Camillo and Violetta to escape from Venice, Jacopo returns to a "scene of violence and deception" (2:157) to confront revolutionary energies now rampant on a national level.

Most centrally indicative of the emergent revolutionism is the aggressiveness of Antonio's fellow fishermen in calling for justice to be dealt to Antonio's murderer. The night following the murder, for example, the fishermen protest at the palace gates. But as opposed to the heroic Revolutionaries of 1776, and consistent with Cooper's suspicions of the unthrottled revolutionism of 1793, the fishermen are presented as misguided and confused, as little more than a mob. Under the sway of a demagogue who, unlike the model revolutionary Lafayette, only "assumed the character of a leader" (2:93), the fishermen "yielded to passion, and moved away toward the palace of St. Mark . . . without any other definite object than a simple indulgence of feeling" (2:97).[65] Such is the fishermen's "ill-regulated zeal" (2:98) and, most crucially, their utter ignorance of Venetian power relationships that they lay the blame for Antonio's murder on the bravo, the readily available scapegoat, whom they believe would kill simply because he lost a gondola race. Like the virtuous Balthazar of *The Headsman* (1833), Jacopo is perceived as an agent of the state who somehow has achieved a degree of autonomy that absolves the state of any complicity in his supposed murderous actions. Of course, this is the use to which the oligarchs have set him up all along, and they eagerly grab at the chance to stigmatize him as a murderous plotter in order to defuse revolutionary energies and reclaim the citizenry's loyalties.

With the account of the arrest and jailing of Jacopo, then, Cooper would seem once again to be exposing the ways in which the oligarchs use their "masonic" cells to preserve and perpetuate their power. But in a narrative move that reflects his contempt for the "breath of the mob" (2:95), Cooper turns his attention to the plight of Senator Soranzo, Gradenigo's replacement on the Council of Three, "who was gifted by nature with feelings that, in any other form of government, would have made him a philanthropist" (2:108–9). Like Violetta, the appealing Soranzo values the home, and he has created within Venice an idyllic domestic retreat. The narrator takes the reader "deep within the walls" (2:171) of Soranzo's abode to present a "small, but lovely family picture" (2:171):

> There was a father [Soranzo], a gentlemen who had scarce attained the middle age, with an eye in which spirit, intelligence, philanthropy, and, at that moment, paternal fondness were equally glowing. He tossed in his arms, with parental pride, a laughing urchin of some three or four years, who rioted in the amusement which brought him and the author of his being, for a time, seemingly on a level. A fair Venetian dame, with golden locks, and glowing cheeks, such as Titian loved to paint her sex, reclined on a couch nigh by, following the movements of both, with the joint feelings of mother and wife, and laughing in pure sympathy with the noisy merriment of her young hope. A girl, who was the youthful image of herself, with tresses that fell to her waist, romped with a crowing infant, whose age was so tender as scarcely to admit the uncertain evidence of its intelligence. (2:171–2)

So infused with the proper domestic values is Soranzo that when summarily called to the Council of Three and informed of Violetta's escape, he "secretly hoped she was in the arms of the Neapolitan" (2:175). Nevertheless, he feels certain that Jacopo murdered Antonio, and he demands his execution. But at the staged trial before the Council of Three, Soranzo experiences a sudden loss of equilibrium when he learns that Jacopo's father is a prisoner of the state. The subsequent death of the father, which occurs during the trial, further complicates matters for Soranzo, as does Jacopo's account of the circumstances surrounding his father's imprisonment and his own conscription. To this surprising news, Soranzo "listened with the interest of one, who was just entering on a noviciate of secret and embarrassing duties" (2:194–5). Having viewed the state unmasked and learned of his own complicitous relationship to power, he departs from the doge's palace a diminished man: "Signor Soranzo hastened to his own luxurious and happy dwelling. For the first time in his life, he entered it with a distrust of himself" (2:200). Within Venice, he realizes, he, like the bravo, is only "an actor" (2:200). His home will be "happy" no more.

Though Cooper unquestionably loathes Venice's corporate governmental machine, his sympathetic presentation of Soranzo's "fall" into knowledge desentimentalizes the novel, dissolving the conventional dis-

tinction between villain and hero central to such Manichean countersubversive texts as Seward's "Address." Many within Venice, high and
low, are "merely the creature[s] of a system" (2:174). Juxtaposed with
the image of the fishermen as fickle mob, however, the portrait of a
compromised but virtuous senator suggests a shift in Cooper's sympathies near the end of the novel, another moment of narrative discovery,
as it were, that momentarily softens the attack on Venice's leaders. This
shift in sympathies, I believe, is an almost inevitable consequence of
Cooper's countersubversive strategies; and I will explore the implications of the shift more fully in the chapter's final section. What I want
simply to note here are the politics implicit in his use of omniscience. As
omnisicent narrator, as master of surveillance, Cooper necessarily shares
his greatest affinities with characters in the know, particuarly those, like
Jacopo and Soranzo, possessive of a "natural" transpolitical virtue. Arguably it is for this reason that Cooper comes to depict the fishermen,
"Antimasons" of sorts whose democratic fervor parallels the democratic
fervor fueling American Antimasonry, as viscious "know-nothings" all
too easily manipulated by demagogues and oligarchs.[66] In Byron's *Marino Faliero* (1821), an important source for *The Bravo,* the citizens of
fourteenth-century Venice flock to see the beheading of Faliero, but at
least those witnessing the execution realize that Faliero is a patriot. In the
words of one witness, Faliero "would have freed us."[67] In contrast, the
citizens of *The Bravo* to the very end remain duped, and self-righteously
so at that.

But duped they are, and just before the scheduled execution of Jacopo,
Cooper effects a turn in the plot that works in part to absolve the fish-
ermen and redirect attention to the Council of Three's invisible and silent
villainy. Gelsomina, who learns of Jacopo's personal history, and the
Carmelite Anselmo, who knows full well that Jacopo is innocent of
Antonio's murder, journey to the doge's palace to petition for justice.
Gelsomina's attempt to save her lover is modeled on Jeannie Deans's
pilgrimage at the end of Scott's *The Heart of Mid-Lothian* and Frances
Wharton's at the end of *The Spy*. Like the queen in Scott's romance and
Washington in Cooper's, the doge is moved by the virtuous woman's
plea for Jacopo and offers to set things right. A familiarity with sentimental conventions naturally leads the reader to believe that the tearful
petitioners have successfully carried out their mission, though an ominous note prevails. At the close of the interview, the doge, "a puppet in
the hands of the nobles" (2:214), consults with a "silent companion"
(2:228), a Fedallah-like member of the Council of Three.

Despite hints at the doge's impotence, the conclusion of the novel
comes as a rude jolt. Jacopo, like Antonio before the race on the Grand
Canal, faces a taunting mob, as Gelsomina pleads for justice. And then

from the palace appears a signal, perhaps of clemency: "Gelsomina uttered a cry of delight, and turned to throw herself upon the bosom of the reprieved. The ax glittered before her eyes, and the head of Jacopo rolled upon the stones, as if to meet her. A general movement in the living mass denoted the end" (2:235). The abrupt axing of Gelsomina's (and the reader's) hopes is adroitly carried out by Cooper. Making use of an onward progression of syntactical events, he conveys the matter-of-fact machine quality of justice and daily life in the subverted republican state: "The Dalmations wheeled into column, the Sbirri pushed aside the throng, on the way to their haunts, the water of the bay was dashed upon the flags, the clotted saw-dust was gathered, the head and trunk, block, basket, ax, and the executioner, disappeared, and the crowd circulated around the fatal spot" (2:228). As at the end of *Benito Cereno* with its beheading, the sun shines "gloriously in the heavens" (2:228) while events on earth mock the glory of the heavens. "Justice is the motto of Venice" (2:226), the doge had assured the now maniacally unhinged Gelsomina, and it is simply that: a motto, part of Venice's ongoing masquerade. Lurking behind Venice's idealized republican façade is an oligarchical corporate machine operating with a "soulless" efficiency to preserve its power. Fully unmasked, this republican state on its self-destructive arc of decline reveals brute malignancy. The informing concern of the novel is that other republics – perhaps even the American republic – may similarly be unmasked and exposed.

"The publick, every where, is proverbially soulless"

As the story goes, Cooper returned to America in 1833 and underwent a transformation. Formerly America's great defender, he suddenly became an inveterate social critic, perceiving little but demagoguery and commercialism all around him. Alan Axelrad writes, "It has become widely accepted in Cooper scholarship that the novelist left for Europe in 1826 a liberal democrat, and only later, after his return in 1833, became disillusioned with popular politics and democratic man." Axelrad rejects the standard plot and in its place installs the less dramatic picture of Cooper as a "lifelong conservative," an interpretation that, to my mind, diminishes the integrity of Cooper's activist republicanism of the early 1830s and, as concerns his art, implies that throughout his career he learned nothing new and said nothing new.[68] I would challenge both the schematic reading of Cooper's political transformation of post-1833 and the ahistorical, extranarrative reading of his political consistency as "lifelong conservative." Let me address the latter issue first, with reference to *The Bravo*.

As is true for his earlier novels, Cooper's avowed intention in writing

The Bravo is anything but socially conservative. According to the Preface, he wants his readers to understand that the "mildest and justest governments in Europe are, at this moment, theoretically despotisms" (2:vii); he wants to show that "a government which is not properly based on the people, possesses an unavoidable and oppressive evil of the first magnitude, in the necessity of supporting itself by physical force and onerous impositions, against the natural action of the majority" (1:vii); and ultimately he wants his Venetian novel to contribute to the "history of the progress of political liberty" (1:vi). Convinced that America is at the forefront of such progress, he assures his American readers, "So long as this vital difference [representative government] exists between ourselves and other nations, it will be vain to think of finding analogies in their institutions" (1:vi). Though he later remarks in *A Letter to His Countrymen* (1834) that *The Bravo* may indeed apply to America and its citizenry – "That some of the facets of this picture were peculiar to the Venetian polity, and to an age different from our own, is true; this much was necessary to the illusion of the tale; but it was believed that there remained enough of that which is eternal, to supply the moral" – he continues to value the unmasking authority of American republicanism: "I determined to attempt a series of tales, in which American opinion should be brought to bear on European facts."[69]

On the basis of the Preface and the *Letter,* we may reasonably conclude that Cooper's damning portrayal of the Venetian oligarchy was intended both to alert Europeans to the subversion of their political institutions and to warn Americans about possible future threats to theirs. What happens in *The Bravo,* however, as in his celebratory novels of the 1820s, is that engagement with narrative, character, and the darker contours of republican discourse leads him toward conclusions that conflict with his stated intentions: If he set out to unmask the Venetian republic, and by extension the sham republic of Louis Philippe, he seems to have discovered "enough of that which is eternal" to perceive the immediate relevance of eighteenth-century Venice to nineteenth-century America. Thus while he may have sought to indict a conspiring oligarchical rule similar to that which he believed was assuming power throughout Europe, it appears that in the course of writing *The Bravo* he also experienced anxieties about the imminent threat of deceit and subversion in even the most promising of republican states. Speaking of machine-corporate pseudorepublican Venice, Don Camillo notes, "It clokes its offences against right in a thousand specious forms, and it enlists the support of every man, under the pretence of a sacrifice for the common good. We often fancy ourselves simple dealers in some justifiable state intrigue, when in truth we are deep in sin" (2:44). This is not simply an indictment of a specific fallen republican state: This is a cautionary warning, and arguably even Cooper's own surprised "discovery," of the dangers inherent in republicanism as an ideology wherever it takes hold.[70] Though certain political and philosophical predispositions, coupled with his suspicion of British aristocrats and French "republicans," may have contributed to the emergence of this insight, I would maintain that Cooper's discovery takes place first and foremost in narrative, that it owes a good deal to the informing power of countersubversive republican discourse, and that to view the novel simply as a stabilized signification of conservative political belief is to diminish its force and sugar-coat its nightmare.

Cooper, nonetheless, makes his own effort at stabilization by exerting a powerful formal control over the nightmarish presentation of the Venetian republic. Like most of his novels, *The Bravo* consists of two volumes, though in this more than most he strives to attain dramatic unity and formal symmetry. The first volume describes but two days in the life of eighteenth-century Venice and concludes with the murder of Antonio. The second volume similarly concludes with the death of a sympathetic character, in this case Jacopo, and covers four days. The novel ends as it begins, with citizens pouring into the Square of St. Mark for nighttime revelry. The tight formalism allows Cooper to make his political points as clearly as possible for those in dire need of a political education – those, like the novel's demagogic fishermen, who remain completely in the dark.

I have argued that Cooper's unflattering picture of the fishermen followed ineluctably from his adoption of a countersubversive narrative presence. Brockden Brown's canny presentation of Sophia's emergence as a "secret witness" in the very act of exposing the machinations of another "secret witness" revealed how the countersubversive can become as manipulative, and as eerily knowledgeable, as the subversives he or she is out to expose. One end result of Cooper's omniscient and intrusive narration in *The Bravo* is to link him, admittedly in odd and uncomfortable ways, with the omniscient and intrusive Venetian oligarchs he seeks to unmask and condemn. Exposing oligarchical manipulations of the people, Cooper becomes a manipulator of the people. And by the end of the novel he expresses a similar contempt for and fear of the masses and a similar desire to keep their disruptive energies in check. In this regard, the fishermen may be viewed as fictional stand-ins for Cooper's implied contemporary readers. For despite the Preface's happy idealization of his readers as a community of "jealous and vituperative" (1:viii) republican guardians, Cooper's coercive narrative techniques in *The Bravo* suggest that he saw himself as one of the few able to penetrate the façades of masquerading republics, one of the few able to discern the difference between a mindless demagoguery and a genuine revolutionary republicanism. His sense of himself as an omniscient and solitary truth teller eventually led him to elevate himself above his own republican community and become, as is typical of the countersubversive, a decrier of corruption who, as a matter of narrative posture, cannot but feel superior to the uninformed reading public he seeks to mobilize and instruct.

If we now reconsider the issue of Cooper's "transformation" of the 1830s, it is apparent that the transformation was a political-rhetorical one, pivoting as it did on his changing attitude toward his democratic reading public. We must recall that despite the controversy over the notorious review of *The Bravo* appearing in the 7 June 1832 *New-York American*, in which one "Cassio" lambasted Cooper's "imbecile efforts of exhausted genius," *The Bravo*, as William Charvat and others have noted, was one of his most popular novels.[71] But rather than let the "Cassio" review fall into oblivion, he kept it alive by assenting to his friend Samuel F. B. Morse's conspiratorial interpretation that the review, in fact the work of New Yorker Edward Sherman Gould, was written by a Frenchman objecting to Cooper's activist republicanism. As a result, Cooper turned the review against his public, attacking his American readers for their docile capitulation to foreign opinion. According to Cooper, the subsequent decline of his contemporary reputation had everything to do with politics: Defending republican and democratic ideals, he was misunderstood in what Marvin Meyers has termed "the Age of Dodge and Bragg."[72] But it may be said in defense of Cooper's contemporary audience that all too often, in his writings of the 1830s and 1840s, his persona resembled that of the didactic and adversarial countersubversive narrator of *The Bravo*. And his readers were perceptive enough to realize that his social criticism, by itself not so extreme, was time and again offered with a barely restrained contempt.

For example, in his valedictory *A Letter to His Countrymen* Cooper lambasts Americans, few of whom probably even read the "Cassio" review, for their credulity and then instructs his readers on the political themes of his European novels.[73] In an unsigned review of the *Letter* in the August 1834 *New-England Magazine,* the writer strenuously and rather sarcastically objects to Cooper's manifest superiority: "The second part of the letter is a sort of political essay upon the powers of the various departments of the government, written apparently with the amiable purpose of enlightening the people of the United States, who have hitherto had no better teachers in constitutional law, than such shallow tyros as John Marshall, Joseph Story, and Daniel Webster, and others." Similarly, in response to Cooper's satirical *Home as Found,* the anonymous reviewer in the January 1839 *New-York Review* again objects less to Cooper's politics than to the tone with which he offers social criticism: "There is a wide difference between faithful rebuke, proceeding from the spirit of true patriotism, and scornful sneers arising from morbid feeling, disaffection, disappointment, and assumed superiority."[74] Cooper's large complaint against his American readers is summed up in a letter of March 1832 to William Dunlap: "There may be better writers than I in the country, but there is certainly no one treated with so little deference." But if, as Steadfast Dodge vaingloriously declares in *Home as Found*, "God never intended an American to kneel,"[75] how could Cooper expect Americans to kneel before him? And yet, failing to obtain the deference he believed Americans would begrudge even God, he could not help experiencing a baffled sense of disillusionment and betrayal. By the late 1830s he was writing with an almost complete disregard for his nonsympathetic readers, fueling hostility by repeatedly insisting on Americans' need for political instruction.

Thus even a thoughtful text like *The American Democrat* could be taken as a deliberate provocation, and with good reason; for in its treatment of the "soulless corporation" we can discern a marked shift in Cooper's thinking about the dangers facing a republic. He warns yet again of aristocratic corporate schemers: "Aristocracies partaking of the irresponsible nature of corporations, are soulless, possessing neither the personal feelings that often temper even despotism, nor submitting to the human impulses of popular bodies." And he calls, hopefully, for a community of republican guardians to detect and unmask such schemers: "All who possess trusts, are to be diligently watched, for there is no protection against abuses without responsibility, nor any real responsibility, without vigilance." But by the end of the text he declares that, though aristocrats may pose a threat to the republic, equally dangerous, and just as iniquitous, are the democratic masses: "The publick, every where, is proverbially soulless." In fact, the "publick" may pose an even greater threat than subversive oligarchs: "The publick, then, is to be watched, in this country, as, in other countries kings and aristocrats are to be watched."[76] By 1838, however, Cooper saw few capable of such dutiful guardianship, and so he abandoned the idealistic hope for a united community of concerned watchers, taking the responsibility for vigilance upon himself.

In *Memorial of James Fenimore Cooper* (1852), Samuel F. B. Morse commented on Cooper's confrontational stance of the 1830s and 1840s: "If he was at times severe or caustic in his remarks on others, it was when excited by the exhibition of the little arts of little minds."[77] Morse speaks well for Cooper's combative mentality during this period. Various social controversies – the dispute over Three Mile Point, his legal battles with the press, his disdain for Anti-Rentism – led him to feel increasingly alienated from the very public he hoped would purchase and read his novels. As a result, though his work of the period shared many of the social concerns of his earlier novels – apprehensions of rootless commercialism, mob violence, and demagoguery are unambiguously present in *The Pioneers,* for instance – he tended to adopt in his later novels a narrative perspective that would keep him relatively sacrosanct and at a knowing remove. Wayne Franklin remarks on *The Crater* (1847), "Cooper in his role as narrator seems almost interchangeable with God."[78] As "God," Cooper in *The Crater* imagines an ideal republic in which his fictionalized persona Mark Woolston governs the Craterinos in curiously "Venetian" fashion: Assisted by a council of three, later expanded to a council of nine, he rules with his council at the huge centralized governmental structure named Colony House. In *The Bravo* such leaders and councils are secretive and despotic; in *The Crater* the idealized leaders, all duly elected, "had no relish for power for power's sake, but only wielded it for the general good."[79] The subsequent decline of Woolston's community is tied not to the excesses of those in power, but to the arrival of fifty new immigrants – including a lawyer, a newspaperman, and four clerics – who bring to Craterino society an insurrectionary demagoguery: Factionalism, sectarianism, and, finally, a democratic election drive Woolston from office. As the narrator loses control of the community, Cooper reasserts his authorial control by subjecting the Craterinos to the "divine" judgment of an obliterating earthquake. In a number of his other novels of the period – the Littlepage manuscripts, *The Ways of the Hour* (1850) – he asserts a similar narrative control and authority, and conveys his contempt for the "soulless" masses, not simply by taking a political stance on such matters as property ownership and the jury system, but by adopting a version of the engaged countersubversive narration of *The Bravo,* or else by employing a first-person narrator so similar to Cooper as to undermine the potential for narrative irony. These narrative tactics diminished the possibility that he could create a community of sympathetic readers.

In short, I am suggesting that Cooper's adoption of the role of countersubversive in *The Bravo* had important ramifications for the shape of his career. Ironically, his sympathetic response to widely shared Antimasonic and Jacksonian fears of conspiracy made him even more elitist, as he came to conceive of the "publick," and not an aristocratic cabal, as the principal source of the greed, self-interest, and ambition threatening to subvert republican ideals. Arguably, countersubversives of the period likewise were made nervous by the energies unleashed by laissez-faire capitalism and Jacksonian egalitarianism. But as opposed to Cooper, and in the spirit of united community, they continued to project their concerns about the breakdown of social boundaries onto conspiratorial organizations. According to Rogin, countersubversive campaigns against aristocratic Masons, monopolies, "corporations," and banks, like the violent campaigns against the Indians occurring during the same period, allowed many Americans to take a heroic pride in their virtuous commitment to the republic even as they self-interestedly "cleared the obstacles to free market relations."[80] Identifying and overcoming subversive "deviants," Americans forged a new consensus for republican expansionism and, so they believed, maintained the purity of their national romance.

In this light we may note a further irony in the shape of Cooper's career. As portrayed by the Antimasons, the Masons were subversives who disdained national borders, universalists whose stated goal was to create one cooperative society of privileged Masonic insiders. Similarly, the Federalists and Congregationalists feared that French-Republican and Illuminati universalism threatened to undermine American nationality. The countersubversive response of both late-eighteenth-century and Jacksonian alarmists was to create borders by invoking the melodramatic opposition between virtuous Americans and villainous others. Whereas Cooper's early fiction, particularly the Leatherstocking novels of the 1820s, shows how the creation of boundaries, or borders, was central to the creation of America, in his writings of 1829–34 he leans toward a republican universalism. To be sure, American republicanism is special to Cooper, but he hardly regards it as an original or distinctive republicanism; it represents the current flowering of a long and great tradition. Convinced of the existence of an international aristocratic conspiracy, then, he counters with an appeal to the principles of a universal republicanism. In doing so, he puts at risk what the Federalists, Jacksonians, and even Cooper himself during the 1820s feared to put at risk – the very notion of American exceptionality.

With his disillusionment increasing into the 1840s, "American republicanism" became for Cooper something of a contradiction in terms. Accordingly, he began to relinquish borders, disencumbering himself, as it were, of America itself. This is apparent in the utopian design of *The Crater*, which is set worlds apart from the North American continent, and I would suggest that it is also apparent in the final two Leatherstocking novels, particularly *The Deerslayer* (1841), with its haunting image of apocalypse-masking Glimmerglass. And though the Anti-Rent novels focus literally on the problem of maintaining borders, they are informed by a despairing sense that the battle against the "soulless" mob is a rearguard and doomed one, as the boundaries between landlord and renter, as well as those between the "savage" Indian and the Anti-Rent "Injin," remain on the verge of collapse. In *The Redskins, or Indians and Injin* (1846), the final novel of the trilogy, we leave the hero Hugh Littlepage as he journeys to Washington to plead the cause of landlords. Should he fail in his mission, Cooper remarks, "he has the refuge of Florence open, where he can reside among the other victims of oppression, with the advantage of being admired as a refugee from republican tyranny."[81]

The bitter irony here suggests that Cooper is prepared to relinquish republicanism; and in his embrace of trinitarian Christianity in the subsequent *The Oak Openings* (1848) and *The Sea Lions* (1849), he indeed bids republicanism farewell. In its stead he envisions a glorious redemptive community – a heavenly community – untainted by corruption and forbidden to the soulless.

3

"A Confusion of Popish and Protestant Emblems"

Insiders and Outsiders in Nathaniel Hawthorne's
The Blithedale Romance

Catholicism wrests from the people the right to choose their own ministers, and the right of election is the very essence of our institutions. It
establishes an aristocratical priesthood, and the whole people are steeped
in republicanism. It withholds the Scriptures, and the age is a reading
one, and reads the more what is forbidden.

> W. E. Channing, *Letter on Catholicism*

"Avoid the convent, my dear friend, as you would shun the death of
the soul!"

> (Kenyon to Donatello)

"I was a prisoner in the Convent of the Sacré Coeur, in the Trinità de'
Monti . . . but in such kindly custody of pious maidens, and watched
over by such a dear old priest, that – had it not been for one or two
disturbing recollections, and also because I am a daughter of the Puritans – I would willingly have dwelt there forever."

> (Hilda to "Hawthorne")

> Hawthorne, *The Marble Faun*

Galvanized by the republican revolutionary ferment of the early 1830s,
Cooper in *The Bravo* sought patriotically to represent the depraved
oligarchy of "republican" Venice as viewed through American eyes. But
when he next wrote about Italy in *Gleanings in Europe: Italy* (1838), the
country that once seemed to him politically corrupt now was worthy of
his highest regard, given the depressing New York political and literary
scene. In *The Bravo* Cooper called attention to a despotism that ensured
sound order through a refined use of military and police force to create an
omnipresent paranoia. In *Italy*, he celebrates the peacefulness of Milan

without questioning the means by which the peace is achieved: "Military patroles march the streets at night, and all night, so that the place is orderly and safe." St. Mark's earlier appeared to him the incarnation of evil, an amalgam of church and state power. By contrast, he fondly remembers the beauty of St. Peter's: "I turned away impressed with the truth that if ever the hand of man had indeed raised a structure to the Deity in the least worthy of his majesty, it was this!" And whereas *The Bravo* portrayed Venice as an aged monster cluttered by its "masonic" palaces, *Italy* offers an acerbic comparison of Rome to New York that reverses the judgment against European decadence: "Rome is a city of palaces, monuments, and churches, that have already resisted centuries; New York, one of architectural expedients, that die off in their generations, like men."[1] Rome, like Cooper himself, attains stature through the act of resistance.

For the most part Cooper writes quietly in *Italy,* recording details while avoiding political and social commentary. But the quietness of the book clearly is part of a rhetorical strategy that enables him to sport with the reading public he had "renounced" only a few years earlier in *A Letter to His Countrymen.* The most striking instances of his arch withdrawal from social analysis occur when he discusses the Roman Catholic church, long associated in America with European imperial powers, long the demon of American millennial ideology. In the Rome section of the book, for example, he cheerfully relays information he recently received about the evangelical intentions of the Catholic church:

> I have ascertained that strong hopes exist here of advancing the religion of this government in America. If this can be done, let it, for I am for giving all sects fair play; but as such expectations certainly exist, it may be well for those who think differently to know it. One of the last things an American would be likely to suspect, is the conversion of his countrymen to the Roman Catholic faith; and yet such result is certainly here brought within the category of possibilities. I would advise you to take large doses of Calvinism, or you may awake some fine morning, a believer in transubstantiation.

By the time Cooper concludes his discussion of the church, he has become so caught up in his gamesmanship that he portrays Roman Catholic institutions as no less democratic than American ones. Describing the office of the Pope, he avows that, contrary to popular belief, it is available to all: "It is usually the case, that the Pope is taken from the Holy College, but it is not constitutionally necessary. You or I might be elected pope." He adds only one small caveat: "Previously to induction or installation, we should be resigned to enter the Romish Church by Roman baptism, and then pass through the several orders of deacon, priest, and bishop."[2]

Writing just four years after the notorious burning of the Ursuline convent in Charlestown, Cooper deliberately remained silent on Americans' renewed fears of a Roman Catholic conspiracy to gain the republic as the crown jewel of the papal kingdom. As he knew full well, the conversion threat to which he casually called his reader's attention had become by the mid-1830s a major subject of evangelical tracts, revivalist sermons, nativistic propaganda, and popular fiction. For Cooper, bitterly estranged from the reigning mood of the moment, an equanimous treatment of the Catholic church emerged as one of his finest jokes at the expense of his self-righteously Protestant American readers.

Two decades later Nathaniel Hawthorne employed a different rhetorical strategy in a key scene of *The Marble Faun* (1860), Hilda's turning to the Roman Catholic confessional for psychological and spiritual solace. Rather than moving Hilda quietly into the confessional, Hawthorne builds dramatically to her decision, developing at some length the New England girl's traumatic journey to her soul-satisfying destination. The scene is especially powerful because the narrative perpetually addresses a skeptical Protestant reader: Hilda's confessional relief thus occurs in defiance of cultural expectations incorporated, as it were, into the text. Revising the standard treatment of confession in America's nativist tracts and convent novels – virginal American Eve at the mercy of satanic European priests – Hawthorne guides the reader to the surprising insight that the confessional, at least in this one instance, has served a redemptive function. Whereas Cooper jests with his contemporary reader from a distance, Hawthorne painstakingly situates a privileged reader in the midst of something wondrous.

Confession in Hawthorne's fiction is both a thematic problem and a cultural trope. His prolonged preoccupation with the guilt-ridden mind expressed his personal concerns that Protestantism and democracy generated painful psychological pressures; similar preoccupations and concerns, Hawthorne's fiction helps us to see, informed the pervasive anti-Catholic literature of his time. This chapter establishes a homology between Hawthorne's fiction and the period's anti-Catholic discourse, and explores as well Hawthorne's more deliberate appropriations and transformations of this discourse. I will not claim that Hawthorne in any simple way was "influenced" by anti-Catholic literature, or even was familiar with its most vulgar manifestations. Rather, I shall argue that the literature of anti-Catholicism constituted an insinuating and tempting cultural discourse available to any author of the period, particularly a writer of historical romance, like Hawthorne, who explicitly addressed the role of Protestant–Catholic conflict in early American history.

Surprisingly, as I shall argue in the main body of the chapter, anti-Catholic discourse also figured significantly in Hawthorne's fictions of nineteenth-century America, most notably *The Blithedale Romance*. Mesmerism, for example, a central motif of his fiction, was often pictured as a form of priestcraft; and anxieties about priestcraft, abundantly expressed in the literature of anti-Catholicism, found a prominent place in *Blithedale*. More important still, nativism and communitarianism had similar social origins and shared a similar countersubversive millennialism. As a result, there were striking intertextual relationships between the apparently opposed discourses of nativist and communitarian propaganda. In order to examine more closely the significance of these relationships, which are central to the literary and cultural concerns of *Blithedale*, we must begin with a consideration of the reemergence of anti-Catholicism, the emergence of reform communitarianism, and the connection of these parallel movements to the history of Brook Farm.

"Into what a place and among what society had I been admitted!"

The debates of the Reformation and England's religious-political crises of the sixteenth and seventeenth centuries inextricably tied the Puritans' desire for a reformational purification to a concomitant desire to expunge "Catholic" pollution from church and state. Central to the Puritans' millennial conception of their sacred mission in America, therefore, was a utopian reformism conjoined to a loathing for what William Bradford called "popish trash."[3] Eighteenth-century republican theory further exacerbated Americans' engrained anti-Catholicism by arousing concerns about the despotic and oligarchical tendencies of such "Romish" imperial powers as France, Spain, and England.[4] However, with the signing of the Declaration came an end to Pope Day, and shortly thereafter the French alliance of 1778 brought America into league with a predominantly Catholic nation. This alliance, along with later constitutional guarantees of religious freedom, quelled overt anti-Catholic activity until the 1820s. Nevertheless, because many Americans agreed, as Adams wrote Jefferson in 1821, "that a free government and the Roman Catholick religion can never exist together in any nation or Country," anti-Catholic discourse retained an explanatory and mobilizing power in the cultural life of the new nation, informing both the political millennialism of the 1790s and the Second Great Awakening of the early 1800s.[5]

A variety of factors contributed to the resurgent anti-Catholicism of the 1820s and 1830s. The evangelical Protestantism of the period, which had contributed significantly to the rise of Antimasonry, gave new life to the millennial typology portraying the Catholic church as the Scarlet Lady of Babylon. The founding of the American Tract Society (1825) and other publishing arms of the "Benevolent Empire," along with the passage in England of the Catholic Emancipation Bill (1829), meant that a blizzard of No-Popery literature descended on the American reading public. Collateral social developments and pressures only reinforced the lessons taught by evangelicals and the suddenly pervasive anti-Catholic texts. As political historian Ann Norton explains, because expansionism in the West had earlier involved Americans in battling Catholic France and Catholic Spain, the antebellum "territorial extension of the United States was identified with the extension of American culture, and thus with the superiority of Protestantism to Catholicism." And yet during a period of jarring economic fluctuations, culminating in the Panic of 1837 and its aftermath, Catholic immigration shot up dramatically: 54,000 Catholics arrived in the 1820s, 200,000 in the 1830s, 700,000 in the 1840s, and 200,000 in the year 1850 alone.[6] Gravitating to the cities and available as cheap labor, Catholics inevitably bore the brunt of a plethora of economic and social frustrations. Viewed as the pawns of Rome and a moral stain on the sanctified fabric of republican culture, Catholics, like the Illuminati and the Free Masons, for a while seemed to many Americans a real conspiratorial threat. To nativist evangelicals in particular, the increasing presence of adulterating Catholics signaled America's compelling need for repurification, reformation, and countersubversion.

As conspiratorial fears recurred in America, the rhetorical strategies and archetypes of countersubversion recurred. The ready availability of such rhetorical currency made it all the easier to cash in on the fear of the moment. Apprehensive that Americans indeed faced an acute moral and political danger, Samuel F. B. Morse, in the first major treatise to unveil the ongoing Catholic conspiracy, drew on the traditional image of the antirepublican infidel that his father, Jedidiah Morse, had so vividly evoked in his anti-Illuminati sermons. Convinced, as his friend Fenimore Cooper was convinced, that "there is a war going on between *despotism* on one side, and *liberty* on the other," Samuel Morse warned Americans, in *A Foreign Conspiracy Against the Liberties of the United States* (1834), that an extremely dangerous group of Roman Catholic conspirators, "despotic, monarchical and aristocratic," had infiltrated America and now sought nothing less than the corruption of Americans' republican ideals and the geographical conquest of the continent. These Jesuitical conspirators, like the expedient Illuminati and Masons, were "proverbial through the world for cunning, duplicity, and total want of moral principle"; and like Brockden Brown's villains and Cooper's Venetians, they were "skilled in all the arts of deception." Most threatening of all, according to Morse, crafty Catholic priests possessed awesome powers of psychological control, a subtle priestcraft, capable of rendering whole peoples, such as the "Catholics of Poland," into "mere passive slaves."[7]

Good Protestant republican that he was, Morse feared that the spread of churches and convents would provide infiltrating convert-seeking priests with the means to enslave unsuspecting Americans; like the Antimasons, he aroused anxieties about a villainous group conspiring behind closed doors. But as dangerous as these walled-in Romish subversives appeared to be, so Morse instructed his readers, Americans possessed the power to defeat them. Jedidiah Morse had told his congregants and readers that moral and civic virtue, along with a vote for the Federalists, would overcome the invisibly infiltrating Illuminati; the Antimasons too located countersubversive power in republican virtue and the ballot box. Samuel Morse informed his readers that aggressive evangelical actions, "AN IMMEDIATE, A VIGOROUS, A UNITED, A PERSEVERING EFFORT TO SPREAD RELIGIOUS AND INTELLECTUAL CULTIVATION THROUGH EVERY PART OF OUR COUNTRY," would ensure victory to the virtuous. "And what are the weapons of this warfare?" he asked. "The Bible, the Tract, the Infant school, the Sunday school, the common school for all classes . . . a free press for the discussion of all questions."[8] Open classrooms to combat the closed convent, a free press to combat secretive psychological manipulations: so much for the awesome contrivances and subtle priestcraft of the contending Catholic empire.

Echoing a number of the themes sounded in Morse's text, Lyman Beecher's *Plea for the West* (1835), perhaps the most widely read nativist tract of the antebellum period, also urged Americans to develop Protestant educational institutions as a way of staving off the conspiratorial Roman Catholic church. Fearing the spread of Catholic convents and parochial schools, Beecher in August 1834 had delivered three anti-Catholic sermons in Boston that possibly inspired the burning of Charlestown's Ursuline convent. Repentant for whatever role he may have played in the burning, Beecher renounced that sort of violent activity. Still, as he argued in *Plea for the West,* Americans needed to know about a "corps of men acting systematically and perseveringly for its own ends upon a community unapprized of their doings, and undisciplined to meet and counteract them." In Beecher's view, Catholic leaders and their minions were *"the inflexible enemy of liberty and conscience and free inquiry, and . . . the main stay of the battle against republican institutions."*[9] Within America, Catholics constituted a separate secretive society conspiring to extend Rome's empire through the subversive art of conversion.

Like Morse, Beecher feared that Americans were all too vulnerable to the wiles of priestcraft, and in what became a dominant theme of countersubversive anti-Catholic texts, he presented the confessional as the prime tool enabling priests to achieve their lordly dominion. Morse touched on the subject in *Foreign Conspiracy:* "Consider, too, the power which these Jesuits and other Catholic priests possess through *the confes-*

sional, of knowing the private characters and affairs of all the leading men in the community; the power arising from their right to prescribe the *kinds and degrees of penance;* and the power arising from the right *to refuse absolution* to those who do not comply with their commands." Beecher enlarged upon the threat of the confessional by detailing the politically subversive uses to which it could be put: "The ministers of no Protestant sect could or would dare to attempt to regulate the votes of their people as the Catholic priests can do, who at the confessional learn all the private concerns of their people, and have almost unlimited power over the conscience as it respects the performance of every civil or social duty." Constrained by their priests to forward the cause of Rome, the church's minions voted as ordered (always for Democrats, lamented the Whig Beecher) and read as ordered (never the tracts of Beecher). That being the case, how could freedom-loving Americans hope to compete against such a unified political-religious body? How could Americans hope to compete against a power that in the not so distant future would know all their secrets too? Clearly, by enrolling their children in the new Protestant schools, by sponsoring further development of Protestant academies throughout the western frontier, and, perhaps most importantly, by reading. As Beecher put it, "Whatever European nations do, our nation must read and think from length and breadth, from top to bottom."[10]

To the Protestant clergy the politics of reading in the new republic paralleled the politics of reading during the Reformation: Protestantism sanctioned the individual's liberty to read; Roman Catholicism, as William Ellery Channing explained, "withholds the Scriptures, and the age is a reading one, and reads the more what is forbidden." Morse, Beecher, and other evangelicals accordingly called on middle-class Protestants to read in "the forbidden"; and during the mid-1830s these Americans began to read with a vengeance. The specter of the Catholic conspirator, like the specter of Jacobin and Masonic conspirators, was both alarming and intriguing: Many Americans desirous of sharing an insider's allegiance to the countersubversive campaign against Catholics became equally fascinated by Catholic insiders. Responsive to and further piquing this fascination were the popular convent novels of the period, which sought to demystify the institutional authority of the Roman Catholic church by penetrating, in Beecher's words, its "exterior of high devotion, great sanctity, and eminent purity" to expose "its track of blood."[11] Lifting the holy veil of the unholy church, the first-person narrators of these texts – entrapped Protestant virgins, the quintessence of sentimentalized republican virtue – offered a restless reading public an intensely captivating experience with conspiracy.

Rebecca Theresa Reed's *Six Months in a Convent* (1835), a fabricated account of a two-year captivity in Charlestown's Ursuline convent, arose out of the tense social situation in Massachusetts and was the first of the popular convent novels. An unassuming physical text, three by five inches with no cover illustration, the novel, like the nativists' image of the unassuming but threatening convent, contains shocking surprises within. Substantiating the warnings of Morse and Beecher, Reed reveals that behind the closed doors of the ever-multiplying Catholic convents reside agents plotting to deliver up America to expansionistic Rome. She tells of how the bishop of the Ursuline convent "had received a long letter from the Pope, in which his Holiness congratulated him for his success in establishing the true religion in the United States, and made him offers of money to advance the interest of the Catholic Church, and more firmly establish it in America." According to Reed, the bishop "thought that America rightfully belonged to the Pope, and that his Holiness would take up his residence here at some future day." But though the threat of imperial conspiracy has an important place in the novel, it is Reed's disclosure of the depraved convent's hidden interiors that constitutes the text's chief fascination. Drawing on the alarmist tropes of the Gothic novel, Reed pictures lascivious priests who reign supreme over their entrapped novitiates. She documents the use of oaths, penances, and regulations that maintain hierarchy and teach the church's most important lesson, one that the mother superior repeatedly impresses upon Reed and the other novices: "Sister, obedience!" After one nun disobeys and unsuccessfully tries to escape, the coldhearted mother superior insists on a murderous torture, which the repulsed Reed describes quite vividly for her readers. Fearing that she will suffer a similar fate and convinced of the need to expose the "startling conspiracy," Reed manages to flee the enslaving nunnery just as it plans to relocate to the Canadian border.[12]

The popular success of *Six Months in a Convent* helped to spawn a number of convent novels, including Maria Monk's notorious *Awful Disclosures of the Hotel Dieu Nunnery* (1836), the expanded second edition of which, also published in 1836, contained several "authenticating" maps detailing the locations in the nunnery of such rooms as the Priests' gaming and feasting area and the specific room (no. 13) used for infant smothering. Describing her escape to America from a Canadian convent (and so echoing Reed's warning about Canadian-based Catholic conspirators),[13] Monk works with the captivity motifs of Reed's novel but presents far ghastlier Catholic crimes. In addition to describing her own torture at the hands of sadistic nuns and priests, she discloses the suffocation of a raped nun's twin babies and, in the most amazing chapter of the book, the bishop-mandated execution of a novice who "would rather die than cause the murder of harmless babes": Festive priests and nuns place the dissenter under a mattress and jump on her until she succumbs to a bruiseless death. Especially frightening about the enslaving convent society is the way church doctrine and institutions legitimize such efforts to compel submission. As Monk explains, "If we thought an act ever so criminal, the Superior would tell us that the Priests acted under the direct sanction of God and *could not sin*." Thus when Monk takes her vows to become a nun, she must assent "to obey the priests in all things."[14] Almost immediately thereafter she suffers a different sort of initiation, but one following ineluctably upon her official vow taking: Three priests rape her in the confessional.

Violated in the confessional, Monk violates its secrecy by confessing the sordid events to her readers. As Monk suffers in the text at the hands of fallen confessors, the reader experiences the moment retrospectively through the medium of a decidedly moral confessional, the text itself, the escaped nun's true confession. Confessing to priests ensures submission and, invariably, confessional violation; confessing to a democratic reading public defends political liberty and ensures confessional intimacy. Sharing secrets, readers of convent novels form a new privileged community of countersubversive insiders; Monk's sensational book of horrors sold upwards of three hundred thousand copies through 1860. Like Monk, her readers would be marveling, "Into what a place and among what society had I been admitted!"[15]

A desire for insidership, for admittance to a purposive community, may well be the crucial informing desire of nativist propaganda and convent fiction. And so while bigoted and expedient anti-Catholic texts reveal once again how countersubversive discourse could serve the ends of power, these texts can also be viewed as jeremiadic efforts by nervous evangelicals and politicians, especially those (like the Whigs) devoted to ideals of unified American community, to reforge a sense of republican identity and millennial purpose during a time of rapid economic fluctuations, western expansion, and increasing immigration.[16] In this respect, I want to argue, there was a strong similarity between the nativist-inclined evangelicals of the 1830s and the reform communitarians of the 1840s. Intent on redeeming the community, nativists attacked Catholic insiders by offering fascinating pictures of insiders; intent on reforming the community, communitarians appealed to Americans to become insiders by likewise offering fascinating pictures of insiders. Reform communitarianism, as both a discourse and social practice, thus played out the desire implicit in the countersubversive discourse of Morse and Beecher and actually rather explicit in the discourse of Reed and Monk: to belong to a purposive community that offered an order and *telos* perceived as missing from Jacksonian America. And it did so from a similar conceptual perspective: While the revivals of the 1820s and 1830s would for some fuel a suspicious nativism and antimodernist fundamentalism, for others a broad impact of the revival movement – with its liberalizing and liberating emphases on immediatism and perfectionism, on human capacity to control the destiny of self and society – was to direct attention toward more modernizing and progressive reforms such as feminism, abolitionism, and communitarianism.[17] As a result of their common cultural origins, however, the same impulses to purify and redeem American society, and the same millennial rhetoric, informed communitarian and nativist discourse. Evangelical nativists and reform communitarians alike spoke in the manner of countersubversives.

Though not as prolific as the nativists, reform communitarians soon developed and disseminated their own canon of central texts, both oppositional and seductive. Important precursors of the communitarian writings of the 1840s were Robert Owen's *A New View of Society* (1813–14) and Frances Wright's *Course of Popular Lectures* (1829), which followed in the republican-millenarian tradition of eighteenth-century revolutionary France. A more distinctively American formulation of the need for communitarian reform was Elizabeth Peabody's "A Glimpse of Christ's Idea of Society" (1841), a millennial paean to the possibilities of Brook Farm. Far more influential, however, even on the Brook Farm community, was the popularization of Charles Fourier's associationist theories in Albert Brisbane's *Social Destiny of Man* (1840), a text responsive to the millenarianism of Fourier, Owen, and Wright but also shaped by the evangelical context of the American 1830s. Brisbane followed *Social Destiny* with *A Concise Exposition of the Doctrine of Association* (1843), and one year later Parke Godwin published *A Popular View of the Doctrines of Charles Fourier*. Horace Greeley devoted numerous columns in the New York *Tribune* to expositions of Fourier's associationism, and the relatively elitist *Dial, Phalanx,* and *Harbinger* presented continuing celebrations of communitarian reform for the Concord–Boston circle. All of these enthusiastic publications of the 1840s championed their ideal communities as needed restoratives for America's ailing body politic. Brisbane's description of the ills afflicting societies throughout the world reflects the tone and mandate of communitarians during this period:

> We assert that the evil, misery and injustice, now predominant on the earth, have not their foundation in political or administrative errors, in the defects of this or that institution, in the imperfection of human nature, or in the depravity of the passions; but in the FALSE ORGANI-SATION OF SOCIETY ALONE. We assert that the present social mechanism is not ADAPTED to the nature of man and to his passions; that its laws are in flagrant opposition to those which regulate or govern their action; that it perverts, misdirects and develops them subversively, and that the selfishness, oppression, fraud, injustice, and crime, which

mark the course of his societies, are attributable to that artificial social misdirection and perversion, and not to any inborn depravity in the human being himself.[18]

Like Finney and other revivalists, Brisbane rejected the Calvinistic notion of "inborn depravity," celebrating instead man's ability to overcome "evil, misery and injustice." And like America's evangelicals and Boston–Concord's transcendentalists, Brisbane was infused with millennial hopes and expectations: "Association, which is declared impossible, owing to the magnificence of its results, is precisely the Order, for which God has created the kingdoms and nature, subject to our industry, and for which above all he has made the passions, now so rebellious to our civilized system of industrial incoherence!" But whereas nativists sought to renew the community's millennial destiny by organizing resistance to the perceived subversive antirepublic of the depraved Catholic church, utopianist reformers calling for "UNITYISM" viewed democratic-republican America as the depraved community in need of purification and redemption; accordingly, throughout *Social Destiny* Brisbane attacked America's "subversive" society.[19] A reformer and "countersubversive," Brisbane sought to demonstrate that associationism offered Americans a prescriptive model for overcoming the "FALSE ORGANISATION" corrupting existing social and economic institutions.

In his utopian appeal for united social action, and in his advocacy of the enclosed institutional space of Fourier's phalanstery, Brisbane therefore seemed to be calling on Americans to throw in their lot with alternative subcommunities similar to those (fascinating) monastic communities vilified in anti-Catholic texts. For example, after commenting on the wasteful competition characterizing America's market economy, Brisbane asked rhetorically: "Suppose that a monastery of thirty Monks had thirty different kitchens, thirty fires, and every thing else in the same ratio; it is certain that, while expending six times as much in materials, cooking implements and hire of servants, they would be infinitely worse served than if there was unity in their household organization." Though Brisbane's reform community would foster Fourier's ideal of Attractive Industry by encouraging individuals to vary their tasks and activities, in a sense it would function – with its enclosing phalanstery, an "architecture of Combination, Unity and Harmony" – like a well-organized monastery.[20] This is not so remarkable, for as Northrop Frye observes, "the influence of the monastic community on utopian thought has been enormous. . . . The conception of the ideal society as a secularized reversal of the monastery . . . appears in Rabelais' scheme for the Abbey of Theleme . . . [and] re-appears in many nineteenth-century Utopias, not only the literary ones but in the most explicitly political schemes of St. Simon, Fourier, and Comte."[21] For just this reason, then, there were also striking parallels between anti-Catholic texts, particularly the convent novel, and texts of communitarian reform. As described in his texts, Brisbane's Fourierist community, like the Catholic monastery or convent, was in search of converts willing to subordinate national allegiances to the larger cause. Like the Catholic church, the reform institution would establish its own walled-in edifices within and without the republican community; Brisbane's and Godwin's books offered detailed floor plans of Fourier's secular-monastic phalanstery, textual parallels to the detailed maps of convent interiors included in alarmist novels of convent captivity. Like the regulated convent (and the Masonic lodge), the reform association would provide purposive order and, in contrast to the leveling tendencies of democracy, the possibility of obtaining individual distinction; Brisbane wanted members to wear "corporate uniforms" and to be guided by officers wearing "badges of honor, such as crosses [!], orders, and medals."[22] Unlike the slavocracy of the convent, however, Brisbane's association would offer a welcome and noncoercive refuge. His utopianist account of social existence behind the walls of the phalanstery was meant not to repulse but to seduce.

But given the homology between monastery and reform community, and given the key structural similarities between anti-Catholic and pro-communitarian texts, it is not surprising that even during the heady utopianism of the early 1840s, reformist subcommunities did not siphon off or convert many Americans to their respective causes. Seductive as they may have appeared with their promises of privilege and distinction, most reform communities during the antebellum period – aspiring as they did to a restrictive and often foreign-derived communitarian ideal – came to be viewed with suspicion or disdain by those many outsiders who remained convinced, like the nativist evangelicals, of America's Manifest Destiny. In fact, reform groups such as Robert Owen's New Harmony community, Frances Wright's Nashoba community, and John Humphrey Noyes's Oneida community were generally regarded, like America's traditional antirepublican enemies, as irreligious and subversive. For example, when the Owen group experienced a brief surge of popularity in the 1820s, a writer for the *National Intelligencer* warned that Owenism threatened "a revival of the blasphemous tenets of the Illuminati, diffused over the continent of Europe in the last century; and the Ghost of Weishaupt has ascended from the Tartarean gulph, breathing the sulpherous flames from the pit from whence he has emerged."[23] Initially a unified and idealistic community, the Owenites responded to outside antagonism and their inability to gain new converts by becoming a factionalized self-enclosed group revolving around a cultish and increasingly authoritarian leader; in effect, they became what they were feared to be.[24]

To a certain extent the Brook Farm community at West Roxbury,

Massachusetts, underwent a similar devolution from a hopeful group of reform communitarians to a self-enclosed cult of Fourierists. Its original 1841 constitution emphasized the voluntaristic character of the joint-stock agrarian community: "No member of the Association shall ever be subjected to any religious test; nor shall any authority be assumed over individual freedom of opinion by the Association; nor by one member over another."[25] But idealistic communalism can exert its own forms of tyranny, and in the name of Unity of Interests, political and social commitments were soon exacted from participants. Octavius Frothingham writes: "Admittance of members was conditioned on pledges of non-resistance, abolition, temperance, abstinence from voting, and such like. Though these conditions were easy enough in themselves, and were expressed in the most conciliatory spirit, they were justly regarded as giving to the community the character of a church or party, much less than world embracing."[26] The group's increasing financial problems, along with its failure to gain a significant body of converts (epitomized by its inability to gain Emerson's allegiance and to retain Hawthorne's), left the community particularly vulnerable to the "evangelical" appeal of Albert Brisbane and other enthusiastic Fourierists, who "converted" the group in 1844. Charles Dana's *Association in Its Connection with Education and Religion* (1844) expressed the more decidedly universalistic and oppositional temper of the newly Fourierist Brook Farmers: "Our ulterior aim is nothing less than Heaven on Earth – the conversion of the globe, now exhaling pestilential vapors and possessed by unnatural climates, into the abode of beauty and health, now so long lost and forgotten."[27] In 1845, with the ground breaking for a phalanstery and the introduction of ritualistic celebrations of Fourier's birthday, the insiders of Brook Farm's "church or party" were well on their way to becoming walled-in "monastic" insiders in search of converts. The first principle of their proposed revised constitution of 1846, a far cry from the initial constitutional call for voluntary association, reads like the mandate of a group – similar to the nativists' feared Roman Catholics – that views conversion as a form of subversion: "To indoctrinate the People of the United States, with the Principles of Associative Unity."[28]

But even while seeking to indoctrinate and convert, a number of Brook Farm's members were contemplating, and actually undergoing, conversions of their own. The community's increasing difficulties in sustaining its insider allegiances led some participants to turn their eyes longingly on America's reviled insiders of the Roman Catholic church. In an 1846 *Harbinger* article titled "The Catholics and Associationists," William Henry Channing called on the Brook Farmers to devote themselves to a monastic life of "renunciation more entire than ever was dreamed of by the most rigid anchorite . . . a life spent without one thought of self, in close and constant relations with his brethren." And he asserted that "advocates [of associationism] must regard with respect and sympathy the Catholic church, as the most successful attempt in the history of the world to bring the race into unity, however mistaken they may deem its measures."[29] Convinced of Roman Catholicism's "mistaken" emphasis on the hierarchical and spiritual authority of its priests, Channing remained true to associationism. Soon after the 1846 fire that destroyed Brook Farm's phalanstery, however, Sophia Ripley, like former Brook Farmers George Leach, Charles Newcombe, and Isaac Hecker, converted to Catholicism. For these communitarians, it would appear, Roman Catholicism delivered on the "UNITYISM" that the pseudoreligion or cult of Fourierist associationism only promised. It offered an insidership that would survive conflagration.

"The type of New England's hereditary spirit"

Hawthorne participated in the Brook Farm community during a seven-month period in 1841; eleven years later he published *The Blithedale Romance*, wherein he suggestively hinted at his awareness of Brook Farm's kinship with a Catholic subcommunity. Before turning to this romance about a writer's effort to find community among reformers, however, I want to consider Hawthorne's initial efforts to find community among his readers. His early tales and sketches, particularly those working with the themes and images central to anti-Catholic discourse, will help us to understand better both his social response to reformism in the 1840s and his literary response in the 1850s.

The year that saw the publication of Beecher's *Plea for the West* and Reed's *Six Months in a Convent* – texts about the nightmare of conversion – also saw the publication of Hawthorne's "Alice Doane's Appeal" (1835), a tale about a storyteller's endeavor to convert "two young ladies" (11:266) into enthusiastic admirers of his artistry. As Reed and Monk disclose terrors in their pursuit of readers, so Hawthorne's teller of the dark tale of witchcraft seeks to alarm his auditors. But when his Gothic story of incest and revenge fails to dispel "the gayety of girlish spirits" (11:268), he decides to make "a trial whether truth were more powerful than fiction" (11:278). On Gallows Hill, he describes the horrors of the Salem witch trials, conjuring a dreadful picture of persecutors and persecuted in frenzied spectral confrontation. He stops at nothing to engage the ladies' interest: "I plunged into my imagination for a blacker horror, and a deeper woe, and pictured the scaffold –" (11:279). At last, Hawthorne's storyteller penetrates their defenses: "But here my companions seized an arm on each side; their nerves were trembling; and sweeter victory still, I had reached the seldom trodden places of their hearts, and found the wellspring of their tears" (11:279–80). Like the sensationalistic authors of his time, the narrator tempts the ladies into the "confessional" of his fiction through invocation and disclosure. But, Hawthorne allows, as his popular counterparts do not, the tale teller's quest for enthusiasts depends upon a kind of priestcraft; confessional intimacy is achieved through a mesmerizing performance that, as in "Alice Doane's Appeal," places the listener – the reader – under the control of an author seeking "sweeter victory still." In this respect the tale can be read as a meditation on Hawthorne's own peculiar relationship to his readers and his art. Cherishing the ambition to achieve celebrity for his literary talents – "In this dismal chamber FAME was won" (8:20), he mused in a well-known 1836 notebook entry – he was constrained by marketplace realities to publish many of his early fictions, including "Alice Doane's Appeal," in Samuel Goodrich's *The Token,* a giftbook annual read predominantly by Protestant "young ladies." In part, the tale conveys Hawthorne's recognition of the need to plot to master Goodrich's genteel readers.[30]

Of course, throughout his career Hawthorne would idealize his relationship to his readers and deny any such plotting. For example, he wrote Cornelius Mathews and Evert Duyckinck in 1841: "I would far rather receive praise from a single individual, than to be deemed a tolerably pleasant writer by a thousand, or a million." Similarly, following the critical success of *The Scarlet Letter,* he informed Horatio Bridge: "The 'bubble reputation' is as much a bubble in literature as in war; and I should not be one whit the happier if mine were world-wide and time-long, than I was when nobody but yourself had faith in me." The diffident tone here would seem to clash with the implicit desire and self-defensive rationalizations of his earlier and more famous letter to Bridge describing the aftermath of reading *The Scarlet Letter* to his wife Sophia: "It broke her heart and sent her to bed with a grievous headache – which I look upon as triumphant success! Judging from its effect on her and the publisher, I may calculate on what bowlers call a 'ten-strike.' Yet I do not make any such calculation. Some portions of the book are powerfully written; but my writings do not, nor ever will, appeal to the broadest class of sympathies, and therefore will not attain a very wide popularity." In his public utterances he covers any disappointment in his lack of "wide popularity" by simply disavowing the pursuit of popularity, declaring in "The Custom-House" that he addresses "the few who will understand him, better than most of his schoolmates and lifemates" (1:3), and preposterously proclaiming in the 1851 preface to *Twice-Told Tales* that "he does not remember or believe to be the case" that "the Author had ever been greatly tormented by literary ambition" (11:4). Several years later, however, in an 1855 letter to William Ticknor, he fulminated against the "d____d mob of scribbling women" and be-seeched his publisher, "What is the mystery of these innumerable edi-tions of the Lamplighter, and other books neither better nor worse? – worse they could not be, and better they need not be, when they sell by the 100,000."[31] Envious and in awe of the scribblers' sales, Hawthorne created his own "lamplighter" in Hilda of *The Marble Faun* and achieved his greatest popular success.

Desiring to achieve the intimacy of America's most popular writers, but wary and at times even scornful of his reading public, Hawthorne in his fiction simultaneously pursues and retreats from intimacy.[32] In an 1836 sketch titled "Churches and Cathedrals," however, he displays an unusually strong desire to demonstrate an insider's allegiance to the con-ventional values of his Protestant reading public. From his perspective as editor and primary contributor to the *American Magazine of Useful and Entertaining Knowledge,* he observes that, although the Church of St. Peter "is the wonder of the world, and undoubtedly the most sublime monument that mankind ever consecrated to the Deity, since the cre-ation," it must not be overlooked that St. Peter's cost the Roman citizen-ry one hundred and sixty million dollars and continues to drain Rome's limited resources: "There are many cracks in the cupola, which has been surrounded by an iron hoop of seven millions of pounds in order to prevent it from breaking down – and . . . large and increasing sums are annually required to make good the dilapidations of each successive year." For Hawthorne the reader-oriented editor, St. Peter's, a church he had yet to see firsthand, testifies to the corruption and degeneration characterizing Roman Catholicism as a sociopolitical power. To make his point as clearly as possible, he provides a general comparison of European and American churches:

> Those grand and noble structures [European cathedrals] are the symbols of an established national religion, and could never have had existence, unless a portion of the public wealth, drawn from the people by other than voluntary taxes, had been devoted to the purpose. They may as justly be numbered among edifices of state, as the royal palaces, the fortresses, and the national prisons. . . . In the United States, on the contrary, every church is a type of the united zeal of private individuals; the building is as much the work of the congregation which worships there, as if each member had laid one of the stones that compose the walls.[33]

American churches manifest the healthy tendencies of a self-reliant dem-ocratic republic, whereas European cathedrals, here as in *The Bravo* ana-logues of "the national prisons," reveal the despotic tendencies inherent in an aristocratic alliance of church and state.

The thematic emphases of the nativistic "Churches and Cathedrals" suggest Hawthorne's shrewd awareness of his contemporary readers' responsiveness to anti-Catholic discourse and his willingness, in this context, to play to the crowd. Though he would later renounce what he called "the middling Magazine articles," refusing permission to reprint them, we must be wary of Hawthorne's insistence on the absolute distinction between his hackwork and his art. He wrote George Hillard in 1844, "If I am to support myself by literature, it must be by what is called drudgery, but which is incomparably less irksome, as a business, than imaginative writing." But literature too is a "business," and the pursuit of that business would involve Hawthorne, as Quentin Anderson remarks, "much more directly with the mess of human circumstances than we admit."[34] Specifically, we will observe that America's pervasive anti-Catholic discourse finds a place in Hawthorne's representations of American history in even his best fiction. Though he surely did not subscribe to the view that a Roman Catholic conspiracy seriously threatened Jacksonian America, at times he revealed the consensual power of anti-Catholic discourse (and his desire to find community with the widest possible readership) when he drew on the typological framework of Bancroft and other contemporary celebrants of the American national character, and linked the Puritan suspicion of Catholicism to the impulses guiding the colonists toward the Revolution.[35] To be sure, Hawthorne developed a perspective on conspiracy mongering far more complex and ironic than the naïve mythmaking of contemporaneous historians and fictionists. But irony need not be equated with a deconstructive poetics, and irony surely does not vouchsafe a transcendent clarity of historical vision.[36]

Thus for all of its implicit demythologizing irony, "The Gray Champion" (1835) first and foremost pictures the Glorious Revolution and the simultaneous overthrow of Governor Andros in America as a triumphal resistance to an Anglo-Catholic conspiracy that typologically predicts the eventual success of the American Revolution. As the narrator informs the reader in the tale's opening paragraph, with the ascent to power of the "popish Monarch" (9:9) James II, the colonists quite sensibly worry about their political and religious freedom, for James has "annulled the charters of all the colonies, and sent a harsh and unprincipled soldier to take away our liberties and endanger our religion" (9:9). The first-person plural encourages the reader to share the fears of the colonists, establishing a countersubversive community of sorts among the Puritans, narrator, and reader. And when Andros, his magistrates and soldiers, and, most disturbing of all to Puritan and implied nineteenth-century reader alike, an "Episcopal clergyman of King's Chapel" (9:13) parade down the streets of Boston, the narrator appeals to this community by invoking, in Morse- and Beecher-like fashion, the millennial and republican significance of the contention for empire between "despotic," "popish" Anglicans and oppressed New Englanders:

> The whole scene was a picture of the condition of New-England, and its moral, the deformity of any government that does not grow out of the nature of things and the character of the people. On one side the religious multitude, with their sad visages and dark attire, and on the other, the group of despotic rulers, with the high churchman in the midst, and here and there a crucifix at their bosoms, all magnificently clad, flushed with wine, proud of unjust authority, and scoffing at the universal groan. And the mercenary soldiers, waiting but the word to deluge the street with blood, shewed the only means by which obedience could be secured. (9:13)

Although the threat to the community's protorepublican character is manifestly clear, the colonists gaze helplessly at crucifix-bearing despots until the Gray Champion steps forward to proclaim that James has been overthrown. Symbolically or actually a regicide judge in residence, the Gray Champion embodies the antidespotic spirit of New England; his announcement that "there is no longer a popish tyrant on the throne of England" (9:16) finally motivates the colonists to express their revolutionary outrage and send the soldiers into retreat. The community-spirited narrator concludes his tale by underscoring for his readers the significance of the Gray Champion's sudden appearance: "His hour is one of darkness, and adversity, and peril. But should domestic tyranny oppress us, or the invader's step pollute our soil, still may the Gray Champion come; for he is the type of New England's hereditary spirit, and his shadowy march, on the eve of danger, must ever be the pledge, that New England's sons will vindicate their ancestry" (9:18).

A worried patriot, the narrator in these final lines offers a heroic, if somewhat disturbing, image of New England vigilance that was highly relevant to the threats of "domestic tyranny" perceived by "New England's sons" during the 1830s. By the logic of the narrator's historical typology and consensual rhetoric, a contemporary reader, if so inclined, could infer that nativism expresses anew the defiant stand against Catholic empire that was earlier embodied by the heroic Gray Champion. To be sure, there are subtle suggestions throughout the tale that a frightening concomitant of the Puritans' suprahistorical understanding of their millennial destiny is their ability to transform will into power. Nonetheless, it should be emphasized that in this particular tale Hawthorne chose to adopt a communal narrative stance and a republican-millennial discourse that appealed to the prejudices of his Protestant republican readers and, hence, diminished the impact (and import) of the deeply embedded demythologizations. Michael Colacurcio argues that "The Gray Champion" convicts the Puritans of succumbing to a "Cosmic Paranoia." Yet it is difficult to ignore that the tale's rhetoric, from beginning to end, calls attention to the *reality* of political difference, confrontation, and incursion.[37]

Even in the more obviously ironic "Endicott and the Red Cross" (1838), Hawthorne again sets up the tale by emphasizing English despotism and, through the communal first-person plural, by taking a sympathetic interest in the concerns of "our forefathers" (9:433). In doing so, he helps his readers to understand why Endicott resorts to alarmist rhetoric after learning that Charles and Laud may send a governor-general to New England. As a public leader, Endicott wants to renew the community's social ideals at a time when he believes New England faces great dangers; accordingly, he summons the image of a horrible enemy threatening to subvert those ideals. Addressing an assembly of soldiers and citizens and, significantly, the vitriolic Wanton Gospeller confined in the stocks for religious nonconformity, Endicott first reminds the Puritans of their vulnerability in America's "howling wilderness" (9:438) and then warns of a terrible new threat to the character and perpetuity of their community: "I tell ye, fellow-exiles, that Charles of England, and Laud, our bitterest persecutor, arch-priest of Canterbury, are resolute to . . . establish the idolatrous forms of English Episcopacy; so that, when Laud shall kiss the Pope's toe, as cardinal of Rome, he may deliver New England, bound hand and foot, into the power of his master!" (9:439–40). Encouraged by his audience's responsive "sound of wrath" (9:440), Endicott speaks "with increasing energy" (9:440): "If this king and his arch-prelate have their will, we shall briefly behold a cross on the spire of this tabernacle which we have builded. . . . We shall hear the sacring-bell, and the voices of the Romish priests saying the mass. . . . Who shall enslave us here? What have we to do with this mitred prelate, – with this crowned king? What have we to do with England?" (9:440). Impelled by the Shakespearean cadences and frightful images of his speech, Endicott hacks from the English banner the Red Cross, symbol of papal pollution. Although Endicott by this point seems nearly out of control, the narrator concludes the tale with a community-oriented interpretation of the historical significance of Endicott's swordsmanship: "We look back through the mist of ages, and recognize, in the rending of the Red Cross from New England's banner, the first omen of that deliverance which our fathers consummated, after the bones of the stern Puritan had lain more than a century in the dust" (9:441).

In the context of the progressive historical typology of Hawthorne's colonial tales, Endicott's bold resistance portends the Gray Champion's, which leads toward the subversive ritual of "My Kinsman, Major Molineux" and then to the heroic Revolution – the spirit of which, to cast a positive light on nativist and revivalist activities of the 1830s, informs the revived republicanism among those of the post-Revolutionary, post-heroic generation. But "Endicott and the Red Cross" dramatizes as well just how easily countersubversive rhetoric can be exploited by those in power. As Hawthorne archly makes clear through Roger Williams's disapproval, Endicott taps into the pervasive fear of papal conquest in order to sustain his own power. With his imposition of strict disciplinary controls over religious nonconformists and other stigmatized dissenters, Endicott emerges as a native authoritarian affronted by foreign authoritarianism. The patriotic moral is that the two forms of authoritarianism differ; the darker moral lies in the likenesses.[38]

In his retellings of "Endicott and the Red Cross" and "The Gray Champion" in *The Whole History of Grandfather's Chair* (1841), however, Hawthorne diminishes historical complexity and irony so that even a child can appreciate the role of anti-Catholicism in the coming of the Revolution; he continues to pursue an insider's relationship to America's conspiratorial dramas. For example, in retelling the story of the Red Cross, Hawthorne has Grandfather point to the connection, not made explicit in "Endicott and the Red Cross," between the cross in the English flag and the cross of the Catholic church. "In the old national banner of England, under which her soldiers have fought for hundreds of years," Grandfather explains, "there is a Red Cross, which has been there ever since the days when England was in subjection to the Pope. . . . Now, whenever the train-band of Salem was mustered, the soldiers, with Endicott at their head, had no other flag to march under than this same old papistical banner of England, with the Red Cross in the midst of it" (6:22). Adopting a phrasing that reflects the Puritan point of view, Grandfather makes far less troubling what in the "adult" story had seemed an unsettling foreshadowing of the Revolution. But the major difference between the two accounts centers on the actions of Roger Williams. In "Endicott and the Red Cross," Williams looks on disapprovingly as Endicott marshals the citizenry; in Grandfather's version, Williams listens respectfully to Endicott's claim that a "stranger, beholding it [the Red Cross], would think that we had undergone all our hardships . . . only to get new dominions for the Pope of Rome" (6:22–3), and then responds somewhat surprisingly by basically supporting Endicott's conspiratorial interpretation: "You speak as an honest man and Protestant Christian should. For mine own part, were it my business to draw a sword, I should reckon it sinful to fight under such a banner. Neither can I, in my pulpit, ask the blessing of Heaven upon it" (6:23). Although an ironic reading is encouraged by Williams's suggestion that Endicott's "business" is "to draw a sword" (and by Grandfather's subsequent account of the banishing of Williams), the narrator questions neither Endicott's motives nor his conception of the

Catholic threat: In the "children's" story Endicott emerges as a patriot and savior when he boldly excises the Red Cross. By simplifying his tale and revising Williams's role from active critic to passive advocate, Hawthorne finds temporary community with readers responsive to Protestant millennial dramas of national purification.

Similarly, in his retelling of the rebellion against Andros, Hawthorne's Grandfather again expands upon the connection of the historical event to anti-Catholic concerns (6:52). Moreover, Grandfather's fuller musings on the relationship between Andros's "absolute despotism" (6:53) and the threat of Catholic despotism underwrites a dramatic change from Hawthorne's earlier account. In this simplified version the fear of Catholic despotic power so mobilizes protorepublicans that the Gray Champion is no longer needed: "Grandfather told how, at the first intelligence of the landing of the Prince of Orange in England, the people of Massachusetts rose in their strength, and overthrew the government of Sir Edmund Andros" (6:54). Reversing the judgment of Cooper's *The American Democrat,* Hawthorne's retelling of Andros's fall celebrates the ability of "the publick" to detect and resist the forces of despotism.[39]

Thus far the tales I have examined align the narrator, at least on the rhetorical surface, with the dominant values of his New England Protestant readers. In several of Hawthorne's early tales, however, a concern about the abuses of countersubversive power led him to identify more sympathetically and explicitly with defeated "outsiders." In "A Bell's Biography" (1836), the narrator describes how the installation of a French bell at the Jesuits' chapel near Lake Champlain arouses fears of a Roman Catholic conspiracy: "It was reported, and believed, all through New-England, that the Pope of Rome, and the King of France, had established this little chapel in the forest, for the purpose of stirring up the red men to a crusade against the English settlers" (11:105). The parenthetical "and believed" calls into question the truthfulness of the conspiratorial claim, and Hawthorne subsequently shows how a countersubversive alarm can serve the interests of conquest: Fearing an imperial papal conspiracy, the Puritans savagely massacre the Jesuits, who achieve a terrible martyrdom. The Puritans are subsequently slaughtered by Indians responding to the bell's ringing summons, and the bell lies abandoned in the wilderness, containing as it were a bloody historical trace of the martyred Catholics. Discovered in the final years of the French and Indian War and brought to Boston, the bell chimes during the Revolution, it welcomes Washington, and it greets Lafayette. From the dialectical (and somewhat genteel) perspective of the narrator's "secret soul" (11:110), the spirit of the martyred Catholics chimes on in the heart of Boston.

"The May-Pole of Merry Mount" (1836) shows conspiratorial fears serving a similarly unattractive function in allowing a powerful majority to conceptualize conquest as a heroic battle against threatening others. Like the nativists of the 1830s, Endicott and his fellow Puritans fear the wiles of a contending community within their midst. The Merry Mount-ers' ceremonial revelry, their transplantation to the New World of "the hereditary pastimes of Old England" (9:60), and, especially, "their ven-eration for the May-Pole" (9:60) remind the Puritans of the ritualization they wanted expunged from the English church and that they disdained in the Catholic church. Regarding the community at Merry (Mary) Mount as nothing less than a contending pagan Catholic empire on the Puritan borders, and believing that the "future complexion of New En-gland was involved in this important quarrel" (9:62), the Puritans all too easily can justify an imperial assault pitting God's warriors against "dev-ils and ruined souls" (9:56). Leading the attack on the Merry Mounters and their May-Pole, Endicott, as in "Endicott and the Red Cross," endeavors to reenact the drama of the Reformation and tighten the bonds of his Puritan community by purging it of the contaminating presence of Anglo-Catholicism. His millennial view of his own attack on the Merry Mounters' "Priest of Baal" (9:63), however, is ironically undercut by the narrator's wry footnote on Endicott's confused identification of the priest as Reverend Blackstone. In the quiet way of a sub-sub-librarian, the narrator manages thus to challenge the legitimacy of Endicott's world view and eventual conquest. And it is a limited conquest: Choos-ing to accept the Lord and Lady of the May into the Puritan community, Endicott places on their heads a wreath of roses "reared from English seed" (9:55). As in "A Bell's Biography," a trace of the "Catholic" past lives on in the midst of "purified" Massachusetts.[40]

Endicott's brutal imperial assault revives the Puritan community and thus fulfills – and this is always implied in Hawthorne's stories of Puritan resistance and conquest – an extreme *need* for community. The search for community is, of course, also a central motif of "The Gentle Boy." As Hawthorne surely knew, the Puritans justified the Quaker executions of 1659, the historical event behind "The Gentle Boy," by analogizing Quakers to plotting Catholics and promoting millennial dramas of con-tention that made persecution seem a social and religious necessity.[41] And yet, while the Merry Mounters are routed against their will, the Quakers of "The Gentle Boy" are involved in a conflict with the Puritans that would appear to serve community needs on both sides. Because Quaker Catharine's sense of her sacred mission depends on the Puritans' cruel attentions, she repeatedly provokes them, going so far as to plead at their meetinghouse, "Reward me with stripes, imprisonment, or death, as ye shall be permitted" (9:83). Her provocations likewise offer second-gener-ation Puritans an opportunity to combat a threatening outsider and reaffirm their sacred mission. Hawthorne's depiction of Quaker–Puritan conflict in the 1660s bears some resemblance to patterns of Catholic–Protestant conflict in the 1830s: During the antebellum period Catholics found that, by participating in a rhetorical drama that depicted them as powerful players in the plot for community, they revitalized their group identity and eased the immigration trauma. Historian R. Lawrence Moore explains, "An outsider identification pursued by a group over time can provide the group with a well-recognized social status within the structure of existing social arrangements."[42] In "The Gentle Boy" the symbiotic conflict between Quaker martyrdom and Puritan cruelty looks ahead, as in "May-Pole" and "A Bell's Biography," to the possibility of assimilation or synthesis. At Catharine's death, we are therefore informed, "a long train of her once bitter persecutors followed her, with decent sadness and tears that were not painful, to her place by Ilbrahim's green and sunken grave" (9:105). The sentimentalizing of the funeral should not obscure the sadder truth, however, of Catharine's lifelong victimization. Before journeying to America, she "had pined in the cells of a Catholic Inquisition . . . and lay in the dungeons of the Puritans" (9:88). In this light, the persecution of Catharine, the death of her son, and the feeble outsidership of the converted Pearsons and their fellow Quakers tell less a sentimental story of mutually beneficial conflict than a brutal story of conquest that implicitly raises the question of whether there is in fact a significant difference between "the cells of a Catholic Inquisition" and "the dungeons of the Puritans."[43]

When Hawthorne drew on Protestant-millennial countersubversive discourse for his tales of the 1830s and early 1840s, at times he seemingly legitimated its authority and at other times he clearly (and not so clearly) challenged its authority. Often he did both simultaneously. Whatever his approach or emphasis, Hawthorne, through an engaged historical re-visioning, showed how countersubversive discourse served not only the interests of power but also the needs of community. In tales such as "The Gray Champion," "Endicott and the Red Cross," and the retellings of *Grandfather's Chair*, Hawthorne expressed his own need for community; that would help to account for their surface nativism. But their darker ironies and those tales, such as "A Bell's Biography," "May-Pole," and "The Gentle Boy," more explicitly critical of the countersubversive temperament ultimately convey a suspicion of community, a desire to linger in the shadows. Hawthorne's typological tales of contending communities suggest again and again that the "type of New England's hereditary spirit" is an alternately revolutionary and persecutory spirit. Like the "shadowy" countersubversive Gray Champion, Hawthorne periodically responded to the spirit's call, but like Goodman

Brown hesitating in the shadows, he also recognized its demonism and his own dark inclinations. Hesitancy led to irony, Hawthorne's characteristic mode for subverting hegemonic discourse.

A conflict between countersubversive and subversive desires is at the heart of "Young Goodman Brown" (1835), a tale that may help us to comprehend more fully Hawthorne's early perspective on conspiracy. Though historicists generally regard the tale as a classic study and critique of Salem's countersubversive mentality of the 1690s, it can also be read as a meditation on America's conspiratorial dramas from the 1620s to the 1830s.[44] Like his first-generation Puritan progenitors, Goodman Brown seeks to revitalize his "Faith" by undertaking a purposive errand into the wilderness. His uncertain situation in the forest reminds us of William Bradford's uncertain situation upon arriving in America: "It was all as lonely as could be; and there is this peculiarity in such a solitude, that the traveller knows not who may be concealed by the innumerable trunks and the thick boughs overhead; so that, with lonely footsteps, he may yet be passing through an unseen multitude" (10:75). A tension between the visible and invisible world, a defining tension of the Puritan mind, informs all conspiratorial fears: Investing the visible world with mysteriously concealed presences makes of life a plot to be decoded and places the interpreter at its center. Throughout the colonial and antebellum period, fears of a contending "unseen multitude" helped to create a visible multitude who, through communal acts of countersubversion, shored up, redefined, and reconsecrated a community putatively under seige. Somewhat anomalously, then, Hawthorne's Goodman Brown remains a solitary figure, his "ocular deception" (10:76) tempting him not to countersubversion but to subversion.

The tale thus calls attention to an unstated, conflicting desire informing the countersubversive persuasion: to belong to an empowered fraternal community not so very different from the demonized subversive community. With its depiction of the seductive appeal of secrecy and power, "Young Goodman Brown" responds not only to Hawthorne's reflections on Bradford and Mather, but also, I believe, to his reflections on the appeal of the Jacksonian (and Antimasonic) attack on aristocratic plotters. Possessing an "indescribable air of one who knew the world" (10:76), Brown's satanic guide lures him on with a typically Antimasonic image of the community's religious, judicial, and political leaders leagued in secretive fraternity: "The deacons of many a church have drunk the communion wine with me; the selectmen, of divers towns, make me their chairman; and a majority of the Great and General Court are firm supporters of my interest. The governor and I, too – but these are state-secrets" (10:77). Brown's decision to venture deeper into the forest expresses the desire both of the countersubversive who wants "to know their secret deeds" (10:87) and of the subversive who feels drawn to "a loathful brotherhood" (10:86). An attraction–repulsion relationship to the perceived conspiratorial community guides him toward the assembled congregants but leaves him uncertain about participation.

Brown discovers a forbidden community in the woods, the tale's ending suggests, because his fears and desires lead him to dream one up. His dreamlike experience suggests a need for community; it compensates for a felt absence. A yearning for purposive community, we have noted, informed evangelical rhetoric of the 1820s and 1830s, which, as Frank Shuffleton has observed, finds an important place in "Young Goodman Brown."[45] The description of the witches' black sabbath parallels contemporaneous descriptions of revivalist camp meetings; this particular frenzied meeting is presided over by "some grave divine of the New-England churches" (10:86) in search of new enthusiasts. "Bring forth the converts!" (10:86), the minister thunders; and Brown responds to the summons by emerging from the shadows and approaching "the proselytes, beneath the canopy of fire" (10:86). But just as the satanic overseer prepares to initiate him into the forbidden community, Brown, a sentimentalist, urges his "Faith" to resist lest he and she become "Polluted wretches" (10:88) and subsequently finds himself "amid calm night and solitude" (10:88). Tempted by the insiders' rite of conversion, he remains to the very end a despondent outsider.

Now, without claiming that the issues treated in Hawthorne's historical fiction always had nineteenth-century contemporaneous inspirations, I will speculate that a key pressure impelling Hawthorne's fictional exploration of "ocular deception" and the temptation to demonic insidership was his personal sense of complicitous participation in the reemergent nativism of the late 1820s and 1830s. For the nightmare vision at the heart of the tale – the image of a contending satanic group hidden from view and tempting a vulnerable American toward conversion – was analogous to the nightmare vision at the heart of the many evangelical tracts, revivalist sermons, nativist texts, and popular fictions warning of the dangers posed to the vulnerable republic by the Roman Catholic church. The evangelicals' response to the Catholic threat was to make conversion to their revived community a social imperative; subversive and countersubversive were locked in a battle for converts. Viewed in this light, Brown's retreat from the baptismal ritual marks an escape from both proselytizing evangelicals and Catholics, from the "loathful brotherhood" of countersubversive and subversive alike. At the same time, the tale enacts a desire for insidership that speaks to Hawthorne's own conflicting desires as he attempted to find community with his nativist-inclined reading public.

Tempted to leave the shadows and evince an insider's relation to community, but dismayed by the character of his community, Hawthorne in 1841 temporarily retreated from Boston's "loathful brotherhood" to join a brotherhood committed to social reform. Of course, his participation at Brook Farm was very different from his fiction writing, but it emerged from impulses quite similar to those underlying the anti-Catholic gestures of his fiction: a desire for admittance to a purposive group of reformers. Moving from Salem-Boston to West Roxbury, he moved from a sporadic rhetorical insidership with nativists to a more permanent and physically defined insidership with communitarians. It was a species of insidership that, even before his Brook Farm admittance, had offered its temptations.

During the 1830s, Hawthorne's search for community expressed itself not only through his rhetorical appeals to the values of communal consensus but also through a rather morbid fascination with self-enclosed Shaker "communitarians": He several times visited their villages, he jokingly wrote his sister Louisa in 1831 that he was considering conversion, and he wrote two tales about their society.[46] His attraction–repulsion relationship to the Shakers, as expressed in "The Canterbury Pilgrims" (1833), may offer an additional clue to his unspoken reasons for trying out life among reform communitarians. In this tale Hawthorne portrays a meeting at a crossroads of arriving and departing members of a Shaker community. Those choosing to join the isolated community are the defeated, the economically unstrung: "They sought a home where all former ties of nature or society would be sundered, and all old distinctions leveled, and a cold and passionless security be substituted for human hope and fear, as in that other refuge of the world's weary outcasts, the grave" (11:131). By way of contrast, the two departing Shakers, young lovers rejecting Shaker celibacy, "went on to mingle in an untried life" (11:131). The tale manifestly criticizes Shaker escapism, but Hawthorne understands full well the forces encouraging retreat into an enclosed community: a sense of homelessness, isolation, poverty, and despair. When eight years later he joined a utopian community that, like the Shakers, wished to level "old distinctions," Hawthorne, still very much the marginal author in search of readers (and money), no doubt counted himself among "the world's weary outcasts."

"The Hall of Fantasy" (1843), a sketch written after his Brook Farm participation, offers a different perspective on his now tested desires for community. Though the sketch satirizes reformism in the abstract as a narcissistic fantasy that, like the edifice of the Hall of Fantasy, "give[s] the impression of a dream, which might be dissipated and shattered to fragments, by merely stamping the foot upon the pavement" (10:172–3), central to the complexity and interest of the sketch is the narrator's admiration for the idealism, energy, and commitment of actual social reformers. Approaching the "noted reformers of the day" (10:180) commemorated in the Hall of Fantasy, the narrator feels his heart "throbbing in sympathy with the spirit that pervaded these innumerable theorists" (10:180); he feels uplifted by their utopian longings: "My faith revived, even while I rejected all their schemes" (10:181). According to the narrator, reformers go astray when they commence viewing the world exclusively through the distorting "pictured windows" (10:181) of their social theories; those so deluded find an appropriate place among the deluded insiders enclosed within the Hall of Fantasy. On these terms Hawthorne himself deserves a place in the Hall, for despite his eventual disillusionment with Brook Farm, the tale suggests that a genuine millennial faith in the possibilities of social reform, and not just economic necessity, was the key factor that led him to join the Brook Farmers. At least for a few months, we may speculate, he was infused, like reformers throughout America, with what Emerson called "the new spirit."[47]

Within seven months, however, frustrated by the routine of manual labor and unable to find the time to write, he was once again an outsider. He married Sophia in July 1842, resigned his position as associate of the Brook Farm Institute in October of that year, and took up residence in the "Saints' Chamber" (10:17) of the Old Manse's erstwhile "old parsonage" (10:3), which for a while provided him a restful (and somewhat monastic) retreat. In 1843 he discussed the Brook Farm community with Emerson, commenting in his notebook: "We have talked of Brook Farm, and the singular moral aspects which it presents, and the great desirability that its progress and developments should be observed, and its history written" (8:371). There is every indication that Hawthorne saw himself as that potential historian, for he continued to keep an eye on Brook Farm during the 1840s. He was particularly struck by the influence of Fourier's social theories on the group, and after Brook Farm's Fourierist conversion of 1844 he caustically remarked in his notebook that an anthill may be "(who knows) the model of a community, which Fourierites and others are stumbling in pursuit of" (7:249). The belittling imagery reflects his increasing suspicion of, and even hostility toward, the group. In 1846 he wrote Bridge: "Brook Farm, I suspect, is soon to see worse times than it ever has yet – at least, so men of business appear to think. Let it sink, say I; – it has long since ceased to have any sympathy from me, though individually I wish well to all concerned." That same year he initiated a lawsuit against the Brook Farm Institute, attempting to recover, with interest, his initial thousand-dollar investment in the joint-stock company. On May 1846, only a week after the burning of the phalanstery, the court ruled in Hawthorne's favor.[48]

When he began work on *The Blithedale Romance* in 1851, Hawthorne borrowed several volumes of Fourier's writings and read them "with a view to my next romance" (8:446). Three days after telling his journal, "I have read Fourier to-day, when I have read anything" (8:457), he made yet another visit to a Shaker community and was repulsed: "Their utter and systematic lack of privacy; their close junction of man with man, and supervision of one man over another – it is hateful and disgusting to think of; and the sooner the sect is extinct the better" (8:465). Drawing on his enchantment and disenchantment with Brook Farm, his skepticism toward the Fourierist developments at the associative community, and his evolving responses to the Shaker "anthill," Hawthorne came to conceive of the fictional Blithedale community in terms of the tropes of conspiracy that had been revived in the culture by anti-Catholic discourse and that were implicit in the millennial discourse of communitarian reform and rather explicit in his own literary discourse. The journey from Rebecca Reed's *Six Months in a Convent,* to Hawthorne's seven months in Brook Farm, to *The Blithedale Romance* is not as tortuous as it may seem. There may be no priests in *Blithedale,* but there are two domineering men who in their own ways seek to enslave through priestcraft; there may be no convent or Catholic headquarters, but there is a community with its own separate grounds and edifices; there may be no nuns and no entrapped novices, but the central women characters appear enslaved to commanding male presences, and both women maneuver behind veils, metaphorical and literal; there may be no empires in typological contention, but there is a clear sense of conflict between the associationists and the community they wish to transform. What has happened is that the tropes of anti-Catholic literature have lost their explicit sectarianism and emerged as seemingly "pure" literary structures. Pure as these structures may seem, however, they are rooted in traditional and contemporaneous sources of cultural anxiety, and they hint at conspiracy.

Frothingham came to believe that there was something suspicious about Brook Farm insiders and, good historian that he was, he had to concede, "The full history of that community can be written only by one who belonged to it, and shared its secret."[49] Hawthorne, who belonged, but retreated, and who agreed with Emerson on the importance of writing Brook Farm's history, addressed the matter of the community's secret and his own Goodman Brown–like temptations to subversive and countersubversive participation in a romance that, as he wrote William Pike, "shall take the Community for a subject, and shall give some of my experiences and observations at Brook Farm."[50] Coverdale is Hawthorne's masterly creation of an insider–outsider seeking confessional intimacy as he plumbs the secrets of the American community and its subcommunities.

"The illustrious Society of Blithedale"

In the preface to *The Blithedale Romance,* Hawthorne allows that during composition he had Brook Farm "in his mind" (3:1),[51] though he maintains that he does not intend to write its history. Instead, in a romance that seeks "merely to establish a theatre" (1), he wishes to convey "the inner truth and spirit of the whole affair" (3). But to convey the "inner truth" of the enterprise, to capture in his text the forces and motivations impelling the "company of socialists" (1) to leave their open democratic community and establish their separate regenerative one, he must be willing to share the insider perspective and in this way make over his readers, as the convent novelist and the propagandist of utopian reform made over their readers, into insiders, at least temporarily. Hawthorne personally establishes his insider credentials in the Preface, when he refers to his past participation at Brook Farm as "the most romantic episode of his own life" (2). But because that participation is a past one, he is once again an outsider, attempting now to achieve community through the mediating agency of his romance.

Hawthorne's insider–outsider relationship to his past utopianist participation, of course, informs his conception of Coverdale's relationship to his. Throughout the romance Coverdale stakes out an ironic distance between himself and all sorts of potential commitments, but he never renounces his initial insider's commitment to Blithedale. Nonetheless, because the romance is retrospectively told by Coverdale, now an outsider, his double perspective appeals both to the few former participants still tending the "chill mockery of a fire" (9) and to the few (or many) who will now participate retrospectively through the mediating agency, "the imaginary warmth" (9), of his narrative. He can thus tell the interlocking stories of community formation and community disintegration as he seeks, through his first-person strategies of confessional intimacy, to create his own community of insiders.[52]

The emphases at the opening of the novel are on the enchantments of insidership. Glorying in the Blithedale mission, Coverdale elevates his decision to participate with rhetoric that, Coverdale the disenchanted outsider well knows, conveys the narcissism and elitism underlying the Blithedalers' brand of reformism. For instance, like all of their social practices, the group dining of "we people of superior cultivation and refinement" (24) is meant to show "mankind the example of a life governed by other than the false and cruel principles, on which human society has all along been based" (19). But the Blithedalers are so taken with their specialness, with their instant ability to transcend "the false and the cruel," that when Hollingsworth and Priscilla arrive during the first of these self-satisfying repasts, no one responds to Hollingsworth's

vehement knocking. Finally, Coverdale hurries to the door and un-
fastens, of all things, a bolt. "At that early period," Hawthorne writes of
seventeenth-century Massachusetts in "The Gentle Boy," "when savages were wandering everywhere among the settlers, bolt and bar were
indispensable to the security of a dwelling" (9:74). Built into the very
structure of the Blithedale community is a barrier between it and the
American "savages" it means to reform.

There are barriers because Blithedale's insiders are enormously suspicious of outsiders. Coverdale's well-known reflection on the associationists' need to compete for markets with Boston's farmers nicely captures the community's oppositional temper:

> It struck me as rather odd, that one of the first questions raised, after our
> separation from the greedy, struggling, self-seeking world, should re-
> late to the possibility of getting the advantage over the outside barbar-
> ians, in their own field of labor. But, to own the truth, I very soon
> became sensible, that, as regarded society at large, we stood in a posi-
> tion of new hostility, rather than new brotherhood. Nor could this fail
> to be the case, in some degree, until the bigger and better half of society
> should range itself on our side. Constituting so pitiful a minority as
> now, we were inevitably estranged from the rest of mankind, in pretty
> fair proportion with the strictness of our mutual bond among ourselves.
> (20–1)[53]

Though the passage is usually read as an outsider's critique of the group's
inability to resist the economic pressures and "selfish competition" (19) of
the market society it deplores,[54] the passage also conveys the insider
mentality that we observed in Brook Farm's millennial-reformist discourse. As an insider Coverdale views himself in rightful opposition to
"the greedy, struggling, self-seeking world"; in the manner of Brisbane
he speaks of the need for conversion, dreaming of the day when "the
bigger and better half of society should range itself on our side." Through
Coverdale's insider perspective, here and in other passages in the opening
chapters, Hawthorne enacts precisely the countersubversive temperament
that tightens the bonds of community by stigmatizing outsiders as "self-
seeking," "greedy" "barbarians." And he points to the social consequences of such projections, for like the reformers in Hawthorne's "The
Procession of Life" (1843), whose "free-masonry of mutual goodness"
(10:217) makes them over into a masonic-like "sect [which] surrounds its
own righteousness with a hedge of thorns" (10:217), the Blithedalers'
"new brotherhood" from the very beginning seems self-enclosing and
prickly.

The group's tight "mutual bond" and self-glorifying millennialism
promote a separateness, it soon becomes apparent, hardly conducive to its

larger reformatory project. And unlike most antebellum associationists, the Blithedalers do not even particularly threaten outsiders, who tend to ridicule their ineptitude as farmers. At least in the first half of the book the associationists are depicted as involved primarily in a more or less personal pursuit of identity and purpose; it is a community, somewhat like the Shakers in "The Canterbury Pilgrims," of the defeated. Anticipating this conception of the group is "The Christmas Banquet" (1844), which Hawthorne wrote not too long after his Brook Farm experience. In this bizarre tale, Hawthorne tells the story of a gentleman who leaves in his will a bequest establishing an annual Christmas banquet "for ten of the most miserable persons that could be found" (10:285). The tale's final banquet configuration foreshadows Blithedale's group configuration: Among the guests at the table sit "a modern philanthropist" (10:303) and "two of the gentler sex – one, a half-starved, consumptive seamstress, the representative of thousands just as wretched; the other, a woman of unemployed energy, who found herself in the world with nothing to achieve, nothing to enjoy, and nothing even to suffer. She had, therefore, driven herself to the verge of madness by dark broodings over the wrongs of her sex, and its exclusion from a proper field of action" (10:303). Presiding over the banquet is the eighty-year-old perpetual guest, whose problem is "a chillness – a want of earnestness" (10:303). At the banquet these early types of Hollingsworth, Priscilla, Zenobia, and Coverdale find community in what the narrator terms "a sad fraternity" (10:301).

In *Blithedale* Hawthorne offers his "sad fraternity" a cheering draught of insider enthusiasm and places its members in a world apart on a more permanent basis; the opening meal, unlike the Christmas banquet, is meant to presage many others, equally self-sustaining and separate, for those in search of bounded community. Coverdale as ironic loner, Hollingsworth as monomaniacal philanthropist, Zenobia as frustrated feminist, Priscilla as poor and endangered seamstress-medium – all seek (and require) the support of a fraternal group. And so Zenobia hopefully declares, "We will be brethren and sisters" (16). Indeed, a generalized yearning for familial order would seem to underlie the community's formulation of "permanent plans" (128) to enclose many of its participants within a housing edifice. Coverdale explains, "One of our purposes was to erect a Phalanstery (as I think we called it, after Fourier . . .) where the great and general family should have its abiding-place" (128).

The image of the Blithedalers as "brethren and sisters" in retreat evokes not only the Shaker community and the "sad fraternity" of "A Christmas Banquet," but also those enclosed "abiding places" replete with brethren and sisters, the Catholic convent and monastery, the traditional structural model for many reform communities, including Fourier's, and in antebellum America a close cousin to the reform community. Blithedale, like the reform and Catholic subcommunity, promises to fulfill desires for a "new brotherhood" by reforging those bonds sundered in democratic American society. It also promises to fulfill desires for purposive order. Although Blithedale's ideology celebrates the freedom of a "vast, undefined space" (36), the community's distribution of labor is governed by a series of rules and regulations. It is significant, therefore, and not simply for the novel's theatrical imagery, that Zenobia asks upon her arrival, "Have we our various parts assigned?" (16). A community with assigned parts will offer place and purpose to the miserable.

But there is, of course, another side to the enclosed subcommunity, as perceived by Protestant Americans of the antebellum period and imaged in anti-Catholic discourse: It may offer itself as a home and refuge, but it is ultimately a false home and an entrapping refuge. As portrayed in the convent novel in particular, the Catholic subcommunity consists of patriarchal priests, lascivious nuns, and vulnerable Protestant virgins; in short, it consists of masters and slaves.[55] Working with the discursive and structural parallels between the reform and Catholic subcommunity, Hawthorne, through Coverdale's "inside" narration, suggests that Blithedale's purposive associative community can also be viewed as a kind of monastic-coventual community that threatens to entrap and enslave the vulnerable.[56]

The opening chapter introduces the motif of entrapment in the person of the possibly entrapped Veiled Lady, a spiritualist's medium, to be sure, but by analogy, in a culture concerned about veiled ladies of the convent, a type of novice. (Zenobia's declaration near the end of the novel that she plans to adopt "the black-veil" [228] and enter a convent makes explicit what is implicit in the veil imagery from the start.)[57] Viewing the Veiled Lady as a type of entrapped novice leads us to view the spiritualist as a type of priest; the spiritualist's stage, accordingly, is a type of confessional whereon he exhibits his patriarchal and psychological mastery. As the motif usually plays itself out, the enslaved medium/novice attempts to flee from a type of conventual imprisonment. That Priscilla is essaying an analogous form of just such a flight, and perhaps is the Veiled Lady (or simply a veiled lady), is hinted at only a few chapters later when she arrives at Blithedale and emerges from her cloak: "The cloak falling partly off, she was seen to be a very young woman, dressed in a poor, but decent gown, made high in the neck, and without any regard to fashion or smartness. Her brown hair fell down from beneath a hood, not in curls, but with only a slight wave; her face was of a wan, almost sickly hue, betokening habitual seclusion from the sun and free atmosphere" (27). Typically in the convent novel the entrapped heroine fashions an escape by hiding within the enclosing nun's cowl that threatens to efface her identity; such is the use to which Priscilla has put her cowl-like hood. Her pale face betrays a "habitual seclusion," with "habitual" pressing us to relate the paleness, by analogy and punning, to the covering veil of a nun's "habit." Furthermore, and emphasizing the political-cultural allegory of her situation, she has not for a while been in a "free atmosphere." Her mysterious identity and plight become even more mysterious when a letter arrives "from one of the city-missionaries" (49), almost certainly Protestant-organized and -directed, containing "a hint, not very intelligible, implying either that Priscilla had recently escaped from some particular peril, or irksomeness of position, or else that she was still liable to this danger or difficulty, whatever it might be" (49). Her repeated acts of "appearing to listen, as if she heard some one calling her name, and knew not precisely in what direction" (60), indicate that she fears reentrapment. Though the "benevolent fraternity" offers her refuge, the question soon arises as to whether she has obtained a protective asylum or has in fact escaped from one imprisoning community only to enter another.

That Blithedale threatens to become an imprisoning, even "conventual," community is suggested by the presentation of Hollingsworth, the former blacksmith and now ardent philanthropist of prison reform, as a type of patriarchal mesmerist quite similar to the mesmerist-"priest" of the opening chapter. When first introduced carrying in his arms the "slim and unsubstantial" (26) Priscilla, the forceful Hollingsworth seems both a liberator and a potential, or actual, enslaver. He seems a priestlike enslaver for his ability to dominate others through a kind of "tenderness . . . which few men could resist, and no woman" (28); he possesses the mesmerical powers that anti-Catholic alarmists ascribed to priests in the confessional. Such are his powers that upon arriving at Blithedale he immediately assumes control over the self-possessed Zenobia; as Coverdale puts it, he "met Zenobia's eyes, and began his influence upon her life" (28–9). In response to his gaze, Zenobia "absolutely changed color, and seemed mortified and confused" (29). When Coverdale later tells Hollingsworth that "your own vocation is evidently to be a priest" (43), it is because he has experienced a similar sense of disorientation during Hollingsworth's ministering visits to his sickbed.

Clearly the increasing confusion and disorientation threatening to subvert Blithedale from within owe a good deal to Hollingsworth's troubling participation. A "bond-slave" (55) to his personal project of building a model prison and contemptuous of Blithedale's communitarian aspirations, Hollingsworth among the Blithedalers resembles an infiltrating and seductive priest in pursuit of converts of his own. His proposed reformatory prison, like the monastic phalanstery, would function as a separate subcommunity, a walled-in edifice housing the leader, "a few disciples" (56), and the "criminal brethren" (56). Indicative of Hollingsworth's commitment to enclosure is his obsession, not with his criminal theories or philanthropic ideals, but with the proposed edifice itself. Coverdale remarks, "I have seen him, a hundred times, with a pencil and sheet of paper, sketching the façade, the side-view, or the rear of the structure, or planning the internal arrangments, as lovingly as another man might plan those of the projected home, where he meant to be happy with his wife and children" (56). Enclosure would ensure the patriarchal authority of the leader; it would create a unified world of insiders under Hollingsworth's command.

Although Blithedale is not yet enclosed within a phalanstery, its separateness works to the seductive Hollingsworth's advantage as he schemes to convert utopianists to his prison project; for characterizing Blithedale throughout the romance is a muted but parallel version of what characterizes the enclosed Catholic subcommunity of the convent novel: an omnipresent and destabilizing sexuality. As Coverdale puts it, Blithedale, as opposed to "conventional society" (72), "seemed to authorize any individual, of either sex, to fall in love with any other, regardless of what would elsewhere be judged suitable and prudent" (72).[58] Coverdale is not exempt from the unsuitable and imprudent: His fantasies reveal desires to master pale Priscilla and to be mastered by the sensual Zenobia. Much to Coverdale's dismay, however, Hollingsworth attracts the liberated libido as he cannot; and it should be noted that the portrayal of Hollingsworth's priestcraft at Blithedale's "conventual" society derives in part from Coverdale's frustrated sexual desires for its "sisters." Troubled by Zenobia's and Priscilla's relative neglect of him, Coverdale deploys the image of the patriarchal cult leader in a mean-spirited effort to account for Hollingsworth's seductive powers: "Hollingsworth, like many other illustrious prophets, reformers, and philanthropists, was likely to make two proselytes, among the women, to one among the men" (68).[59] When Priscilla later chooses to sit with Hollingsworth after Coverdale mocks her gaiety, Coverdale eases his discomfort by again projecting onto Hollingsworth a lordly mastery: "Indeed, it was a sight worth gazing at, and a beautiful sight too, as the fair girl sat at the feet of that dark, powerful figure. Her air, while perfectly modest, delicate, and virginlike, denoted her as swayed by Hollingsworth, attracted to him, and unconsciously seeking to rest upon his strength" (77). The "beautiful sight" of Priscilla's submission speaks to the desire for purposive submission implicit in the trope of the patriarchal priest; it speaks to the desire implicit in Blithedale itself. But the picture of the submissive virgin also evokes the alarmist image of priestly domination and suggests the potential dangers of Hollingsworth's magnetic charms.

These dangers are underscored through the novel's plot, an unfolding melodrama of flight and entrapment that emphasizes the extreme (but

analogous) threat posed by the diabolically magnetic Professor Westervelt to the "virginlike" Priscilla. In quest of Priscilla, whom Coverdale
senses is the Veiled Lady, the "fashionably dressed" (92) Westervelt
resembles both a spiritualist in pursuit of an escaped medium and a priest
in pursuit of an escaped novice. As shaper of the melodrama, as teller of
the tale, Coverdale presents Westervelt's pursuit of Priscilla as the archetypal pursuit of a virtuous and innocent American by villainous, depraved "Europeans." He does so by linking Zenobia to the aristocratic,
European-seeming Westervelt, with whom she really is enmeshed, and
by sentimentally insisting on the unbridgeable moral chasm between the
sexually experienced Zenobia and the virginally innocent Priscilla (and
this despite details suggesting that the seamstress may once have been a
whore).[60] Coverdale's early pointed remark that there is "a luxuriant
growth in Zenobia's character" (15), along with his observation of her
exposed shoulder and fresh hothouse flower, would lead the antipapist
among the crowd to view her as a Scarlet Lady now in retreat.[61] She is a
decidedly fallen Scarlet Lady, for in his sick chamber Coverdale concludes that she has lost the purity vouchsafed by virginity – "There is no
folded petal, no latent dew-drop, in this perfectly developed rose!" (47) –
and that she accordingly is a fraud (48). Within "conventual" Blithedale
she can be viewed as its lascivious nun: As fraudulent as Westervelt's false
teeth, to follow Coverdale's thinking on the matter, she would be the
perfect coconspirator for either "priest" of the novel.

   I am suggesting, then, that a dominant motif of Blithedale and other
"spiritualist" novels of the period, "the subjugation and rescue of the
mesmerist's clairvoyant,"[62] has important sources in the Gothic and convent novel's dominant motif of the subjugation and rescue of the priest's
novice. Thus given the homology of reform subcommunity and Catholic subcommunity, Hawthorne's appropriation of this motif cannot but
imply the sorts of discursive parallels I am pursuing. George Lippard's
phenomenally popular The Quaker City; or The Monks of Monk Hall
(1844), inscribed to the memory of Charles Brockden Brown, stands as a
particularly illuminating example of the intertextual relationship between the convent and spiritualist novel. A mansion in Philadelphia that
formerly served as a nunnery and monastery, Monk-hall houses no
Catholic monks or nuns, just a motley group of aristocrats, spiritualists,
and perverts. And yet, as the title suggests, all of Monk-hall's members
by analogy resemble plotting monks at an urban monastery. Reigning
over Monk-hall is the inquisitorial Devil-Bug, whose practice of dropping his tortured victims' bodies through the mansion's basement pit
recalls Poe's similar use of inquisitional tropes in "The Pit and the Pen-
dulum" (1842). And as is typical of the nativists' convent, Monk-hall
houses an entrapped virtuous "novice," Mary, who is viciously raped by

the hall's "monks," and a promiscuous betraying "nun," Dora, who, when mortally wounded, is described, like the Anglo-Catholic revelers of "May-Pole," as a pagan: "Zenobia, on her throne, with the spoils of all the nations scattered around her feet, could never have looked, more sternly beautiful."[63]

Blithedale's unfolding melodrama presents Hawthorne's pagan–Catholic Zenobia as similarly tempted to turn against the novice-like Priscilla, or, to put it another way, as tempted to step into the villainous role of lascivious nun implicitly ascribed to her by Coverdale. Her "helpless sort of moan" (104) in response to Westervelt's plea for complicity, however, reveals that affairs are not as simple as Coverdale's melodramatic conception would indicate. Nevertheless, soon after Westervelt's departure, Zenobia herself resorts to melodrama when she tells the "illustrious Society of Blithedale" (106) the legend of "The Silvery Veil," a tale of the subjugation and aborted rescue of a mesmerist's clairvoyant. As the veil imagery suggests, the Veiled Lady of Zenobia's legend can be viewed as an enslaved medium-novice who, like Priscilla, takes refuge, even as she remains greatly endangered, "amid a knot of visionary people . . . seeking for the better life" (114). Significantly, Zenobia projects herself into the legend as a nunlike lady aligned with a priestly spiritualist. Tempted by his promise that her betrayal of the Veiled Lady would further her "pursuit of happiness" (115), the lady reenslaves the Priscilla figure by dropping a veil over her head; Zenobia likewise drops a veil of gauze over Priscilla's head at the conclusion of her legend. Clearly a confessional statement of her temptation to plot with the priestly Westervelt so that she might align herself with Hollingsworth, her melodramatic tale presses us to ask whether Coverdale's melodramatic account of Blithedale's "priests" and "veiled ladies" might not similarly confess to his unstated temptations.

We can best address the confessional nature of Coverdale's melodramatic narrative by reconsidering its insider–outsider perspective. As enchanted insider, Coverdale participates with the Blithedalers in the oppositional, or "countersubversive," gesture of identifying a corrupt enemy – the ruthless marketplace society of self-interested Americans. As disenchanted outsider, he presents a much different picture of corruption, with his melodramatic tropes suggesting that the equally ruthless unconventional society he initially finds so appealing in fact bears a close resemblance to the "inside" communities of anti-Catholic discourse. His narrative, then, like the conventual narrative of the entrapped republican virgin, seemingly takes on a more traditional "unveiling" function in alerting America's Protestant republican readers to the threatening secretive societies within their midst. What is not so traditional, however, is the way in which he unveils the community; despite his many ironies, he is an infinitely more willing participant than the entrapped virgin. Unlike Cooper's narrator in *The Bravo* and Brown's Sophia, Coverdale to the end of the novel resists assuming the declamatory posture of the alarmist outsider. Although disenchanted, he remains enchanted. His melodramatic portrayal of Blithedale's "priests" and "veiled ladies" confesses to a conflict of desires.

Coverdale obliquely touches on the nature of his desires at the narrative's opening. As he informs the reader, on the day before his departure from the city he attends a public performance of the famed medium, the Veiled Lady, whose veil serves as an emblem for the associative community he plans to join: "It was white, with somewhat of a subdued silver sheen, like the sunny side of a cloud; and falling over the wearer, from head to foot, was supposed to insulate her from the material world, from time and space, and to endow her with many of the privileges of a disembodied spirit" (6). Unlike his bachelor apartments, the Blithedale community offers a purifying, spiritual insulation, attractive in part because, like the veil, it is tantalizingly enigmatic. As he gazes at the veil he cannot resist speculating on the identity of the mysterious young woman who, rumor declares, is trapped behind it. In this way Coverdale conveys his wish to lift the veil, a wish enacted analogously through his decision to retreat behind Blithedale's "veil" and become a purposive insider endowed with "privileges." Mounting the communitarian "stage" and surrendering his bachelor's freedom to leave at the end of each performance, he becomes a kind of Veiled Lady.

An escape from the individualistic orientations of the "material world," a wish for privilege, an attraction to the secretive and the spiritual – all motivate the spectatorial urbanite to gaze at the Veiled Lady and then to assume an analogous role. The dynamic at work here, I want to suggest, resembles the dynamic at work in American countersubversion, particularly antebellum anti-Catholicism. In an essay titled "Secret Societies – The Know-Nothings," which appeared in the January 1855 issue of *Putnam's,* an anonymous antinativist author addressed this dynamic in his effort to understand how the intolerable Know-Nothings had managed to gain so many followers. The source of their society's popularity, he posited, lay in their adoption of secret rituals which appealed to "the love of our poor human nature for mystery itself – mystery which is consubstantiate, if we may so express it, with the infinite depth and yearnings of our souls." Yearning for a version of "Catholic" mystery and ritual because anguished by the "obvious inability of existing society to meet the wants of the human soul," Protestant Know-Nothing countersubversives, the author concluded, became somewhat "Catholic" themselves. The line between subversion and countersubversion, enchantment and disenchantment, entanglement and disentanglement, as Hawthorne dramatically showed in "Young Goodman Brown," is a thin one.[64]

Certainly if Coverdale confesses to anything in the opening of his narrative, it is to the "inability of existing society to meet the wants of the human soul." The urban world of Blithedale is populated by ghostly, broken men, like Moodie, who sustain themselves through alcoholic inebriation, idle fantasy, and decadent entertainments. When Coverdale acts on his deeper longings and becomes one of Blithedale's "veiled ladies," he expresses, like the Know-Nothings, a yearning for "Roman Catholic" mystery, spirituality, and foundational purpose. Nonetheless, and in this way he resembles the countersubversive "outsider," he continues to pride himself on his spectatorial distance from the subcommunity, "my private theatre" (65). Believing his own role at Blithedale to be "singularly subordinate" (97), merely an interpretive one, he loses sight of his insider's status and desires. To be sure, he intimates the possibility of entanglement when, aloft in his hermitage following the visits of Moodie and Westervelt, he views a wild grapevine that "had caught hold of three of four neighboring trees, and married the whole clump with a perfectly inextricable knot of polygamy" (98). But even while contemplating the polygamous knot, Coverdale applauds his "inviolate" (99) individuality. At "conventual" Blithedale, those who are enmeshed, enchanted, and endangered are its "sisters."

Coverdale thus increasingly chooses to present himself as a disengaged chronicler of the mysteries of Blithedale, a chronicler who focuses on a limited cast of characters and a limited danger: the threat posed to the vulnerable and innocent Priscilla by the novel's contending patriarchal masters. Viewed in relation to Zenobia's confessional narrative, however, and viewed in a larger discursive relation to the insider desire informing convent novels, texts of utopian reform, and countersubversive discourse generally, Coverdale's melodramatic account of Priscilla's plight can be taken as an equally confessional account of his own entanglement in plot and community. It is evident from the start that Coverdale, who fled the city and soon feels entrapped at Blithedale, is as much tempted by the priestly Hollingsworth's influence as any of the other Veiled Ladies of the community, and is at much at risk.

As in the alarmist convent novel, the pursuit of the individual convert simultaneously endangers and exalts that individual, and we sense that Coverdale – minor author, anonymous drifter, Veiled Lady – takes enormous pleasure in the fact that he matters to the forceful philanthropist. Hollingsworth's kindly visits to his sickbed especially please him, until he realizes the extent of his vulnerability. In an ironic aside to the reader that couples his "naïve" suspicions with the knowledge that his

suspicions eventually will be borne out, he relates his fear that Hollingsworth's "more than brotherly attendance" (41) may in fact be less than
brotherly: "I wondered whether it were possible that Hollingsworth
could have watched by my bedside, with all that devoted care, only for the
ulterior purpose of making me a proselyte to his views!" (57). Coverdale's
jocular remark to the ministering Hollingsworth that "your own vocation
is evidently to be a priest, and to spend your days and nights in helping
your fellow-creatures to draw peaceful dying-breaths" (43), evokes the
alarmist image of the expedient priest willing to exploit even the intimacy
of the sickbed to gain converts to the cause.

We see just how strenuously Hollingsworth seeks converts, and how
vulnerable are all of Blithedale's participants, during a later scene at
Eliot's pulpit, the rock where apostle John Eliot reputedly sought to
convert the Indians and where Hollingsworth now regularly addresses
"his few disciples" (119). Coverdale by this point has become so en-
tranced with Hollingsworth, so taken with his hypnotically soothing
voice, that he regularly requests to hear him speak on various subjects.
As he confesses soon after his recovery, "I loved Hollingsworth, as has
already been enough expressed" (70). Nevertheless, he continues to perceive him as a "high-priest" (71) devoted to the "false deity" (71) of his
prison project; and as on his sickbed, at Eliot's pulpit Coverdale again
discerns the power masked by Hollingsworth's philanthropic façade:
When Zenobia boldly ascends the pulpit to inveigh against injustices
done to women, Hollingsworth immediately asserts that "true wom-
anhood" (123) belongs at man's side as "Sympathizer" (122) and that he
would use "physical force, that unmistakeable evidence of sovereignty,
to scourge them back within their proper bounds!" (123). Like the priests
in *Six Months in a Convent*, he demands of his disciples: "Sister, obedience!" Priscilla's "glance of such entire acquiescence and unquestioning
faith" (123) seems the glance of a brain-washed or brainless slave. As
Zenobia's impassioned pressing of Hollingsworth's hand further suggests, at conventual Blithedale the "sisters" remain in thrall.

But Hollingsworth also wants a "brother," and soon after the scene at
Eliot's pulpit he once again turns his sights on Coverdale, the man in
search of holy brotherhood. Like Brockden Brown's priestly Ludloe
attempting to convert Carwin to the Jesuitical Illuminati, he promises to
reinvest the life of the drifting Coverdale with what he has all along been
seeking, "a purpose in life, worthy of the extremest self-devotion –
worthy of martyrdom, should God so order it!" (133). Offering him an
insider's fraternity, he seemingly invites Coverdale inside his "monastic"
prison project: "Be my brother in it!" (133). He then makes a particularly
seductive appeal:

Strike hands with me; and, from this moment, you shall never again feel the languor and vague wretchedness of an indolent or half-occupied man! There may be no more aimless beauty in your life; but, in its stead, there shall be strength, courage, immitigable will – everything that a manly and generous nature should desire! We shall succeed! We shall have done our best for this miserable world; and happiness (which never comes but incidentally) will come to us unawares! (133)

His hands outstretched, his eyes welling with tears, he beseeches in Christ-like fashion: "Coverdale . . . there is not the man in this world, whom I could love as I could you. Do not forsake me!" (133).

Hollingsworth's offer of fixed and sacred purpose tempts the "aimless" Coverdale for the same reason that monastic/reformist Blithedale tempts him, and there is a palpable tension as Coverdale considers the possibility of conversion. But fearing that he, like the submissive Priscilla, is more or less entrapped within the community and a potential victim of a priestly mesmerist at that, he feels a growing resistance to Hollingsworth's demand for a total surrendering commitment. Recalling his successful resistance from the outsider perspective, Coverdale offers a striking picture of his precarious situation: "As I look back upon this scene, through the coldness and dimness of so many years, there is still a sensation as if Hollingsworth had caught hold of my heart, and were pulling it towards him with an almost irresistible force. It is a mystery to me, how I withstood it. . . . Had I but touched his extended hand, Hollingsworth's magnetism would perhaps have penetrated me with his own conception of all these matters" (133–4). Seemingly a veiled lady on the verge of entering the trance state (or a novice on the verge of succumbing to the confessional wizardry of a priest),[65] Coverdale makes the monumental effort and finally wills a response to the priestly mesmerist's direct demand for him to join the cause: "No!" (135). Having summoned the energy to dismount the confessional stage and feeling "an absolute torture of the breast" (135), he soon after takes leave of Blithedale's "brethren . . . [and] sisterhood" (141), returning to the city and resuming his outsidership.

Like the formerly entrapped republican virgin, whose resistance to papal authority allows her to interpret her experiences in her own terms and for her own readers, Coverdale, a professional author, in resisting Hollingsworth's demands for conversion reasserts his individual freedom to view experience through his "own optics" (135). Considered from this perspective, Coverdale's resistance enacts a classically Protestant reclaiming of the sovereignty of the unshackled imagination. And yet despite the romancer's insistence on his imperial outsidership, Coverdale's obsession with secrecy, his fantasy imaging of Hollingsworth and Zenobia kissing across his hotel bed, and especially his melodramatic presentation of Priscilla's plight suggest that he too courts pursuit and wishes to be an insider, if not of an ideal community then of a real conspiracy; he wants to be entangled. Discovering Westervelt, Zenobia, and Priscilla in the boardinghouse adjacent to his hotel, he therefore eagerly resumes his double role as spectator and narrator of melodramatic romance, the role he would have relinquished had he converted to Hollingsworth's cause. But as at Blithedale he continues to waver between an engaged insidership and a spectatorial outsidership. In Zenobia's legend of "The Silvery Veil," the Veiled Lady demands of the voyeuristic Theodore, "Dost thou come hither, not in holy faith, nor with a pure and generous purpose, but in scornful scepticism and idle curiosity?" (113). This question, which a Catholic could put to a prurient nativist, could also be put to the prurient Coverdale and his "Protestant" art. Lacking the religiovisionary foundation of an Emerson (or contemporaneous Transcendentalist), he finds that his account of "the knot of characters . . . upon my mental stage as actors" (156) all too often turns upon the promptings of his idle speculations. The unshackled imagination, Coverdale seems uneasily to be intimating, is a decadent, "unhumanizing" (154) imagination. In the manner of a bored theatergoer for whom nothing is "real," he self-parodically confesses to his reader, "I began to long for a catastrophe" (157).

Catastrophe appears imminent because he uses his dramaturgic "insulating" method, as he did at Blithedale, to conceptualize the still highly mysterious plot as an "entertaining" melodrama of flight and entrapment in which the endangered medium Priscilla continues to seem a Protestant virgin endangered by plotting Catholics.[66] Emphasizing her virtue and purity, Coverdale compares Priscilla, through juxtaposition, to the solitary white dove on the peak of her boardinghouse, a country dove that should be "nestling in a warm and comfortable dove-cote" (152). Unlike "birds of city-breeding" (149), which would know "how to guard themselves against the peculiar perils of their position" (149), Priscilla would be especially vulnerable to the "cat-like" (158) Westervelt, who is compared to the city cat creeping along roofs "with murderous purpose against its feathered citizens" (149). Where Priscilla appears the vulnerable American innocent of "country" republican discourse, Zenobia in the city is presented as a pagan queen whose luxurious trappings, as popular iconography would have it, are wastefully decorative in the Catholic mode. Wearing "costly robes" (163) and "flaming jewels on her neck" (163), residing in a dazzling room whose furniture and accoutrements offer Coverdale "more shapes of luxury than there could be any object in enumerating" (164), Zenobia moves Coverdale to a republican (and rather priggish) vituperation on her aristocratic veneer: "In the gorgeousness with which she had surrounded herself – in the redundance of personal ornament, which the largeness of her physical nature and the rich type of her beauty caused to seem so suitable – I malevolently beheld the true character of the woman, passionate, luxurious, lacking simplicity, not deeply refined, incapable of pure and perfect taste" (164–5). Linking Zenobia to the priestly, citified spiritualist, and emphasizing the contrast between Zenobia's luxury and Priscilla's pure innocence, Coverdale guides the reader toward an alarmist reading of Priscilla's plight. Thus when Zenobia, Westervelt, and Priscilla ride off in a carriage and, as the chapter title ominously declares, "They Vanish" (168), we suspect that Priscilla, like Hilda who "vanishes" into conventual captivity in *The Marble Faun,* has suffered a similar form of imprisonment.

That possibility makes the melodramatist Coverdale, who throughout the novel projects his confused desires onto Priscilla's situation, acutely feel his outsidership, and so he decides to seek out the unfortunate Moodie, ostensibly "for the purpose of ascertaining whether the knot of affairs was as inextricable, on that side, as I found it on all others" (174). What he more urgently desires, however, is to go inside or, so it seems, to return inside. We should recall that when Coverdale fends off Moodie in the opening chapter he terms him "an acquaintance" (6); when he later observes him at Blithedale, he tells Hollingsworth, "I know this old gentleman . . . that is, I have met him a hundred times, in town" (82). Or does he mean "in tavern"? For when he enters the tavern he offhand-edly remarks, "I had often amused myself with watching the staid hu-mors and sober jollities of the thirsty souls around me" (174).[67] Though ostensibly cruel, his protestations of amused outsidership, as with his similar protestations of outsidership from the Blithedale commu-nitarians, mask authentic desires for an insider's fraternity with "thirsty souls." Plying Moodie with wine, he does so in secret sympathy as he marvels at the alcohol's ability to make toper into utopian: "It was wonderful, however, what an effect the mild grape-juice wrought upon him. It was not in the wine, but in the associations which it seemed to bring up" (181). Whether at tavern or at Blithedale, communitarian inebriation induces regenerative "associations" possessing "an inde-scribable, ideal charm" (176).

These particular "associations" – Moodie-Fauntleroy's tale of his two fragmented families and economic fall – allow Coverdale both to get inside the plot and to heighten the sentimental contrast between Priscilla and Zenobia central to his melodramatic conception. The offspring of Moodie's superficial first marriage to a wealthy beauty, Zenobia is re-garded by Moodie, "already rich in gems" (182), as just "another jewel" (182). After perpetrating a secret economic crime in an attempt to preserve his dwindling wealth, Moodie retreats to the cramped Irish quarters of a colonial governor's degenerated mansion, marries a feeble seamstress, and fathers feeble Priscilla, whose renowned spiritualistic gifts eventually attract the attentions of an enslaving spiritualist.[68] While Zenobia grows to adulthood amidst great wealth, Priscilla "was enthralled in an intolerable bondage, from which she must either free herself or perish" (190). Underscoring the contrast between Zenobia's power and Priscilla's vulnerability, Coverdale appends to Moodie's history a sketch of a meeting between Zenobia and Moodie, drawn, Coverdale confesses, "mainly from fancy, although with some general grounds of surmise in regard to the old man's feelings" (190). As Coverdale presents the scene, Moodie beholds the bejeweled Zenobia, asks the puzzled heiress to treat Priscilla kindly as a sister, and, upon her departure, shouts in his lonely chamber: "Zenobia take heed! Priscilla shall have no wrong!" (193). Linking this imagined scene to the unfolding narrative of Priscilla's entrapment, Coverdale suggests that Zenobia may well have betrayed her familial trust: "That very evening, so far as I can adjust the dates of these strange incidents – Priscilla – poor, pallid flower! – was either snatched from Zenobia's hand, or flung wilfully away!" (193).

As the adoption of Moodie's point of view makes clear, the account of Moodie's precipitous loss of financial and familial stability quite unexpectedly makes an impact on Coverdale, who in his own way had been adrift in the open democratic marketplace before finding temporary sanctuary among the "brethren and sisters" of Blithedale. While with Moodie, Coverdale, against his will, experiences his strongest sense of fraternity in the romance. His intuition of his kinship with the broken Moodie staggers him: "Well! I betook myself away, and wandered up and down, like an exorcised spirit that had been driven from its old haunts, after a mighty struggle" (194). In his fraternal responsiveness both to Moodie and to his own "old haunts" of the tavern, he seems to realize why he had thrown in his lot with the "thirsty" communitarians in the first place, and he subsequently privately reaffirms his initial commitment to the association (195). Even so, only a fortuitous meeting at the lyceum hall performance of the Veiled Lady recalls the timid insider-outsider to the vortex of the community, and to the vortex of the melodramatic plot.

The move from the spirit lovers of the tavern to the spiritualists of the lyceum represents a move from a broken to a decadent community of idealists. Although the New England country audience possesses "a generally decent and respectable character" (197), it is a restless audience that, when bored by the purple-bespectacled impressario, "signified their desire for the entertainment to commence by thump of sticks and stamp of boot-heels" (199). Like the "acidulous-looking gentleman" (11:52) and his cohorts in "Main-street" (1849), the villagers are cynical and voracious, and there is a sense that Hawthorne's initial sympathies in the scene lie with Westervelt, the artist who must appease the crowd. The spiritualist's displaying of the Veiled Lady to "all those straining eyes" (201), after all, parallels Hawthorne's displaying of the Veiled Lady to his readers. Like the entrepreneurial convent novelist, and like the spiritualist, Hawthorne, as romancer behind the romancer, entices a restless democratic readership with melodrama and mystery; and Coverdale, the novel's "limited" first-person narrator, takes the blame![69]

Nonetheless, the central reality of Westervelt's performative art is that it depends upon enslaving a woman behind a veil; it depends upon his priestcraft. Hollingsworth possesses similar powers of mesmerical control, an analogous priestcraft. And so he mounts the confessional platform, ritually waves his hand, and liberates Priscilla, who, Coverdale sentimentally suggests, has remained untainted by her experiences (203). But while she would seem to have achieved a glorious freedom, it is difficult to ignore just how dependent she is upon Hollingsworth's priestcraft. According to Coverdale, when Priscilla removes her veil we realize that for some time now she has been under his influence: "Within that encircling veil, though an evil hand had flung it over her, there was as deep a seclusion as if this forsaken girl had, all the while, been sitting under the shadow of Eliot's pulpit, in the Blithedale woods, at the feet of him who now summoned her to the shelter of his arms" (203). Hollingsworth, who "often ascended Eliot's pulpit," had assumed at Blithedale the priestly role and at Eliot's pulpit was at his most despotic. From an alarmist perspective, then, Priscilla passes hands from the patriarchal master of the stage to the patriarchal master of the pulpit, and remains enslaved.

But informing the alarmist presentation, I have been arguing, is an implicit desire for insidership; and informing the alarmist trope of the patriarchal priest is a temptation to purposive refuge and submission. The chapter concludes in this way: "[Priscilla] uttered a shriek and fled to Hollingsworth, like one escaping from her deadliest enemy, and was safe forever!" (203). Despite the equivocating simile, Coverdale's description of Priscilla's eternal safety in Hollingsworth's sheltering arms conveys a resonant envy: He too has sought asylum both at Blithedale and at tavern and, as the "crisis" conversion scene dramatized, has been tempted toward surrender and submission, toward a coconspiratorship of sorts, by Hollingsworth's simultaneously brotherly and priestly appeal. Enslaved to a patriarchal spiritualist and threatened by her jealous sister, the impoverished Priscilla has very clear needs for shelter and community. But from what does Coverdale, the confessional melodramatist, seek shelter so as to be "safe forever"? And why does he so waver between his enchanted insidership and disenchanted outsidership? The answer, I would suggest, is implicit in the lyceum scene, which would have us reevaluate Blithedale's spiritualistic/monastic brotherhood as a revolutionary brotherhood less Catholic than Protestant.

A backward glance at Lippard's *The Monks of Monk Hall* helps to disclose the revolutionary implications of *Blithedale*'s lyceum scene. Lippard's novel, anticipating Hawthorne's, similarly builds to a showdown between contending patriarchal spiritualists who seem, sexually domineering "monks" that they are, altogether priestly. Ravoni the Sorcerer, an aristocratical showman and a possible source for Westervelt, mesmerically commands numerous enslaved novice-mediums and, for most of the novel, the equally mesmerized Devil-Bug. In the confrontation scene Devil-Bug finally stabs the heretofore omnipotent Ravoni, but Ravoni still manages to command his enslaved mediums to worship him after his death. They respond instantaneously: "'Hail Ravoni!' shouted the band of enthusiasts, and the group of lovely women, the vacant-eyed maniacs and the voluptuous forms of Ravoni's harem, went whirling over the floor in a bounding dance." At his death, then, the patriarchal Ravoni quite literally leaves his mesmerized followers in a perpetual state of revolution. The mediums' maniacal "whirling" points to another way of viewing the "Catholic" spiritualists both at Monk-hall and at Blithedale: as invisibly linked spirits infused with a ceaseless revolutionism.[70]

A crucial source for the conception of spiritualism as a form of revolutionism lies in eighteenth-century responses to the theories of Franz Anton Mesmer. Like the newly discovered phenomena of electricity and oxygen, mesmerism focused attention on the invisible world and bolstered confidence in man's ability to control that world. Thus it was regarded by many as a reformatory science promising to bring man and his institutions into a state of perfect harmony. But because mesmerism achieved its first great popularity around the time of the French Revolution, European conservatives came to view it as a revolutionary science promoting social instability. The specter of mesmerical revolutionaries invisibly shaping history contributed to the pervasive conspiratorial fears of the 1790s; not surprisingly, concerns about conspiring mesmerists found a prominent place in Abbé Barruel's anti-Illuminati *Memoirs of Jacobinism*.[71] Anxieties about invisibly plotting mesmerists resurfaced during the revolutions of 1848–9, and they are central to Orestes Brownson's *The Spirit-Rapper* (1854), a novel intent on exposing the conspiratorial-revolutionary dimensions of spiritualism and reformism that he felt Hawthorne's *Blithedale* had ignored.

For Brownson, who concluded in a review of *Blithedale* that Hawthorne failed to document fully "the actual goings-on at Brook Farm," utopian reformers, with their mesmerical and spiritualistic activities, were in fact satanic subversives responsible for the revolutions of the past sixty-five years.[72] As the narrator of *The Spirit-Rapper* confesses on his deathbed, after mastering the art of mesmerism and joining forces with the spiritualist Priscilla (!), a Satan worshiper and international revolutionary, he learns, for example, that the French Revolution occurred when the Illuminati and other mesmerical "spirit-rappers" exercised an invisible control over defenseless citizens: "Weishaupt, Mesmer, Saint-Martin, and Cagliostro, did far more to produce the revolutions and convulsions of European society at the close of the century, than was done by Voltaire, Rousseau, D'Alembert, Diderot, Mirabeau, and their associates. . . . The masses were possessed, they were whirled aloft, were driven hither and thither, and onward in the terrible work of demolition, by a mysterious power they did not comprehend, and by a force they were unable, having yielded to it, to resist." The revolutionary situation of the 1840s arose when unwary European peoples, like Ravoni's mediums, were once again "whirled aloft" by enslaving mesmerical forces: "The same phenomena, only on a reduced scale, were observable in the revolutions of 1848. Everywhere there seemed to be an invisible power at work." And yet the revolutions ultimately failed, not, as many Americans believed, because of Catholic and aristocratic reactionism, but because of God's saving intervention. As Brownson's revolutionary-spiritualist declares: "Our magic failed us; a more powerful magician than we intervened."[73] The novel concludes with the narrator's saving conversion to Roman Catholicism.

A convert himself to Roman Catholicism, Brownson hardly regarded spiritualists as types of Catholic priests; rather, he viewed them as satanic Protestant revolutionaries. Significantly, the novel's anti-Protestant narrator first learns about mesmerism from Mr. Winslow, a Unitarian minister who, "after hesitating a while, began to try experiments himself, and found that he had a wonderful magnetic power."[74] For Brownson, Winslow's petty drive to mastery embodies, on a small scale, what is most blasphemous about nineteenth-century Protestant reformism: its Mesmer-like insistence on man's ability to shape and control his destiny. To enlarge the historical frame, Brownson saw spirit-rapping, mesmerism, and other types of spiritualism as following inevitably from the revolutionary "humanism" of the Protestant Reformation. Though his fervent Catholicism guided him toward an alarmist notion of spiritualism as a form of conspiracy, his view of Protestantism's revolutionary spirit is essentially accurate and, as indicated by the more complex typology of such tales as "Endicott and the Red Cross," "The Gray Champion," and "My Kinsman, Major Molineux," not so very different from Hawthorne's.[75] Neither a political alarmist nor a Catholic dogmatist, Hawthorne in *Blithedale* nonetheless echoes Lippard's *Monks* and, contrary to Brownson's review, anticipates Brownson's own countersubversive *The Spirit-Rapper* by calling attention to the Protestant revolutionary energies informing the utopianists' communitarian project "to begin the reformation of the world" (39).

Crucial to the presentation of Blithedale as a revolutionary community is the very spiritualism–reformism analogy that has all along encouraged our reading of the group's "Catholic" character; for if we look again at the climactic lyceum scene, we observe that Westervelt, a priestly spiritualist, is also a demonic revolutionary. At Westervelt's introduction, for example, the impressario celebrates the spiritualist's invisible mesmerical-sexual power for its ability to destabilize and subvert "natural" human relationships: "At the bidding of one of these wizards, the maiden, with her lover's kiss still burning on her lips, would turn from him with icy indifference; the newly made widow would dig up her buried heart out of her young husband's grave, before the sods had taken root upon it; a mother, with her babe's milk in her bosom, would thrust away her child" (198). As in Brownson (and as in anti-Illuminati tracts), this particular revolutionary is amoral and expedient. Sounding a bit like a Congregationalist minister of the 1790s, a revulsed Coverdale observes: "Human character was but soft wax in his hands; and guilt, or virtue, only the forms into which he should see fit to mould it. The religious sentiment was a flame which he could blow up with his breath, or a spark that he could utterly extinguish" (198).[76] In the context of the impressario's introduction, Westervelt's utopianist salute to a "new era that was dawning upon the world . . . that would link soul to soul" (200) suggests an equally dark image of helpless "mediums" linked together by an expedient plotter "into one great, mutually conscious brotherhood" (200).

This "mutually conscious brotherhood" recalls the "loathful brotherhood" of "Young Goodman Brown." In that tale the satanic traveler whom Brown meets in the woods, like Westervelt whom Coverdale meets in the woods, carries a cane – at once a magician's wand and an emblem of his patriarchal authority. Like Westervelt, the satanic traveler promises to initiate his followers into the world of demonic revolutionism, teaching them "how many a woman, eager for widow's weeds, has given her husband a drink at bed-time, and let him sleep his last sleep in her bosom; how beardless youths have made haste to inherit their fathers' wealth; and how fair damsels – blush not, sweet ones! – have dug little graves in the garden, and bidden me, the sole guest, to an infant's funeral" (10:87). In this regard the analogy developed in Blithedale between the brotherhood of spiritualists and the brotherhood of utopian reformists, reinforced by the analogy between Westervelt and Hollingsworth, presses us to see that the Blithedalers' reformism too relies on an invisible linkage of spirits and may itself tend toward a Westervelt-like demonism.

Early in the novel, however, Coverdale deploys an imagery more of secrecy than of demonism, crediting the burgeoning of Blithedale's "apostolic society" (39) to the fact "that this idea of a Community had been growing up, in silent and unknown sympathy, for years" (62). He later elaborates on this "sympathy," describing it as a "species of nervous sympathy" (139) so intense that if "one of us happened to give his neighbor a box on the ear, the tingle was immediately felt, on the same side of everybody's head" (139); consequently, the Blithedalers know immediately of Coverdale's break with Hollingsworth. Coverdale's uneasy awareness that there is a "general brain of the Community" (140) – that the community is "one great, mutually conscious brotherhood" – contributes to his decision to return to the city. And it contributes to his growing perception of Blithedale as a revolutionary community: "It was impossible, situated as we were, not to imbibe the idea that everything in nature and human existence was fluid, or fast becoming so; that the crust of the Earth, in many places, was broken, and its whole surface portentously upheaving; that it was a day of crisis, and that ourselves were in the critical vortex" (140).

That the Blithedalers are subversive revolutionaries akin to Westervelt's demonic revolutionaries is further suggested by Coverdale's description of the festive masquerade following Priscilla's liberation from Westervelt. Returning to the community after his prolonged absence, Coverdale encounters a changed and charged "spiritual" landscape: "The atmosphere had a spirit and sparkle in it. Each breath was like a sip of ethereal wine" (204). At first he yields "to the lively influences of air and motion" (204) but soon he suffers from "a sickness of the spirits" (206), a kind of hangover. Climbing to his grape-laden hermitage, he tries to restore his spirits by sustaining his drunkenness: As insider he devours grapes he imagines would produce a wine of "passionate zest, and endowed with a new kind of intoxicating quality" (208). But when he finally descries the reveling group, masqueraders whose costumes invoke a sum of mythic and American history while revealing only "portentous red noses" (210), Coverdale, like Robin in "My Kinsman, Major Molineux," finds himself thoroughly disoriented.[77] In a passage that manifests a discomfort like Endicott's with pagan-Catholic ritual, a fascination like Lippard's with spiritualistic depravity, and a fear like Brownson's of Protestant revolutionism, Coverdale describes the intoxicated masqueraders' "whirling": "So they joined hands in a circle, whirling round so swiftly, so madly, and so merrily, in time and tune with the Satanic music, that their separate incongruities were blended all together; and they became a kind of entanglement that went nigh to turn one's brain" (210). Like Robin in the midst of a revolutionary conspiracy with which he unconsciously sympathizes, the drunken Coverdale, upon hearing the group's "roar of laughter" (210), cannot refrain from offering his own complicitous (fraternal) "burst of laughter" (210). Aloft and hidden in his hermitage, listening to "the Satanic music," he is simultaneously, and painfully, within and without; he is Goodman Brown in the shadows.

He is also a "Catholic" in the shadows. Earlier in the text Coverdale had referred to his hermitage as "a perfect nest for Robinson Crusoe or King Charles" (98). The Crusoe image aptly conveyed Coverdale's initial escapist desires; the association with the secret Catholic Charles II, whose father was the victim of revolutionary reformers – the victim, as it were, of the Reformation – now reveals his uncertainty about the wisdom of pursuing a "restoration" of his place within the community. In Brownson-like fashion, as the identification with King Charles suggests, Coverdale views the carnivalesque masquerade as the manifestation of a subversive revolutionism that, as in *The Spirit-Rapper,* has its historical sources in the Protestant Reformation and its first great expression in the English civil war. In this respect the group's increasing commitment to Fourierism, despite Hollingsworth's disdain for its negative metaphysics, places the Puritan revolution, as Brownson surely would have placed it, near the beginning of an unbroken line running from the Reformation up to the French Revolution and Europe's revolutionary nineteenth century. Emerson's belief that "Fourier carried a whole French Revolution in his head, and much more," led him to fear that Fourierism at Brook Farm would appeal to "a lawless crew who would flock in troops to so fair a game, and, like the dreams of poetic people on the first outbreak of the old French Revolution, so theirs would disappear in a slime of mire and blood."[78] Looking down from his hermitage on "a fantastic rabble" (211), Coverdale views a ritual enactment of just such a revolutionary outbreak in which he becomes, as enforced outsider, a contemporary substitute for the Catholic monarchs Charles II and Louis XVI. Returning as a sympathizer, Coverdale watches the revelers comically and frighteningly plot three different versions of his death (211). Unhinged by a revolutionary spectacle in which he plays chief victim, Coverdale finds his world turning upside down: "I was like a mad poet hunted by chimaeras" (211).

With its echoing of the Merry Mounters' Anglo-Catholic mirthmaking and its evocation of "whirling" revolutionism, the masquerade scene reveals Blithedale as a community torn between opposing sides of its character. Behind the community's reformational zeal, as in the apocalyptic "Earth's Holocaust" (1844), lies "a confusion of popish and protestant emblems" (10:399). Over the course of the novel the community simultaneously turns inward in cultish implosion and outward in revolutionary explosion: It is itself a contending empire of "Catholic" and

"Protestant" energies. Coverdale too is torn between a "Catholic" desire for monastic retreat and a "Protestant" desire to join with the revolutionary brethren; and in the masquerade scene he suddenly, and seemingly for the first time, has to confront his own revolutionism, his own status as intoxicated insider. His "Catholic monarchical" anxieties, then, point to what is implicit in his narrative all along: that he seeks shelter in conventual/monastic Blithedale, as Constantia sought shelter in her father's "temple," to escape from a subversive revolutionism apprehended in self and society. When Blithedale's (and his own) invisibly lurking revolutionism reveals itself in what Coverdale perceives as a demonic eruption, he flees the disorderly "merriment and riot" (211) and attempts a return, as Robin Molineux can never return, to a prerevolutionary world of order and authority; he flees, suitably enough, to Eliot's pulpit, where the world comes back into focus: "I looked up, and found myself nigh Eliot's pulpit, at the base of which sat Hollingsworth, with Priscilla at his feet, and Zenobia standing before them" (212).

But it is a focus that is out of focus, as Coverdale's melodramatic clarity begins to blur. Zenobia, whose feminism has been regularly undercut by Coverdale as a nunlike sexuality bestowed only upon the priestly, now boldly confronts the group as an antipatriarchal revolutionary at odds with the priestly. Wearing a luxurious costume of "fanciful magnificence" (213), she defiantly attacks "you men" (215) who "bring a woman before your secret tribunals, and judge and condemn her" (215). Imaging her as a "sorceress . . . fair enough to tempt Satan with a force reciprocal to his own" (214), Coverdale links the antiauthoritarian Zenobia to the threatening Protestant revolutionary energies of the "Satanic" masqueraders. Clearly Zenobia threatens Coverdale, as Ormond threatens Constantia, with "sexual sensations" that would bring on "a case of more entire subversion and confusion of mind than any other."[79] Zenobia intoxicates, and it is no coincidence that Coverdale's language of drunkenness parallels his language of sexual fantasy. His desire to taste Zenobia's otherworldly "richest and spiciest dishes . . . between draughts of intoxicating wine" (48) looks forward to the simultaneously tempting and discomforting intoxications of the masqueraders' sensual and destabilizing merriment. Troubled by the ways in which Zenobia and the masqueraders stimulate his imagination and passions – concerned, as it were, that Blithedale has not done its office – Coverdale enacts in his melodramatic narrative a literary act of projection and containment: Imaging the subversive Zenobia, and the Blithedalers en masse for that matter, as pagan Catholics, he maintains control over his body by keeping it inviolate, thereby reclaiming his status as Crusoe.

Thus while Zenobia by the end of the novel seems an altogether modern feminist revolutionary, there are good reasons for continuing to view her as a type of Catholic, particularly within the context of Coverdale's melodramatic narrative. Coverdale reinvokes Scarlet Lady imagery at Eliot's pulpit by referring to Zenobia's "cheeks [which] had each a crimson spot" (213), an image that echoes an earlier image of Zenobia out "a-maying" (58) for maple twigs, "the leaf of which looks like a scarlet-bud" (58). Coverdale's continual hinting at her "Catholicism," I want to suggest, involves him in an act of projection typical of antebellum Protestant reformers uncomfortable with their "Catholic monarchical" anxieties. Ann Norton writes, "The ascription of femininity to the Catholic church and Catholic immigrants was a Northern mode of signifying people whose natural passions and appetites have been released from conventional bonds." As we noted in the convent novel in particular, nativist discourse regularly emphasized the Catholics' unrestrained sexuality and violence; and these emphases, as I discuss in greater detail in the next chapter, had important social consequences: In the late 1820s and 1830s there emerged an institution-oriented urban reformism that sought to restrain, transform, or enclose the threatening sexual and violent passions of the immigrants, many of whom were Catholic, in order, so the reformers professed, to "protect existing institutions and those they encompassed."[80] The point I would make here is that Coverdale's melodramatic strategies are intimately tied to a very restrictive (and restricting) notion of psychological, corporeal, and institutional order. Like the first several generations of America's Puritan fathers, to whom he explicitly compares the Blithedalers, Coverdale seeks to rein in his (and his community's) inherent revolutionism by locating the subversive, as the Puritans of *The Scarlet Letter* located the subversive, in a scarlet outsider.

From this cultural-historical perspective we may view Hollingsworth, who stands before Zenobia at Eliot's pulpit as "a Puritan magistrate, holding inquest of life and death in a case of witchcraft" (214), as an incarnation in extreme of the Puritan/Protestant tendency to pursue reformism through exorcism – a revolutionary become inquisitorial persecutor, he is "the type of New England's hereditary spirit." Like Hawthorne's Endicott and antebellum countersubversives, he professes a disinterested commitment to the "reformation of criminals" (36) on the one hand, while on the other hand millennially conceiving of the world in terms of insiders and outsiders, friends or foes. Ironically, then, Hollingsworth's "Puritan" inquest over the "witch" Zenobia, like the Puritans' persecution of Quaker Catharine in "The Gentle Boy," reenacts the historical abuses of Catholic despots that the Puritan reformers prided themselves on transcending. As in that tale, and as in "May-Pole" and "A Bell's Biography," the perception of threatening others as subversives leads the Protestant reformers to become "Catholic" authoritarians themselves.[81] But where Hollingsworth, like Hawthorne's other authoritarian reformers, differs essentially from a Catholic priest, Coverdale repeatedly reminds us, is in the fact that the only foundation for his priestcraft lies in his "all-devouring egotism" (71). As Zenobia famously remarks on his prison project, "It is all self!" (218). Accountable to no "pope," to no sense of spiritual absolutes, Hollingsworth, like the "illustrious Society of Blithedale" (and Brownson's litany of spiritualistic reformers, including the Illuminati), fully expects to illuminate the world through the light of his own reason. Frustrated in his efforts to do so, he invariably imposes his will as power.

Coverdale's final use of mesmerical imagery, then, like his earlier uses, calls attention to the prescriptive, invasive, and priestly aspects of that power. As in the lyceum scene, Hollingsworth summons Priscilla to his side: "Priscilla . . . come!" (219). In a world of such masterful patriarchs, Zenobia might remark, women are in need of a sisterly retreat, a convent without priests. Priscilla expresses a need literally for a sisterly community when she resists Hollingsworth's summons, walks to Zenobia, and gasps, "We are sisters!" (219). Exhibiting her own "mesmerical" powers, the grimly realistic Zenobia waves Priscilla back to Hollingsworth and then, viewed only by Coverdale, falls to her knees and "sobbed convulsively; dry sobs, they seemed to be such as have nothing to do with tears" (221).

With the collapse of community and the failure of melodrama to tell the whole story, there remains the redemptive possibility of confessional intimacy, the creation of an ideal community of two. But Zenobia's outsidership, and seeming availability, only tempt forth the slumbering priest in Coverdale. Desirous of transforming his Hollingsworth-like (and Westervelt-like) invasive and egotistical artistry into something sacred – desirous, that is to say, of leaving behind the confessional wizardry of the artist for the confessional sanctitude of the true priest – Coverdale rhetorically confides to his reader, "Was it wrong, therefore, if I felt myself consecrated to the priesthood, by sympathy like this, and called upon to minister to this woman's affliction, so far as mortal could?" (222). Throughout the novel Zenobia obliquely seeks just such an auditor, ironically confessing to Coverdale when he first leaves the community, for example, "Do you know, Mr. Coverdale, that I have been several times on the point of making you my confidant, for lack of a better and wiser one? But you are too young to be my Father Confessor" (141). In their final meeting Coverdale claims sympathetically to feel Zenobia's "self-same pang" (222) – as perhaps he does, for he too loves Hollingsworth – but he quickly concludes that any effort to comfort her "would be a mockery and an anguish" (223). Too self-absorbed to be a father confessor, and too uneasy with his body, he continues to picture confessional intimacy as a form of confessional violation and chooses to do nothing. Thus in a last ironic parry that conceals her suffering, Zenobia announces her intention of retreating to the sanctum of real father confessors: "I intend to become a Catholic, for the sake of going into a nunnery. When you next hear of Zenobia, her face will be behind the black-veil; so look your last at it now – for all is over!" (227–8). In a parodic echo of Sophia Ripley's conversion (and the trajectory of Brook Farm), Zenobia would retreat from one subcommunity to another, from a community that offers no assurances to a community that promises everything. The "black-veil," however, images not her salvation but her death, and it signifies as well her frustrated confessional needs.

The romance itself stands as testament to Coverdale's frustrated confessional needs. He can later forgive Hollingsworth for the role he may have played in Zenobia's apparently suicidal drowning, thereby distinguishing for the reader the difference between Hollingsworth and the forever loathsome Westervelt: One of the "priests" has a heart, even if that better priest, according to Silas Foster, "wounded the poor thing's breast" (235). But who will forgive Coverdale for a series of disentangling evasions and demeaning projections that arguably play an equally complicitous role in Zenobia's death?[82] Failing to achieve any sort of intimacy at Blithedale, as he also fails in the city, Coverdale confides his tale to a community of fellow outsiders whom he attempts to make over into insiders of his confessional text. Hawthorne added the final chapter, "Miles Coverdale's Confession," after completing the initial draft of the romance; it represents Coverdale's desperate effort to obtain confessional relief by lifting the veil of his melodramatic account to reveal its underlying truth. But Coverdale's pitiful concluding lines – "I – I myself – was in love – with – PRISCILLA!" (247) – should perhaps be taken as a confession of his love not for Priscilla but for her situation. Priscilla takes refuge with the masterful Hollingsworth in a country cottage; in fact, in a fine reversal, the "protective and watchful" (242) Priscilla offers the self-professed murderer a vigilant guardianship. Coverdale drifts on.

Although the tropes generated by anti-Catholic literature centrally inform the conception of Blithedale as a secretive society in (counter)subversive relation to democratic America, they also convey the culturally "representative" Coverdale's hidden attraction to an ordered, selfless community that would provide shelter from a pervasive, destabilizing, and tempting "Protestant" revolutionism.[83] Throughout the romance Coverdale refrains from stating just why he seeks refuge among communitarians; his spectatorship permits strategic retreats. But when he ironically expresses an attraction to Catholicism during the debate on women's rights at Eliot's pulpit, his irony here, as throughout the novel, masks authentic longings for a mediating relationship, a consoling submission, a glimpse of the spiritual. He self-mockingly declares to the "knot of characters," "I have always envied the Catholics their faith in that sweet, sacred Virgin Mother, who stands between them and the Deity, intercepting somewhat of His awful splendor, but permitting His love to stream upon the worshipper, more intelligibly to human comprehension, through the medium of a woman's tenderness" (121–2). The Virgin Mother, as opposed to Zenobia, offers sensuality cleansed of sexuality and gently redeems. She absorbs the self-absorbed. A yearning for "sweet" intercession, for the "privileges of a disembodied spirit" during "the epoch of annihilated space" (195), permeates Coverdale's romance. It is the yearning of a timorous pilgrim in search of a refuge from "whirling" bodies – a refuge from *internal* subversion.

"The emerging from their lurking-places of evil characters"

Writing to Sophia approximately a year before journeying to Brook Farm, Hawthorne shared with his future wife a most disturbing dream: "Dearest, thou didst not come into my dreams, last night; but, on the contrary, I was engaged in assisting the escape of Louis XVI and Marie Antoinette from Paris, during the French Revolution. And sometimes, by an unaccountable metamorphosis, it seemed as if my mother and sisters were in the place of the King and Queen."[84] The dream anticipates that double perspective of revolutionism and victimization informing *Blithedale*'s masquerade scene. A year away from "assisting" reformers, he dreams a revolutionary drama that aligns him, the heroic protector, with endangered Catholic monarchs – his mother and sisters, "sweet, sacred Virgin mother[s]." Perplexed and disturbed by the "unaccountable" specter of revolution he himself could dream up, Hawthorne nevertheless eventually joined the reformers at Brook Farm. However, shortly after quitting the associationists, he jotted in his notebook a nightmarish germ for a future tale or sketch: "The emerging from their lurking-places of evil characters, on some occasion suited to their action – they having been quite unknown to the world hitherto. For instance, the French Revolution brought out such wretches" (8:240). The notebook jotting would suggest, along the lines of his French Revolutionary dream, that even during his short-lived personal participation in Brook Farm, he continued to remain deeply suspicious of a social revolutionism that threatened to summon from hidden "lurking-places," not the solitary heroic antipatriarchal Gray Champion, but a wretched mob. Conveying in a dream description, a notebook entry, and (later) the guillotining scene of "The Custom-House" a "monarchical" dread of "evil characters" who would make of him too a victim or, even more frighteningly, a regicide and matricide, Hawthorne can seem to possess, like Coverdale (and like Charles II and Louis XVI), a yearning for "Catholic" forms of order and community.[85]

But this sort of psychobiographical reading would move us much too easily to what I believe would be an overly schematic (and containing) interpretation of Hawthorne as ambivalent Protestant yearning for institutional and hierarchical order, yearning, in effect, for "Catholic" conversion. Rather than embodying his utter distance from and disdain for a Protestant reformational politics that tends toward conspiracy, *Blithedale* enacts in a very complex way Hawthorne's dispiriting notion that a Protestant revolutionary attack on rigid institutions, particularly given Protestantism's traditional unease with the unconstrained body, can yield its own new rigidities. In this respect we can interpret Coverdale's retreats to the unmediated and unenclosed space of the hermitage as self-defensive responses to Blithedale's increasingly monastic/imprisoning character. Arguably, in his strenuous desire to resist the pressures of a group increasingly under Hollingsworth's command, Coverdale emerges as a proud Puritan among fallen Pilgrims, committed, as I believe Hawthorne was committed, to the antiauthoritarian ideals of the original Protestant reformers. Thus despite *Blithedale*'s alternately satirical and anxious view of communitarian reformers, it would be mistaken to view the novel, in the words of communitarian John Noyes, as "a poetico–sneering romance."[86] Rather, it is a romance that, through its insider–outsider perspective, expresses Hawthorne's deeply conflicting attitudes toward the "revolutionary" reformism that for a while he so sympathetically embraced.

But it is a romance too that raises troubling questions about the teleology of Protestant reform. Hawthorne's doubts about Brook Farm/Blithedale's reformism, doubts relevant as well to a variety of earlier Protestant "re-formations" – from Quaker persecutions, to witch executions, to political revolutionism, to crusading nativism – can be phrased in the following terms. If, as historian William G. McLoughlin observes, the perfectionist reformism of the 1830s and 1840s promoted the idea that "human nature is open to total renovation in the twinkling of an eye, and so, then, is the nature of society"; and if, as a result, there arose among Protestant reformers the belief that "society is totally malleable to the power that works in harmony with God's will," how then ensure the parallelism between reformism and God's will?[87] When we sense the lack of such parallelism in, among other works, "Endicott and the Red Cross," "The Gentle Boy," "A Bell's Biography," and *Blithedale*, we are in accord with Hawthorne's mistrust of millennial reformers who do not seem to have been vouchsafed even an inkling as to God's providential plan. It is tempting to view such concerns and hesitations as "sneering," but foundational doubts about reform and revolution are quite different from an alarmist reactionism. To take the more extreme case, when the self-assured Roman Catholic Orestes Brownson addresses the matter of

Protestant reform in his countersubversive *The Spirit-Rapper*, he unhesitatingly insists upon his ability to discern a fundamental lack of congruence between God's plot and the social plottings of America's and Europe's reformers. Given that Hawthorne shares some of Brownson's concerns about the potentially destabilizing effects of Protestant reform, and given too that he surely shares some of Coverdale's concerns about the bases (and worth) of his "unshackled" art, it is noteworthy that he manages to invest *Blithedale* with such idealistic and even revolutionary insider energies. Though an anxious romance, *Blithedale* is not polemically or mean-spiritedly alarmist, for Hawthorne, unlike Brownson, never faithfully claims to possess an untroubled ability to read God's plans and purposes.

Where Hawthorne does seem to place some faith, however, as reflected in the "romance" ending of *The House of the Seven Gables,* is in the regenerative and redemptive possibilities of reconstituted family. That is why, as with Cooper's idealization of Senator Soranzo's whole and loving family in the midst of fragmented Venice, Coverdale, after fleeing the fragmenting "great and general family" at Blithedale, likewise idealizes a blithesome family prospering in the midst of the city. Cooper had written of Venice in *The Bravo,* "While nearly every dwelling has one of its fronts on a canal, there are always communications by the rear with the interior passages of the town."[88] Similarly, within his rented hotel room, the appropriate residence for such a spectral interpreter, Coverdale views the New England city "Venetianly": "Realities keep in the rear, and put forward an advance guard of show and humbug" (3:149). He then peers through the "show and humbug" of a boardinghouse's rear window to descry the "real":

> At the window of the next story below, two children, prettily dressed, were looking out. By-and-by, a middle-aged gentleman came softly behind them, kissed the little girl, and playfully pulled the little boy's ear. It was a papa, no doubt, just come in from his counting-room or office; and anon appeared mama, stealing as softly behind papa, as he had stolen behind the children, and laying her hand on his shoulder to surprise him. Then followed a kiss between papa and mamma, but a noiseless one; for the children did not turn their heads. (3:150–1)

Significantly, this sentimentalized picture prompts Coverdale's one unambiguously passionate affirmation in the novel: "I bless God for these good folks!" (3:151). As in *The Bravo,* and as in many of the novels written by America's "scribbling women," the imaging of the enclosed family as a restorative and stabilizing haven in a heartless world calls attention to outside instabilities, confusions, and plottings.

For the typical countersubversive – Brockden Brown's Sophia being the best literary example – melodramatic conceptions make sense of the world's plots by offering easy distinctions between heroes and villains, and clear political imperatives. Though Hawthorne's early appropriations of nativist discourse preserved the rhetorical form of that discourse even while challenging its Manichean totalizations, his work increasingly reveals, particularly by the mid-1840s, "a confusion of Popish and Protestant emblems" that ultimately breaks down the distinction between heroes and villains and complicates political imperatives. Accordingly, we must be wary of imputing to his work a stable or univocal ideological perspective. *The Scarlet Letter,* for example, could be read as an anticipatory expression of the nostalgia for Catholicism putatively informing *The Marble Faun.* Encouraging this line of interpretation are Hawthorne's many sympathetic references to Hester's "Catholicism": The Puritans may view the "gorgeous luxuriance" (1:53) of her scarlet letter as sacrilegious, but her sumptuary artistry reflects the gorgeousness of Anglo-Catholic art (and links her to Hawthorne the artist); the Puritans may punish her for the crime of adultery, but her loving commitment to Pearl on the scaffold evokes "the image of Divine Maternity" (1:56); she may settle on the outskirts of the Puritan community as a social pariah, but her continued good works within the community eventually lead her to be regarded as a "Sister of Mercy" (1:161) whose "scarlet letter had the effect of the cross on a nun's bosom" (1:163).[89] To a large extent, of course, the "Catholicizing" of Hester is generated less by Hawthorne than by the Puritans, who in effect demonize and marginalize her threatening sexual energies by labeling them "Catholic." As we become aware that the Puritans' disciplinary relation to Hester finds its conceptual justification in the imaging of her as, in Governor Bellingham's words, "a scarlet woman, and a worthy type of her of Babylon!" (1:110), we become highly suspicious of a millennially inclined community that tends "to interpret all meteoric appearances, and other natural phenomena . . . as so many revelations from a supernatural source" (1:154).

Such is Hawthorne's skepticism of the ability of any reform group to obtain access to divinity, and such is his dark view of the ways in which "men no worse than their neighbours . . . [can] grow cruel, merely because they possessed the power of inflicting harm" (1:40–1), that his representation of the Puritans' "Utopia of human virtue and happiness" (1:47) ultimately discloses its "Catholic" character. After all, with their prisons, courts, and governmental structures, the Puritans, like their descendant Hollingsworth, are thoroughgoing institutionalists committed to hierarchy and social control. Furthermore, the luxurious embellishments to Governor Bellingham's mansion, Hawthorne remarks, "might have befitted Aladdin's palace, rather than the mansion of a grave old Puritan ruler" (1:103). In fact, when the Puritan leaders participate in public ceremonies, they can seem, like the English rulers of Hawthorne's revolutionary tales, both aristocratic and Catholic: "Deep ruffs, painfully wrought bands, and gorgeously embroidered gloves, were all deemed necessary to the official state of men assuming the reins of power; and were readily allowed to individuals dignified by rank or wealth, even while sumptuary laws forbade these and similar extravagances to the plebeian order" (1:82).

As opposed to these hierarchical aristocrats who use their institutions, as Cooper's Venetian oligarchs use theirs, to maintain an "inquisitorial watch" (1:81) over the community's stigmatized deviants, Hester seems anything but Catholic. In the anti-institutional spirit of seventeenth-century Protestant reformers, and in the antinomian spirit of Anne Hutchinson, she finds the "world's law was no law for her mind" (1:164).[90] Accordingly, like Cromwell's fellow Puritans, and like Hawthorne's New England Blithedalers, she views her conventional society as a fallen society and concludes that reform requires revolution: "As a first step," she decides, "the whole system of society is to be torn down, and built up anew" (1:165). To be sure, such extreme revolutionism, the narrator remarks, threatens to isolate Hester "without rule or guidance, in a moral wilderness" (1:199); and thus, from the perspective of Hawthorne the Victorian moralist, her antipatriarchal revolutionism "taught her much amiss" (1:200). We might argue, then, that the similarity between Hester's world-historical antimonarchical revolutionism, as revealed in Chapter 13, and the French Revolutionism of "The Custom-House," which claims Hawthorne as monarch-like victim, encourages a reading of *The Scarlet Letter* as a Burkean antirevolutionary text (or even a Brownsonian anti-Protestant text) that, on balance, sanctions the "Catholic" institutional impositions of the Puritan reformers as necessary acts of social control.[91]

But I would maintain that what is true for *Blithedale* is also true for *The Scarlet Letter:* Revolution so unnerved Hawthorne because he was imaginatively responsive to it. Like Coverdale, he was simultaneously an insider and an outsider, and that double perspective informs his oscillating portrait of Hester as Catholic/Protestant. Certainly if Hawthorne were unsympathetic either to Hester's "Catholic" artistry or to her "Protestant" revolutionism, there would be little sense of conflict in the novel. And if he were not concerned that the very revolutionism that he finds so tempting could bring to the fore, as he wrote in "Another View of Hester," "shadowy guests, that would have been as perilous as demons to their entertainer" (1:164), there would be little tension in the novel as well.

Certainly a novel that is generally seen as lacking tension is *The Marble Faun* (1860), Hawthorne's postconsular romance of corruption and redemption in Catholic Rome of the 1850s. With its numerous descriptions of famous paintings and sculptures, the romance seems to give full and explicit expression to the attraction to "artistic" and "sumptuary" Catholicism implicit in *The Scarlet Letter*. The attraction to Catholic art extends in the novel to other aspects of Roman Catholicism, particularly its institutional availability of confession. In *The Scarlet Letter* Dimmesdale's need for confessional relief eventually "drove him to practices, more in accordance with the old, corrupted faith of Rome" (1:144): He begins whipping himself with a scourge. Does Hawthorne mean to suggest that Catholic confession would have provided Dimmesdale with a needed escape from the guilt-ridden culture of the Protestants? That is the suggestion of James Russell Lowell, who reported in a letter of 1860 to Jane Norton: "I have seen Hawthorne twice. . . . He is writing another story. He said also that it had been part of his plan in 'The Scarlet Letter' to make Dimmesdale confess himself to a Catholic priest. I, for one, am sorry he didn't. It would have been psychologically admirable."[92] Hawthorne himself remarked in an 1858 notebook entry on the confessionals of St. Peter's: "If I had had a murder on my conscience or any other great sin, I think I should have been inclined to kneel down there, and pour it into the safe secrecy of the confessional. What an institution that is!" (4:59). When, in a climactic scene of *The Marble Faun*, Hawthorne has Hilda, the self-proclaimed "daughter of the Puritans" (4:54), actually enter one of St. Peter's confessionals in search of psychological and spiritual solace, it would appear that we have come a long way indeed from Hawthorne's nativistic "Churches and Cathedrals" and, as noted in the preface to this chapter, that a deliberately self-conscious rhetoric means to emphasize that distance. We are told, for example, that Hilda, who "had not always been adequately impressed by the grandeur of this mighty Cathedral" (4:348), regarding it as "a gay piece of cabinet-work on a Titanic scale" (4:349), now suddenly perceives it "as a magnificent, comprehensive majestic symbol of religious faith" (4:350). Tormented by having witnessed Donatello's murder of Miriam's model, she finds a receptive priest and "poured out the dark story which had infused its poison into her innocent life" (4:357). In doing so, she experiences, unlike Dimmesdale, a soothing and restorative sense of relief: "When the hysteric gasp, the strife between words and sobs, had subsided, what a torture had passed away from her soul!" (4:357–8).

But it passes not without the taint of confessional violation. Just before Hilda's confession, Hawthorne warns of the possibility of Catholic expediency: "Had the Jesuits known the situation of this troubled heart, her inheritance of New England puritanism would hardly have protected the poor girl from the pious strategy of those good Fathers" (4:344). As it turns out, soon after the confession Hilda is betrayed by her selected priest and, so it appears, is subsequently used as blackmail to coerce Miriam and Donatello into surrendering to papal authorities. These authorities – priests and armed soldiers – are ubiquitous in the novel; and it must be stressed that despite Hawthorne's seeming attraction to Roman Catholic rituals and institutions in certain scenes, the repeated descriptions of French and Italian militia suggest that he remains concerned about Roman Catholicism's tendencies toward despotism.[93]

Hawthorne's wavering attraction–repulsion relationship to Catholicism, as enacted in *The Marble Faun,* reflects a similar wavering in American culture during the 1850s. This was the decade that saw the astonishing, albeit short-lived, political power of the nativist Know-Nothings and the publication of such shrilly anti-Catholic texts as Edward Beecher's *The Papal Conspiracy Exposed* (1855) and the anonymous *Pope, or President?* (1859). But the 1850s also saw cultural commentators ranging from Hawthorne's friend George Stillman Hillard to James Jackson Jarves discovering in Rome a glorious artistry that prompted a revaluation of the city's supposedly despotic trappings. As Jarves remarked on the Sistine Chapel in *Italian Sights and Papal Principles* (1856), "No one can enter this beautiful chapel, and behold the multitudes kneeling in silent adoration before the sacrament, without feeling stirred within him the spirit of devotion."[94] In part, the Gothic revival and Catholic nostalgia of the 1850s reflected concerns among social elites that the institutions of antebellum (Victorian) culture were no longer regarded by "the multitudes" with a "spirit of devotion." To these elites, the Roman Catholic church presented itself as an institutional model of hierarchical control during a decade, as the next chapter explores in fuller detail, that saw an increasing realization of such control in prisons, factories, and plantations.

From Hawthorne's point of view, however, it cannot be overlooked that the church's advocacy of hierarchy, in the context of the European revolutions of 1848–9, smacked of reactionary priestcraft. There is thus a strong current of sympathy in *The Marble Faun* for Miriam as anti-patriarchal revolutionary. Sympathetic to Miriam's revolutionary energy and imagination while simultaneously made uneasy by the prospect of an actual social revolution, Hawthorne presents the Roman carnival near the end of the novel as a possible safe outlet for revolutionism. "Everyone seemed lawless," he writes of the gaiety; yet "nobody was rude" (4:441). Like the Roman Catholic confessional, the Roman carnival allows for a ritual release of throttled energies within a setting that keeps them in check. It is true that a safeguard against these energies breaking loose is maintained by "a strong patrol of Papal dragoons" (4:441). As Hawthorne remarks, "Had that chained tiger-cat, the Roman populace, shown only so much as the tip of his claws, the sabres would have been

4

"Follow Your Leader"

Captains and Mutineers in Herman Melville's Benito Cereno

Though experience has shown that revolutions and political movements – unless when they have been conducted with the most guarded caution and moderation – have generally terminated in results just the opposite of what was expected from them, the angry ape will still play his fantastic tricks, and put in motion machinery, the action of which he no more comprehends or foresees than he comprehends the mysteries of infinity.

William Harper, *Memoir on Slavery*

Who aint a slave? Tell me that.

Melville, *Moby-Dick*

Benito Cereno, Herman Melville's unsettling novella of black revolutionary conspiracy, was serialized in the October–December 1855 issues of *Putnam's,* a widely circulating periodical whose editors took care, so they assured, "that nothing in the remotest degree offensive to propriety or good taste defaces these pages."[1] Though accorded but scant notice in reviews of *Piazza Tales* (1856), wherein the novella was reprinted, *Benito Cereno* now seems an obviously central literary meditation on the problem of slavery in antebellum culture. Less obvious, at least for a while, was Melville's attitude toward slavery and rebellious blacks. F. O. Matthiessen initiated debate on the subject in 1941, judging the novella to be "superficial" because its presentation of "the embodiment of good in the pale Spanish captain and of evil in the mutinied African crew" obscures the fact that Babo and his compatriots "were slaves and that evil had thus originally been done to them." Sidney Kaplan's 1957 reappraisal of Babo as "a maritime Nat Turner" offered but a partial revision of Matthiessen's reading, for Kaplan followed Matthiessen in regarding Melville's attitude toward the blacks as fundamentally racist.[2] By the 1960s, however, with the civil rights movement stimulating scholars to take a second look at *Benito Cereno*'s racial politics, critical thought swung full circle: Matthiessen was rejected outright and Kaplan was seen to have "erred badly on occasion" in failing to perceive Melville's ironic uses of black stereotypes. Emerging from a flurry of activity during the 1960s and 1970s was a new critical consensus that saw *Benito Cereno* as a scornful attack on Delano's blinding innocence, a damning indictment of the evils of chattel slavery, and a rousing celebration of black rebellion.[3] And with the issue of the novella's politics seemingly settled once and for all, Melville suddenly towered over American culture as a Jeremiah who with bold certainty fashioned a progressive symbolic action vilifying racism and endorsing rebellion.

Yet while post-1960s commentators were generally right in identifying an antislavery thematics in *Benito Cereno,* they may very well have diminished our experience of the text as a literary event and as an act of the historical imagination. Reading *Benito Cereno* has become an exercise in certainty, in literary mastery, an occasion to offer pious denunciations of Delano and Cereno and fraternal embraces to Babo and his fellow conspirators. As a result, a dynamic and threatening text has been almost entirely stripped of any felt anxiety, implicating presence, and, ironically, transhistorical power. Robert Lowell's verse-drama *Benito Cereno* (1964) played an especially influential role in this development. Presenting Delano as a self-avowed racist standing in righteous opposition to blacks conceived unambiguously as freedom fighters, Lowell built his play to a moment of revelation, not of black conspiracy but of white malevolence: At the play's conclusion Delano shoots the revolutionary "Babu" and, as the lights dim, pumps five more bullets into his lifeless body. By placing the audience at a revulsed spectatorial distance from Delano, and by linking the sea captain's violence to his imperial claims to power, Lowell writes out of the play what I will argue is absolutely central to Melville's novella: the way in which Delano's interpretive uncertainties undergird a relative reluctance to use power. And by stigmatizing Captain Delano as a malign other with whom we share no common ground, Lowell consequently frees the enlightened spectator, as revisionary readings of *Benito Cereno* free the enlightened reader, from any taint of Delano-like complicity and blindness and thus from the perils of participating in Delano's anxious effort to see his way past the nightmare of a black mutinous conspiracy.[4]

But Melville would have insisted – such, I believe, was his historicism – that during the American 1850s there was no escape for white Americans from insurrectionary nightmares. Fears of rebellious slaves were regularly voiced by Southern proslavery writers, who defended the institution of slavery as the best possible means of containing and controlling black violence. While Northern celebrants of "free labor" saw themselves as worlds apart from Southern enslavers, they too remained fearful about the prospect of black violence, for it was a tenet central to antislavery writing that the presence of chattel slavery in republican America only exacerbated the potential for a "war of extermination" between the races. Furthermore, and posing a challenge to easy schematic generalizations about sectional difference, Northern elites possessed their own related fears of insurrectionary violence. These fears contributed to the rise of urban-reform institutions – such as prisons, mental asylums, and almshouses – which were celebrated as the best possible means of containing and controlling potential violence, not of the black slaves, but of the urban poor, especially Catholics and other European immigrants, who likewise were feared as incipient insurrectionaries.

Significantly for interpretation of *Benito Cereno,* both the debate on slavery and the debate on the reform institution found their way into the antebellum sea narrative, which served as a laboratory for testing the desires and concerns inherent in the idealization of institutions in both sections of the country. Like the simultaneously loathsome and appealing Catholic monastery, and like Hollingsworth's proposed prison, the ideal ship of many antebellum sea narratives was a hierarchical and familial order containing a kindly paternal captain and a willingly submissive childlike crew. A similarly idealized image of hierarchical and familial order informed proslavery and urban-reform tracts, and the discourse of all these texts shared a broadly Victorian evocation of organic community and a concomitant anxiety that conspiratorial irruptions from below could precipitate social collapse.[5] The most dreaded form of insurrectionary subversion within the South was black revolt; within the ghettos of expanding Northern cities, riots; and within the isolated, self-contained society of the ship, mutiny.

In this chapter I propose to investigate the ways in which the social and interpretive concerns underlying the idealization of the slave and reform institution took expression in contemporaneous sea narratives, texts that typically imaged the seaman as slave and prisoner, the captain as slave driver and prisonkeeper, and the ship as plantation and prison. An examination of Melville's depictions of mutiny within the ship as institution will set the stage for an extended discussion of *Benito Cereno,* his dread-filled novella of subversion. The issues central to the antebellum sea narrative and to the transsectional debate on institutionalism are central as well to *Benito Cereno* and affect in crucial ways Melville's representation of a slave revolt. We tend to ignore the institutional context and concerns of this troubling text that, most importantly, unfolds from the point of view of a sea captain. I want therefore to challenge the tendency to read *Benito Cereno* as a transcendingly assured attack on enslavers and racists. By considering the black conspiracy in *Benito Cereno* in connection with contemporaneous fears of subversive insurrectionism, I hope to disclose the ways in which the social-critical force of the text emerges from Melville's construction of an implicating narrative that addresses his and his readers' complicitous entanglement in a web of anxiety, desire, and power.[6]

"Perfect sea order"

Although historians of the antebellum period have traditionally agreed that irreconcilable differences in sociopolitical values characterized North and South and contributed to the coming of the Civil War, generalizations about absolute differences between the sections have recently been rigorously questioned. In a study of their social, political, and economic structures, for example, Edward Pessen concludes that the sections actually had a good deal in common: "The South's political system of republicanism and limited democracy, like its hierarchical social structure, conformed closely to the prevailing arrangements in the North, as they also did to the classic features of a capitalistic order."[7] Though fully aware of the differences between Southern defenders of slavery and Northern reformers, abolitionist and otherwise, historians have noted as well that spokespersons on both sides "found no fault with the social hierarchy."[8] In fact, by the 1830s these spokespersons became mutually obsessed with the possibility that insurrections from below could overturn such hierarchy. Thus William Gilmore Simms could aggressively maintain in "The Morals of Slavery" (1837) that fears of what he termed "mutiny and revolt" were not simply the province of Southerners wary of potentially subversive slaves:

> But, even did there exist among the people of Charleston and the South generally, an apprehension of mutiny and revolt among their serviles, to what would it amount? What would it prove? . . . Suppose we grant it, and in what then does our condition as a community, and our relations with our slaves, differ from that of any European people? . . . Why are the walks of the great city garrisoned with spies to report the sayings and doings of the populace? Why does England growl at the bare mention of Ireland, and present her bayonets, if she but stirs, in her stagnating sleep? And why does France burden herself with the support of half a million of armed men? Why does Russia the same? Why is Austria only a great camp? Why does New-York call out its militia to support the sheriff and collect the rents of the Patroon –

and unavailingly? . . . It is because authority every where dreads the revolt of the inpatient, toiling, vexed, weary and ignorant inferiority.[9]

Simms simultaneously evokes and betrays the social anxieties informing the American (and European) mentality of the time. In both North and South, those of the middling and upper classes were haunted by fears of insurrectionary subversion, of "mutiny," to work just a bit longer with Simms's felicitous metaphor, that kept these uneasy "sea captains" perpetually on the lookout for plotters in the ship of state.

Although post-Revolutionary America saw only three large-scale slave conspiracies – the Gabriel Prosser conspiracy of 1800, the Denmark Vesey conspiracy of 1822, and the Nat Turner rebellion of 1831 – each plot horrified Southerners and summoned the nightmare of the San Domingo slave revolt of the 1790s, "the bloodiest and most shocking insurrection ever recorded in the annals of history," as the prominent proslavery spokesman Thomas Dew put it. The specter of a slave uprising in which more than sixty thousand people died and the first black republic was established came to exemplify the worst that could happen if whites failed to maintain a vigilant watchfulness over their slaves. Consequently, the Nat Turner slave rebellion, the only black revolt resulting in a substantial loss of white lives – approximately sixty, including women and children, were killed – dealt an especially jolting blow to Southerners. As Dew observed in his widely read *Review of the Debates in the Virginia Legislature of 1831–32* (1832), in the wake of Turner's rebellion "the imagination was suffered to conjure up the most appalling phantoms, and picture to itself a crisis in the vista of futurity, when the overwhelming numbers of the blacks would rise superior to all restraint, and involve the fairest portion of our land in universal ruin and desolation." Such a crisis, Dew prophesied with melodramatic flair, would lead to the utter collapse of Southern civilization:

> But one limited massacre is recorded in Virginia history; let her liberate her slaves, and every year you would hear of insurrections and plots, and every day would perhaps record a murder; the melancholy tale of Southampton would not alone blacken the page of our history, and make the tender mother shed the tear of horror over her babe as she clasped it to her bosom; others of a deeper die [*sic!*] would thicken upon us; those regions where the brightness of polished life has dawned and brightened into full day, would relapse into darkness, thick and full of horrors.

However, Dew believed that slavery had little to do with such "ruin and desolation," for the slaves, he asserted, were absolutely content with their lot. They became killers only when abolitionists meddled, constraints were lifted, and a freedom to which they did not aspire was forced upon them. Within the slave plantation, Dew assured his readers, "a merrier being does not exist on the face of the globe, than the negro slave of the United States."[10]

From Dew's idealizing (and ahistorical) perspective, the institution of slavery contained the black's savage energies and nurtured his merriment; "domestic slavery," he insisted, "seems to be the only means of . . . moderating his savage temper." Like most proslavery writers, then, he failed to entertain the possibility that the enslavement of blacks was an originating act giving rise to the blacks' "savage temper." Instead, by staking out a dualistic opposition between the merry and the savage slave, he perpetuated the already deeply held notion that the slave was essentially a savage. Merriment was perhaps but a cloaking mask; and Dew wanted Southerners to realize that beneath the mask lurked the threat of a terrible insurrectionary violence. That a surface calm might be cloaking an incipient rebellion – and could even be taken as chief evidence for impending trouble – was also suggested by Thomas Gray, who declared in his preface to *The Confessions of Nat Turner* (1831), "It will thus appear, that whilst every thing upon the surface of society wore a calm and peaceful aspect; whilst not one note of preparation was heard to warn the devoted inhabitants of woe and death, a gloomy fanatic was revolving in the recesses of his own dark, bewildered, and overwrought mind, schemes of indiscriminate massacre to the whites."[11]

Anxious about such "schemes" and determined to "moderate" the "merriment" of the slaves, Dew called for increased vigilance and supervision on the plantation. His widely reprinted text encouraged proslavery writers throughout the South to speak with renewed fervor about the benefits of slavery and the responsibilities of the master. These writers believed, George Fredrickson explains, that if "the control of the master was firm and assured, the slave would be happy, loyal, and affectionate; but remove or weaken the authority of the master, and he would revert to type as a bloodthirsty savage."[12] In an effort to obscure the authoritarian and disciplinary character of slavery, proslavery writers regularly appealed to reigning Victorian ideals of domesticity, picturing the slave plantation as a "merry" community very much resembling a happy family: In numerous post-1830s tracts the slaveowner was imaged as a kindly but firm paternal authority who beneficently watched over his sometimes refractory childlike slaves. And like communitarian reformers, who also pictured their societies as familial, proslavery writers proclaimed that the slave institution, as opposed to the fallen institutions of Northern market society, offered status and place to all of its members. William John Grayson wrote in *Letters of Curtius* (1851), "Every plantation is an organized community, a phalanstery, as Fourier would call it – where all work, where each member gets subsistence and a home and the

most industrious larger pay and profits to their own superior industry."
As George Fitzhugh explained in *Sociology for the South* (1854), the slave
plantation, like Fourier's phalanstery, provided a refuge from the heartless marketplace: "The poor man is burdened with the care of finding a
home, and procuring employment, and attending to all domestic wants
and concerns. Slavery relieves our slaves of these cares altogether." But
clearly where Fitzhugh's and Grayson's vision foundered was on the
stark truth that the plantation contained masters and slaves, and invariably the masters were white and the slaves black. "We need never have
white slaves in the South," Fitzhugh trumpeted, "because we have black
ones."[13] Vigilant, paternal "white ones" over suspiciously merry "black
ones," the proslavery writers averred, would help to contain the savage
irruption of "mutiny and revolt" and, hence, preserve the social order.

Southerners, Simms rightly contended, were not alone in fearing mutinous rebellions and in searching for means to contain such rebellions.
Concerned about the large-scale immigration of the 1830s and 1840s, the
strains of industrialization, and the diminishment of the traditional authority of church and family, many Northerners began to fear that the
stability of the republic was threatened by an insurrectionary energy
lurking just beneath the surface of what came to be regarded as the
mysterious and wicked city. Especially worrying to cultural elites – and
also to many middle-class tradesmen, workers, and villagers, and even
those of the working classes seeking to identify themselves with consensus values as a way of achieving middle-class "American" identity –
were the markedly increased number of riots in major Northeast cities
between 1830 and 1860. These riots, along with an upsurge "of almost
continuous disorder and turbulence among the urban poor," historian
Paul Boyer observes, "seemed simply part of a frightening, intensifying
cycle of violence – a cycle perhaps presaging that cataclysmic social
collapse which some believed the inevitable result of urbanization."[14]

Exacerbating Northern concerns about "a crisis in the vista of futurity" was an aggressive countersubversive rhetoric, adopted by radical
labor spokespersons during the late 1820s and 1830s, that imaged managers and owners as types of aristocratic slaveholders and workers as victims of "wage slavery."[15] Fueled by the Antimasonic/Jacksonian attack
on aristocracy, this oppositional working-class rhetoric soon became a
regular feature of popular texts. At the center of Lippard's bestselling
The Monks of Monk Hall, for example, was a prophetic dream vision of
an utterly subverted Philadelphia in 1950, wherein "the slaves of the city,
white and black. . . . the slaves of the cotton Lord and the factory Prince . . . and by their sides the grim overseer" march grimly through the
city on "the anniversary of the death of freedom." Culminating with an
apocalyptic image of God wreaking His vengeance on "Sodom," the

novel's dream vision clearly was intended by Lippard to promote resistance to what its ghostly spirit calls "Priest-craft, and Slave-craft, and Traitor-craft."[16]

In the South the infamous rhetorical manifestation of slave resistance was former slave David Walker's *Appeal . . . to the Coloured Citizens of the World* (1829), first published in Boston, which urged enslaved blacks to "kill or be killed."[17] In the North the attack on "wage slavery," especially by leaders of the New York Workingman's Party and other such organizations, found its millennial fulfillment in Orestes Brownson's "The Laboring Classes" (1840). Arguing that those who work for wages are just as enslaved as those who toil on the plantation, and going so far as to suggest, as Fitzhugh would suggest in the 1850s, that "the slave system [is] decidedly preferable to the system at wages," Brownson lambasted capitalistic managers for their villainy: "Wages is a cunning device of the devil, for the benefit of tender consciences, who would retain all the advantages of the slave system, without the expense, trouble, and odium of being slave-holders." Declaring himself an enemy to all forms of slavery, however, whether practiced on the plantation or in the city, Brownson called for the abolition of the national bank, monopolies, and hereditary property rights. And in the spirit of David Walker he advocated violent resistance on the part of the "slave" to bring about these revolutionary changes:

> The rich, the business community, will never voluntarily consent to it, and we think we know too much of human nature to believe that it will ever be effected peaceably. It will be effected only by the strong arm of physical force. It will come, if it ever come at all, only at the conclusion of war, the like of which the world as yet has never witnessed, and from which, however inevitable it may seem to the eye of philosophy, the heart of Humanity recoils with horror.[18]

For Brownson before his conversion to Roman Catholicism, as for Lippard and other champions of America's "white slaves," rebellion was a form of countersubversion, a merited attack on corrupt aristocrats who, like Cooper's oligarchical Venetians, duplicitously espoused republican ideals while exploiting the labor of others for their own economic ends. Accordingly, rebellion against the standing order could be justified as nothing less than a reenactment of the American Revolution against antirepublican oligarchical despots.

The appeal to Revolutionary tradition, Jacksonian ideals of individual sovereignty, and millennial apocalyptic violence were also central to Northern abolitionist writings, particularly Garrison's texts of the late 1820s and 1830s, which no doubt informed and helped to shape the radical labor discourse of the period. In late 1831, for example, Garrison asserted that Nat Turner and his coconspirators "deserve no more censure than the Greeks in destroying the Turks, or the Poles in exterminating the Russians, or our fathers in slaying the British." And he declared several months later, "Despotism in a republic is as sure of punishment, as in a monarchy." That punishment, so he prophesied, would come in the form of an apocalyptic slave revolt. "Woe to the safety of this people!" he proclaimed in his Fourth of July Address of 1829. "The nation will be shaken as if by a mighty earthquake. A cry of horror, a cry of revenge, will go up to heaven in the darkness of midnight, and re-echo from every cloud. Blood will flow like water – the blood of guilty men and of innocent women and children. Then will be heard lamentations and weeping, such as will blot out the remembrance of the horrors of St. Domingo."[19]

Not surprisingly, the symbiotic rhetoric of working-class and abolitionist spokespersons heightened fears among many Northerners of the prospect of confronting rebellious "slaves" in their own region. The specter of a revolutionary and apocalyptic violence from which, in Brownson's words, "the heart of Humanity recoils with horror" contributed to at least three major defensive strategies on the part of elites who felt threatened by such challenges to social hierarchy and stability. The first, and one that proved successful for quite some time, was an effort to define labor "combinations" as illegal forms of conspiracy; the period from 1800 to 1835 saw the establishment of several such precedents.[20] The second was the depiction, by the Whigs in particular, of labor radicalism and urban violence as linked forms of conspiracy that had as their common origin the "popish" plotting of the Roman Catholic church; countersubversive claims of this sort helped to keep alive nativist activity during the 1840s and 1850s. The third strategy, and one that was ostensibly apolitical but intimately related to both the nativism and communitarianism of the period, was the rise in the 1830s and 1840s of an urban reformism that sought to perpetuate republican ideals, and, for that matter, to preserve the Republic, through the creation of re-formative "total institutions." Erving Goffman writes, "A total institution may be defined as a place of residence and work where a large number of like-situated individuals, cut off from the wider society for an appreciable period of time, together lead an enclosed, formally administered round of life."[21] In antebellum America these institutions included prisons, mental asylums, almshouses, juvenile delinquent homes, and, relatedly, schools and factories. Sentimentalized as familial institutions, but with their insistence on the importance of separation, hierarchy, and paternalistic discipline bearing similarity to the "familial" slave plantation, these new institutions of social reform, so argued their promoters, would make model republicans of the dangerous working classes. As John Kasson observes, "The total institution represented the ultimate form in this period of the search for institutions of republican community."[22]

But though a case can be made that Northern urban reformers were motivated by a less than malevolent desire to preserve republican ideals of "free labor" and virtuous community, they nevertheless participated with Southern defenders of slavery in a drama of anxiety and social control that pivoted on the idealization of institutions as a necessary means of containing the irruption of socially threatening energies. From the reformers' apocalyptic perspective, as a historian of the movement notes, "nothing less than the safety and future of the republic was at issue, the triumph of good over evil, of order over chaos."[23] Like Southerners fearful of the slaves' savage violence, Northern reformers were concerned, as William Ellery Channing wrote in "Ministry for the Poor" (1835), that the working poor, when intemperate, would "take their place among the brutes" and inevitably threaten the republic with a brutish violence. The challenge facing urban reformers, then, was to find new ways of channeling to positive purposes the "savage" energies of potential rebels. In the Federalist tradition of Noah Webster, education reformer Horace Mann, who in the 1830s helped to establish a public mental hospital in Worcester, advocated well-ordered "Americanizing" public schools and other such institutions as a way of simultaneously controlling and refashioning the "mutinous" disposition of the restless laboring classes. "The favored classes may think they occupy favored apartments in the ship," he warned his constituents, "but, if it does founder, the state will go down with the steerage." Prison reformer Dorothea Dix expressed similar concerns about the "mutinous" tendencies of the incarcerated. Addressing the issue of "punishment by the lash," usually regarded by Northern reformers as an evil special to the slave plantation (or tyrannous ship), she allowed that at times harsh discipline might become a social necessity: "I am certain that I could never subdue my instinctive horror and disgust of punishment by the lash, as a means of producing submission and obedience. I could never order, witness, or permit its application; but I am forced, with unspeakable reluctance, to concede that I believe it may be sometimes *the only* mode, under the Auburn, or congregated system, by which an insurrectionary spirit can be conquered."[24]

Southerners idealized their hierarchical and disciplinary plantations because they were concerned about the "insurrectionary spirit" of their slaves. Northerners concerned about subversive insurrectionism similarly idealized their hierarchical and disciplinary total institutions as familial institutions that, more often than not, would rely not on force but on moral suasion; both Mann and Dix, it is only fair to note, in principle opposed corporal punishment.[25] Of course, the Northern urban-reform institution, unlike the plantation, was meant to "rehabilitate" the foreign, the poor, and the deviant – potential rebels all, in the eyes of social elites – and to produce loyal citizens who would work hard and "merrily" in the cities' expanding factories. But though celebrated in the 1830s and 1840s for their regenerative capabilities, by the 1850s these reform institutions, particularly the prison and asylum, had become custodial institutions that, like the slave plantation, really did seek to contain the "savage." To be sure, some reformers clung to their social-environmental belief that grim material conditions corrupted the poor; as Robert Hartley put it in 1853, "Degrade men to the condition of brutes, and they will have brutal propensities and passions."[26] But an increasing fear of the working poor led many others to conclude that those persons perennially exhibiting "brutal propensities and passions" could never be rehabilitated and so should be permanently shut away. Like the abolitionists who supported colonization for free and enslaved blacks, reformers at their most nervous wanted to gather up a perceived rebellious and vengeful poor, especially recent immigrants, and, in effect, return them to the ships by which they had arrived. Indeed, with their emphases on discipline, hierarchy, and custodial isolation, the new asylums, prisons, and other self-contained "familial" total institutions resembled not only the slave plantation but also the institution afloat of nautical romance – the well-ordered ship at sea.

Popularized by James Fenimore Cooper's nautical romances of the 1820s, antebellum sea narratives, particularly those written after the Panic of 1837, present the ship as an asylum that, for a while at least, fulfills the mutual needs of captains and seamen. At its most idealized and romanticized, the hierarchical ship, like the idealized reform institution, endows the impoverished young men seeking out its interiors with a renewed sense of place and purpose; it offers a substitute, and more adequate, familial order for those who have been cast adrift. Henry Mercier begins his *Life in a Man-of-War* (1841) with the confession that he joined the navy because he lacked the funds to pay his rent. In Charles Briggs's popular and aptly titled *The Adventures of Harry Franco, A Tale of the Great Panic* (1839), Franco takes to sea to escape bankruptcy; some twenty years earlier Briggs himself took to sea after his father went bankrupt. In *Working a Passage; or, Life in a Liner* (1844), a sequel to *Harry Franco*, Briggs explains why he offers the reading public yet another sea narrative: "My motive, then, in writing and publishing this little book, is to furnish a hint to those young men, very numerous I fear they are, who sometimes find themselves suddenly deprived of their accustomed means of support, and before they become used to standing alone, fall so heavily to the ground, as to be unable ever to rise again." Even Richard

Henry Dana, Jr.'s *Two Years Before the Mast* (1840), the most widely read
and influential sea narrative of the period, had as its genesis just such
social and economic concerns. As he confesses in his "Autobiographical
Sketch" (1842), he signed on with the *Pilgrim* in 1834 because "my father
was at this time embarrassed in his pecuniary condition, & I felt that I
was a burdn [sic] upon him." Writing to his brother after nearly seven
months at sea, Dana underscores the satisfactions obtained from serving
on the purposive ship: "I feel that I have done my duty in coming to sea,
and I can truly say that I am, at heart, lighter and happier, than I was
during my last year of idleness which I spent at home."[27]

Like America's communitarian societies of the antebellum period, the
ship as familial institution offers the promise of what Dana calls "perfect
sea order."[28] Central to the ship's "perfect" order, however, was a hierarchical social structure and disciplinary authority that, as numerous sea
writers warned, made the seaman over into a kind of slave. In an influential text, *Evils and Abuses in the Naval and Merchant Service, Exposed*
(1839), nautical reformer William McNally works explicitly with the
analogies of sailor to slave, ship to plantation, to press his call for the
abolition of flogging. Furthermore, he asserts that the practice of flogging on board Northern ships exposes the hypocrisy of abolitionists:

> Never let American citizens in the Northern states rail at slavery, or the
> punishment inflicted on slaves, or say that it is wrong, so long as their
> own sons, their own flesh and blood, their own seamen, their own free
> citizens, and the men to whom they look for protection in case of war,
> are daily subject to the same treatment as the slaves, whose degraded
> situation in the Southern states calls forth, so justly, the warmest sen-
> sibilities of the heart and nature of philanthropists.

McNally concludes his tract with the ominous suggestion that unjust
flogging may incite revenge and encourage mutiny: "Seamen know that
they are born free, and freemen will never submit to the lash of slavery."[29] The insider warning of "slave revolt," reminiscent of David
Walker's *Appeal*, makes *Evils and Abuses* one of the most provocative
texts of its kind.

Dana, of course, also works with the trope of the sailor-slave, depicting his fellow "common sailors" in *Two Years* as types of wily slaves:
"Jack is a slave aboard ship; but still he has many opportunities of
thwarting and balking his master." His fraternal sympathies underlie the
harrowing presentation of Captain Thompson's flogging of John and
Sam. In a scene looking forward to Simon Legree's flogging of Uncle
Tom in the hell of his slave plantation, the captain ferociously applies the
lash while blasphemously taunting the martyred John: "Don't call on
Jesus Christ. . . . *Call on Captain T[hompson].*" He then glares at his
potentially mutinous crew and reminds them of the essential reality of

their status on board ship, the reality that McNally had disclosed. "You've got a driver over you!" he declares. "Yes, a *slave-driver* – a *negro-driver!* I'll see who'll tell me he is n't a negro slave!" As a "slave," then, the outraged Dana entertains thoughts of a slave revolt: "The first and almost uncontrollable impulse was resistance." But he quickly controls this "uncontrollable impulse," renounces mutiny, and subsequently moralizes on his situation: "Bad as it was, it must be borne. It is what a sailor ships for." He thus offers what he wants his readers to take as an insider's defense, a defense from below in the forecastle, of the captain's actions: Tyrannical or not, Thompson acted to preserve the "perfect sea order" that "a sailor ships for." Dana explains, "I never knew a sailor who found fault with the orders and ranks of the service; and if I expected to pass the rest of my life before the mast, I would not wish to have the power of the captain diminished an iota."[30]

But while Dana in this scene suggests that he argues from the forecastle and for his fellow common sailors, by the time he wrote *Two Years* his attitude toward mutiny and revolt more accurately was a captaincy-oriented one, that of a nervous Boston Brahmin who came to value hierarchy and discipline as necessary constraints on the very "slaves" seemingly gaining his fraternal sympathies. This captain-like perspective informs the text's overall narrative; for as imaged in *Two Years,* the *Pilgrim* is an asylum that, like the new asylums of social reform, separates the dangerous poor from the rest of society, in this case by taking them off to sea. With its "crew of swearers," its overcrowded conditions that lead to petty quarrels, and its abundance of drunken "foreigners" – "It is to be remembered that more than three fourths of the seamen in our merchant vessels are foreigners" – the *Pilgrim* adopts the disciplinary controls characteristic of the urban total institution: "In no state prison are the convicts more regularly set to work, and more closely watched." Manifesting the alarmism of an anxious reformer, Dana explains to his readers why sea captains must keep their crews under constant surveillance:

> As things are now, many masters are obliged to sail without knowing anything of their crews, until they get out at sea. There may be pirates or mutineers among them; and one bad man will often infect all the rest; and it is almost certain that some of them will be ignorant foreigners, hardly understanding a word of our language, accustomed all their lives to no influence but force, and perhaps nearly as familiar with the use of the knife as with that of the marline spike. No prudent master, however peaceably inclined, would go to sea without his pistols and handcuffs.

Portraying the common seaman as in dire need of "religion and moral improvement" and as potentially violent, Dana, in the apocalyptic mode of Northern and Southern defenders of institutional control, concludes his text with a defense of the legal authority delegating to captains the most extreme disciplinary powers: "These are provided to meet exigencies, which all hope may never occur, and yet by possibility may occur, and if they should, and there were no power to meet them instantly, there would be an end to the government at once."[31]

As opposed to Cooper's early nautical romances, then, which extol the revolutionary Byronism of self-reliant sailors, Dana places supreme value on the ship as corporate-republican institution, fearing as he does, like other Northern reformers of the period, that revolutionary energies from below could precipitate social anarchy, "an end to the government at once." Yet because he also conveys a genuine fraternal concern for the rights of common sailors, *Two Years* appealed to a range of constituencies and emerged as the dominant sea narrative of the 1840s. Dana himself, following the publication of *Two Years,* became something of a celebrity and was deferred to as the principal spokesman for the values inscribed in the antebellum sea narrative. Thus it was perfectly consistent with his public persona and role that in early 1843 he should have taken it upon himself to decide for Americans whether on board another ship at sea – the U.S. naval brig *Somers* – the sort of "exigencies" he had warned about in *Two Years* had actually arisen to merit the absolute disciplinary response available to sea captains: capital punishment. Let us briefly review the widely publicized and debated *Somers* affair, a "sea narrative" of sorts that brings to a revealing focus the captain-like perspective on mutiny and revolt in antebellum culture.

In November 1842, Captain Alexander Slidell Mackenzie believed he detected on board the *Somers* an incipient mutiny and, after consulting with his officers, including Melville's first cousin Lieutenant Guert Gansevoort, ordered hanged three sailors: Philip Spencer (the son of President Tyler's secretary of war, John Canfield Spencer) and his two alleged accomplices, Elisha Small and Samuel Cromwell. Significantly, the ship at the time was not only overcrowded – 120 were aboard a ship meant for 90 – but it was also "manned" by apprentice sailors, a number of whom were under sixteen. The *Somer's* demographics thus in a sense literalized the familial metaphor central to the idealization of the ship as institution, providing Mackenzie and his officers with good reason to conceive of themselves as officer-fathers. Acting as firm parental guardians, the officers administered an unusually large number of floggings – forty-three – before ordering the executions. The hangings themselves were intended to serve as lifelong examples to impressionable "children" of what can befall the disobedient; they were also intended to preserve the jeopardized familial order. As Guert Gansevoort explained to his own family: "'It was not only the public property, the Flag of my country; & my own life that was in the utmost jeopardy; but the lives of the crew, (those that were true); but of those apprentices, those *children,* entrusted to the care of the Officers; for whose safety we were responsible . . . I had pledged myself, to extend parental care and advice.' "[32] Two weeks after the hangings, the *Somers* docked in New York and debate on the officers' "parental" actions ensued.

On the evidence of his empathy for the flogged sailors in *Two Years* and his contemporaneous reputation as the "Seaman's Friend," Dana might have been expected to side with the flogged and executed apprentice sailors. In *The Seaman's Friend* (1841), after all, he soberly urged captains to proceed with cautious deliberation before imposing discipline: "In many cases prudence may require a postponement of the proper punishment. The authority of the master, being in its nature parental, must be exercised with a due regard to the rights and interests of all parties." He noted too just how difficult the detection of an impending mutiny could be: "Every little instance of disobedience, or insolent conduct, or even force used against the master or other officer, will not be held a revolt or an endeavor to make a revolt."[33] But when confronted with allegations of an actual mutiny, Dana's anxieties as "captain" led him to view Mackenzie as a masterly disciplinarian who could do no wrong. His influential public defense of Mackenzie, a letter published in the 13 January 1843 New York *Evening Post* and reprinted in several other newspapers, expressed these anxieties by presenting Mackenzie and his officers as vulnerable gentlemen in the midst of an urban ghetto: crowded, restless, mysterious. Reporting on his inspection tour of the docked and deserted *Somers,* for example, Dana evoked the claustrophobia and fears of an elite outsider who had strayed into a dark alleyway wherein distinctions between the governed and the governors had almost completely broken down:

> You would hardly believe your eyes if you were here to see, as the scene of this dreadful conspiracy, a little brig, with low bulwarks, a single narrow deck flush fore and aft, and nothing to mark the officers' quarters but a long trunk-house, or companion, raised a few feet from the deck to let light and air in below, such as you may have seen in our smaller packets which ply along the seaboard. You feel as though a half a dozen resolute conspirators could have swept the decks and thrown overboard all that opposed them before aid could come from below.[34]

Such was Dana's imaginative sympathy for Mackenzie's situation that it can seem, not only in this passage but throughout the defense, that Dana himself was about to fall victim to mutineers. The effectiveness of the defense, then, owed a good deal to his narrative skill in drawing the reader "inside" the perspective of a vulnerable captain who, for the sake of the ship's community, must maintain a vigilant watchfulness. Within the overcrowded *Somers*, Dana wanted his landed readers to realize, the detection of mutinuous intent had to be swift and preemptive or all would have been lost.

Given the *Somers*'s vulnerability to conspiracy, Dana concluded, the naval brig required officers skilled in the interpretive art of countersubversion – skilled, as it were, in "reading." It was the contention of James Fenimore Cooper, embroiled in a nasty personal dispute with Mackenzie over their conflicting interpretations of Oliver Perry's role in the Battle of Lake Erie, that the *Somers*'s captain was anything but a skillful reader. Crucially, three years before the executions, Mackenzie had damningly reviewed Cooper's *History of the Navy* (1839) in the *North American Review*. Victimized by Mackenzie's review, Cooper took the side of the *Somers*'s victimized sailors, even though his *Ned Myers* (1843) and *Afloat and Ashore* (1844) certainly endorsed Dana's ideal of the ship as corporate institution. Just as Mackenzie misread Perry's nautical participation (and Cooper's *History*), so, Cooper asserted, had he misread the situation on board the *Somers*, thereby promoting a general paranoia among the officers that eventually impelled the murderous executions: "After the arrest of Mr. Spencer, it is evident from the testimony that Messrs. Mackenzie and Gansevoort began to see an enemy in every bush. We do not wish to say that they were frightened in the abject sense, but, that their minds were in that condition in which they were most disposed to exaggerate."[35]

To counter such charges, Mackenzie and his defenders asserted that interpretation on board the *Somers* was rather straightforward and that ultimately interpretation may be ratified by the social claims of character. Mackenzie himself testified that he and his officers took note of suspicious eye signalings and coded documents and, as interpreters sharing an allegience to a common-sense epistemology, acted as a community to save the community: "[The officers] observed the ominous appearances from hour to hour and from day to day, and watched with care their fearful progress. . . . To reject their united evidence as fabulous or imaginative, would be to destroy that faith which man, from his social relations, is bound to place in the testimony of his fellow men." Dana too presented Mackenzie as a prudent, self-controlled leader, "more noted for conscientiousness, order and thoroughness, than for imagination or enthusiasm," who was altogether capable of dispassionately assessing evidence "significant only to naval men." He therefore resoundingly supported Mackenzie's appeal to the united testimony of his officers: "*Every man on board the Somers of known fidelity and of superior experience and intelligence, thought that execution was necessary.*" Inspired by Dana's defense, Charles Sumner, the future senator, went one step further and, three months after Mackenzie's acquittal, argued in the July 1843 *North*

American Review that whenever a captain "has *reasonable grounds* to believe his life in danger" he must act preemptively to save the community, even if "it should afterwards appear that no such design existed." Thus, Sumner paradoxically insisted, because the naval ship *clearly* faced the *possibility* of danger, "the guilt of Spencer, Cromwell and Small . . . is irrelevant to the determination of the merits of the defence."[36]

The defense of Mackenzie's use of force played on fears of faceless conspirators, expressed political and social insecurities, and justified the (literal) power of interpretation. In this respect, the defense was similar not only to the Northern defense of disciplinary practices within the "familial" urban-reform institution, but also to the Southern defense of disciplinary force within the "familial" slave plantation. In fact, much of the rhetoric surrounding the *Somers* case suggests that, when Mackenzie and his officers decided to act, they believed they were protecting the ship from the sort of violence that Southern writers warned would accompany a slave revolt. Mackenzie, for example, offered as a key piece of evidence for the probability of an impending mutiny his observation of a sailor "sharpening . . . the African knife and battle-axe"; and he told of how he overheard "the declaration by one of the conspirators that he would like to get the African knife into the hands of Mr. Spencer, and that the knife would yet have to do a great deal of slaughter."[37] Actually, there was good reason for Mackenzie to perceive the alleged mutineers as potentially rebellious slaves, for as we have seen, such "common sailors" as McNally and even Dana tended to represent themselves as slaves. That the *Somers* was returning from a cruise to West Africa, the mission of which was to discourage the illegal slave trade, may have additionally made Mackenzie nervous about his own conspiratorial "slaves." Moreover, the most famous mutinies at sea before the alleged mutiny on board the *Somers* were highly publicized black mutinies on slavers: the 1839 revolt on board the Spanish slaver *Amistad* (a revolt that may have been in the back of Melville's mind when he wrote *Benito Cereno*) and the 1841 revolt on board the brig *Creole*. In a passage from his *North American Review* defense that could have been lifted from a proslavery tract warning of black rebellion, Sumner, perhaps sensing Mackenzie's fears of a slave revolt and almost certainly reflecting his own fears of similarly subversive urban insurrectionaries, warned of the consequences of "the crime of mutiny" on board the *Somers* or, for that matter, within any well-ordered ship of state: "It unlooses the bonds of social order, it subverts the authority of law, and inflames the worst passions of man."[38] From the point of view of Mackenzie and his supporters, on the captain's willingness to interpret and, subsequently, to act on his (mis)interpretation rests the survival of the social state. Like nervous "sea captains" throughout America, these captains – even those, like Dana and Sumner, who became abolitionists – feared the prospect of "mutiny and revolt" and placed their faith in "perfect sea order."

"Wild thoughts"

In his sea narratives of the 1840s, Melville decidedly is not a captain. Rather, as in *Typee* (1846), his first published book, he sympathetically explores the common seaman's desire to subsume self to a "perfect sea order" in which personal autonomy and responsibility are greatly diminished. Enjoying "a perfect freedom from care and anxiety" (T, 86) among the Typee islanders, Tommo seems little more than the adopted son of Marheyo, "a most paternal and warm-hearted old fellow" (T, 84). As "one tranquil day of ease and happiness follows another in quiet succession" (T, 149), he manages to recapture the "delightful, lazy, languid time" (T, 9) he earlier enjoyed aboard the whaler *Dolly*, where, under its "paternal" (T, 30) and "fatherly" (T, 30) captain, "there was nothing to be done; a circumstance that happily suited our disinclination to do anything" (T, 9). But childhood does not last forever, and Tommo's eventually dire condition on board the *Dolly* anticipates his eventually dire condition among the islanders: In both cases the surrendering of self leads to an imprisoning of self. Fleeing what becomes an oppressive whaler for the "indulgent captivity" (O, 3) of Typee society, Tommo at the conclusion of the narrative flees what becomes an equally oppressive community; we leave him clinging to the hope that his new situation aboard the ordered world of the Australian whaler *Julia* will provide a saving refuge. In *Omoo*, however, we learn that he flees this whaler too when it proves to be oppressive, only to return eventually to yet another whaler, the *Leviathan*, which he again invests with his deepest regressive desires: "Like all large, comfortable old whalers, she had a sort of motherly look: – broad in the beam, flush decks, and four chubby boats hanging at the breast" (O, 290). Accordingly, the whaler promises the best possible of situations: "A cosier craft never floated; and the captain was the finest man in the world. There was plenty to eat, too; and, at sea, nothing to do but sit on the windlass and sail" (O, 313).

The seaman's rather risky desire to escape from the marketplace world of "cares and anxiety" to the more bounded space of "indulgent captivity" – similar to the desire informing convent novels and texts of communitarian reform – may be taken as a reflection of Melville's own desires following his father's mental breakdown and death in 1832. Like Dana before he went to sea, Melville during the 1830s and early 1840s became something of a burden to his financially struggling family. Gansevoort reported to his brother Allan in November 1840: "Herman is still here – He has been & is a source of great anxiety to me – He has not obt^d a situation." Two months later, having already tried his hand at banking and teaching, Melville signed on as a common seaman on board the whaler *Acushnet*. His mother could thus reassure his concerned sister, "Gansevoort says he never saw him so completely happy as when he had determined upon a situation and all was settled."[39]

The need for, in Maria and Gansevoort's apt word, a "situation" is shared by most of Melville's roving sailors; usually the need goes un-stated or, as in Redburn's Ishmaelean confessional remarks, quietly un-derstated: "Sad disappointments in several plans which I had sketched for my future life; the necessity of doing something for myself, united to a naturally roving disposition, had now conspired within me, to send me to sea as a sailor" (R, 3).[40] Whether they say so or not, the very presence of Melville's sailors on board ship speaks for their initial willingness to surrender to its hierarchical order; as in *Typee* and *Omoo,* what William Gilman calls the "rebellious flight to the ocean"[41] actually represents a less than rebellious search for familial asylum. From this perspec-tive Redburn's ludicrous insistence on presenting himself as a well-established young gentleman, his outsider status as participant in the "Juvenile Abstinence Association" (R, 42), his naïve expectation that affairs on board ship will be conducted in accordance with liberal dem-ocratic principles, and his seeming inability to realize that the ship pro-vides a shipboard family that substitutes for his fallen family – all contribute to the humor and pathos of the book and, for a while at least, challenge Redburn's status as reformer and social critic. Even in the manifestly reformist *White-Jacket,* the narrator, like the comically limited Redburn, denounces authority from a compromised position. Surely the opening of the book, with its meticulous examination of the naval ship's well-defined hierarchy and division of labor, testifies to just how well the ship serves the institutional needs of the vaguely defined narrator. To denounce this social structure as rigid and antidemocratic is to announce one's own status as self-assured, economically secure, and altogether naïve landsman: Those down and out who sign on with a naval ship crave the distinction, order, and station attending what promises to be a saving refuge. As White-Jacket remarks, "The navy is the asylum for the perverse, the home of the unfortunate" (WJ, 74).

The asylum analogue is not an isolated one: Institutional and urban comparisons abound in *White-Jacket.* White-Jacket reports that the naval ship is "a city afloat" (WJ, 74); one character calls the ship "a sort of state prison afloat" (WJ, 175). Shakings, formerly incarcerated at Sing Sing state prison, signs on with the *Neversink* in an effort to recapture the "freedom" he enjoyed in prison, wherein, like Tommo among the Typee islanders, "he was relieved from all anxieties about what he should eat and drink, and was supported, like the President of the United States and Prince Albert, at the public charge" (WJ, 175).[42] In addition to resembling a prison, the ship "is something like . . . a large manufactory. The bell strikes to dinner, and hungry or not, you must dine" (WJ, 35).

Like Dana's *Pilgrim* and the total institutions of America's urban centers, the *Neversink* adopts the order of the factory and the prison, not only because it houses sailors like Shakings (and White-Jacket) who desire to surrender to an idealized familial social structure, but also because it houses the disorderly poor that urban reformers wanted isolated and enclosed. In what I take to be a parody of Dana's nervous outsidership, Melville's White-Jacket informs the reader that the ship's crew consists of "scores of desperadoes" (WJ, 39), predominantly foreigners (WJ, 380), who regard the navy "as the asylum for all drunkards" (WJ, 54). And in the mode of a nervous reformer, White-Jacket offers a wonderfully nightmarish, Lippardian image of the ship as enclosed urban den of iniquity: "With its long rows of port-hole casements, each revealing the muzzle of a canon, a man-of-war resembles a three-story house in a suspicious part of town, with a basement of indefinite depth, and ugly looking fellows gazing out at the windows" (WJ, 75). Given the ship's overcrowded conditions (WJ, 222) and the "morbidness of mind [that] is often the consequence" (WJ, 222), the ship's strict regulations, as in the total institution, serve the fundamental purpose of preserving the social order: "Were it not for these regulations a man-of-war's crew would be nothing but a mob" (WJ, 9). As nervous "gentleman" among the rogues, White-Jacket is thus prepared to abide by the ship's institutional structure and to follow its leader. Unfortunately, at the command of the *Neversink* is not the idealized and idolized British main-top-man Jack Chase, a "stickler for the Rights of Man" (WJ, 17) who is also "a little bit of a dictator" (WJ, 15), but Captain Claret, a disciplinarian who is also a type of slave master.

As in Dana's *Two Years,* a flogging scene makes explicit the connection between captain and slave master, sailor and slave, ship and slave plantation. Like Captain Frank Thompson, Claret sadistically flogs an apparently innocent sailor while blasphemously asserting his shipboard supremacy: "I would not forgive God almighty!" (WJ, 138). And as in Dana the cruel flogging promotes the narrator's rapid transformation from nervous insider to fraternal insider: Realizing that flogging "convert[s] into slaves some of the citizens of a nation of freemen" (WJ, 144), White-Jacket begins to turn against the corporate ideal of "perfect sea order" that informs the opening of the text. But whereas Dana backs away from mutiny, taking refuge in his insider desire for submission and his outsider fear of the sailors' insurrectionary energies, White-Jacket's emergent belief that the captain's authority rests on "arbitrary laws"

(WJ, 138) leads him to develop a rationale for resistance that appeals to a higher law, "the Law of Nature" (WJ, 145) – the Law, according to his reading of Blackstone, " 'coeval with mankind, dictated by God himself, [and] superior in obligation to any other' " (WJ, 145). Convinced that flogging is an affront to God's Law, he proclaims, "Every American man-of-war's man would be morally justified in resisting the scourge to the uttermost; and, in so resisting, would be religiously justified in what would be judicially styled 'the act of mutiny' itself" (WJ, 145).[43]

Eventually, White-Jacket's principled defense of resistance is put to the test when the captain orders him flogged for failing to report to his proper station – an unfair charge, it turns out. In effect, then, on "planta-tion" *Neversink,* where "you see a human being, stripped like a slave; scourged worse than a hound" (WJ, 138), White-Jacket must entertain the possibility of a slave revolt. His "inside narrative" of mutiny and revolt, a meditation on his building revolutionism, is worth quoting at some length:

> There are times when wild thoughts enter a man's heart, when he seems almost irresponsible for his act and his deed. The Captain stood on the opening of the lee-gangway, where the side-ladders are suspended in port. Nothing but a slight bit of sinnate-stuff served to rail in this opening, which was cut right down to the level of the Captain's feet, showing the far sea beyond. I stood a little to windward of him, and, though he was a large, powerful man, it was certain that a sudden rush against him, along the slanting deck, would infallibly pitch him head-foremost into the ocean, though he who so rushed must needs go over with him. My blood seemed clotting in my veins; I felt icy cold at the tips of my fingers, and a dimness was before my eyes. But through that dimness the boatswain's mate, scourge in hand, loomed like a giant, and Captain Claret, and the blue sea seen through the opening at the gangway, showed with an awful vividness. I can not analyze my heart, though it then stood still within me. But the thing that swayed me to my purpose was not altogether the thought that Captain Claret was about to degrade me, and that I had taken an oath with my soul that he should not. No, I felt my man's manhood so bottomless within me, that no word, no blow, no scourge of Captain Claret could cut me deep enough for that. I but swung to an instinct in me – the instinct diffused through all animated nature, the same that prompts even a worm to turn under the heel. Locking souls with him, I meant to drag Captain Claret from this earthly tribunal of his to that of Jehovah, and let Him decide between us. (WJ, 280)

White-Jacket may have morally, religiously, and politically justified the "act of mutiny itself," but when personally confronted with an imminent flogging something more powerful comes into play: "wild thoughts," an instinctual, visceral resistance that White-Jacket believes would build in all "animated nature." It is a resistance that threatens to unhinge him; hence the Gothic descriptions – the iciness, the dimness. When Colbrook and Chase use their influence to save White-Jacket from the flogging, they therefore save him not only from becoming "a murderer and suicide" (WJ, 281), but also from embracing a disintegrative revolutionary energy not so very different from that empowering and unhinging Brockden Brown's revolutionary murderess Constantia. Relieved at the dissipation of the threat to his mind and body, White-Jacket "almost burst into tears of thanksgiving where I stood" (WJ, 281).

Developing the analogues of ship to urban-reform and slave institutions in order to enlarge the significance of what might otherwise be read as an isolated, or marginal, moment of revolutionary defiance, Melville takes the reader "inside," or down below, to experience firsthand what it means psychologically, socially, and physically to be subjected to the ship's institutional and judicial authority. White-Jacket's close encounter with flogging therefore prompts him to project himself "inside" the situation of those whom he suddenly regards as fellow victims of the Articles of War, the men hanged aboard the brig *Somers:*

> What happened to those three men on board the American armed vessel a few years ago, quite within your memory, White-Jacket; yea, while you yourself were yet serving on board this very frigate, the Neversink? What happened to those three Americans, White-Jacket – those three men, even as you, who once were alive, but now are dead. *"Shall suffer death!"* those were the three words that hung those three men.
>
> Have a care, then, have a care, lest you come to a sad end, even the end of a rope; lest, with a black-and-blue throat, you turn a dumb diver after pearl shells; put to bed forever, and tucked in, in your own hammock, at the bottom of the sea. (WJ, 294)

Hanged by "three words" – the death penalty as prescribed by the Articles of War – the doomed men of the *Somers,* White-Jacket imagines in this lyrical, Shakespearean meditation on "dumbness," confronted the real beneath the ideal: Placing their faith in the familial order of the ship, they unwittingly submitted themselves to a brute enslaving power. In *Working a Passage,* Briggs terms the *Somers* case "the foulest, darkest, bloodiest spot upon our national history . . . because it was the legitimate result of our national LAW."[44] The radical implication of Melville's challenge to the captain's disciplinary authority, whether on board the *Neversink* or *Somers,* is thus to challenge the very legitimacy of the legal codes upholding that authority. And to do so is to perceive how the languages of authority – in this case the Articles of War – construct and preserve the institutions of authority; it is to "see through" the familial idealizations of ship, urban-reform institution, and slave institution to perceive the fundamental reality of power.

The text's Carlylean unclothing of the ship's various forms of authority fuels White-Jacket's building rebelliousness. Michael Rogin comments on that rebelliousness as it develops over the course of the narrative: "Attacking flogging, the officer corps, and the *Somers* executions, White-Jacket is working himself up to a slave revolt."[45] Although his incipient revolt against Claret is finally made unnecessary by Colbrook and Chase's intervention, his challenges to the "arbitrary laws" (WJ, 138) and domestic rhetoric upholding the institution of the ship suggest that White-Jacket could support a mutinous "slave revolt" in other contexts as well. As he boldly declares, "I was not born a serf, and will not live a slave!" (WJ, 295). Still, White-Jacket, like virtually all of Melville's other rebellious sailors, stops short of rebellion, even when, by the end of the novel, the horrible flogging of the noble Ushant would appear to call for an active resistance. Michael Bell remarks, "Again and again, in Melville's writings, rebellious defiance is turned into repressive evasion, guilty self-destruction, or – increasingly – a curious sort of passive enervation."[46] Why should this be so?

Perhaps Melville's resistance to mutiny, or, more precisely, to representing acts of mutiny, can be tied to a desire to resist ideological appropriation. In texts like *Mardi* and *White-Jacket* he invests such an abundance of verbal and intellectual energy in demystifying social and institutional ideologies that ultimately he seems to destabilize the grounds for constructing an absolute foundation to any ideology, even an ideology of resistance. *Mardi,* for example, offers a dialogue on the problem of slavery in "free-and-equal" Vivenza (M, 512) in which Yoomy champions slave revolts, Babbalanja expresses fears of revolutionary disorder, and "Vivenza" holds out the hope that "Time – all-healing Time – Time, great Philanthropist! – Time must befriend these thralls!" (M, 535). Though Yoomy may posit the most inspiring solution, Melville makes it clear that Yoomy is a poet who waxes free with his revolutionary sentiments. By the same token, Babbalanja as royal historian reads slavery as it suits his needs, and "Vivenza" as it suits the needs of a liberal, hopeful nation. What we are left with, then, is an uncomfortable lack of direction on the practical matter of action. Similarly, in *White-Jacket* the dialogical play of a number of voices and positions keeps alive the question of Melville's attitude toward active rebellion. To be sure, he opposes flogging – "I am offering up devout jubilations for the abolition of the flogging law," he wrote Evert Duyckinck soon after publication of *White-Jacket* – but he does so, in the several polemical passages addressing the issue, less in his own voice than in the voice of John Lockwood's *An Essay on Flogging* (1849).[47] This voice is quite different from that of the opening, which is so responsive to the insider promise of the ship, and from that of the conclusion, which finds in "The Great Massacre of the Beards" (WJ, 355) an occasion for mock-epic narration and a silly punning on the barbarity and barbarousness of the navy's barbers. Within this larger rhetorical context, the account of the sailors' short-lived rebellious defiance lacks a sense of fraternal conviction.

A resistance to ideological appropriation, and thus to formulating a univocal politics of mutiny and revolt, is in large part a natural consequence of Melville's epistemology and style. Perhaps having even more influence on his hesitations in representing or advocating mutiny, especially given his own experiences as landsman and seaman, is the countervailing implicit desire for "perfect sea order" informing the sea narrative as a genre. Although for many antebellum sea writers mutiny has as its analogue the rebellion of the slave, most of these writers, no matter how genuine their sympathies for their abused fellow seamen and no matter what their politics, retained a trace of their troubled desire for the ideal "situational" order of the purposive and fraternal ship. Accordingly, sea narratives necessarily remained a problematic arena for challenging hierarchical authority, even the kind of authority that "enslaves." McNally, for all his revolutionary outrage at the evils of flogging, nevertheless repudiates the notion of full democratization on board ship: "I am one of the last men that would wish to deprive a master of a merchant vessel of the power sufficient to preserve his authority." The protagonist of Briggs's *Working a Passage* may likewise compare the abusive authority of the shipmaster to "that of a slave-master," but upon returning to land he laments the loss of the ship's community: "Spite of the hardships I had endured on board the _____, I left her with a feeling of regret; and I could scarce part with my forecastlely companions without a tear for the loss of their fellowship."[48]

Although there is much in *White-Jacket* that challenges and revises the politics of popular nautical romances, there is an equally strong sense that what is true for other sea writers of the time is also true for Melville: The desire for familial order and fraternal asylum deeply informs all of his sea narratives of the 1840s. Rebellion and desire thus remain perpetually in conflict and contribute to that "passive enervation" characterizing Melville's rebellious sailors. It is an enervation that White-Jacket notes in extremity in his fellow seamen. On shore for three days "in penniless drunkenness" (WJ, 390), most of the sailors, defeated by landedness, return of their own volition to the authoritarian ship, which they continue to regard as an accommodating asylum. As White-Jacket explains, on the *Neversink* "they have plenty to eat; spirits to drink; clothing to keep them warm; a hammock to sleep in; tobacco to chew; a doctor to medicine them; a person to pray for them; and to a penniless castaway, must not all this seem as a luxurious Bill of Fare?" (WJ, 383). Despite the rather bitter irony here, it is clear that for a number of Melville's protagonists a ship like the *Neversink* helps to keep those at the drowning point afloat.

Nonetheless, as Melville's seamen always learn, the romanticized ship can enslave. Invariably, the fall from the ideal to the real induces a sense of betrayal, and then a hesitant, rebellious defiance. If one reason for the hesitation can be tied to a resistance to ideological appropriation and if another can be tied to an implicit desire for order and asylum, perhaps a third reason can be tied to an uneasiness with the "wild thoughts" that would lead to an anarchic irruption of sea disorders. To return to the key moment in *White-Jacket* when we actually get an "inside" view of impending revolt: As described by White-Jacket, the revolt would have been an instinctual one involving a simultaneous affirmation and destabilization of his humanity. I read this inside account as a frightening moment in White-Jacket's career pointing to Melville's own discomfort with the personal and social destabilization that would accompany a full-scale "slave revolt."

Arguably, this is also a captain-like fear of revolt, a discomforting fear of social destabilization that, in Melville's early work, is most explicitly manifested in *Typee*'s Appendix, a defense of Lord George Paulet's imposition of disciplinary restraints upon the Sandwich Islanders. As with Dana's defense of Mackenzie, Melville insists that Paulet's use of forceful measures was prompted by "unusual exigencies" (T, 258) – the missionaries' political meddling and the governor's operation of a prostitution ring. Taking control, Paulet restores order through the assumption of captaincy; he governs the Islanders "in the same firm and benignant spirit which marked the discipline of his frigate" (T, 256). When the French later precipitately release the Islanders from Paulet's command, the result is just what Melville fears: a grotesque social unraveling. Somewhat prudishly (and self-mockingly), he reports: "The spectacle of universal broad-day debauchery, which was then exhibited, beggars description. The natives of the surrounding islands flocked to Honolulu by hundreds, and the crews of two frigates, opportunely let loose like so many demons to swell the heathenish uproar, gave the crowning flourish to the scene. It was a sort of Polynesian saturnalia. Deeds too atrocious to be mentioned were done at noon-day in the open street" (T, 258). Consequently, Melville informs his readers, the Sandwich Islanders realize that Paulet's "captaincy" had been in their best interests: "To this hour the great body of the Hawiian [*sic*] people invoke blessings on his head, and look back with gratitude to the time when his liberal and paternal sway diffused peace and happiness among them" (T, 258).

Although White-Jacket may challenge such paternalism as it informs the familial idealization of the *Neversink,* he nevertheless reveals as well a fear of social disorder, a fear that has its sources not only in his intimation of his own progression to an instinctual revolutionism but also in his captain-like discovery of what happens when the crew is precipitately released, as the Hawaiian Islanders of *Typee* were precipitately released, from disciplinary restraints. White-Jacket portrays two such moments, one benign and one not so benign. The first occurs when the captain permits the seamen to engage in theatricals on Independence Day, and they choose to perform a revolutionary drama culminating in Jack Chase's glorious rescue of "fifteen oppressed sailors from the watch-house" (WJ, 94). So pleased are the sailors with the performance that their spontaneous festive celebration produces a "temporary rupture of the ship's stern discipline" (WJ, 95). White-Jacket muses: "This now is as it should be. It is good to shake off, now and then, this iron yoke round our necks" (WJ, 95).

Only two chapters later, however, during "The Dog-days off Cape Horn" (WJ, 100), discipline is even more abruptly terminated with the order from the officers: "*All hands skylark!*" (WJ, 102). The sailors are subsequently permitted "perfect license" (WJ, 102), and as with the theatricals, the abrupt cessation of discipline allows for a carnivalesque release of revolutionary energies. White-Jacket describes the scene: "It was a Babel here, a Bedlam there, and a Pandemonium every where. The Theatricals were nothing compared with it. . . . Gangs of men, in all sorts of outlandish habiliments, wild as those worn at some crazy carnival, rushed to and fro, seizing upon whomsoever they pleased – warrant-officers and dangerous pugilists excepted – pulling and hauling the luck-less tars about, till fairly baited into a genial warmth" (WJ, 102). But unlike Hawthorne's Roman carnival, whose participants are lawless but not rude, this "din frightened the sea-fowl" (WJ, 102), as "genial warmth" boils over to heated violence. "While the 'skylarking' was at its height," White-Jacket relates, "one of the fore-top-men – an ugly-tempered devil of a Portuguese, looking on – swore that he would be the death of any man who laid violent hands upon his inviolable person. This threat being overheard, a band of desperadoes, coming up from behind, tripped him up in an instant. . . . Presently, disengaging his hands from those who held them, the enraged seaman drew from his bosom an iron belaying pin, and recklessly laid about him to right and left" (WJ, 102–3). The ruckus, with its violent denouement, puts a permanent end to sky-larking, "further head-breaking," a relieved White-Jacket reports, "being strictly prohibited" (WJ, 103).

Concerns about insurrectionary disorder lie submerged but present in Melville's sea narratives and implicitly challenge the antiauthoritarian sentiments of these works. Rather than programmatically use his fiction to articulate a Brownson-like revolutionary mandate for "slave" resistance, Melville presents the reader with seamen–narrators who simultaneously attack the ship as institution even as they turn to its institutional structures for an ordering, and defining, asylum. Tempted toward revolutionism, they can only hover at the brink, perpetually fearful of those mutinous "wild thoughts" threatening to lead self and community toward a suicidal, murderous, and anarchic "head-breaking." *White-Jacket* in particular seems haunted by the possibility that revolutionary energies could explode in an insurrectionary fury reminiscent of the French Revolution, the rebellion in San Domingo, and those unnamed and sporadic riots in America's Northern urban centers: The man-of-war is like "the lodging-houses in Paris, turned upside down" (WJ, 75), occupied at the top level "by a whole rabble of common people" (WJ, 75); the "jolly Africans" (WJ, 58) serving as the ship's cooks sing "remarkable St. Domingo melodies" (WJ, 58); White-Jacket fears that should the crew have to fight a real naval battle, "*then* our bulwarks might look like the walls of the houses in West Broadway in New York, after being broken into and burned out by the Negro Mob" (WJ, 69). Outraged by the tyrannical Claret and the enslaving Articles of War, and yet fearful of what might accompany a mutinous revolt of the ship's "slaves," Melville, even in the "reformist" *White-Jacket,* remains in conflict between his political sympathies and his social anxieties. Although more democratic and idealistic than Dana – more intent on demystifying, resisting, and redefining authority – he nevertheless implies a politics of "nautical" order that resembles the more aggressively institutionalist politics of Dana's *Two Years.*

The problem of maintaining order, of course, was central to debate not only on reform and slave institutions but also, and more generally, on the state of the Union. This was especially true of the late 1840s and 1850s; for with the military triumphs of the Mexican War came a renewal of the sectional controversy on slavery and expansionism and a heightening of concerns about Americans' ability to hold together as one. Harking back to a dominant metaphor of the Puritan migration and revolution, Northern political rhetoricians in particular, fearing national disaster, regularly imaged America as a federated "ship of state" careening toward cataclysmic shipwreck. Fearful of national shipwreck, Longfellow revised an early draft of a poem on mutiny and, in the final version of "The Building of the Ship" (1849), depicted a lordly "Master" constructing a ship that promises to remain intact as it sails through stormy waters: "Sail on, O Ship of State! / Sail on, O UNION, strong and great!" A supporter of Mackenzie's actions on board the *Somers,* Longfellow adopted a poetics of Unionism that, just a few months later, would achieve its political actualization in the Compromise of 1850.[49] It is not surprising, then, that Longfellow would be attacked by abolitionists for anticipating and apparently justifying a compromise that, through its enactment of the Fugitive Slave Law, further enmeshed "free soil" Northerners with Southern enslavers; and it is not surprising that critics of the compromise would continue to draw on ship-of-state imagery to dramatize their sense of America's precarious situation. Thus while Longfellow's "Ship," much reprinted during the 1850s, advised its readers, "Fear not each sudden sound and shock, / 'T is of the wave and not the rock; / 'T is but the flapping of the sail, / And not a rent made by the gale," Theodore Parker, in language typical of the compromise's dissenters, warned his auditors and readers: "The Fugitive Slave Bill is a long wedge, thin at one end, wide at the other; it is entered between the bottom planks of our SHIP OF STATE; a few blows thereon will 'enforce' more than the South thinks of. A little more, – and we shall go to pieces."[50] Given the pervasiveness of ship-of-state imagery in the discourse of the period, Melville's representations of mutiny during the 1850s would take on an even greater urgency and political significance.

Although *Moby-Dick*'s perspectival narrative offers resistance to political-allegorical readings, I want nevertheless to speculate on the text's politics of mutiny by considering its two mutinies and its one near mutiny. The text's most dramatic representation of mutiny occurs in "The Town-Ho's Story," narrated by Ishmael in Peru several years after his experiences on board the *Pequod* and inserted into the text near its midpoint. According to Ishmael, at "some really landless latitude" (MD, 211) the Nantucket whaler *Town-Ho* develops a leak. Especially fretful about keeping the ship afloat is the mate Radney, a co-owner of the ship who, not incidentally, is as "ugly as a mule" (MD, 211). Fearing for the health of a ship in which he owns stock and, Claggart-like, developing a hatred for the handsome seaman Steelkilt, who jokes about his leaking investment, Radney decides to impose a strict and humiliating discipline upon this "tall and noble animal" (MD, 211). Steelkilt, we have been told, remains "harmless and docile" (MD, 210) if treated with "inflexible firmness, only tempered by that common decency of human recognition which is the meanest slave's right" (MD, 210). In response to Radney's lack of "decency," therefore, a "nameless phantom feeling . . . fell over Steelkilt" (MD, 213), who resists Radney's order to sweep the planks. When Radney subsequently grazes his cheek with a club hammer, Steelkilt lashes back with a nearly murderous blow – the active resistance that White-Jacket can only imagine in his "wild thoughts" – thereby initiating a full-scale mutiny that is also "a paradigm," as Carolyn Karcher points out, "of slave insurrection."[51]

It is a mutiny that has been celebrated by some of the most perceptive readers of *Moby-Dick*'s political symbolism. Charles Foster hails it as "radically democratic"; Alan Heimert asserts that it is an "exemplary mutiny," an allegory of the Barnburner Revolt leading to Free-Soil Democracy.[52] The rhetoric describing the revolt, however, indicates that Melville may well regard Steelkilt, the man who, we should keep in mind, deliberately provoked Radney's rage, as a demonic revolutionary. A leader of "sea Parisians" (MD, 216) who vows murderous vengeance should he or his accomplices be flogged, Steelkilt, when eventually captured, speaks, as does the satanic Fedallah (and later Claggart), "in a sort of hiss" (MD, 219). Thus when Moby Dick surfaces to kill Radney, who dares to flog Steelkilt after the captain fearfully declines, I think we have to take as ironic the assertion by Ishmael, the *Pequod*'s one surviving "orphan," that in the appearance of the malignant Moby Dick "Heaven itself seemed to step in to take out of [Steelkilt's] hands and into its own the damning thing he would have done" (MD, 221). If anything, Moby Dick acts as the final participant in a revolutionary mutiny against the ship's hierarchical order that, hardly productive of a new democracy, serves instead to complete the disintegration of the sinking ship and to initiate Steelkilt's career as a roving pirate.

And yet parallels between White-Jacket's "wild thoughts" and Steelkilt's "phantom feeling" suggest an affinity between Melville's autobiographical persona, on the one hand, and his hissing revolutionary, on the other, as does the imaging of both White-Jacket and Steelkilt as types of slaves. According to Karcher, in Steelkilt's mutiny we observe once again "the same conflict on Melville's part between identifying with the rebellious slave or acknowledging the authority of his oppressor."[53] And I would add that we also observe the same conflict between identifying with the revolutionary claims of the aggrieved individual or the corporate claims of the larger social community – the conflict, that is to say, central to numerous nautical romances of the period. Although Melville sympathetically portrays the impulses behind Steelkilt's rebellion, we cannot ignore the fact that he portrays as well its dire social consequences; on the evidence of the *Town-Ho*'s story, mutiny exacts a high social cost indeed. In his subsequent account of the mutiny on board the *Jeroboam,* Melville, in his apparent revulsion at this particular mutiny, resorts to the rhetoric characteristically employed by late-eighteenth-century conservatives to warn of the debilitating infectiousness of revolutionism: The *Jeroboam,* a "mutinous boat" (MD, 269), is stricken with "a malignant epidemic" (MD, 265). Revolutionary fevers have led to the displacement of the ship's captain and the ascension of the mad Shaker "Gabriel," who, despite his obvious fanaticism, has "gained a wonderful ascendency [*sic*] over almost everybody in the Jeroboam" (MD, 266). Enslaved to the will of a usurpative madman, the *Jeroboam*'s crew is fated to sail along aimlessly until all aboard succumb to disease.

Within the larger narrative of *Moby-Dick,* Melville depicts two acts of mutiny, both of which precipitate social breakdown. If these ships are meant allegorically to represent ships of state, then mutiny, one might conclude, augurs national disaster. Yet on the *Pequod* itself, mutiny appears to be a social desideratum, perhaps the only way to preserve the ship from shipwreck. Captain Ahab, however Promethean, is also a monomaniac only recently out of the straitjacket. And in terms of the text's ironically deployed Christian typology, the captain too is a kind of satanic mutineer, rebelliously seeking to wreak his vengeance on an authoritarian captain-like God in the name of Adam and his descendants, the world's "shipmates" (MD, 50), as Father Mapple terms the mass of humanity. On a ship that, with its representative Indians and blacks, Northerners and Southerners, American-born officers and foreign-born seamen, is a microcosm of the American ship of state, Ahab taps into the revolutionary energies of his "Anarcharis Clootz deputation" (MD, 108) of "*Isolatoes*. . . . federated along one keel" (MD, 108) to create a purposive community sworn to the destruction of a fearsome plotting enemy. In this respect the odd Ahab is not so odd at all: Typically in antebellum culture those at the political helm mobilized support by warning the populace of the dangers posed to the republic by a submerged and ubiquitous enemy possessing, as the submerged and ubiquitous Moby Dick is said to possess, "great ferocity, cunning, and malice" (MD, 155). The charismatic and despotic Ahab eventually gains sway over the allegiances of nearly the entire crew; as Ishmael confesses, "Ahab's quenchless feud seemed mine" (MD, 155).[54]

Only Starbuck takes conscious note of the threat posed to the shipboard community by such a single-minded quest. Fearing Moby Dick's blind power, appalled by Ahab's blasphemous conception of his quest, and concerned that the *Pequod* is neglecting its principal aim of accumulating sperm oil, Starbuck emerges as the typical Melvillean rebel in conflict. "Oh! I plainly see my miserable office," he soliloquizes, " – to obey, rebelling; and worse yet, to hate with a touch of pity!" (MD, 148). But when, in an echo of "The Town-Ho's Story," a leak, in this case in the oil casks, threatens the economic fortunes not just of the owners but of all the sailors paid according to the lay, Starbuck decides to act, urging upon Ahab prompt corrective measures. Scornful of mere worldly profits, Ahab points a musket at Starbuck and, in language resembling that of such lords of the lash as Dana's Captain Thompson and Melville's Captain Claret, pridefully declares, "There is one God that is Lord over the earth, and one Captain that is lord over the Pequod" (MD, 394). Shortly thereafter, a more politic Ahab orders the casks repaired, but not before his overbearing authority has pushed Starbuck toward rebellion. When Starbuck later boldly speaks out against Ahab's theatrical burning of the lightning rods on the ship's mastheads – "God, God is against thee, old man; forbear!" (MD, 418) – the possibility of a full-fledged mutiny suddenly becomes a real one. Ishmael reports: "The panic-stricken crew instantly ran to the braces. . . . For the moment all the aghast mate's thoughts seemed theirs; they raised a half mutinous cry" (MD, 418).

And for a moment it appears that Starbuck may act after all to free the community from Ahab's lordly dominion. He enters Ahab's cabin, finds Ahab asleep, and faces his great temptation. During Nat Turner's night-time rebellion a number of the murdered white victims met their fates upon awakening from sleep; within Ahab's cabin Starbuck himself seems something like a slave in the master's great house readying for the kill. The cabin is called a "state-room" (MD, 421); on the forward bulkhead stands Ahab's last resort to authority, a rack of loaded muskets. Starbuck, still smarting from the indignity suffered at the hands of his master, suddenly contemplates exacting a liberating revenge. Experiencing an "evil thought" (MD, 421) paralleling White-Jacket's "wild thoughts" and Steelkilt's "phantom feeling," Starbuck, in a nautical recasting of Hamlet's temptation to murder Claudius at prayer, aims a musket at the sleeping Ahab and reasons that, if he pulls the trigger, he would be killing "the wilful murderer of thirty men and more, if this ship come to any deadly harm" (MD, 422). "Wrestling with an angel" (MD, 423), but ultimately fearing eternal damnation, he decides against the homicidal mutinous act and puts his faith not in institutions but in heaven. For the time being, Ahab's federated community, unlike the communities on board the *Town-Ho* and the *Jeroboam,* remains intact.

Thus when the *Pequod* finally encounters Moby Dick, the crew battles the whale as a united community under Ahab's command. As Ishmael puts it, during the apocalyptic three-day battle "they were one man, not thirty" (MD, 454). Such a formulation, especially within a sea fiction, implies an idealized conception of purposive community, just what the Ishmaelean seaman is looking for. The image speaks as well to the uto-pian ideal of America itself, recalling the originating vision of John Winthrop, who warned his shipmates on board the *Arbella* that "the onely way to avoyde this shipwracke and to provide for our posterity is to . . . be knitte together in this worke as one man."[55] Significantly, it is precisely because the *Pequod* remains "knitte together" that it comes undone; and we may posit that, if Melville is indeed making a specific political-allegorical point here, it is that the knitting together of the sections under the millennial Unionism of the Compromise of 1850 promises to bring a similarly disastrous "shipwracke" – especially if citizens continue to "obey, rebelling" in the face of such a national moral wrong as slavery.

Yet during the period from 1851 to 1855 rebellions against the com-promise's Fugitive Slave Law became a regular occurrence in Massachusetts, and to many observers the American ship of state seemed even more endangered than before the compromise, precisely because so many disobeyed, rebelling. Arguing that their fundamental loyalty was not to the Constitution but, as Garrison, Seward, Thoreau, and many others asserted, to a "higher law" of justice and morality, abolitionists were increasingly willing to use violent means to oppose efforts to return fugitive slaves to the South. In the spirit of White-Jacket's appeal to God's "Law of Nature," Thoreau proclaimed in "Slavery in Massachusetts" (1854): "Whoever has discerned truth, has received his commission from a higher source than the chiefest justice in the world, who can discern only law. He finds himself constituted judge of the judge."[56] One of the judges being judged, of course, was Melville's father-in-law, Lemuel Shaw, chief justice of the Massachusetts supreme court, who, despite his personal opposition to slavery, ruled in the 1851 trial of escaped slave Thomas Sims and in the 1854 trial of the fugitive slave Anthony Burns to uphold the claims of their respective "owners." Both trials were punctuated by escape attempts and riots; and during the trial of Sims, which occurred shortly after antislavery forces engineered the successful escape from the courthouse of the fugitive slave Shadrach, Shaw's court was ringed in with protective chains. For Shaw, then, riots only underscored the need to address sectional problems institutionally and juridically. As Robert M. Cover remarks (with proleptic reference to *Billy Budd*): "Sectional strife simply reinforced [Shaw's] belief in the necessity of a 'Mutiny Act' for the fugitive."[57]

Because several of Melville's short stories of the 1853–6 period address quite critically the claims of enslavers and racists, it is tempting to view Melville as a harsh critic of Shaw, who, in turn, can be viewed as a type of legal-formalist sea captain. But we should at least entertain the possibility that Shaw's central role in enforcing the Fugitive Slave Law would have complicated Melville's response to developments of the 1850s, dividing his sympathies between "liberal" leaders agonizingly enforcing the law of the land, corrupt as it may be, and "higher law" abolitionists, absolutely convinced of their ability to discern the truth, rioting on the steps of the Massachusetts supreme court. Melville's Shaw-like perspective, I believe, informs the treatment of slavery and mutiny in Sketch Seventh of "The Encantadas" (1854), "Charles's Isle and the Dog-King," a meditation on the cycle of violence and vengeance arising from the introduction of slavery into a political economy. The sketch tells the history of a Creole adventurer who fights on the side of Peru against imperial Spain and is eventually paid for his services with Charles's Isle, like millennial America a "promised land" (PT, 789). At first the Creole invites immigrants to populate his new nation; but when they fatally succumb to his tyrannous, enslaving authority – he watches over them with "canine janizaries" (PT, 790) and executes rebels – he replenishes the state with deserters from whaling ships. Eventually the whalers conspire with the enslaved populace to resist his rule, and there ensues a massive slave revolt, "a terrible mutiny" (PT, 791), as the narrator terms it, which leads to the banishing of the Creole and the establishment of a democratic republic. According to the skeptical narrator, however, Charles's Isle "was no democracy at all, but a permanent *Riotocracy,* which gloried in having no law but lawlessness" (PT, 791).

Melville offers a troubling picture of the riots engendered by a mutinous "slave revolt," not because he lacks concern for the plight of black chattel slaves, but because the isle's former slaves are suggestively imaged less as blacks than as types of Northern reformers: Massachusetts's erstwhile predestined Calvinists become self-liberated and self-righteous Perfectionists. Melville wants to show how these white former slaves to Jehovah now glorify themselves through their embrace of the black fugitive slave, the "runaway tar": "Charles's Island was proclaimed the asylum of the oppressed of all navies. Each runaway tar was hailed as a martyr in the cause of freedom, and became immediately installed a ragged citizen of this universal nation. In vain the captains of absconding seamen strove to regain them" (PT, 792). Working with the analogy central to all of his sea fiction – seaman to slave – Melville suggests that the "higher law" mentality threatens to become a mentality of self that gives rise to an uncontrolled and unfocused revolutionism. He therefore concludes the section, in an echo of Hawthorne's French Revolutionary nightmare of desperate characters emerging from their "lurking-places," with the wry observation that the island became "the unassailed lurking-place of all sorts of desperadoes, who in the name of liberty did just what they pleased" (PT, 792). In his account of Charles's Isle, Melville is at his most like the King Charlesean Coverdale in the hermitage, at his most like Hawthorne, or, more pertinently, at his most like a sea captain.

Melville's mutinies are indeed double-edged swords: They threaten "captains" and "seamen" alike, promising to put an end to a sea order that was never perfect by installing in its place a recurring cycle of insurrectionary violence. Concerned about the prospects for a ship of state infected by both the coercive order of slavery and the anarchic disorder of "mutiny and revolt," Melville remains contemptuous of enslaving captains and yet fearful of mutiny, fully aware – and I want to insist upon this, because it is here that Melville differs significantly from Hawthorne – that the fear of mutiny is an empowering fear of sea captains. Sharing the fear of mutiny, he becomes a sea captain of sorts; he becomes complicitous in the standing order, its authoritarian abuses, and its "legitimating" ideologies. In order to plumb this complicity he would have to do what he had never before done in his fiction: He would have to adopt the perspective of a sea captain in the midst of a mutinous conspiracy.

"Spectacle of disorder"

In 1817, at the height of the jingoistic nationalism accompanying America's celebrated "victory" over Britain in the War of 1812, a former sea captain soberly observed, "National prejudices, to a certain extent, may be very useful and possibly necessary, but they are always attended by considerable evils in the narrow and intolerant spirit which they perpetuate, and in the contentions which they produce." Among these "considerable evils," so argued the captain, were imperialism and, as manifested by the Spanish in their interactions with South American Indians, slavery:

> Some [of the Indians] are made slaves by being taken prisoners in time of war, or by [the Spanish] purchasing them from their enemies. I have been struck with horror to hear a Spanish priest call them brutes; telling me at the same time they were not Christians, and no better than cattle; when that same arrogant man's countrymen had robbed and despoiled the unfortunate Indian of all that was dear to him. Thus, 'thinks I to myself,' goes the world: – one man robs another his country, his wealth, and his liberty; and then says he is a brute, and not a Christian. In such cases as these, I will say with the meritorious physician, to whom Bonaparte made the proposition to poison his soldiers at Jaffa, or Joppa: 'If those be the requisites necessary to form a great man, I thank my God I do not possess them.'

The writer here is Captain Amasa Delano of Duxbury, Massachusetts. The text is his *Narrative of Voyages and Travels, in the Northern and Southern Hemispheres,* Melville's principal source for *Benito Cereno.* Now, while Melville's appropriation of a key episode from this text has led to Delano's negative apotheosis as villainous racist and imperialist, a consideration of Delano's *Narrative* as a whole would suggest that the captain's appeal for Melville lay less in his villainy than in his geniality and liberality. Nonetheless, it must be emphasized that Delano is a sea captain. Although in the passage cited above we see him capably marshaling the sort of liberal–progressive rhetoric currently used to denigrate the fictional Delano's racism and imperialism, upon his captaincy his liberalism founders. He candidly confesses as much early in the *Narrative:* "I have a great horror of the crime of mutiny, and feel as every master of a vessel naturally will upon this subject. The bias of my mind, which my office in my profession has produced, is against whatever may tend to rebellion in the subject, and in favour of whatever may secure the prerogative of the commander." It is for this reason above all others that the historical Delano, despite his "humanitarian" objections to slavery, aids Cereno in suppressing a slave revolt: For Delano, rebellious slaves are mutineers who threaten captains with a horrible disorder.[58] One large aim of *Benito Cereno,* I will argue, is to explore the historical conditions and consequences of the sea captain's biases.

Thus although I will emphasize the importance of considering the relationship of *Benito Cereno*'s discourse to the sociopolitical discourse of the 1850s, we must keep in mind that *Benito Cereno* is a historical novella, a text about a time when "ships were then not so plenty in those waters as now" (PT, 673)[59] and a text that has as its principal source a chapter from an 1817 travel narrative. My reading of the novella is guided in part by R. G. Collingwood's notion of enactive historical narrative as set forth in *The Idea of History.* Collingwood proposes that the most powerfully illuminating historical narrative seeks to convey both "the outside and the inside of an event" – the event understood "in terms of bodies and their movements" and the event understood "in terms of thought."[60] What this requires of the historian is an imaginative effort to reenact the past event in his own mind and then the narrative skills to impel the reader toward a similar reenactment. In *Benito Cereno,* for reasons I will elaborate later, Melville as historian places special privilege on the bodies of the blacks and the thoughts of Delano, as he seeks to provide the reader with an "inside" look at the mentality of an American sea captain. And yet, as Eric Sundquist remarks on Melville's narrative strategies in the novella, "it is clear that we are not exactly in Delano's shoes, but rather are suspended between 'the sardonic, third-person intelligence' . . . that offers an extravagant and increasingly potent array of figurative clues and the American captain, to whom the very creation of those clues is often ascribed but who nonetheless fails . . . to interpret them correctly."[61] But it is precisely such suspension and uncertainty, I believe, that tempts us, as it were, to step into Delano's shoes and experience the consequences. Perhaps sensing that a first-person account, as in the original *Narrative,* would promote resistance among readers prone to suspect confessional narratives as inherently self-interested and unreliable, Melville instead lures the reader into adopting the perspective of a sea captain in the midst of a conspiracy by, in effect, situating the reader in the midst of a conspiracy. As in Hawthorne's "My Kinsman, Major Molineux," in *Benito Cereno* Melville enacts a double plot – one against Delano, another against the reader – that means to ambush both unawares.

Given its alternately reportorial and sardonic narrator who insists on maintaining an ironic distance from character and event, and given its plot that so long remains in a state of enigmatic suspense – given, in short, *Benito Cereno*'s conspiratorial form – I want to underscore, then, that first-time readers intent on interpretation are closely linked to Delano, himself a "first-time reader" intent on interpretation, because no matter how many "clarifying" hints are offered over the course of the narrative, it simply is impossible to be absolutely certain about what is going on aboard the *San Dominick* until events have completely unfolded. This is the central enactive strategy of Melville's narrative of conspiracy. To push my argument even further, I want also to insist on the primary importance of retaining, even after numerous rereadings, a memory of "first-time reading" for achieving the fullest historical understanding of Delano's inability to make sense of his situation. Otherwise we can always presume knowledge as experienced readers that frees us from any taint of implication in Delano's confusions and hence rise in self-congratulatory and, I will argue, self-blinding triumph over a character who, no matter how often we reread the text (and, for that matter, read the narrative of history running from Delano to the Civil War and beyond), remains a perpetually entangled and historically bound first-time reader.

To be sure, Delano's interpretative efforts are often naïve and racist, for he is set up as an American bumpkin seemingly unaware of the darker realities of power and history. Certainly, experienced readers of Melville would be wary of a character described as unable to "indulge in personal alarms, any way involving the imputation of malign evil in man" (673). But in a comment on historical re-envisioning especially pertinent to Melville's implicating use of Delano's limited point of view, Collingwood writes: "We must be able not only to re-enact another's thought but also to know that the thought we are re-enacting is his. But so far as we re-enact it, it becomes our own . . . [it] therefore cease[s] to be past."[62] In *Mardi*, "Vivenza" pointedly complains of outsiders who self-righteously attack those enmeshed in a slave culture: "Easy it is to stand afar and rail. All men are censors who have lungs" (M, 534). As we shall see, the narrative demands of Melville's novella make it difficult indeed for the new reader of *Benito Cereno* "to stand afar and rail."

At the risk of rehearsing the familiar, let us begin at the beginning of *Benito Cereno*, with Delano, captain of the *Bachelor's Delight*, facing a potentially dangerous predicament. The genial New England captain, the narrator reports, "commanding a large sealer and general trader, lay at anchor with a valuable cargo, in the harbor of St. Maria – a small, desert, uninhabited island toward the southern extremity of the long coast of Chile" (673). On his second day there, amidst ominous gray shadows and "troubled gray fowl" (673), an unidentified "strange sail" (673) approaches the harbor, the sun eerily shining through its cabin "not unlike a Lima intriguante's one sinister eye" (674). As Delano peers through his spyglass, he nervously wonders why a ship sailing in a lawless part of the world should choose not to show its colors. The image of the spyglass reminds us that, as Delano "continue[s] to watch" (674) the ship, we watch it too, in part, through his vigilant eye. At first he perceives it as a monastery carrying "a ship-load of monks" (675); he identifies them as "Black Friars pacing the cloisters" (675). But as the ship moves closer it comes into focus for Delano: It is "a Spanish merchantman of the first class; carrying negro slaves, amongst other valuable freight, from one colonial port to another" (675). Mysteriously, the ship betrays a "slovenly neglect" (675) and "sad disrepair" (675); and mysteriously, blacks far outnumber the whites on board what Delano soon sees is the San Dominick. Mysterious too are the ship's stern piece, which displays the arms of Castile and Leon and a masked satyr stepping on the neck of a writhing masked figure, and its canvas-covered figurehead, which has painted or chalked beneath it the slogan " 'Seguid vuestro jefe' (follow your leader)" (676). And perhaps most mysterious of all, when Delano actually boards the San Dominick, he meets the puzzling Benito Cereno, an "undemonstrative invalid" (681) with "a dreary, spiritless look" (678), attended by the slave Babo. Although not more than thirty, Cereno, who appears to be the ship's captain, is "almost worn to a skeleton" (679).

Within the context of teasing enigma, the masking imagery hints at a ubiquitous masking of power relations and so implies the potential for an unmasking: As in the carnival world of The Bravo and the theatrical world of Blithedale, masks arouse suspicion and fuel interpretive desires of protagonist and reader alike. Clearly, Melville meant to exacerbate suspicion among certain contemporary readers, and in this way further link these readers to Delano, through the novella's political imagery, an amalgam of conspiratorial languages hinting at any number of possible threats to the Duxbury captain and his crew. Delano's initial perception of the approaching San Dominick as a "ship-load of monks," for example, would alert the Protestant republican reader to a particular danger: This is a shipload of plotters. The subsequent shift in perceptions that correctly identifies the ship as a Spanish slaver alerts this reader to another, though related, conspiratorial threat, that emanating, as in The Bravo, from a European "republic" in decline; hence the comparison of the ship to "superannuated Italian palaces" (675) and, as suggested by the description of its "tenantless balconies [hanging] over the sea as if it were the grand Venetian canal" (676), to subverted republican Venice.[63]

For the contemporary Northern reader, a reader both implied and "constructed" by the narrative, such imagery would also associate the Spanish slaver with the putatively conspiratorial Southern "Slave Power." As David Brion Davis has shown, during the 1840s and 1850s many Northerners became convinced that Southern slave interests had secretly infiltrated and taken control of America's political and social institutions.[64] Significantly, by the late 1840s the rhetoric of nativists and Slave Power countersubversives began to overlap, for in the aftermath of the 1848 European revolutions the Roman Catholic church emerged in popular accounts, particularly in Northeast newspapers and journals, as perhaps the most dangerous threat to the ideals of republican liberty; the church itself came to be imaged as a Slave Power, which, unmasked, was the church of the Inquisition. Because the church in Spain had been particularly active in the Inquisition and had also initiated the importation of slaves to the New World, the Southern Slave Power was often compared to Spain. Theodore Parker, for example, traced the origins of the Southern Slave Power's expansionism in the Southwest territories back to Spanish expansionism in colonial America; and his angry response to the Kansas–Nebraska Act may well have provided Melville with a catalog of resonant imagery for his novella:

> Long before the Anglo-Saxons, the Spaniard came to America; greedy of money, hungering for reputation – the glory of the Gascon stock. He brought the proud but thin and sickly blood of a decaying tribe; the traditionary institutions of the past – Theocracy, Monarchy, Aristocracy, Despotocracy, the dominion of the master over the exploitered slave. He brought the mass-book and legends of unnatural saints, – the symbols of superstition and ecclesiastic tyranny; the sword, – the last argument of Spanish kings, the symbol of military despotism; fetters and the bloodhound.[65]

In *Benito Cereno,* the conjoining of oligarchical Catholic Spain to the Southern Slave Power is enacted through Delano's opening crisscrossing perceptions and is developed through Melville's emphasis on Cereno's "thin and sickly blood," "exploitered slave," Catholicism, and masquerade sword. The sickly leader of a declining slave power, the Northern stereotype of the Southern cavalier, and a Catholic who looks "like some hypochondriac abbot" (679), Cereno would be viewed by a republican countersubversive as an altogether suspicious representative of a Southern papistical Slave Power.[66] As Delano himself reflects, "The very word Spaniard has a curious, conspirator, Guy-Fawkish twang to it" (710).

The conspiratorial languages of the American 1850s thus press Melville's implied (Northern) contemporary reader to suspect the Spanish slaver that Delano too suspects. But they also play a major role in keeping alive the mystery central to the novella's plot: What is going on aboard the *San Dominick?* Should Delano be wary of Cereno, the archetype of the conspiring Catholic European (Southern) Slave Power leader, and thus be wary as well of the Spaniard's slaves, analogized to the restless Catholic masses controlled by the priestcraft of a "hypochondriac abbot"? Or should black slaves, long suspected in America of constituting a violent rebellious potential, be feared in and of themselves? As a number of critics have pointed out, Melville hints at this particular threat by setting the novella in 1799, a small but significant departure from his source in Delano's *Narrative,* which recounts events of 1805, and by renaming the ship the *San Dominick,* as opposed to the *Tryal.* Melville thus alerts the reader to the threat posed not only by "Catholic" slaves, but also by insurrectionary slaves such as those of San Domingo, whose bloody revolt, among other things, led to the expulsion of the Spanish presence from the islands before 1800.[67]

In various ways, then, *Benito Cereno* asks the reader to become a countersubversive attempting to make sense of a most problematic text, the doubloon of the enclosed ship at sea, "a strange house with strange inmates in a strange land" (667). It does so through its political symbolism, and most importantly it does so through its development of Delano's "apolitical" perspective as a sea captain. Drawing on the conception in contemporary sea narratives of the ship as an institutional space separating "inmates" from outsiders, Melville describes Delano's meditation on the enigma of the ship *qua* ship: "Both house and ship, the one by its walls and blinds, the other by its high bulwarks like ramparts, hoard from view their interiors till the last moment; but in the case of the ship there is this addition; that the living spectacle it contains, upon its sudden and complete disclosure, has, in contrast with the blank ocean which zones it, something of the effect of enchantment" (667). It is an enchantment to which Delano must not succumb, for as all sea captains know, interpretation "in a strange land" may be a matter of economic and social survival.

Two enigmatic narratives develop simultaneously, exacerbating Delano's unease about the possibility of survival and, because enigmatic, involving Melville's readers too in the act of captain-like interpretation. First, in an effort to construct "the whole story" (682) of what happened on board the *San Dominick,* Delano elicits from a hesitating Cereno information about the ship's disasters at Cape Horn; he then tests the "facts" against his knowledge of normal practices and occurrences at sea and against Cereno's retellings of the same story. The other narrative is, of course, the disturbing narrative unfolding before Delano's eyes, as a series of interruptions to Cereno's storytelling suggests that the whole story may be but a partial story. Both the construction of narrative and the unfolding of narrative make Delano uneasy. Like Robin Molineux seeking authority in the revolutionary (and conspiratorial) city, his perception that something may be awry leads him to cling to the "innocence" and values that, at least to this point in his life history, have managed to preserve him. These are the values of a sea captain, which throughout the novella shape his responses and interpretations.

Because Delano is a self-satisfied and strong captain, he latches onto evidence of poor leadership as the key to the *San Dominick*'s past catastrophes and present disorders. For example, as he listens to Benito Cereno's account of the "heavy gales" (683) and scurvy that, "by a luckless fatality" (684), killed fifteen sailors and every remaining officer, he smugly imputes Cereno's difficulties "both to clumsy seamanship and faulty navigation" (686), the result of "youth, sickness, and gentility united" (686). When Cereno timidly suggests that they ascend the ship's poop to get clear of the noisy hatchet polishers, Delano contemptuously wonders "why such an interruption should be allowed" (687). An unpunished instance of black insubordination that, Delano pridefully remarks, on his ship would bring "instant punishment" (688) prompts the self-righteous reflection, "I know no sadder sight than a commander who has little of command but the name" (688). Troubled by the *San Dominick*'s "prominent breaches, not only of discipline but of decency" (682), Delano soon takes it upon himself to tell Cereno how to run his ship: "Keep all your blacks employed" (688), he instructs him. Eventually he will take the helm of the ship and guide it ashore. From Delano's perspective as a sea captain, the *San Dominick* could profit from the order and discipline characteristic of older European slave powers; Cereno seems deficient as a leader because he is not "Spanish" enough.

Delano's evolving responses to the Spanish slaver pivot on a homology and *telos* central to the institutionalist mentality of America's antebellum "sea captains": "In armies, navies, cities, or families, in nature herself, nothing more relaxes good order than misery" (679). His interpretive framework therefore focuses attention on what can be called the "reformist" concerns of the narrative: the captain-like fear of "urban" disorders and the concomitant desire for discipline and authority to restore "perfect sea order." As Delano nervously views various acts of black insubordination, he decides that "what the *San Dominick* wanted, was what the emigrant ship has, stern superior officers" (682). Compared to a "belittered Ghetto" (686), the *San Dominick* needs the protective services vouchsafed by what Delano terms a "police department" (682). Ideally, however, this commissarial "police department" would maintain order over the ship's "emigrants" through the assumption of a "natural" paternal authority; hence Delano's conjoining of "house and ship" and, more tellingly, "armies, navies, cities, or families." Confronted with the disorderly "emigrant ship" of the ghettos, nervous Northern reformers extolled their hierarchical and discipline-oriented prisons and asylums as familial, as grounded in "nature herself"; similarly, Delano's conception of the well-ordered ship as familial serves the double purpose of legitimizing institutional authority and quelling anxiety.[68] Yearning for "the quiet orderliness of [his] sealer's comfortable family of a crew" (682) and troubled by Cereno's apparent lack of command, Delano essays to place his faith in all vestiges of the San Dominick's "health" and "authority," even the slaver's hierarchical ideal of good order: white over black.

Like many late-eighteenth-century (and nineteenth-century) Americans, Delano regards the relationship between master and slave as a reassuringly natural one, wholly analogous to that between captain and seaman, father and child, man and dog. As the narrator famously puts it, "Captain Delano took to negroes . . . just as other men to Newfoundland dogs" (716).[69] It is not surprising, then, that initially he should "take to" the San Dominick's apparently happy and faithful blacks or that he should jocularly offer to purchase Babo. Yet rifts in the unfolding narrative increasingly suggest that Delano – regarded by most recent critics as stupidly naïve and blind to the possibility of black conspiracy – in fact wills his blinding romantic racialism and familial institutionalism in the face of an intimated threat of riotous eruption from the San Dominick's black "emigrants." Crucially, as "insiders" we realize that Delano time and again experiences unsettling intuitions of white vulnerability. He perceives the "continuous, low, monotonous chant" of the junk pickers as a "funeral march" (677). He may romanticize the ominous hatchet polishers as exemplars of "the peculiar love in negroes of uniting industry with pastime" (678), but when he later walks past them and conceives of himself as "running the gauntlet" (687), we wonder, as it seems Delano himself is wondering, about the peculiarity of "the peculiar love in negroes." Nevertheless, when the muscular, enchained black king Atufal arrives to stand before Cereno while refusing to beg forgiveness for his past insubordination, Delano cannot help feeling that all is well aboard the San Dominick. The "mulish mutineer" (691) is padlocked, and Cereno wears the key around his neck. "Away with suspicion," Delano tells himself (694). He then dreams the restful dream of a sea captain: Cereno "restored to health" (700) and "restored to authority" (700). "Such were the American's thoughts," the narrator observes. "They were tranquilizing" (700).

As mysteries remain in a murky suspension, though, one thing is clear: The "tranquilized" Delano is in need of further sedation. Viewing Cereno and Babo whispering between themselves, "Captain Delano thought he observed a lurking significance in it, as if silent signs of some Freemason sort had that instant been interchanged" (696).[70] He fears that Cereno's apparent lack of command may in fact mask a conspiratorial design, in which "every soul on board, down to the youngest negress, was his carefully drilled recruit in the plot" (699). Moreover, in a reflection that recalls the image of Fedallah and his confederates, he wonders if Cereno has Malay pirates lurking in the ship's hold, "a hundred spears with yellow arms ready to upthrust them through the mats" (698). Seeking to reinforce bonds between the captain-like reader of the novella's creation and the putatively "singularly undistrustful" (673) Captain Delano, Melville, whose arch narrative voice throughout the novella plays fast and loose with the reader, repeatedly intervenes to belittle Delano's fears of plotters, remarking, for example, that Delano generally "heightened whatever, upon a staid scrutiny, might have seemed unusual" (677). In this way he attempts to con the reader into an acceptance of Delano's racialist and institutionalist idealizations and hence surprise the "un-distrustful" reader, as the captain himself is surprised, by conspiracy.[71]

At the same time, however, Melville continues to emphasize the threatening otherness of blackness within the ship as "urban" institution and Delano's anxious perception of that threat. The forward part of the mainmast, for example, is "wholly occupied by the blacks" (686). Thus Delano's glimpse of a "spectacle of disorder" (701) – two blacks beating a white – exacerbates his fears of white defenselessness should such disorder eventually have free reign. Taking command, he decides to speak with one of the few white Spanish sailors to be found in the black "Ghetto":

> Descending the poop, he made his way through the blacks, his move-ment drawing a queer cry from the oakum-pickers, prompted by whom, the negroes, twitching each other aside, divided before him; but, as if curious to see what was the object of this deliberate visit to their Ghetto, closing in behind, in tolerable order, followed the white stranger up. His progress thus proclaimed as by mounted kings-at-arms, and escorted as by a Caffre guard of honor, Captain Delano, assuming a good-humored, off-handed air, continued to advance; now and then saying a blithe word to the negroes, and his eye curiously surveying the white faces here and there sparsely mixed in with the blacks, like stray white pawns venturously involved in the ranks of the chess-men opposed. (702)

The chess imagery conveys the cerebrally calculating world of power Delano has entered and the color polarities of that world. A white king surrounded by black knights and vulnerable to checkmate, he tries to maintain his confident bluster even as he notes that all of the white sailors, like Delano, are completely encircled by blacks. A sailor working with tar has attracted "blacks squatted round him inquisitively eying the process" (703). An older sailor at work on a Gordian knot is assisted by "two sleepy-looking Africans" (703). Just as the masking imagery im-plies the possibility of an unmasking, so the sleepiness implies the pos-sibility of an awakening. Not for nothing does Delano ask himself, in the sort of language typically used to warn of impending mutinies, riots, and slave revolts, "Might not the *San Dominick*, like a slumbering volcano, suddenly let loose energies now hid?" (698).

Yet even as Delano assesses a multitude of unsettling signals that point to the possibility of Spanish or black conspiracy, he refrains from taking the sort of preemptive self-defensive action that Mackenzie and his supporters argued was morally incumbent upon a sea captain. "In short," the narrator explains, "to the Spaniard's black-letter text, it was best, for awhile, to leave open margin" (695). Given Delano's access to the martial power of his ship and crew, to interpret is to act; to continue to "read," even when the elderly Spanish sailor tosses him the Gordian knot and urges him to "undo it, cut it, quick" (707), suggests a generous, albeit confused, willingness to entertain for a while longer the possibility that he may "be murdered here at the ends of the earth" (709). But his anxiety necessarily fuels an ongoing meditation on "four curious points" (710) about the Spanish slaver: two acts of black insubordination, Atufal's strange defiance/penance, and "the cringing submission to their master of all the ship's underlings, mostly blacks; as if by the least inadvertence they feared to draw down his despotic pleasure" (710). All of these "curious points" are, of course, curious points about chattel slavery itself, and the captain's meditations therefore provide us with an "inside" view of his essential blind spot: a recognition of the blacks' humanity and intelligence.

But again we must ask the question: How blind is he? Because Delano, unlike the typical Northerner, finds himself in a situation in which a slave revolt would actually result in his death, his idealization of the "natural" hierarchical relation of master to slave can be viewed as a close parallel to the proslavery idealization, as a betrayal, I think we are meant to realize, of a similar willed blindness. For example, in William Harper's *Memoir on Slavery* (1838), published only seven years after Turner's rebellion, Harper lauds the natural loving relationship between master and slave and then for some odd reason feels called upon to scoff at the very idea of black conspiracy: "Of all the impossible things, one of the most impossible would be a successful insurrection of our slaves, originating with themselves." The possibility is so impossible that he must dwell on the prospect at length: "Though experience has shown that revolutions and political movements – unless when they have been conducted with the most guarded caution and moderation – have generally terminated in results just the opposite of what was expected from them, the angry ape will still play his fantastic tricks, and put in motion machinery, the action of which he no more comprehends or foresees than he comprehends the mysteries of infinity." Similarly, although Delano perceives that the hatchet polishers have the "air of conspirators" (696), he rejects the notion that blacks independent of Cereno would or could plot a violent rebellion on their own. He assures himself, "They were too stupid" (707).[72]

Nevertheless, he cannot repress his sense that on board the *San Dominick* he views a form of theater in which the director is other than the captain. His initial suspicion that Cereno may be "one of those paper captains" (688) had led him to surmise, as Redburn surmised about the ungentlemanly Captain Riga, that the "man was an imposter" (694). Reflecting on how Cereno supposedly belongs to a renowned Spanish family, "a sort of Castilian Rothschild" (694), he posits that this effete Cereno may be "playing a part above his real level" (694). Significantly, when Delano later tries to impose order on blacks exulting "in disorderly raptures" (711) at the arrival of the provision-laden *Rover,* his self-conscious perception of his own theatricality reveals that he is beginning to regard himself as an actor lacking any naturally sanctioned authority. He orders the blacks to back off, "making use of a half-mirthful, half-menacing gesture" (711); and then it appears he will learn the true limits of his captaincy. The blacks pause in their places, "a rapid cry came from Don Benito" (711), and Delano's submerged fears of rebellious blacks suddenly surface as he prepares himself "to be massacred" (711). Although even here he continues to believe that the blacks, if conspirators, must be under Cereno's command, when the oakum pickers intervene and push back the crowd, Delano, ever the competitive sea captain, assuages his shaken psyche by pitying Cereno for his loss of "self-command" (712).

The problem of command is at the center of the novella's most famous scene, Babo's shaving of Cereno, which Delano again senses is a form of theater, "some juggling play" (720). Clinging as best he can to the racialist belief that "most negroes are natural valets and hair-dressers" (716), Delano finds that this particular shaving hardly provides him with calming reassurances of black servility. From his unsettled perspective (and this is anticipated in his opening perception of the blacks as Catholics), the *San Dominick's* cuddy — with its "small, meager crucifix" (715) and settees like "inquisitors' racks" (715) — resembles the inquisitorial torture chamber that nativists advised could be found within America's convents and monasteries. Indeed, as Babo deliberately "search[es] among the razors, as for the sharpest" (717), holds up "the gleaming steel" (717), places Cereno's head in a shaving basin, and nicks him, he seems to become "Spanish" himself, a sadistic, priestly enslaver. Arguably, then, the initial impact of the scene is to exacerbate captain-like anxiety as to who, in fact, is in command;[73] for as Delano observes the shaving he sees only the black man's razor and the white man's throat: "Altogether the scene was somewhat peculiar, at least to Captain Delano, nor, as he saw the two thus postured, could he resist the vagary, that in the black he saw a headsman, and in the white a man at the block" (717–18). But as with Delano's earlier intimations of black power and white vulnerability, the narrator encourages the reader to dismiss Delano's better intuitions as mere vagaries of the imagination: "This was one of those antic conceits, appearing and vanishing in a breath, from which, perhaps, the best regulated mind is not always free" (718).

To the very end, however, Delano's "regulated mind" remains rather perceptive and nervous about Babo's headmanship and the possibility of black conspiracy. After eliciting yet another rehearsal of Cereno's narrative of events at sea, Delano spots a white surrounded by blacks and "felt a slight twinge, from a sudden indefinite association in his mind of Babo with Atufal" (727). Preparing finally to return to his aptly named *Bachelor's Delight,* he experiences one last fearful moment. He hears the bell on the *San Dominick* sounding, "as of the tolling for execution in some jail-yard" (730). The image of execution, along with the "beheading" at the shaving basin, speaks to the prospect of a "Jacobin" revolutionary conspiracy; the image of the jailyard speaks to his sense of entrapment. He then realizes that to leave the *San Dominick*'s "jail-yard" he must walk past the enchained "inmate" Atufal; and after considering various conspiratorial threats, he asks himself a key question: "Was the negro now lying in wait?" (731). Summoning all of his will and courage, Delano, "with clenched jaw and hand" (731), hastens past Atufal and upon disembarking lifts his eyes toward the heavens and reflects on the protection offered by "the ever-watchful Providence above" (731). Then he boards his ship, the two ships begin to part ways, and suddenly Cereno leaps onto Delano's deck, followed by Babo, and the threatening energies Delano had intimated all along abruptly manifest in an explosive unmasking of "mutiny and revolt."

So quickly does the unmasking take place that Delano initially overpowers both Cereno and Babo. He exhibits a brute power that links him with the grinning satyr on the *San Dominick*'s masthead: "The left hand of Captain Delano, on one side, again clutched the half-reclined Don Benito, heedless that he was in a speechless faint, while his right foot, on the other side, ground the prostrate negro" (733). Delano's obtuseness kept him at an interpretive distance; when he cannot help untying the knot inside his head, which, ironically, is what the reader wants him to do all along, he rediscovers his fraternal connection to his fellow sea captain: "With infinite pity he withdrew his hold from Don Benito" (734).[74] Now aligned as one, the captains, outsiders of the black conspiracy, together confront unchained, vengeful blacks, "not in misrule, not in tumult, not as if frantically concerned for Don Benito, but with mask torn away, flourishing hatchets and knives, in ferocious piratical revolt" (734). There ensues a "spectacle of disorder."

The presentation of the racial clash is of a piece with the darkest imaginings of racial conflict in antebellum America. In pursuit of Cereno, *his* fugitive slave, Babo triggers a mass explosion of fury that evokes the "volcanic" eruption at San Domingo: "Meantime, the whole host of negroes, as if inflamed at the sight of their jeopardized captain, impended in one sooty avalanche over the bulwarks" (733). As in a horrible nightmare, the shroud is lifted from the *San Dominick*'s stern piece to reveal the skeleton of its former captain, Alexandro Aranda, above the injunction to "*Follow your leader*" (734). Unmasked, the stern piece calls for a mass slaughter of whites; unmasked, Delano's idealized childlike slaves become seemingly horrifying demons. From the perspective we have been following, that of Delano, we are temporarily blinded to the larger social issues impelling the blacks to seek revenge. We have become sea captains, confronted with an implacable insurrectionary fury. The blacks are imaged as an astonishingly hateful mass of energy: They are called "delirious black dervishes" (734). Perhaps modeled on the vengeful Indians of Francis Parkman's *The Conspiracy of Pontiac* (1851), they cut off a white's fingers when "Indian-like, they hurtled their hatchets" (736). The violence builds to an apocalyptic bloody climax that, from the whites' terrified perspective, conceives of the blacks as savage beasts: "Their red tongues lolled, wolf-like, from their black mouths" (738). Confronted with such alarmist imagery, it is not so remarkable that a critic as discerning as Matthiessen should have viewed the novella as racist. The past, in Collingwood's terms, has become present, and we still see like captains.

To this point my reading of *Benito Cereno* has been a temporally based one that follows Delano from intimation to recognition of black conspiracy and argues for the implicating function of the captain's "inside" perspective. James Kavanagh writes that "analysis of 'Benito Cereno' must begin by breaking absolutely the seductive grip of identification between the reader and Amasa Delano."[75] I am maintaining that for post-1960s readers the break with Delano has become such an easy, de facto, and essentially extratextual gesture – the "correct" response as mandated by critical consensus – that the reverse is in order: We need temporarily to relinquish our political right-mindedness and certainties so that analysis may *begin* by considering the grip of the reader's initial identification with the captain. Only when we contemplate our temptation, however short-lived, to experience with the captain both his fear of conspiracy and his pursuit of tranquility can we truly come to understand the seductiveness of captaincy and, I would suggest, our similar temptations toward analogous forms of captaincy in our own time.

    At the conclusion of the discussion I will take up what I regard as *Benito Cereno*'s transhistorical cultural thematics. Before doing so, however, I want now to depart from the temporal reading, as the novella itself, following the revelation of black conspiracy, departs from its temporal unfolding, to address a problem central to our overall study of romance and conspiracy: the relationship between the romancer's critical appropriation of countersubversive discourse and his implication in the fears and desires inscribed in such discourse. More specifically, I want to consider the interpretive problems raised by Melville's seeming adoption in the novella of what Brook Thomas terms "a proslavery perspective."[76] Though Melville unquestionably remains skillfully in control of the unsettling ironies emerging from his use of a conspiratorial form that links reader to Delano, at the unmasking of the blacks' plot, I believe, he betrays some of his own anxieties about the potentially violent consequences of America's racial situation. T. Walter Herbert comments on Melville's narrative method in *Typee:* "Melville is able in effect to dismantle the civilized self and give its constituents play, toying with its root anxieties without giving way to the chaos that threatens to erupt."[77] As noted earlier, this is not exactly true for *Typee's* Appendix; and it may be even less true for *Benito Cereno,* in which an eruption of chaos brings to surface all sorts of fears inherent in the discursive formations and social practices of the antebellum period, particularly the fear, to use the parlance of the times, of an apocalyptic "war of extermination" between the races. In light of the violence surrounding the Fugitive Slave Law and the Kansas–Nebraska Acts, what Tocqueville observed about the American 1830s was even truer for the American 1850s: "The more or less distant but inevitable danger of a conflict between the blacks and whites of the South of the Union is a nightmare constantly haunting the American imagination."[78] *Benito Cereno's* implicating narrative would suggest that the nightmare haunted Melville's imagination as well.

The nightmare of slave revolt, we recall, took particular rhetorical forms and served particular sociopolitical purposes. Central to the nightmare of black conspiracy informing virtually every Southern defense of slavery, and central to the analogous nightmare of revolt informing texts of urban reform, was an (often familial) idealization of the hierarchical institutional structures that would keep insurrectionary energies in check. Those at the lower rungs of the social ladder were therefore generally presented in terms of an insidiously deployed alarmist dualism: Contained within institutional structures, so the argument went, they were happy and content; uncontained, they became miserable and vicious. With specific reference to the proslavery argument: Contained, so Dew and many others argued, the slaves were Sambos; uncontained, they became savages. And yet so pervasive and endemic were fears of black conspiratorial revolt that Southerners came to believe that the Sambo in fact masked the savage. This dualistic conception without a middle ground – shared too by Northerners advocating colonization as a bloodless solution to the supposed black rage for vengeance – surely played a major role in encouraging Americans to skirt political solutions to the problem of slavery; it prompted slaveholders in particular to translate conspiratorial fears into power. What Melville ultimately reveals through Delano's uncannily insightful perspective, then, is that those most aware of restlessness down below are America's various "captains."

Where Melville is implicated in all of this is in his appropriation of key alarmist tropes for his re-presentation of a slave revolt. Structured around the Sambo–savage dualism and building to a nightmarish racial clash, *Benito Cereno,* it can be argued, seems to imply a politics similar to the politics informing alarmist proslavery writing. To illustrate what I mean in the baldest possible terms, when Fenimore Cooper in *The American Democrat* (1838) attacks slavery as "an evil" while at the same time warning that emancipation would inevitably lead to an interracial "war of extermination,"[79] he in effect works against his antislavery position, for the last thing he would want to advocate is apocalyptic annihilation. Moreover, his specter of a "war of extermination" is precisely the specter evoked by proslavery writers to justify the continuation of slavery. Compare Cooper's crisis mentality in *The American Democrat,* for example, with William Harper's in *Memoir on Slavery,* also written in 1838. Like Cooper, Harper cannot imagine a postemancipated America that is not engulfed in violence and so he warns: "Released from the vigilant superintendence which now restrains them, they [emancipated slaves] would infallibly be led from petty to greater crimes, until all life and property would be rendered insecure. Aggression would beget retaliation, until open war – and that a war of extermination – were established."[80] Though at odds in their avowed politics, the alarmism of their prophecies makes their implied politics nearly commensurate.

Two nautical romances that, like Melville's novella, conjoin the Sambo–savage dualism with depictions of an interracial "war of extermination" shed additional light on the interpretive problems raised by *Benito Cereno's* alarmist discourse. In Edgar Allan Poe's *Narrative of Arthur Gordon Pym* (1838), Pym and his crew put their trust in black Tsalalian islanders who "evinced the most friendly manner." But the seemingly slavish Too-Wit, the islanders' ingratiating leader, is actually a Babo-like master intelligence determined to rid his island of the whites' polluting presence. Thus, after duplicitously leading the credulous explorers into a ravine, he orders his fellow Tsalalians to bury the whites alive, bringing about what Pym calls "the day of universal dissolution." As Pym retrospectively observes, "A very short while sufficed to prove that this apparent kindness of disposition was only the result of a deeply laid plan for our destruction, and that the islanders for whom we entertained such inordinate feelings of esteem, were among the most barbarous, subtle, and bloodthirsty wretches that ever contaminated the face of the globe."[81] Although the disasters befalling the explorers could be interpreted as Poe's attack on their blinding sense of cultural and racial superiority, it is not far-fetched to suggest that in the wake of Nat Turner's rebellion, as Harold Beaver remarks, "Poe deliberately played on Southern hysteria, by suggesting that blacks, far from timid, were both a sly and warlike people; that quite apart from subversion without, the South should be constantly on its guard against treachery from within."[82] And it is not far-fetched to suggest that, for many of Poe's contemporary Southern readers, the romance's alarmism, whatever Poe's intentions, simply would have confirmed their belief in the need to keep a close watch over their own "bloodthirsty wretches."

Fenimore Cooper teaches a similar countersubversive lesson in *Afloat and Ashore* (1844). Sailing along the northwest coast of South America in the aptly named *Crisis* during the crisis year of 1799, Miles Wallingford's crew encounters a group of apparently friendly South American Indians with whom they negotiate exploitative barter exchanges. Reflecting the "scientific" racialism of the time (and hence linking South American Indian to North American black), Wallingford takes special note of the Indians' stupidity: "I had seen beasts in cages that appeared to me to be quite as intelligent, and members of the diversified family of human caricatures or of the baboons and monkeys, that I thought were quite as agreeable objects to the eye." Convinced of the Indians' friendliness and idiocy, the less than vigilant North Americans leave themselves vulnerable to a bloody plot, which, true to the novel's use of alarmist dualism, unmasks the fiction of the Indians' slavish stupidity to reveal their malignant savagery. The leader of the plot, Smudge, who initially "seemed to be almost without ideas," turns out, like the theatrical Too-Wit and Babo, to have been "the principal actor in this frightful scene." As Wallingford fearfully confesses during the pitched battle between the races, "I was astonished at seeing the intelligence that gleamed in the baboon-like face of Smudge."[83] As with *Pym,* it is tempting to read the account of the Indians' attack on unsuspecting whites as a reflection of Cooper's disdain for racist and expansionistic North Americans. The novel as a whole, however, emphatically conveys Cooper's acute fear of mutinous revolt and insists on the need for strong captains and obedient seamen in order to preserve the shipboard community from further disorders. Accordingly, soon after the lamentable execution of Smudge, who nobly saved Wallingford from drowning, Cooper indulges in the utopian fantasy that would inform *The Crater* and has the Cooper-like Wallingford ascend to the captaincy of a ship in which the crew members, unlike Cooper's loathed anti-Renters, submit completely to his authority. In the remainder of the novel everyone obeys Captain Wallingford, and every command from the captain upholds the commonwealth of the ship. Despite the tragic hanging, then, the presentation of the conspiratorial revolt at sea suggests that the captain-like need to be wary and protective of the social order, the need to keep the "beasts in cages," outweighed in Cooper's mind even the legitimate claims of the mutinous plotters with whom he could also sympathize.

An abolitionist polemic that far more strenuously upheld the claims of revolutionary slaves, and that also conjoined the dualistic conception of blacks with an apocalyptic image of interracial violence, appeared in *Putnam's* only a few pages before the final installment of *Benito Cereno*. In the anonymous sketch titled "About Niggers," a genial first-person narrator describes the delightful characteristics of "Niggers" in stereotypical fashion, seemingly oblivious to the limitations of his racialist idealizations. But at the sketch's conclusion the narrator abruptly turns against his racism, and that of an implied complacent reader, to warn of the distinct possibility of a violent slave rebellion:

> But with all this charming jollity and waggishness, the nigger has terrible capacities for revenge and hatred (which opportunity may develope, as in St. Domingo), and which ought to convince the skeptic that he is a man, not a baboon; and whenever our southern partners quit us, and begin to take care of their niggers themselves, they will learn that they are no joke.[84]

Of interest here is the way the author argues the cause of the black by proferring and then subverting the stereotype of the waggish "nigger," installing in its place what had become an equally stereotypical image of the "nigger" as vengeful arch conspirator. By relating American blacks to the rebels of San Domingo and by endowing them with "terrible capacities for revenge and hatred," the writer insists upon the imminence in America of an explosive black violence. If read just before the concluding section of *Benito Cereno*, the sketch would guide the reader to regard the novella's unmaskings as an illustration of blacks taking a well-deserved revenge on white enslavers. And yet the revolutionary blacks of "About Niggers" and *Benito Cereno* are also the duplicitously violent blacks feared by America's proslavery writers and are similar to the dangerous poor feared by America's nervous defenders of urban-reform institutions: evincing "charming jollity" on the surface, nurturing homicidal vengeance beneath the veil. These are the insurrectionaries feared by Northern and Southern "captains" alike.

From a rhetorical perspective, then, the revolt in *Benito Cereno* provides a horrifying culmination of the novella's development of the masking motif that would seem to suggest, along the lines of Thomas Dew,

William Harper, Edgar Allan Poe, and even Fenimore Cooper, that blacks are either content valet-barbers or vicious headsmen; stupid brutes or intelligent plotters; enslaved or enslaving. At least on the surface of things, Melville, having appropriated for his novella the alarmist and countersubversive discourse of slave revolt, necessarily reproduces the perceptual (and conceptual) limitations of the very discourse he wishes to scrutinize and critique. Accordingly, he takes the risk of appearing to imply a racist and institutionalist politics not essentially different from he politics of enslavers and sea captains. Bakhtin comments on the lialogical novelist's need to take such risks:

> The prose writer as a novelist does not strip away the intentions of others from the heteroglot language of his works, he does not violate those socio-ideological cultural horizons (big and little worlds) that open up behind heteroglot languages – rather, he welcomes them into his work. The prose writer makes use of words that are already populated with the social intentions of others and compels them to serve his own new intentions, to serve a second master.[85]

It is precisely because Melville preserves the intentions and horizons of his culture's alarmist discourse of mutiny and revolt, I would maintain, that he can seem to be more historically limited and complicitous than he actually is. But does his dialogical responsiveness to a range of cultural discourses really bring with it a new form of mastery?

On the one hand, then, with the selective parallel examples from Harper, Poe, and Cooper, I have been pursuing a "new historical" reading of *Benito Cereno* that implicates Melville in the containment strategies of his culture. On the other hand, following Bakhtin, I have adopted a "dialogical" reading that places Melville at an ironic and critical distance from such strategies. And yet, as I have emphasized throughout this study, irony does not necessarily liberate the writer from the taint of implication, nor is there any reason it should aspire to do so. In *Benito Cereno*, I want to suggest, as with Melville's troubling account of *Omoo*'s "dark, moody savage" (O, 72) Bembo, "a man, or devil, if you will" (O, 72), the depiction of alarmingly vengeful blacks speaks in a nonpatronizing and disarmingly honest fashion to a white author's unwillingness to domesticate black rage; it speaks honestly to a white author's social and racial anxieties. It also speaks to the pessimism dominating Melville's works of the 1850s, which would lead him to find such a grimly antiutopian episode from Delano's *Narrative* to be a more appropriate source than, say, a progressive and providential episode from a slave narrative like Frederick Douglass's. Melville's appropriated alarmist tropes and discourse thus keep the novella true not only to its source in Delano's text, but also to the social situation, concerns, and sensibility of its producer, a "second master" but not an absolute master.

Certainly Melville is nervous about the prospects for interracial violence and is implicated by the very rhetoric he "welcomes" into his work. What sets him in opposition to countersubversive alarmists is that he understands how and why this should be so and accordingly makes the matter of implication *the* central matter of the novella. He does this, in large part, through his use of the captain's perspective, which, we come to realize as rereaders, plays a fundamental role in compelling us to view events in terms of alarmist dualisms and institutionalist solutions. When Delano watches Babo "changing his previous grin of mere animal humor into an intelligent smile" (697), for example, we suspect that, as opposed to Harper and Poe, the shift from "animal humor" to "intelligent smile" is less a betrayal of Melville's conceptual tendencies than a portrayal of Delano's.

In the same way the black women too are presented in terms of an alarmist dualism. Viewed through the lens of Delano's romantic racialism, a "slumbering negress" (704) and "the other negresses" (704) are initially idealized as "noble savage" mothers: "Unsophisticated as leopardesses; loving as doves. Ah! thought Captain Delano, these perhaps are some of the very women whom Mungo Park saw in Africa, and gave such a noble account of" (704). The contrastive view of awakened black women is provided in the court deposition, which reports that "the negresses, of age, were knowing to the revolt, and . . . had the negroes not restrained them, they would have tortured to death, instead of simply killing, the Spaniards slain by command of the negro Babo" (750).

As with the portrayal of Babo and his male compatriots, the unveiling of the black women's homicidal rage frightfully exposes the bankruptcy of Delano's romantic idealizations while at the same time – and this is the novella's most unsettling irony – "legitimizing" his, the captain-like reader's, and, eventually, the Spanish authorities' recourse to a containing institutionalism. In *Benito Cereno* Melville relates the "peculiar institution" of slavery to the familial institution of the ship as part of a brilliant historical perception of the relationship between the legitimizing of racial and ethnic stereotypes and the legitimizing of institutions of social control in the South and in the North.[86] Essential to Melville's portrayal of the legitimation process, to underscore the argument of this chapter, is his presentation of the revolutionary slave conspiracy as a "mutiny" (735) that threatens to subvert the "perfect sea order" of captains. Viewing the ideal order of the ship as analogous in significant ways to the ideal order of the antebellum total institution allows us to relate Delano's efforts to negotiate his way past the fear of mutiny to similar efforts by Southern enslavers and Northern urban reformers. Like these land-bound captains, Delano clings to a way of seeing that keeps him at the helm. Intimating the disruptive presence of black mutineers, he idealizes the good order of master over slave and grounds that order in nature. His faith in the microhierarchical order of captain over seaman extends to the analogous order of master over slave and thus serves to authorize the macrohierarchical "familial" order of both the institution of the ship and the institution of slavery. Idealizing these institutions whenever he senses a threat to his self-command, he manages for the longest while to keep his world intact.

Secondary institutions and their concomitant ideologies, sociologists Peter Berger and Thomas Luckmann suggest, serve this tranquilizing function for those in command. Institutions alleviate tension by providing a structure wherein predictable behaviors and roles are maintained; they fend off the terror of chaos and death by giving rise to ideologies that put "everything in its right place."[87] Delano's captaincy-based assumptions and values continually allow him to do just that. Even when he finally realizes that he is in the midst of a slave revolt, he instantly "rereads" the day's events in terms of mutiny, and all that was mysterious suddenly makes sense: "Across the long-benighted mind of Captain Delano, a flash of revelation swept, illuminating in unanticipated clearness his host's whole mysterious demeanor, with every enigmatic event of the day, as well as the entire past voyage of the San Dominick" (734). Apprehending the slave revolt as a form of mutiny, he need not put to any sort of test the assumptions undergirding his racialism and institutionalism. Rather, for Delano, as for other defenders of total institutions, a violent mutiny merely reinforces "in unanticipated clearness" the need for those ordered institutions that keep "everything in its right place."

The novella, however, through its discursive appropriations, theatricalizations, and unmaskings encourages us to regard Delano's seemingly naturalized and objectified orderings as man-made fictions that participate in the world of power. It does so, as numerous critics have pointed out, through Babo's subversive revolutionism, which can be regarded as a surrogate for Melville's subversive artistry. Michael Rogin writes: "By forcing Don Benito to play the part of master, Babo has forced him to mistrust the patriarchal, domestic relations which had constituted his identity. By overthrowing slavery and then staging it as a play, Babo has conventionalized the supposedly natural relations of master and slave." He adds, making clear the connection between Babo and Melville, "Against an ideology that saw slavery as the most organic of social relations, Melville conventionalized, as stage props, the symbols of authority which slaveowners insisted were theirs by nature."[88] But while we eventually learn that Babo's is the masterminding intelligence behind the novella's conspiratorial plot – that he is "the plotter from first to last" (749–50) – the challenging and profoundly disturbing aspect of *Benito*

Cereno is the way Melville keeps that intelligence a silent and yet controlling presence that, contrary to Collingwood's historicist imperatives, we
can never really get "inside." Given our narrative distance from Babo, it
may be mistaken to view his actions as forms of ideological analysis and
criticism, particularly if we ourselves are involved in ideological analysis
and criticism. Though not as invidious as Delano's imaging of a black
rebel as a Newfoundland dog, the ideological critic's rendering of Babo as
ideological critic performs a similar act of domestication and containment
that makes the "lividly vindictive" (734) Babo rather too much like us.

And yet the very absences and uncertainties that, as first-time readers,
exacerbate our anxieties of plotting blacks beg us as rereaders to adopt, as
best we can, the point of view of black revolutionaries. There are textual
encouragements toward this end – the narrator's teasing dark ironies, the
enactive plot that perpetually revictimizes readers unwilling to break
from Delano – but finally, and this is what makes *Benito Cereno* so
subversive of the order it can seem to "legitimate," the impulse to adopt
the blacks' perspective must come from both within and without the
text; in effect, when we resist the seductions of Delano's perspective and
values, we involve ourselves in the sort of risky resistance to shipboard
authority and hierarchy that regularly accompanies mutiny in Melville's
nautical romances. Identifying with Babo, projecting ourselves inside his
point of view, may be regarded then as an act of "mutiny" analogous to
White-Jacket's near act of mutiny: It occurs within an antebellum sea
narrative but is motivated by values at odds with, and posing a radical
challenge to, the values inscribed in the dominant sea narratives of the
period. Accordingly, our mutinuous perspective is not necessarily a con-
flict-free or untroubling perspective, for it asks us to relinquish the very
ideals and desires that, as we have seen, inform even Melville's earlier
nautical romances.

Nevertheless, when we imagine ourselves "inside" the mutineer perspective, whether governed by a perception of the narrator's ironic distance from Delano, or by an *a priori* belief in the evil of slavery and the
humanity of the black rebels, or even by a critical consensus that insists
on the moral imperative of seeing like Babo, to a large extent all does
appear "in unanticipated clearness." We recognize and admire the blacks'
brave and impassioned desire for liberty; we perceive Babo as a brilliant
trickster whose verbal resourcefulness and inventive role playing nearly
succeed in liberating his fellow blacks; and we come to realize that Delano's "innocent" racialist and institutionalist idealizations are inextricably intertwined, as Kavanaugh puts it, with a "violent, somewhat
vicious, defense of privilege, power, and self-image."[89] With our animus
now directed against the captain, a rather horrific novella can become for
its "knowing" rereaders somewhat comic, as Delano, the butt of the
artful plot, remains forever in the dark.

Certainly from our "mutinuous" perspective the Spanish court transcript on the black revolt is especially appalling for its absences. Like the social institutions we have examined in this chapter, the transcript contains and makes sense of a feared and fearful violence through an act of framing enclosure; it is a Spanish Catholic document of slavery writ large that legitimizes the Spaniards' practice by grounding it in the historical, economic, and religious ideals securing the state. The court deposition from the vice-regal court in Lima, Peru, is signed in the name of "His Majesty's Notary for the Royal Revenue, and Register of this Province, and Notary Public of the Holy Crusade of this Bishopric, etc." (739). Like the alleged transcript of *The Confessions of Nat Turner,* which similarly promises to provide "an authentic account of the whole insurrection" and is likewise officially framed by the legal seal of the "Clerk of the County Court of Southampton" and the verdict of *"the Commonwealth,"* the Spanish transcript tells what the narrator ironically calls the "true history of the *San Dominick*" (738) by remaining blind to the blacks' point of view.[90] The deposition thus silences the already self-silenced Babo by offering an account of the conspiracy in a formalistic language that attends primarily to the unfolding of the revolt as experienced by the whites, particularly Captain Benito Cereno. Inserting the Spanish court transcript into the novella almost immediately after the unmasking of the black revolt, at that crucial point in the novella when all has seemed to burst asunder, Melville focuses attention on the way a state's official language acts to pull things back together through a juridical willed blindness paralleling Delano's willed blindness.

Enclosed with the official seals of the transcript, as in Nat Turner's *Confessions,* is an account of the bloody circumstances attending a ferocious slave revolt that, so framed, is intended by the Spanish to put on display not black desires for freedom but the "fact" of black savagery and the need to contain it. Like those Virginians who prided themselves on their "liberal" slave practices, so the paternalistic first-captain Alexandro Aranda was shocked that the blacks he "liberally" left unchained should have seen fit to revolt even as trusting whites lay asleep. His shock parallels that of the similarly trustful, and victimized, Captain Barnard of Poe's *Pym.* With his enthusiastic support for pitilessly hurling whites into the sea, Babo resembles Poe's black cook, the plotter behind the uprising on board Barnard's *Grampus;* and by refusing to murder with his own hands, he also resembles Turner, who took credit for only one killing in the Southampton rebellion. When Babo later has Aranda's white skeleton attached to the prow in place of the ship's figurehead – Christopher Colon – his wickedly ironic remarks on the whiteness of the skeleton and on the whites' need to follow his orders lest they "Follow your leader" (744), again in the context of the framing deposition, are meant to testify to the sadistic energies unleashed by the black rebellion.[91] From the Spaniards' cultural-legal perspective, then, the blacks' bloody deeds speak to the urgency of imposing upon them an absolute form of recontainment: state-ordered tortures and executions.

Of course, it has become clear to most modern readers that, as Matthiessen realized (and believed Melville did not), the ferocity of the black revolt, both as witnessed by Delano's crew and as reported in the deposition, ultimately testifies to the slaves' very human response to the crime of slavery – this was also quite explicitly the point of the *Putnam's* piece "About Niggers." Hardly an indication of a particularized black "savagery," the blacks' violent resistance to their enslavement is rightly taken as the novella's most cogent evidence that Spanish/Southern crimes were committed against a people possessive of memory, dignity, and intelligence. The blacks' ferocity, and the prospects for future ferocity, therefore challenge the silences and concealments of Spanish and American legal discourse.[92]

I want to emphasize, however, that there is no revolutionary and highly personalized White-Jacket in the novella to make this challenge or political perspective explicit; instead, the burden of political analysis is bequeathed to the reader. But the novella, it should be noted, also bequeathes to the reader multiple spectacles of disorder indicative of a generalized "savagery" shared among blacks and whites. The presentation of the interracial "war of extermination" had limned the horror of a black–white confrontation as witnessed by white officers appalled by black mutineers. The court deposition, in addition to providing an overview of the initial black uprising, offers a dispassionate account of the later bloody battle between blacks and whites at St. Maria, and through its measured language reveals an equally horrid picture of whites succumbing to a sadistic retributive violence. We learn from the deposition, for example, that the whites, upon regaining control of Cereno's ship, proceeded to torture and stab recaptured blacks already "shackled to the ring-bolts on deck" (752). According to the deponent Cereno:

> These deaths were committed by the sailors, ere they could be prevented. That so soon as informed of it, Captain Amasa Delano used all his authority, and, in particular with his own hand, struck down Martinez Gola, who, having found a razor in the pocket of an old jacket of his, which one of the shackled negroes had on, was aiming it at the negro's throat; that the noble Captain Amasa Delano also wrenched from the hand of Bartholemew Barlo, a dagger secreted at the time of the massacre of the whites, with which he was in the act of stabbing a shackled negro, who, the same day, with another negro, had thrown him down and jumped upon him. (752)[93]

Whites too are enslaved by the institution of slavery and are "savages" barely contained within it. As in the antislavery writings of Richard

Henry Dana, Jr., and numerous other abolitionists, who feared that slavery made both the despotic enslaver and the victimized slave what Harriet Beecher Stowe's St. Clare called "brute beasts," at the heart of Melville's novella is a dark vision of transracial savagery that simultaneously challenges the institution of slavery while exacerbating anxieties about the imminence of apocalyptic "head-breaking."[94]

Critical as *Benito Cereno* is of slavery and its concomitant ideologies, the novella is haunted by the fear, not so very different from the fear haunting *White-Jacket* (or *Two Years* and *Uncle Tom's Cabin*), of the imminent irruption, in the words of Captain Mackenzie's supporter Charles Sumner, of "the worst passions in man." Such is *Benito Cereno*'s ironic and demystifying power, however, that we resist the nostalgic retreat to an enslaving institutionalism; we are innocent no more. At the same time, as Bernard Rosenthal observes of Melville's parodic uses of Christic, Marian, and Spanish/American political imagery, such is the novella's insistence "that we see the failure of all religious systems and all political systems," that we are left grasping for some sort of regenerative possibility.[95] Hardly a progressive or glibly postmillennial jeremiad, *Benito Cereno* portrays a macabre cycle of crime and revenge which suggests that the achievement of a "solution" to America's racial situation – however much desired and morally imperative – remains only a distant possibility when we assess, as Delano cannot, "the imputation of malign evil in man." As is true for most of Melville's writings of the middle to late 1850s, in *Benito Cereno* there would seem to be little hope indeed for the emergence of an ideal fraternal community – a community, as imaged in *Moby-Dick*'s "A Squeeze of the Hand," of "abounding, affectionate, friendly, loving feeling" (MD, 348). We remain stranded in an unregenerate world of separateness, expediency, and tyranny.

In this regard the slogan "Follow your leader," under its "proper figure-head" (744) of Christopher Colon, resonates not only as a grim prophecy on republican America's inability to transcend imperial Spain's historical crimes, but also as a grimly ironic reminder of Babo's willingness to assume a Spanish-like captaincy, and not just in "deceit and defense" (746). The slogan thus speaks to the novella's Hawthornean sense of history as a cyclical repetition of victimization and tyranny; there are no villains and heroes, only those in power and those victimized by power. Neither the two captains nor Babo and his compatriots are "essentially" evil or good. It is significant, for example, that Atuful should have been a king in his own country and that Babo, himself formerly enslaved by blacks, should have been striving to take the *San Dominick*'s blacks to Senegal, a country wherein blacks traditionally enslaved blacks. Given the novella's dark perspective on man's will to power and potential for "savagery," and given the unsettling logic of its alarmist discourse, "Follow your leader" ultimately resonates as a desperate call for a model republican leader, like the revolutionary and yet pragmatically institutionalist Jack Chase, capable of bringing about what *Benito Cereno,* and arguably all of Melville's nautical romances, suggest may well be an impossibility: containment without enslavement. The novella is Melville's despairing, Longfellow-like call – the call of a writer of nautical romances unwilling to relinquish the genre's implicit desires and ideals – for a simultaneously authoritarian and fraternal captain who could guide Americans past the shipwreck of the civil and racial "war of extermination" he truly feared. It is a call, so the novella's final scene suggests, that makes Melville altogether uneasy.

In a scene that occurs chronologically before the court tribunal but that Melville reserves as a coda on the seductions and pitfalls of captaincy, the two captains, "during the long, mild voyage to Lima" (753), discuss the disturbing events of recent days. Comforted by a teleological faith in good order, Delano thanks God for His guardianship and looks forward to new voyages. In contrast, Cereno, plagued by memory and nearly wasted away by his ordeal, cannot struggle free from the shadow he calls "The negro" (754). As envisioned in Melville's novella, the negro is an absence that casts a shadowy presence, and so Cereno's despair – the despair of one who has experienced – remains truer to the novella's enactment of black revolutionary fury than does Delano's happier "innocence." Nevertheless, the stark description of Babo's severed head, "that hive of subtlety, fixed on a pole in the Plaza" (755), suggests why Delano would adopt his blindness: It allows him to turn from "shadows present, foreshadowing deeper shadows to come" (673), so as to pursue the "bright sun" (754) of future prospects. Those who on first reading are duped with Delano reenact his self-protective blindness and are surprised by conspiracy. But even readers who come to scorn Delano can, with Melville's "inside" help, at the very least understand Delano's desire to avert his eyes from Babo's. The novella closes with the lifeless Babo still seemingly gazing hatefully at his "leader" Cereno; when Delano at the opening of the novella peers through his telescopic lens at the *San Dominick,* meeting his eye, we realize as rereaders, is the resurrected gaze of Babo. Peering with Delano, we meet Babo's hateful eyes head-on. Nervously, we contain that gaze by offering Babo our fraternal embrace and subjecting the captain to a disdainful scrutiny.

As rereaders we turn against Delano's "innocent" and blinding racism and institutionalism. Yet our participation in his willed blindness compels us to contemplate our own desires for good order and our own desires to "take to" Babo and thus to contemplate the ways in which our own pursuit of the "bright sun" may depend upon an assumption of captaincy. "Who aint a slave?" (MD, 15), Ishmael rhetorically demands at the beginning of *Moby-Dick*. The equally troubling rhetorical question posed by *Benito Cereno*'s conclusion is "Who aint a captain?" The social-critical force of Melville's attack on slavery, and on the institutional practices idealized by America's various captains, emerges, I believe, from his sense of his own inability to rise above the pervasive fear of "mutinous" disorders, his own inability to claim an untainted perspective on the political and social crises of his time, and his own inability, as fearful and relatively privileged Northeast white, to assume a non-complicitous relationship to antebellum forms of captaincy and power. *Benito Cereno* is not simply an antislavery tract that "shows" the evils of slavery; rather, it is a crisis-ridden work that winds around on the strands of America's Gordian knot and asks of even its most enlightened readers to participate with Delano, however unwillingly, in the anxious and blinding desire for "perfect sea order" that could sanction so insidious an institution as slavery. By linking first-time readers to Delano, and by historicizing the problem of slavery through the representation of the late-eighteenth-century captain's mentality, Melville suggests how difficult it would be for any "captain" at that time to relinquish the fear of the alien and the comforts of power, and thus presses his readers to reflect on their own fear of the alien and their own complicitous relationship to power. *Benito Cereno* transcends its historical moment, then, in part by refusing to offer a higher consolation to its interpreters. Shortly before his death Cereno remarks to Delano: "You were with me all day; stood with me, sat with me, talked with me, looked at me, ate with me, drank with me; and yet, your last act was to clutch for a monster, not only an innocent man, but the most pitiable of all men" (754). Cereno is perceptive on this matter: He is simultaneously "innocent," "pitiable," and monstrous. So is Delano and so is the reader; such is the uneasy situation, Melville suggests, of the civilizers and the civilized.[96]

"The story . . . is no romance"

Drawing on contemporaneous discourse warning of the dangerous laboring classes, Slave Power subversives, and rebellious slaves, and enacting his sociopolitical drama of black conspiracy in a sea narrative – dedicated as the genre was to idealized (and conflicting) notions of good order – Melville brought to bear on *Benito Cereno* the desires and anxieties informing the moral dilemma and sectional impasse of the 1850s. The novella itself, I have been arguing, reaches its own impasse, as Melville manipulates the reader both to seek authority and containment and to resist authority and containment. The text transforms the reader into a self-conscious sea captain desirous of restoring the ship of state even as he or she remains aware of, and mutinously identifies with, an otherness subsumed and enslaved by the "consensual" demands of community.

Melville had not always been so pessimistic about the possibility of remedial action. In *White-Jacket* he asserted that the end of the seaman's "enslavement" could come about through an embrace of natural law, "'coeval with mankind, dictated by God himself.'" The suggestion of *Benito Cereno,* however, reinforced by the political developments of the 1850s and Melville's theological despair of the same period, is that a belief in the congruence between the individual and God is idealistic and naïve, a version of Pierre's "country" innocence. Pierre's comically inadequate innocence, of course, soon gives way to a feeling that "all the world, and every misconceivedly common and prosaic thing in it, was steeped a million fathoms in a mysteriousness wholly hopeless of solution" (P, 128). As a result, the more mature author Pierre, like Melville of the 1850s, turns against the closure strategies of "the countless tribes of common novels [which] laboriously spin vails of mystery, only to complacently clear them up at last," and instead pursues "profounder emanations" that "never unravel their own intricacies, and have no proper endings; but in imperfect, unanticipated, and disappointing sequels (as mutilated stumps), hurry to abrupt intermergings with the eternal tides of time and fate" (P, 141). *Benito Cereno*'s "mutilated stump" of an ending – with its representation of mutilated Babo, despairingly self-conscious Cereno, and "naïvely" re-empowered Delano – dangles but does not unravel three strands of the Gordian knot. The ending conveys Melville's Pierre-like lament that things may be "wholly hopeless of solution" in a world, not so different from the captainless "NO TRUST" (CM, 5) world of *The Confidence-Man,* in which there is an absence of moral and spiritual authority.

The absence of authority can generate desires, like Delano's, for a return to authority. Such desires were central to the American 1850s. Forgie writes: "In terms of political institutions, the desire for return manifested itself in the appearance of both the Republicans and the nativist Know-Nothings. Both claimed that the nation was being changed beyond recognition by insidious forces; both called for a return to the purity of the beginning."[97] For the secretive and fraternal Know-Nothings, the pure beginning was a nation that, according to Brockden Brown, never existed: a nation devoid of plotting, self-interested aliens. Experiencing, as Delano would experience, a breakdown of "fidelity on the one hand and confidence on the other" (PT, 685), the Know-Nothings crusaded to save the republic from the "corrupting" presence of the Roman Catholic church and its emigrants – a "slave power" that, so the Know-Nothings argued, threatened republican ideals of free labor and virtuous community. In *The Confidence-Man* Melville mocks the

Know-Nothings' nativism through his portrayal of an alarmist who warns his auditors of "those Jesuit emissaries prowling all over our country" (CM, 92). Although the alarmist admits that his warnings lack the support of empirical evidence, he justifies his countersubversive practices with a series of maxims: "Suspect first and know next. True knowledge comes but by suspicion or revelation" (CM, 92). Like Melville's alarmist, the Know-Nothings claimed to have identified the conspiratorial forces undermining the stability of America's expanding cities. Arguing that their homogeneous and hierarchical organization would eventually restore the order and deference they deemed essential to the state, the Know-Nothings offered their followers the privileges of "knowledge" and "revelation" in a world many believed no longer offered privilege to anyone. Captain Delano's values and fears reflect the corporate sensibilities and concerns of Know-Nothing leaders; his perception of the blacks as "black friars" exemplifies the ways in which fears of Catholic immigrants and blacks permeated one another in the mid-1850s.[98] At the very least, Melville's narrative strategies in *Benito Cereno* play with a trope of Know-Nothingism: Central to the enactive unfolding of the novella is an effort to link reader and Delano as a community of captain-like "know-nothings" yearning for a return to the hierarchical order and purposive unity of the familial ship.

The Know-Nothing yearning for an ordered ship of state, as with other countersubversive movements of antebellum culture, was an expression in extreme of the desire for order and community held by even those who rejected the party's nativism. Similar desire, as Forgie notes, informed the program of the emergent Republican Party; and a brief look at Lincoln's effort to restore and repurify the state will help to suggest a way past the impasse of *Benito Cereno*.

For Lincoln, the political crisis of the 1850s taught several key lessons: that the exchange of "rational" discourse between the nation's contending sections and interests threatened only to prolong the crisis; that, as Robert Ferguson puts it, "knowledge alone will not bring better understanding"; and that there was a need less for a return to an older social order than for the development of a new social order.[99] In important ways Melville's *Benito Cereno* shares these beliefs. Babo's silence, for example, speaks to the imperative for pragmatic, or even revolutionary, action guided by truths morally intuited rather than rationally proved. "Seeing all was over," the narrator remarks when Babo is brought to trial, "he uttered no sound, and could not be forced to. His aspect seemed to say, since I cannot do deeds, I will not speak words" (PT, 755). The Spanish court decrees words, formulating the sentences that, with a repulsive rationality, condemn the blacks to an eternal silence. Melville's sentences, however, vouchsafe the reader responsive to his ironies knowledge of the ways in which an enslaving institutional authority can idealize its authority and, in so doing, uphold its claims to authority. Yet it cannot be ignored that the novella's most acutely self-conscious and "knowledgeable" character, Benito Cereno, perversely and rather narcissistically luxuriates in his self-consciousness until he wastes away. Construed at its most radical, then, the novella, by emphasizing the limits of words, rationality, and "knowledge," encourages the reader to make a redoubled effort to redefine political vocabulary and institutions through "deeds" and not "words" and to reject out of hand the enslavers' and captains' – the know-nothings' – recourse to containment. But at its most anxious – and this is what separates Melville from Lincoln in the 1850s – the novella foresees perpetual tensions between a community's "insiders" and those "outsiders" feared as aliens, perpetual displays of "malign evil in man," and, most despairingly of all, perpetual and essential meaninglessness in a world absent of God.

In his 1852 campaign biography of Franklin Pierce, Hawthorne spoke of God's presence in the world as he urged abolitionists to put aside their antislavery efforts. Slavery, he advised, is "one of those evils which divine Providence does not leave to be remedied by human contrivances, but which, in its own good time, by some means impossible to be anticipated, but of the simplest and easiest operation, when all its uses shall have been fulfilled, it causes to vanish like a dream."[100] In contrast, Lincoln embraced a millennialism that conceived of evil as God's test of His people's contrivances. Accordingly, action to combat evil was needed and necessary, even if that meant abandoning the dream of distant abolition for the nightmare of war; for the Civil War, as Lincoln explained in his Second Inaugural Address (1865), drawing on Psalms 19:9, was a nightmare both meaningful and deserved:

> Fondly do we hope – fervently do we pray – that this mighty scourge of war may speedily pass away. Yet, if God wills that it continue, until all the wealth piled by the bond-man's two hundred and fifty years of unrequited toil shall be sunk, and until every drop of blood drawn with the lash, shall be paid by another drawn with the sword, as we said three thousand years ago, so still it must be said, "the judgments of the Lord, are true and righteous altogether."[101]

In *Benito Cereno* violence occurs in the spiritual wasteland of St. Maria and does not save. For Lincoln, violence in the hallowed battlefields of America was redemptive, promising to bring forth a reconsecrated community in which the sorts of problems complicating *Benito Cereno* would have disappeared. Under the duress of war and in the name of glorified consensus, so Lincoln hopefully imagined, "aliens" would become "friends," Americans would discover "the better angels of our nature."

institutions would serve the interests of the commonwealth, and there would be "malice toward none." Whereas Hawthorne saw the Civil War sweeping Americans "into a Limbo where our nation and its polity may be as literally the fragments of a shattered dream as my unwritten Romance," Lincoln's writings of the Civil War period expressed, to recall Frye's formulation, a "wish-fulfillment dream," an effort to reconstitute the shattered fragments of the American romance while eliding the problem of boundary drawing that we noted in Washington's romance.[102]

The majesty of Lincoln's Civil War writings, Ferguson proposes, "flows from his virtually unique ability to wrap political explanation in divine mystery."[103] In the 1850s Melville lacked Lincoln's ability to appropriate "divine mystery" and would mock those, like *Pierre*'s Plotinus Plinlimmon, who pretended that they could. By the time of the Civil War, however, Melville shared Lincoln's hopes that violence would sanctify the nation, as he departed significantly from his portrayal of unregenerate violence in *Benito Cereno*. Nevertheless, he continued to lack Lincoln's ability to harness the divine for the political, and that, I would suggest, is what makes *Battle-Pieces* (1866) so disconcerting. Unlike Lincoln in his visionary writings, Melville in the Civil War poems cannot avert his eyes from dark human passions and the specter of the alien. For example, although "Lee in the Capitol" concludes with the hopeful couplet "Heaven shall the end ordained fulfill, / We march with Providence cheery still" (BP, 237), its principal focus, as is true for many of the poems in the volume, is on the real problem of Northern vengeance. Concerned that a spiteful North would "in Union's name forever alienate" (BP, 236), Melville celebrates what he demystifies in *Benito Cereno*, the "sounder fruit" of "re-established law" (BP, 235). Similarly, in "The House-top," a meditation on the "draft riots" of 1863, a three-day massacre of blacks in lower Manhattan, the poet gazes upon a city undone by "the Atheist roar of riot" (BP, 86) and muses that only "Wise Draco" (BP, 87), by implementing "code corroborating Calvin's creed" (BP, 87), could contain and redeem base human passions. Melville captures the depravity of the disorder through his use of nautical imagery: "Balefully glares Red Arson – there – and there. / The Town is taken by its rats – ship-rats – and rats of the wharves" (BP, 86). By the end of the poem the poet rejects the notion that "Man is naturally good, / And – more – is Nature's Roman never to be scourged" (BP, 87). Abandoning the idealism of *White-Jacket*, Melville sanctions flogging.

Although "The House-top" was occasioned by the massacre of blacks, *Battle-Pieces* for the most part conveys little sympathy for the blacks, who are imaged as aliens bearing signal responsibility for the Civil War: "Can Africa pay back this blood / Spilt on Potomoc's shore?" (BP, 242). In the volume's "Supplement" Melville addresses the problem of postbellum

"Re-establishment" (BP, 259) and presents the South, not the blacks, as the war's principal victims. As in *Mardi,* he argues that Southerners "were not the authors" of slavery, but rather were its "fated inheritors" (BP, 266). Victims of history and Northern power, Southerners, like the victimized blacks of *Benito Cereno,* have been effectively silenced, "stricken down and unavoidably debarred, for the time, from speaking through authorized agencies for themselves" (BP, 264). Urging that the North not "perilously alienate" (BP, 267) the South, that there be "malice toward none," Melville chooses to alienate the blacks, as he calls on Northern legislators to exhibit kindness "to communities who stand nearer to us in nature" (BP, 267). Fearing the irruption of violent "exterminating hatred of race toward race" (BP, 268), he appeals, as did Hawthorne in 1852, to the wisdom of community and to God: "Something may well be left to the graduated care of future legislation, and to heaven" (BP, 269). Within Melville's reconsecrated America, blacks will continue to be alien outsiders inscribed by the whites' laws and institutions, though he hopefully, and jarringly, concludes: "Our institutions have a potent digestion, and may in time convert and assimilate to good all elements thrown in, however originally alien" (BP, 269).

The problem of the "alien" haunts all of the romances we have examined, all of which build to the death of the character most threatening to the standing order. Melville's corporeal rhetoric of "potent digestion" simultaneously exposes the power cloaked by the body politic's romance of sanctified community while naturalizing and affirming that power. He uses a similar corporeal image in *Billy Budd.*[104] In that later text the narrator comments on British and American fears of the French Revolution's "red meteor of unbridled and unbounded revolt" (BB, 54) and then refers to the Nore mutiny "as analogous to the distempering irruption of contagious fever in a frame constitutionally sound, and which anons throws it off" (BB, 55). By the end of the novella, however, what is "thrown off" the *Bellipotent*'s frame is the body of the archetypally innocent Billy Budd. To be sure, Billy Budd, who is referred to in the "authorized" naval chronicle as "one of those aliens adopting English cognomens" (BB, 130), participates in sanctifying Vere's decision – "God bless Captain Vere!" (BB, 123). Nevertheless, it is difficult not to wonder about the appropriateness and "naturalness" of Captain Vere's punitive actions; for while Vere advocates "forms, measured forms" (BB, 128), the narrator insists that "truth uncompromisingly told will always have its ragged edges" (BB, 128). One inescapable implication of the novella is that the trimming away of raggedness may well involve "the abrogation of everything but brute Force" (BB, 122).

And yet the narrator repeatedly calls attention to the very real potential for widespread mutinous disorders. As he remarks, because of the recent mutinies at Spithead and Nore, "it was not unreasonable to apprehend some return of trouble sporadic or general" (BB, 59). Consequently, the officers are especially vigilant in watching out for subversive mutineers: "At sea, precautionary vigilance was strained against relapse" (BB, 59). Such overprotective straining, however, leaves the ship vulnerable to the plottings of a malevolent countersubversive, who cannily waits until the *Bellipotent* is at its "furthest remove from the fleet" (BB, 90) before accusing Budd of mutiny. The master-at-arms Claggart, compared to the notorious countersubversive Reverend Dr. Titus Oates, who warned of the factitious Popish Plot, shrewdly plays on Vere's anxiety by hinting that Budd's alleged mutinous activities could result in another Nore mutiny: "God forbid, your honor, that the *Bellipotent*'s should be the experience of the _____" (BB, 93). In making his charges, the countersubversive gains an inquisitorial power over the accused – Budd is compared to "a condemned vestal priestess in the moment of being buried alive" (BB, 99) – which is instantly abrogated by the stuttering Budd's mortal blow.

The burden of judgment falls to Captain Vere, who initially covers his face as if to flee responsibility, and then "unmasks": "Slowly he uncovered his face; and the effect was as if the moon emerging from eclipse should reappear with quite another aspect than that which had gone into hiding. The father in him, manifested toward Billy thus far in the scene, was replaced by the military disciplinarian" (BB, 100). Not only does the father, as is typical of Melville's early nautical romances, emerge as a disciplinarian, but at the drumhead court he also emerges, like Claggart, as a type of priestly inquisitor: Vere's officerial "vows of allegiance to martial duty" are compared to the "vows of monastic obedience" of the "true monk" (BB, 104). And when his arguments for the execution of Budd reach their climax, he resorts to the same countersubversive tactics as Claggart, as he likewise appeals to the officers' fears of "the recent outbreak at the Nore" (BB, 112). Altogether successful as an alarmist rhetorician, he brings the officers "to something more or less akin to that harassed frame of mind which in the year 1842 actuated the commander of the U.S. brig-of-war *Somers* . . . to resolve upon the execution at sea of a midshipman and two sailors as mutineers" (BB, 113). A disciplinarian, a priest, and a manipulative countersubversive, Vere at the drumhead court seems at his most expedient and monstrous.

But he is sanctified by Billy Budd, who, unlike the typical "subversive," accepts his fate. "True knowledge comes but by suspicion or revelation," the *Confidence-Man*'s alarmist proclaims. In *Billy Budd* there is a suggestion that, although Vere understandably experiences the generalized anxiety of mutiny and then exploits countersubversive warnings to arouse further anxiety, he, as opposed to the demonic Claggart, is ultimately guided by revelation. In this respect, Vere resembles less Captain Mackenzie or Judge Shaw, the historical figures to whom he is usually compared, than Lincoln; for immediately following Budd's killing of Claggart, Vere has a vision. To the surprise of the level-headed and skeptical surgeon, Vere points to Claggart's dead body and proclaims: "It is the divine judgment on Ananias! Look!" (BB, 100). Subsequently, after "standing absorbed in thought" (BB, 101), he vehemently exclaims: "Struck dead by an angel of God! Yet the angel must hang!" (BB, 101). Lincoln envisioned the sacrifices of the Civil War giving birth to "the better angels of our nature"; Vere envisions the sacrifice of God's better angel as the eternal price of liberty. Budd's stutter, the narrator remarks on his allegorical and melodramatic characterization of the Handsome Sailor, "should be evidence not alone that he is not presented as a conventional hero, but also that the story in which he is the main figure is no romance" (BB, 53).

Melville perceived the world as horologically unsuited to God's angels, and in the posthumous *Billy Budd,* his compellingly enigmatic "farewell address," he uses the conventions and discourse typifying America's literary romances to peer beneath the idealizing rhetoric sustaining Lincoln's consecrating romance. The romance of America is no romance – that may be the darkest truth revealed by America's romancers.

per classes, and racial anxieties were heightened in all regions of the country. In addition to fearing subversion from below, many Americans, responding to late-nineteenth-century incorporations and consolidations of power, came to suspect plotters from above. Renewed suspicions of a Masonic-like "money power," which was believed to be corrupting the character of the nation, contributed to the rise of populism as a significant political force. To look ahead only briefly: As a result of America's participation in the war effort, the period from 1917 to 1921 was "unmatched in American history for popular hysteria, xenophobia, and paranoid suspicion."[2] The tensions surrounding the Red Scare of the period carried over into the McCarthyite campaigns of the 1940s and 1950s and beyond. Racial, religious, and other political anxieties continued to play a major role in twentieth-century American culture.

Nevertheless, it would appear that the most obviously "major" fictionists of the postbellum period, unlike those of the antebellum period, were less attentive to local conspiratorial fears and their accompanying discourses. Realism and naturalism were international movements that encouraged American authors to broaden their literary and philosphical bases. Moreover, the very idea of conspiracy, as the writings of Henry Adams (and, later, Thomas Pynchon) suggest, was itself becoming more broadly conceived in relation to larger historical forces and transformations. That said, recent historicist studies of late-nineteenth-century fiction have disclosed the ways in which the naturalists and realists were also engaged with various discourses of subversion and countersubversion. Henry James's *The Princess Casamassima* (1885) draws on Anglo-American concerns about spies and secret societies and, through its distinctive omniscient narration, to some extent reproduces the surveillance tactics of modern policing agencies. In this respect, James's narrative tactics resemble those of Cooper in *The Bravo*. Mark Twain's *A Connecticut Yankee in King Arthur's Court* (1889) draws on anti-Catholic, "slave power" discourse and, in its portrayal of Hank Morgan as despot and slave, evokes a despairing sense of historical repetition reminiscent of *Benito Cereno*. Moreover, *Connecticut Yankee*'s movement from utopia to apocalypse, pivoting as it does on conflicting reponses to Catholicism, reminds us of the movement and conflict informing *Blithedale*. To take one other example, William Dean Howells's *A Hazard of New Fortunes* (1890) draws on widely shared concerns about insurrectionary irruptions in the city, particularly as articulated in Josiah Strong's popular *Our Country: Its Possible Future and Its Present Crisis* (1885). Although sympathetic to the claims of the exploited working classes, Howells's fear of subversion, coupled with his urge as "realist" to explore America's social geography, led him to place special narrative emphasis on delineating, and ultimately demarcating, the existing boundaries between workers and managers, lower and upper classes, ethnics and "Americans." The interplay between conspiratorial anxieties and boundary drawing, central to *Hazard* and Strong's more alarmist *Our Country*, recalls the similar interplay and anxieties characterizing Sophia's narrative strategies in *Ormond*.[3]

Although we can discern important continuities and parallels between antebellum and postbellum fictionists' engagement with conspiracy, there is at least one significant underlying difference that allows us to "periodize" American romance as an early national and antebellum literary phenomenon. In the decades following the Civil War, John Higham observes, there were numerous conspiratorial crises in which, centrally, "confidence in the homogeneity of American culture broke down."[4] During the early national and antebellum period, in contrast, it was confidence in the perpetuity of "America" that broke down. If we view the creation of America as itself an expression of the imaginative energies central to romance, we may conclude that the (melo)dramatic quest animating the national romance was fulfilled with the Union forged by the Civil War. The achievement of the national romance, the transformation of limitation into power, in effect quelled the rhetorical and social tensions from which had arisen the romancer's restless art.

Notes

Introduction

Epigraph: Wendell Phillips, *Public Opinion* (speech before the Massachusetts Antislavery Society, 1852), rpt. in *Speeches, Lectures, and Letters* (Boston: Redpath, 1863), p. 52.

1. Charles Brockden Brown, *Edgar Huntly; or Memoirs of a Sleep-Walker,* ed. Sydney J. Krause and S. W. Reid (Kent, Ohio: Kent State University Press, 1984), p. 3.
2. James Fenimore Cooper, for example, conceded to his European readers that the American writer suffered from "a poverty of materials" (*Notions of the Americans* [1828], rpt. in *The Native Muse: Theories of American Literature from Bradford to Whitman,* ed. Richard Ruland [New York: Dutton, 1976], p. 224). In the preface to *The Marble Faun: or, The Romance of Monte Beni,* ed. William Charvat, Roy Harvey Pearce, Claude M. Simpson, Matthew J. Bruccoli, Fredson Bowers, and L. Neal Smith (Columbus: Ohio State University Press, 1968), p. 3, Nathaniel Hawthorne worried over America's absence of antiquities and ruins.
3. Henry James, *Hawthorne* (Ithaca, N.Y.: Cornell University Press, 1956), p. 34; James, "Preface to 'The American,'" in *The Art of the Novel: Critical Prefaces by Henry James,* ed. Richard P. Blackmur (New York: Scribner, 1934), pp. 34, 33.
4. Richard Chase, *The American Novel and Its Tradition* (Garden City, N.Y.: Doubleday, 1957), pp. 38, 22, 39. Chase was also considerably influenced by Lionel Trilling, who declared in his Jamesian "Manners, Morals, and the Novel" (1948) that the "novel in America diverges from its classic intention, which . . . is the investigation of the problem of reality beginning in the social field. The fact is that American writers of genius have not turned their minds to society" (*The Liberal Imagination: Essays on Literature and Society* [Garden City, N.Y.: Doubleday, 1950], p. 206). For sophisticated extensions and revisions of James and Chase, see Joel Porte, *The Romance in America:*

Studies in Cooper, Poe, Hawthorne, Melville, and James (Middletown, Conn.: Wesleyan University Press, 1969); and Michael Davitt Bell, *The Development of American Romance: The Sacrifice of Relation* (University of Chicago Press, 1980). On the limitations of Trilling's and Chase's romance theories, see David H. Hirsch, *Reality and Idea in the Early American Novel* (The Hague: Mouton, 1971), pp. 32–48; Nicolaus Mills, *American and English Fiction in the Nineteenth Century: An Antigenre Critique and Comparison* (Bloomington, Ind.: Indiana University Press, 1973), pp. 11–31; and Robert Merrill, "Another Look at American Romance," *Modern Philology*, 78 (1981): 379–92. For useful overviews and critiques of romance theorists' ahistorical orientations to nineteenth-century American literature, see Carolyn Porter, *Seeing and Being: The Plight of the Participant Observer in Emerson, James, Adams, and Faulkner* (Middletown, Conn.: Wesleyan University Press, 1981), pp. 3–22; Amy Kaplan, "'Absent Things in American Life,'" *Yale Review*, 74 (1984): 126–35; and Russell Reising, *The Unusable Past: Theory and the Study of American Literature* (New York: Methuen, 1986), pp. 92–162.

5. M. M. Bakhtin, *The Dialogic Imagination*, ed. Michael Holquist (Austin: University of Texas Press, 1982), p. 293. Bakhtin's ideas on "dialogic" intertextuality have greatly influenced my approach to American romance.

6. In *A World Elsewhere: The Place of Style in American Literature* (New York: Oxford University Press, 1966), Richard Poirier writes, "The classic American writers try through style temporarily to free the hero (and the reader) from systems, to free them from the pressures of time, biology, economics, and from the social forces which are ultimately the undoing of American heroes and quite often of their creators" (5). This is especially true, I think, of America's classic romancers. Where I depart from Poirier is in placing the interpretive emphasis on the inescapable presence of such political and social pressures.

Notable recent historicist studies of nineteenth-century American fiction include Harry B. Henderson III, *Versions of the Past: The Historical Imagination in American Fiction* (New York: Oxford University Press, 1974), esp. pp. 3–50; Porter, *Seeing and Being*; Robert Clark, *History, Ideology and Myth in American Fiction, 1823–52* (London: Macmillan Press, 1984); Philip Fisher, *Hard Facts: Setting and Form in the American Novel* (New York: Oxford University Press, 1985); and Jane Tompkins, *Sensational Designs: The Cultural Work of American Fiction, 1790–1860* (New York: Oxford University Press, 1985).

7. See, for example, William C. Spengemann "What Is American Literature?" *Centennial Review*, 22 (1978): 119–38; and Spengemann, "American Writers and English Literature," *ELH*, 52 (1985): 209–38. Nina Baym observes that for reviewers during the 1840–60 period, "the term romance was deployed simply as a synonym for the term novel" ("Concepts of Romance in Hawthorne's America," *Nineteenth-Century Fiction*, 38 [1984]: 430); see also Baym, *Novels, Readers, and Reviewers: Responses to Fiction in Antebellum America* (Ithaca, N.Y.: Cornell University Press, 1984), esp. pp. 225–35. In *The Development of American Romance* Bell argues that nineteenth-century writers used the term "romance" to emphasize the fictionality of their literary texts;

see esp. pp. 7–36. See also Perry Miller, "The Romance and the Novel," *Nature's Nation* (Cambridge, Mass.: Harvard University Press, 1967), pp. 241–78; and George Dekker, *The American Historical Romance* (Cambridge University Press, 1987), pp. 14–18.

8. Evan Carton, *The Rhetoric of American Romance: Dialectic and Identity in Emerson, Dickinson, Poe, and Hawthorne* (Baltimore, Md.: Johns Hopkins University Press, 1985), p. 1.

9. James, "Preface to 'The American,'" p. 32. My sense of America as "creation" and "invention" draws on Gordon S. Wood, *The Creation of the American Republic, 1776–1787* (1969; rpt. New York: Norton, 1972); and Gary Wills, *Inventing America: Jefferson's Declaration of Independence* (Garden City, N.Y.: Doubleday, 1978). See also Edmundo O'Gormon, *The Invention of America* (Bloomington: Indiana University Press, 1961); and Brook Thomas, "*The House of the Seven Gables:* Reading the Romance of America," *PMLA,* 97 (1982): 195–211.

10. George Washington, "Farewell Address," in *American Thought and Writing: The Revolution and the Early Republic,* ed. Russel B. Nye and Norman S. Grabo (Boston: Houghton Mifflin, 1965), pp. 168, 169.

11. Carton, *The Rhetoric of American Romance,* pp. 47, 58.

12. Washington, "Farewell Address," p. 178.

13. Northrop Frye, *Anatomy of Criticism: Four Essays* (Princeton, N.J.: Princeton University Press, 1957), p. 186.

14. Fredric Jameson, *The Political Unconscious: Narrative as a Socially Symbolic Act* (Ithaca, N.Y.: Cornell University Press, 1981), pp. 117, 115; Jameson, "Magical Narratives: Romance as Genre," *New Literary History,* 7 (1975): 140.

15. Washington, "Farewell Address," p. 169.

16. David Brion Davis, *The Slave Power Conspiracy and the Paranoid Style: Images of Conspiracy in the Slavery Controversy* (Baton Rouge: Louisiana State University Press, 1969), p. 6.

17. Richard Hofstadter, *The Paranoid Style in American Politics and Other Essays* (New York: Random House, 1967), p. 29. Relatedly, see Seymour Martin Lipset and Earl Raab, *The Politics of Unreason: Right-Wing Extremism in America, 1790–1970* (New York: Harper & Row, 1970). My thinking on conspiratorial fears and discourse in American history has been very much influenced by David Brion Davis, "Some Themes of Countersubversion: An Analysis of Anti-Masonic, Anti-Catholic, and Anti-Mormon Literature," *Mississippi Valley Historical Review,* 47 (1960): 205–24; Davis, *The Slave Power Conspiracy;* and *The Fear of Conspiracy: Images of Un-American Subversion from the Revolution to the Present,* ed. Davis (Ithaca, N.Y.: Cornell University Press, 1971). See also Richard O. Curry and Thomas M. Brown (eds.), *Conspiracy: The Fear of Subversion in American History* (New York: Holt, Rinehart & Winston, 1972); and Michael Paul Rogin, *Ronald Reagan, the Movie: and Other Episodes in Political Demonology* (Berkeley and Los Angeles: University of California Press, 1987), pp. 272–300.

18. William Bradford, *Of Plymouth Plantation,* ed. Harvey Wish (New York: Capricorn, 1962), p. 25.

19. Richard Slotkin, *Regeneration through Violence: The Mythology of the American Frontier, 1600–1860* (Middletown, Conn.: Wesleyan University Press, 1973), p. 117. See also Ann Kibbey, *The Interpretation of Material Shapes in Puritanism: A Study of Rhetoric, Prejudice, and Violence* (Cambridge University Press, 1986).

20. Cotton Mather, *The Wonders of the Invisible World: Being an Account of the Tryals of Several Witches Lately Executed in New-England* (1692; rpt. London: John Russell Smith, 1862), pp. 13, 74, 14; John Winthrop, "A Modell of Christian Charity," in *The Puritans: A Sourcebook of Their Writings,* 2 vols. ed. Perry Miller and Thomas H. Johnson (New York: Harper Torchbooks, 1963), 1:199. On the Salem witch trials see Paul Boyer and Stephen Nissenbaum, *Salem Possessed: The Social Origins of Witchcraft* (Cambridge, Mass.: Harvard University Press, 1974); and John Demos, *Entertaining Satan: Witchcraft and the Culture of Early New England* (New York: Oxford University Press, 1982). In *Purity and Danger: An Analysis of the Concepts of Pollution and Taboo* (1968; rpt. London: Routledge & Kegan Paul, 1978), Mary Douglas argues that the fear of social "pollution is a type of danger which is not likely to occur except where the lines of structure, cosmic or social, are clearly defined" (113). I am arguing in addition that the social act of creating lines of structure may just as readily generate concerns about the threat of pollution and the need to expunge it. On the ways in which the Puritans firmed cosmic and social boundaries by directing themselves against subversive others, see also Kai T. Erikson, *Wayward Puritans: A Study in the Sociology of Deviance* (New York: Wiley, 1966); Michael Zuckerman, "The Fabrication of Identity in Early America," *William and Mary Quarterly,* 36 (1977): 183–214; and Andrew Delbanco, "The Puritan Errand Re-Viewed," *Journal of American Studies,* 18 (1984), 343-60. As A. N. Kaul writes in his excellent *The American Vision: Actual and Ideal Society in Nineteenth-Century Fiction* (New Haven, Conn.: Yale University Press, 1963), the "great type of American social experience" was the "separation from a corrupt society to form an ideal community" (35).

21. Notable studies of millennialism in American history include Ernest Lee Tuveson, *Redeemer Nation: The Idea of America's Millennial Role* (University of Chicago Press, 1968); Cushing Strout, *The New Heavens and the New Earth: Political Religion in America* (New York: Harper & Row, 1973); and Ruth H. Bloch, *Visionary Republic: Millennial Themes in American Thought, 1756–1800* (Cambridge University Press, 1985). The perception of the New World as a type of Eden inevitably bred fears of the corrupt, plotting Old World devil; see Charles Sanford, *The Quest for Paradise: Europe and the American Moral Imagination* (Urbana: University of Illinois Press, 1961), esp. pp. 162–3; and Cushing Strout, *The American Image of the Old World* (New York: Harper & Row, 1963), esp. pp. 1–106.

22. Gordon S. Wood writes, "Far from being symptomatic of irrationality, this conspiratorial mode of explanation represented an enlightened stage in Western man's long struggle to comprehend his social reality" ("Conspiracy and the Paranoid Style: Causality and Deceit in the Eighteenth Century," *William and Mary Quarterly,* 39 [1982]: 411). On the tension between providential and

human agency as it informs the rise of the novel, see also Leo Braudy, "Providence, Paranoia, and the Novel," *ELH,* 48 (1981): 619–37; and Leopold Damrosch, *God's Plots and Man's Stories: Studies in the Fictional Imagination from Milton to Fielding* (University of Chicago Press, 1985). For an excellent discussion of the way in which Lockean epistemology generated anxieties about the deceptiveness of appearances, see Jay Fliegelman, *Prodigals and Pilgrims: The American Revolution against Patriarchal Authority, 1750–1800* (Cambridge University Press, 1982), pp. 235–48. On the duplicities and uncertainties attending economic exchange in the "placeless" market, see Jean-Christophe Agnew, *Worlds Apart: The Market and the Theater in Anglo-American Thought, 1550–1750* (Cambridge University Press, 1986); and on the transformative significance of the rise of modern printing, see Elizabeth L. Eisenstein, *The Printing Press as an Agent of Change: Communications and Cultural Transformations in Early-Modern Europe,* 2 vols. (Cambridge University Press, 1979).

23. On the colonists' attitudes toward the French and Indian War, see Nathan O. Hatch, "The Origins of Civil Millennialism in America: New England Clergymen, War with France, and the Revolution," *William and Mary Quarterly,* 31 (1978): 407–30.

24. Bernard Bailyn, *The Ideological Origins of the American Revolution* (Cambridge, Mass.: Harvard University Press, 1967), p. 95; "The Declaration of Independence," in *American Thought and Writing,* ed. Nye and Grabo, p. 54. See also Gordon S. Wood, "Rhetoric and Reality in the American Revolution," *William and Mary Quarterly,* 23 (1966): 3–32. On the influences of Florentine, Commonwealthean, and Whig political science on the Revolutionary mentality, see Caroline Robbins, "European Republicanism in the Century and a Half before 1776," in *The Development of a Revolutionary Mentality,* ed. Richard B. Morris (Washington, D.C.: Library of Congress, 1972), pp. 31–55; J. G. A. Pocock, *Politics, Language and Time: Essays on Political Thought and History* (New York: Atheneum Publishers, 1973), pp. 80–147; and esp. Pocock, *The Machievellian Moment: Florentine Political Thought and the Atlantic Republican Tradition* (Princeton, N.J.: Princeton University Press, 1975). On the impact of millennialism on the countersubversive countours of Revolutionary ideology, see Nathan O. Hatch, *The Sacred Cause of Liberty: Republican Thought and the Millennium in Revolutionary New England* (New Haven, Conn.: Yale University Press, 1977); James West Davidson, *The Logic of Millennial Thought: Eighteenth-Century New England* (New Haven, Conn.: Yale University Press, 1977); and Bloch, *Visionary Republic.*

25. Such reenactments therefore resembled, and arguably were in the tradition of, the Puritan jeremiad. As Sacvan Bercovitch explains in *The American Jeremiad* (Madison: University of Wisconsin Press, 1978), the jeremiad reinforced communal consensus beliefs in the nation's redemptive mission by promoting concerns about declension that, as part of a ritual process, inspired a recommitment to the goals and ideals of the Puritans' nation-originating errand into the wilderness. As in the European jeremiad, anxiety played a major role in rallying Americans around a common cause. "But the American jeremiad went much further," Bercovitch writes. "It made anxiety its end as well as its

means. The very concept of errand, after all, implied a state of *unfulfillment*" (23). Bercovitch, of course, emphasizes the "affirmative energies" (xv) of the jeremiad. In my study of "jeremiadic" countersubversive writings, I will emphasize the ways in which these energies were also used to repress and marginalize threatening others.

26. Jefferson to Lafayette, letter of 2 April 1790, in *The Writings of Thomas Jefferson*, ed. Andrew A. Lipscomb (Washington, D.C.: Thomas Jefferson Memorial Association, 1903), p. 13. According to Paul C. Nagel, *This Sacred Trust: American Nationality, 1798–1898* (New York: Oxford University Press, 1971), "American nationality was tainted by uncertainty throughout the nineteenth century" (7). See also Benjamin T. Spencer, *The Quest for Nationality: An American Literary Campaign* (Syracuse, N.Y.: Syracuse University Press, 1957); and Curtis Dahl, "The American School of Catastrophe," *American Quarterly*, 11 (1959): 380–90.

27. Erikson, *Wayward Puritans*, p. 64.

28. Robert H. Wiebe, *The Opening of American Society: From the Adoption of the Constitution to the Eve of Disunion* (New York: Knopf, 1984), p. 367. Similarly, Daniel Walker Howe writes, "George Washington, who warned of a conspiracy to deprive colonists of their rights, and Abraham Lincoln, who warned of a conspiracy to nationalize slavery, were not isolated cranks but responsible leaders in tune with their people" (*The Political Culture of the American Whigs* [University of Chicago Press, 1979], p. 79).

29. The republican revisionism of the past two decades or so – with its emphases on discourse and mentality – merits the close attention of literary scholars. Key works include Gordon S. Wood, *The Creation of the American Republic;* and Pocock, *The Machievellian Moment.* See also Robert E. Shalhope, "Toward a Republican Synthesis: The Emergence of an Understanding of Republicanism in American Historiography," *William and Mary Quarterly,* 29 (1972): 49–80; Shalhope, "Republicanism and Early American Historiography," *William and Mary Quarterly,* 39 (1982), 334–56; and William L. Hedges, "The Myth of the Republic and the Theory of American Literature," *Prospects: An Annual of American Cultural Studies,* 4 (1979): 101–20. For important critiques of the failure of republican revisionists to integrate economic developments and conflicts into their historical interpretations, see Isaac Kramnick, "Republican Revisionism Revisited," *American Historical Review,* 87 (1982): 629–64; and Joyce Appleby, *Capitalism and a New Social Order: The Republican Vision of the 1790's* (New York: Oxford University Press, 1984). For an interesting polemical attack on the revisionists' putative idealization of republican virtue as a political reality, see John Patrick Diggins, *The Lost Soul of American Politics: Virtue, Self-Interest, and the Foundations of Liberalism* (New York: Basic, 1984).

Hierarchical and patriarchal, republicanism often served the ends of power. To a certain extent, then, as Linda K. Kerber argues, "republican ideology primarily concerned a single sex rather than an American community of both sexes" (*Women of the Republic: Intellect and Ideology in Revolutionary America* [Chapel Hill: University of North Carolina Press, 1980], p. 7). According to Lester H. Cohen, however, republican conceptions of the conflict between virtue and corruption, liberty and power appealed to many women and informed popular sentimental and melodramatic novels, as well as Mercy Warren's *History of the American Revolution* (1805) (see Cohen's "Mercy Otis Warren: The Politics of Language and the Aesthetics of Self," *American Quarterly*, 35 [1983]: 481–98). The threat republican ideology posed to women, as both Kerber and Cohen point out, is in denying them a public sphere and thus relegating them to the home as idealized republican mothers.

   Though republicanism served the economic interests of the upper class, it also spoke powerfully to those of the working class who saw themselves "enslaved" to corrupt aristocrats. Sean Wilentz brilliantly shows how the concept of "artisan republicanism" informed the rise of labor radicalism in antebellum New York; see *Chants Democratic: New York City & the Rise of the American Working Class, 1788–1850* (New York: Oxford University Press, 1984), esp. pp. 61–103.

30. *The Federalist Papers,* ed. Clinton Rossiter (New York: New American Library, 1961), p. 149.

31. On the tropes and anxieties generated by the image of the confidence man, see Susan Kuhlmann, *Knave, Fool, and Genius: The Confidence Man as He Appears in Nineteenth-Century American Fiction* (Chapel Hill: University of North Carolina Press, 1973); Warwick Wadlington's somewhat abstruse *The Confidence Game* (Princeton, N.J.: Princeton University Press, 1975); Gary Lindberg, *The Confidence Man in American Literature* (New York: Oxford University Press, 1982); Karen Halttunen, *Confidence Men and Painted Women: A Study of Middle-class Culture in America, 1830–1870* (New Haven, Conn.: Yale University Press, 1982); and William E. Lenz, *Fast Talk & Flush Times: The Confidence Man as Literary Convention* (Columbia: University of Missouri Press, 1985).

32. James H. Huston, "The Origins of 'The Paranoid Style in American Politics': Public Jealousy from the Age of Walpole to the Age of Jackson," in *Saints and Revolutionaries: Essays on Early American History*, ed. David D. Hall, John M. Murrin, and Thad W. Tate (New York: Norton, 1984), pp. 372, 353; Washington, "Farewell Address," p. 169. Historians continue to debate the issue of whether republicanism persisted into the nineteenth century. Wood argues that the late eighteenth century saw the end of classical republicanism and that by the nineteenth century conspiratorial explanations came to seem "increasingly primitive and quaint" ("Conspiracy and the Paranoid Style," 441). Appleby argues that Jefferson, influenced by his reading of John Locke and Adam Smith, detached "republicanism" "from its classical context and made it a synonym in common usage for democracy or popular government" (*Capitalism and a New Social Order,* 63). But the end of "classical" republicanism, I am suggesting, allowed republicanism to live on as an explanatory discourse and communitarian social ideal, in part because it could more easily be appropriated and put to use by a range of political and social groups. Pocock argues in *Politics, Language and Time* that the republican "concept of corruption came to form part of the American vocabulary, and in a sense remains so to this day" (97). On the persistence of republican rhetoric and its attendant conspiratorial modes of interpretation, see also Pocock, "The Americanization of Virtue," *The Machievellian Moment*, pp. 506–52; Howe,

The Political Culture of the American Whigs; Jean H. Baker, *Affairs of Party: The Political Culture of Northern Democrats in the Mid-Nineteenth Century* (Ithaca, N.Y.: Cornell University Press, 1983), esp. chap. 4, "The Revival of Republicanism," pp. 143–76; Dorothy Ross, "Historical Consciousness in Nineteenth-Century America," *American Historical Review,* 89 (1984): 909–28; Wilentz, *Chants Democratic;* and Wiebe, *The Opening of American Society.* On the influence of republican ideology on Thoreau's major works, see Leonard N. Neufeldt, "Henry David Thoreau's Political Economy," *New England Quarterly,* 57 (1984): 359–83.

33. Chase, *The American Novel and Its Tradition,* pp. ix, 21, 41. The best discussion of melodrama in American countersubversive discourse is Davis, "Some Themes of Countersubversion." See also David Grimsted, *Melodrama Unveiled: American Theater and Culture, 1800–1850* (University of Chicago Press, 1968). On melodrama as an aspect of fiction that should be taken seriously as literary and cultural expression, see Peter Brooks, *The Melodramatic Imagination: Balzac, Henry James, Melodrama, and the Mode of Excess* (New Haven, Conn.: Yale University Press, 1976); John G. Cawelti, *Adventure, Mystery, and Romance: Formula Stories as Art and Popular Culture* (University of Chicago Press, 1976), esp. pp. 44–7, 260–95; and Tompkins, *Sensational Designs.*

34. Sacvan Bercovitch, "The Problem of Ideology in American Literary History," *Critical Inquiry,* 12 (1986): 642. On ideology and rhetoric see also Clifford Geertz, *The Interpretation of Cultures* (New York: Basic, 1973); Gordon S. Wood, "Rhetoric and Reality in the American Revolution"; Wood, "Intellectual History and the Social Sciences," in *New Directions in American Intellectual History,* ed. John Higham and Paul K. Conkin (Baltimore, Md.: Johns Hopkins University Press, 1979), pp. 27–41; Peter Berger and Thomas Luckmann, *The Social Construction of Reality* (Garden City, N.Y.: Doubleday, 1967); and Pocock, *Politics, Language and Time.*

35. Bakhtin, *The Dialogic Imagination,* p. 33.

36. My readings of romances in subsequent chapters pay especially close attention to the unfolding of plot. On the importance of plot to antebellum writers and readers, see Baym, *Novels, Readers, and Reviewers,* pp. 63–81. See also Peter Brooks, *Reading for the Plot: Design and Intention in Narrative* (New York: Knopf, 1984).

37. Geertz, *The Interpretation of Cultures,* p. 20.

38. Reising, *The Unusable Past,* p. 229. For a wide-ranging though somewhat too insistently taxonomic study of relationships among myriad antebellum texts, see David S. Reynolds, *Beneath the American Renaissance: The Subversive Imagination in the Age of Emerson and Melville* (New York: Knopf, 1988).

39. I want to emphasize, then, that though I speculate on the cultural significations of American romances, I am not attempting to recover the responses of "actual" readers. In *History and Criticism* (Ithaca, N.Y.: Cornell University Press, 1985), Dominick LaCapra shrewdly remarks on the limitations and pitfalls of reception theory: "The restriction of a study of reception to an empirical and analytic account of past readings or uses of texts is a neo-positivistic attempt drastically to curtail one's own exchange with the past and, by the same token, to transcend the contemporary conflict of interpreta-

tions. It is also a blatant return to a narrowly documentary model of knowledge – one that threatens to identify all interpretation as anachronistic" (130). Accordingly, he argues for "the importance of critical reading itself as a context of reception" (130): "Only through an attempted critical reading can one acquire some perspective on what occurs in the 'reception' of texts in given contexts. And one simultaneously confronts the problem of the location of one's own reading in the contemporary critical scene" (130). On the risks and pitfalls of contextualization, see also LaCapra, *Rethinking Intellectual History: Texts, Contexts, Language* (Ithaca, N.Y.: Cornell University Press, 1983), pp. 23–71.

1. *"The Defencelessness of Her Condition"*

Epigraph: Charles Brockden Brown, *Wieland; or, The Transformation: An American Tale* and *Memoirs of Carwin the Biloquist,* ed. Sydney J. Krause and S. W. Reid (Kent, Ohio: Kent State University Press, 1977), p. 301.

1. Brown, *Wieland,* p. 68; Brown, *Ormond; or, The Secret Witness,* ed. Sydney J. Krause, S. W. Reid, and Russel B. Nye (Kent, Ohio: Kent State University Press, 1982), p. 111; Brown, *Edgar Huntly; or, Memoirs of a Sleep-Walker,* ed. Sydney J. Krause and S. W. Reid (Kent, Ohio: Kent State University Press, 1984), p. 15; Brown, *Arthur Mervyn; or, Memoirs of the Year 1793,* ed. Sydney J. Krause and S. W. Reid (Kent, Ohio: Kent State University Press, 1980), p. 49.
2. "On a Scheme for Describing American Manners," *Monthly Magazine,* July 1800, p. 8.
3. Charles Brockden Brown, "Advertisement for 'Sky Walk'" (1798), in *The Rhapsodist and Other Uncollected Writings,* ed. Harry R. Warfel (New York: Scholars' Facsimiles, 1943), p. 136. The best discussion of Brown's villains as types of socially deviant artists is Michael Davitt Bell, *The Development of American Romance: The Sacrifice of Relation* (University of Chicago Press, 1980), pp. 6–61; the early influential version is Bell, "'The Double-Tongued Deceiver': Sincerity and Duplicity in the Novels of Charles Brockden Brown," *Early American Literature,* 9 (1974): 143–63. See also Robert A. Ferguson, "Literature and Vocation in the Early Republic: The Example of Charles Brockden Brown," *Modern Philology,* 78 (1980): 139–152; and Maurice J. Bennett, "Charles Brockden Brown's Ambivalence toward Art and Imagination," *Essays in Literature,* 10 (1983): 55–69. Useful discussions of the impact of Scottish Common Sense philosophy on American literary aesthetics can be found in William Charvat, *The Origins of American Critical Thought, 1810–1835* (1936; rpt. New York: Barnes, 1961), pp. 1–58; and Terence Martin, *The Instructed Vision: Scottish Common Sense and the Origins of American Fiction* (Bloomington: Indiana University Press, 1961). In an important challenge to the prevailing view that Brown wrote during a time of enormous antinovel sentiment (and hence perceived himself as a type of social deviant), Robert B. Winans observes that by "the 1780s and 1790s the amount of fiction printed in the magazines far outweighed the number of

essays denouncing it" ("The Growth of a Novel-Reading Public in Late-Eighteenth-Century America," *Early American Literature*, 9 [1975]: 267).

4. John R. Howe, Jr., "Republican Thought and the Political Violence of the 1790s," *American Quarterly*, 19 (1967): 150. Valuable analyses of the heightened political debates of the late 1790s can be found in Marshall Smelser, "The Federalist Period as an Age of Passion," *American Quarterly*, 10 (1957): 391–419; Richard Hofstadter, *The Idea of a Party System: The Rise of Legitimate Opposition in the United States, 1780–1840* (Berkeley and Los Angeles: University of California Press, 1969), pp. 1–121; J. Wendell Knox, *Conspiracy in American Politics, 1787–1815* (New York: Arno, 1972); and Richard Buel, Jr., *Securing the Revolution: Ideology in American Politics, 1789–1815* (Ithaca, N.Y.: Cornell University Press, 1972), pp. 137–261. On political ideology and rhetoric during the early national period, see also Linda K. Kerber, *Federalists in Dissent: Imagery and Ideology in Jeffersonian America* (Ithaca, N.Y.: Cornell University Press, 1970); and Lance Banning *The Jeffersonian Persuasion: Evolution of a Party Ideology* (Ithaca, N.Y.: Cornell University Press, 1978). For a brilliant intellectual history, see Henry May, *The Enlightenment in America* (New York: Oxford University Press, 1976).

5. Cited in James Morton Smith, *Freedom's Fetters: The Alien and Sedition Laws and American Civil Liberties* (Ithaca, N.Y.: Cornell University Press, 1956), p. 106.

6. Throughout this section I am indebted to Vernon Stauffer, *New England and the Bavarian Illuminati* (New York: Columbia University Press, 1918). For an account of the clergy's participation in political debate, see Gary Nash, "The American Clergy and the French Revolution," *William and Mary Quarterly*, 22 (1965): 392–412; and Ruth H. Bloch, *Visionary Republic: Millennial Themes in American Thought, 1756–1800* (Cambridge University Press, 1985), pp. 202–31.

7. J. M. Roberts, *The Mythology of the Secret Societies* (New York: Scribner, 1972), p. 119.

8. James H. Billington, *Fire in the Minds of Men: Origins of the Revolutionary Faith* (New York: Basic, 1980), p. 94. Ironically, the Illuminati writings published by the Bavarian government intrigued European radicals. As a result, Billington writes, "Illuminism gained a paradoxical posthumous influence far greater than it had exercised as a living movement" (99).

9. Roberts, *The Mythology of the Secret Societies*, p. 193. For Edmund Burke's early reference to the Illuminati, see *Reflections on the Revolution in France*, ed. Conor Cruise O'Brien (Harmondsworth: Penguin, 1976), p. 265.

10. John Robison, *Proofs of a Conspiracy Against all the Religions and Governments of Europe, Carried on in the Secret Meetings of Free Masons, Illuminati, and Reading Societies, Collected from Good Authorities* (1797; rpt. New York: Forman, 1798), p. 14.

11. Jedidiah Morse, *A Sermon, Delivered at the New North Church in Boston, in the Morning and in the Afternoon at Charlestown, May 9th, 1798, Being the Day Recommended by John Adams, President of the United States of America, for Solemn Humiliation, Fasting, and Prayer* (Boston: Hall, 1798), pp. 12, 21.

12. Timothy Dwight, *The Duty of Americans, at the Present Crisis, Illustrated in a Discourse, Preached on the Fourth of July, 1798* (New Haven, Conn.: Thomas and Samuel Green, 1798), pp. 8, 12, 13, 15, 13, 19. For a good discussion of Dwight's politics, see Kenneth Silverman, *Timothy Dwight* (New York: Twayne, 1969), pp. 81–110. Writing in defense of Dwight and Morse, K. Alan Snyder asserts that to label these ministers reactionaries is to ignore both their genuine fears and their genuine commitment to liberty; see "Foundations of Liberty: The Christian Republicanism of Timothy Dwight and Jedidiah Morse," *New England Quarterly*, 56 (1983): 382–97. As Emory Elliott more sensibly observes, Dwight in the 1790s, though at times alarmist, was engaged in an honest effort "to cope with the bafflement and confusion that Brackenridge, Freneau, Brown, and all thinking men agreed were a threat to the republic" (*Revolutionary Writers: Literature and Authority in the New Republic, 1725–1810* [New York: Oxford University Press, 1982], p. 273). See also Lewis P. Simpson, "Federalism and the Crisis of Literary Order," *American Literature*, 32 (1960): 253–66. On the similarities between the fear of the Illuminati and the traditional fear of "the classic Jesuitical foe," see David Brion Davis, *The Fear of Conspiracy: Images of Un-American Subversion from the Revolution to the Present* (Ithaca, N.Y.: Cornell University Press, 1971), p. xvii; and on the similarities between alarmist Federalist writing and the rhetorical structure of the jeremiad, see Sacvan Bercovitch, *The American Jeremiad* (Madison: University of Wisconsin Press, 1978), pp. 132–41. For a comprehensive list of sermons and tracts inspired by the Illuminati fear, see Stauffer, *New England and the Bavarian Illuminati*, pp. 368–73; and Buel, *Securing the Revolution*, pp. 346–9.

13. George Washington, "Farewell Adress," in *American Thought and Writing*, ed. Russel B. Nye and Norman S. Grabo (Boston: Houghton Mifflin, 1965), pp. 173, 177, 176.

14. Susanna Rowson, *Charlotte Temple: A Tale of Truth*, ed. Clara M. Kirk and Rudolf Kirk (New Haven, Conn.: College & University Press, 1964), p. 58. In William Hill Brown's *The Power of Sympathy* (1789), ed. William S. Kable (Columbus: Ohio State University Press, 1969), the Reverend Mr. Holmes suggests a parallel between the situation of the new American republic and the situation of the innocent, virtuous maiden by drawing on the conventional language used to describe America's rising glory: "BEHOLD the youthful virgin arrayed in all the delightful charms of vivacity, modesty and sprightliness – Behold even while she is rising in beauty and dignity, like a lily of the valley, in the full blossom of her graces, she is cut off suddenly by the rude hand of the Seducer. Unacquainted with his baseness and treachery, and too ready to repose confidence in him – she is deluded by [his] promises and flattery" (116). Useful discussions of popular novels of the period include Herbert Ross Brown, *The Sentimental Novel in America, 1789–1860* (1940; rpt. Freeport, N.Y.: Books for Libraries Press, 1970); Alexander Cowie, *The Rise of the American Novel* (New York: American Book, 1948); and Henri Petter, *The Early American Novel* (Columbus: Ohio State University Press, 1971). Especially recommended for their provocative readings are Leslie A. Fiedler, *Love and Death in the American Novel* (New York: Stein &

Day, 1966); William C. Spengemann, *The Adventurous Muse: The Poetics of American Fiction, 1789–1900* (New Haven, Conn.: Yale University Press, 1977), pp. 68–118; Cathy N. Davidson, "Flirting with Destiny: Ambivalence and Form in the Early American Sentimental Novel," *Studies in American Fiction*, 19 (1982): 17–39; and Davidson, *Revolution and the Word: The Rise of the Novel in America* (New York: Oxford University Press, 1986). Jay Fliegelman provides excellent analyses of the political anxieties implicit in early American fiction and in Washington's writings; see *Prodigals and Pilgrims: The American Revolution against Patriarchal Authority, 1750–1800* (Cambridge University Press, 1982), esp. pp. 197–267.

15. Morse, *A Sermon, Delivered at the New North Church in Boston*, p. 21; David Tappan, *Discourse, Delivered in the Chapel of Harvard College, June 19, 1798, Occasioned by the Approaching Departure of the Senior Class from the University* (Boston: Manning & Lorring, 1798), p. 27; Dwight, *The Duty of Americans*, pp. 20, 21. On the linkage of religious infidelity to libertinism in the political rhetoric of the period, see Shirley Samuels, "Infidelity and Contagion: The Rhetoric of Revolution," *Early American Literature*, 22 (1987): 183–191.

16. Buel, *Securing the Revolution*, p. 172.

17. On the tension between republicanism and liberalism, see Joyce Appleby, *Capitalism and a New Social Order: The Republican Vision of the 1790s* (New York: New York University Press, 1984).

18. Jedidiah Morse attempted to rekindle interest in the Illuminati, announcing on 25 April 1799 that he possessed a list of 100 members of a Virginia branch of the Illuminati; his fraudulent charges were not taken seriously. See Morse, *A Sermon, Exhibiting the Present Dangers, and Consequent Duties of the Citizens of the United States of America* (Charlestown, Mass., 1799).

19. Letters of 14 June 1813 and 30 June 1813, in *The Adams–Jefferson Letters: The Complete Correspondence Between Thomas Jefferson and Abigail and John Adams*, ed. Lester J. Cappon (New York: Simon & Schuster, 1971), pp. 329, 347.

20. See Buel, *Securing the Revolution*, pp. 175–83.

21. [John C. Ogden,] *A View of the New-England Illuminati: Who Are Indefatigably Engaged in Destroying the Religion and Government of the United States; Under a Feigned Regard for their Safety – And Under Impious Abuse of True Religion* (Philadelphia: James Carey, 1799), pp. 3, 16, 15, 20. See also Alan V. Briceland, "The Philadelphia *Aurora*, the New-England Illuminati, and the Election of 1800," *Pennsylvania Magazine of History and Biography*, 100 (1976): 3–36.

22. Philip Freneau, *Letters on Various Interesting and Important Subjects*, ed. Harry Hayden Clark (New York: Scholars' Facsimiles, 1943), pp. 48–9, 41–2.

23. Alan Axelrod, *Charles Brockden Brown: An American Tale* (Austin: University of Texas Press, 1983), p. 16.

24. William Hedges, "Charles Brockden Brown and the Culture of Contradictions," *Early American Literature*, 9 (1974): 135–6. See also Hedges, "The Old World Yet: Writers and Writing in Post-Revolutionary America," *Early American Literature*, 16 (1981): 3–18. On the Friendly Society see James E. Cronin, "Elihu Hubbard Smith and the New York Friendly Club," *PMLA*, 64 (1949): 471–9; and especially May, *The Enlightenment in America*, pp. 233–

6. Vernon L. Parrington, *The Romantic Revolution in America, 1800–1860* (New York: Harcourt Brace & World, 1927), pp. 180–4; and David Lee Clark, *Charles Brockden Brown: Pioneer Voice in America* (Durham, N.C.: Duke University Press, 1952), champion Brown as a political radical; their arguments gloss over the social tensions and complexities of the 1790s. In a well-known assessment, Warner Berthoff suggests that Brown lacked a systematized political ideology and that his fiction was thus "an instrument for *discovering* ideas, for exploring and testing them out" (see " 'A Lesson on Concealment,' Brockden Brown's Method in Fiction," *Philological Quarterly*, 37 [1958]: 46). David H. Hirsch takes a similar approach in "Charles Brockden Brown as a Novelist of Ideas," *Books at Brown*, 20 (1965): 165–84. Other useful discussions of Brown's politics and fiction include Harry W. Warfel, *Charles Brockden Brown: American Gothic Novelist* (Gainseville: University of Florida Press, 1948); Donald Ringe, *Charles Brockden Brown* (New York: Twayne, 1966); and Lawrence J. Friedman, *Inventors of the Promised Land* (New York: Knopf, 1975), pp. 79–105. See also William Dunlap, *The Life of Charles Brockden Brown: Together with Selections from the Rarest of His Printed Works, from His Original Letters, and from His Manuscripts before Unpublished*, 2 vols. (Philadelphia: Parke, 1815); and Paul Allen, *The Life of Charles Brockden Brown*, ed. Charles E. Bennett (New York: Scholars' Facsimiles, 1975).

25. Charles Brockden Brown, *Alcuin: A Dialogue*, ed. Lee R. Edwards (New York: Grossman, 1971), pp. 86, 9.

26. Cathy N. Davidson, "The Matter and Manner of Charles Brockden Brown's *Alcuin*," in *Critical Essays on Charles Brockden Brown*, ed. Bernard Rosenthal (Boston: Hall, 1981), p. 82. On Brown and Wollstonecraft, see also Linda K. Kerber, *Women of the Republic: Intellect and Ideology in Revolutionary America* (Chapel Hill: University of North Carolina Press, 1980), pp. 224–5; and Fritz Fleischmann, "Charles Brockden Brown: Feminism in Fiction," in *American Novelists Revisited: Essays in Feminist Criticism*, ed. Fleischmann (Boston: Hall, 1982), pp. 6–41.

27. See *The Diary of Elihu Hubbard Smith*, ed. James E. Cronin (Philadelphia: American Philosophical Society, 1973), pp. 454–9. In the August 1799 issue of his *Monthly Magazine and American Review*, Brockden Brown praised Timothy Dwight's anti-Illuminati *Nature and Danger of Infidel Philosophy* as "natural and judicious" (369). In the same issue he also printed "Sketches of Distinguished Characters: Dr. Dwight" (388–90). The May 1799 issue applauded Jedidiah Morse "as a sensible well-informed and correct writer" (127), and the July 1799 issue, discussed in the final section of the chapter, commented on Barruel's *Memoirs*.

28. Entry of 14 September 1798, *Diary of William Dunlap (1766–1839): The Memoirs of a Dramatist, Theatrical Manager, Painter, Critic, Novelist, and Historian*, 3 vols. (New York: New York Historical Society), 1:338–9. For an early discussion of Brown's treatment of the Illuminati, see Lillie Deming Loshe, *The Early American Novel, 1789–1830* (1907; rpt. New York: Ungar, 1958), pp. 41–3. In *American Gothic: Imagination and Reason in Nineteenth-Century Fiction* (Lexington: University Press of Kentucky, 1982), Donald A.

Ringe proposes that additional important influences on Brown's treatment of secret societies were German Gothic novels of the 1790s, such as Johann Christoph Friedrich von Schiller's *The Ghost-Seer* (1796) and Karl Friedrich August Grosse's *Horrid Mysteries* (1796). A large difference between these novels and Brown's *Ormond* and *Memoirs of Carwin*, however, is that Brown makes use of a contemporary setting.

29. Brown, *Wieland*, pp. 67, 130.
30. Ibid., pp. 179–80, 179, 190.
31. For an excellent reading of the relationship of Lockean epistemology to Clara's "transformation," see Fliegelman, *Prodigals and Pilgrims*, pp. 237–40. See also Arthur G. Kimball, *Rational Fictions: A Study of Charles Brockden Brown* (McMinnville, Ore.: Linfield Research Institute, 1968).
32. Brown, *Wieland*, p. 32.
33. Ibid., pp. 201, 54, 90, 205, 212.
34. Ibid., p. 66. In *Sensational Designs: The Cultural Work of American Fiction, 1790–1860* (New York: Oxford University Press, 1985), Jane Tompkins argues that "*Wieland* is a patriotic novel . . . [that] in an attempt to alert people to the dangers of mob rule, realizes the Federalist nightmare" (58). Although I think she is right in calling attention to the novel's "Federalist" social anxiety, I believe that the appealing qualities of Carwin, the limitations of Clara's narrative, and the peculiarities of Theodore Wieland make the romance something very different from "a political tract" (44). On historical themes in the novel, see also Edwin Sill Fussell, "*Wieland:* A Literary and Historical Reading," *Early American Literature,* 18 (1983): 171–86.
35. M. M. Bakhtin, "Discourse in the Novel," in *The Dialogic Imagination: Four Essays by M. M. Bakhtin,* ed. Michael Holquist (Austin: University of Texas Press, 1981), p. 314.
36. Brown, *Wieland*, pp. 241, 244. On the importance of the Stuart-Maxwell story to the overall novel, see Tompkins, *Sensational Designs*, pp. 54–61.
37. Paul C. Rodgers, Jr., argues that Brown wrote *Ormond* in an improvisatory manner ("Brown's *Ormond:* The Fruits of Improvisation," *American Quarterly,* 26 [1974]: 4–22); and Sydney J. Krause has shown that the novel may well have been written in approximately one month ("*Ormond:* How Rapidly and How Well 'Composed, Arranged and Delivered,'" *Early American Literature,* 13 [1978–9], 238–49). See also Russell B. Nye's "Historical Essay" and S. W. Reid's "Textual Essay" in the Kent State *Ormond*, pp. 295–354. Nye's observation that *Ormond* is "a brilliantly bungled book" (*Ormond,* p. 307) reflects the consensus view. For a comprehensive analysis of the novel's many obscure references, see Sydney J. Krause's "Historical Notes," pp. 389–478. A path-breaking and still valuable discussion of *Ormond* is Ernest Marchand, "Introduction," *Ormond* (New York: Hafner, 1937).
38. Brown, *Ormond*, p. 7. Subsequent parenthetical page references are to the Kent State edition.
39. For a provocative discussion of familial themes in early American fiction, see Shirley Samuels, "The Family, the State, and the Novel in the Early Republic," *American Quarterly,* 38 (1986): 381–95. On the "shape-shifting nature of social exchange in the new world of commodities" (61), see Jean-

Christophe Agnew, *Worlds Apart: The Market and the Theater in Anglo-American Thought, 1550–1750* (Cambridge University Press, 1986). On social exchange in Brockden Brown, see Tompkins, *Sensational Designs,* pp. 62–93.

40. Berthoff, " 'A Lesson on Concealment,' " p. 47. Brown's use of analogy as a structuring device brings coherence to a seemingly "improvised" text. In "Walstein's School of History" (1799), Brown writes: "Systems, by being imperfectly attended to, are liable to beget error and depravity. Truth flows from the union and relation of many parts" (*The Rhapsodist and Other Uncollected Writings,* p. 151). Used as a critical barometer, this statement presses us to reconsider the generally low value critics have placed on *Ormond's* artistry, a book that more than any of the other major romances successfully eschews "system" and develops its vision through a coherent presentation of disparate parts. A novel like *Wieland,* by comparison, can seem thesis–ridden.

41. Brown, letter of 25 October 1796, in David Lee Clark, *Charles Brockden Brown,* p. 156; George Cabot, letter of 1798, cited in Shirley Samuels, "Plague and Politics in 1793: *Arthur Mervyn,*" *Criticism,* 27 (1985): 225; Barruel, *Memoirs of Jacobinism,* cited in Stauffer, *New England and the Bavarian Illuminati,* pp. 226–7. Barruel's alarmist linking of plague to subversive revolutionism is suggestive of a similar linking in *Ormond* and, later, *Arthur Mervyn.* My understanding of Brown's conception of yellow fever has profited from Robert A. Ferguson, "Yellow Fever and Charles Brockden Brown: The Context of the Emerging Novelist," *Early American Literature,* 14 (1979–80): 293–305. Ferguson argues that the fever, by overturning conventional patterns of life, in effect liberated Brown from a fixed social role and made it easier for him to become an author. See also William L. Hedges, "Benjamin Rush, Charles Brockden Brown, and the American Plague Year," *Early American Literature,* 7 (1973): 295–311; Norman S. Grabo, "Historical Essay," *Arthur Mervyn,* pp. 447–75; and Samuels, "Plague and Politics in 1793," 225–45.

42. In *Women of the Republic,* Linda K. Kerber writes that in the late eighteenth century the "model republican woman was a mother" (228). Brown's characterization of Constantia boldly establishes the heroine's nonmotherly virtues. For a good discussion of the ways in which the Gothic novel in America "enlarged the arena in which the heroine could realize her nature" (282–3), see Cathy N. Davidson, "Isaac Mitchell's *The Asylum;* or Gothic Castles in the New Republic," *Prospects,* 7 (1982): 281–99.

43. See Brown, "The Man at Home," *The Rhapsodist and Other Uncollected Writings,* pp. 44–56. Brown's rational perspective on fever is also reflected in his "Extract of a Letter from a Gentleman in Philadelphia to His Friend in England, Dated July 7, 1799," *Monthly Magazine,* August 1799, pp. 324–30. In this piece Brown's narrator argues sensibly that yellow fever results from poor sanitation methods. On art allegory in the novel, see Paul Witherington, "Charles Brockden Brown's *Ormond:* The American Artist and His Masquerades," *Studies in American Fiction,* 4 (1976): 111–19.

44. Brown writes in "Walstein's School of History," "Marriage is incident to all; its influence on our happiness and dignity, is more entire and lasting than any other incident can possess" (*The Rhapsodist and Other Uncollected Writings,* p. 153).

45. This is precisely the alarmist lesson on France taught by the Federalists and Congregationalists. As Jedidiah Morse declared in *A Sermon Preached at Charlestown, Nov. 29, 1798, on the Anniversary Thanksgiving in Massachusetts* (Boston, 1798), "The conduct of the government of France towards this country, ever since the commencement of our connexion with that nation, has been a series of selfish cunning, masked with the *name* of friendship" (56). On the debate between the Federalists and Jeffersonians on France's conduct, see Buel, *Securing the Revolution*, pp. 28–49. The debate on gratitude and neutrality informed the early American novel. In Hannah W. Foster's popular *The Coquette* (1797), for example, the heroic Eliza Wharton faces marriage dilemmas similar to Constantia's, and the dilemmas reflect similar political concerns. On the republican politics of marriage in post-Revolutionary American writings, see Jan Lewis, "The Republican Wife: Virtue and Seduction in the Early Republic," *William and Mary Quarterly*, 44 (1987): 689–721. Also useful is Walter P. Wenska, "*The Coquette* and the American Dream of Freedom," *Early American Literature*, 12 (1977): 243–55.

46. In addition to the artistic identification, we learn from Smith's diary that Brown, like Ormond, had a mistress, one Susan Potts (*Diary of Elihu Hubbard Smith*, p. 440). Brown, of course, also read widely in radical Enlightenment thought; and Marchand thus speculates that "Brown assigned his more daring opinions to his obvious villains as a convenient way of putting them before the public, without bearing the onus of holding them himself" ("Introduction," *Ormond*, p. xxix).

47. For this invasive aspect of Ormond's "secret witnessing," Brown may have drawn on Robison, who printed what he claimed to be Weishaupt's directive that the Illuminati infiltrator "look around him, and . . . notice the conduct of other men, and part of his weekly rescripts must consist of all interesting occurrences in the neighborhood, whether of a public or private nature" (*Proofs of a Conspiracy*, p. 97).

48. Robison, *Proofs of a Conspiracy*, pp. 18–19.

49. Brown, *Wieland*, p. 147.

50. Norman S. Grabo posits that Sophia and Constantia have sexual designs on one another; see *The Coincidental Art of Charles Brockden Brown* (Chapel Hill: University of North Caroline Press, 1981), pp. 47–55.

51. For an interesting poststructuralist analysis of the problematics of the text's authority, see William J. Scheick, "The Problem of Origination in Brown's *Ormond*," *Critical Essays on Charles Brockden Brown*, ed. Rosenthal, pp. 126–41.

52. Davidson, *Revolution and the Word*, p. 164; Brown, *Monthly Magazine and American Review*, February 1800, pp. 98–9.

53. Brown's distrust of the rationalist is made clear in "Walstein's School of History": "Mere reasoning is cold and unattractive" (*The Rhapsodist and other Uncollected Writings*, p. 151). In *An Enquiry Concerning Political Justice* (1793) (ed. Raymond A. Preston, 2 vols. [New York: Knopf, 1926], 1:159), an important source of Brown's wavering radicalism, William Godwin disavows the sort of secrecy employed by Ormond: "There cannot be a more unworthy idea than that truth and virtue should be under the necessity of seeking alliance with concealment."

54. By bestowing money and property on Helena, Ormond in effect makes her the pathetic character he comes to despise. His degradation of Helena once again puts him in league with Robison's Illuminati. Robison had asked: "Are not the accursed fruits of Illumination to be seen in the present humiliating condition of women in France? pampered in every thing that can reduce them to the mere instrument of animal pleasure" (*Proofs of a Conspiracy*, p. 197).

55. For a discussion of Brown's literalizations in *Wieland*, see Mark Seltzer, "Saying Makes It So: Language and Event in Brown's *Wieland*," *Early American Literature*, 13 (1978): 81–91.

56. Similarly, the text of the Alien and Sedition Laws warned that the nation needed protection against a supposed "army of spies and incendiaries scattered throughout the Continent" (cited in Buel, *Securing the Revolution*, p. 180).

57. John C. Cleman, "Ambiguous Evil: A Study of Villains and Heroes in Charles Brockden Brown's Major Novels," *Early American Literature*, 10 (1975): 195.

58. Washington, "Farewell Address," p. 168; Dwight, *The Duty of Americans*, p. 16.

59. Northrop Frye, *Anatomy of Criticism: Four Essays* (Princeton, N.J.: Princeton University Press, 1957), pp. 186, 189. James R. Russo argues, to an extreme, that the novel's sentimental structure conceals the surprising truth of Constantia's homicidal villainy; see "The Tangled Web of Deception and Imposture in Charles Brockden Brown's *Ormond*," *Early American Literature*, 14 (1979): 205–22.

60. Brown, *Alcuin*, p. 76.

61. Sydney J. Krause, "Ormond: Seduction in a New Key," *American Literature*, 44 (1973): 578. Also saluting Ormond as a heroic Enlightenment figure is Carl Nelson, "A Just Reading of Charles Brockden Brown's *Ormond*," *Early American Literature*, 8 (1973): 163–78. When Krause reconsidered the matter for "Historical Notes," however, he wrote that Ormond "is an exemplar of the human intellect run amuck with its own enlightenment" (*Ormond*, p. 454).

62. Peter Brooks, *The Melodramatic Imagination: Balzac, Henry James, Melodrama, and the Mode of Excess* (New Haven, Conn.: Yale University Press, 1976), p. 20.

63. My reading of Martinette owes a good deal to David H. Hirsch, *Reality and Idea in the Early American Novel* (The Hague: Mouton, 1971), pp. 97–9. For an excellent discussion of the impact of the French Revolution on representations of revolution in the Gothic novel, see Ronald Paulson, "Gothic Fiction and the French Revolution," *ELH*, 48 (1981): 532–54. On the French Revolution and Brown, see Hedges, "Charles Brockden Brown and the Culture of Contradictions"; Robert S. Levine, "Arthur Mervyn's Revolutions," *Studies in American Fiction*, 12 (1984): 145–60; and Samuels, "Plague and Politics in 1793."

64. *Monthly Magazine and American Review*, July 1799, pp. 289, 290. Brown's remarks on Barruel appeared in his review of Reverend William Brown's *An*

Oration, Spoken at Hartford, in Connecticut, on the Anniversary of American Independence (1799). Gordon S. Wood discusses the review in "Conspiracy and the Paranoid Style: Causality and Deceit in the Eighteenth Century," *William and Mary Quarterly*, 39 (1982): 436–7.

65. Brown, *Edgar Huntly*, pp. 192, 278.
66. Brown, *Arthur Mervyn*, pp. 114, 332.
67. Brown, *Ormond*, p. 178; Brown, *Memoirs of Carwin*, p. 269; Robison, *Proofs of a Conspiracy*, p. 109 (Brown's description of Carwin's apprenticeship draws on Robison's chapter in *Proofs of a Conspiracy* describing the Novice and his Mentor, pp. 94–106); Brown, *Memoirs of Carwin*, pp. 284, 305, 285.
68. *The American Review, and Literary Journal, for the Year 1801* (New York: Swords, 1801), p. vi; Charles Brockden Brown, *Clara Howard and Jane Talbot*, ed. Sydney J. Krause, S. W. Reid, and Donald A. Ringe (Kent, Ohio: Kent State University Press, 1986), pp. 3, 24, 302, 407. On the late novels, see Paul Witherington, "Brockden Brown's Other Novels: *Clara Howard and Jane Talbot*," *Nineteenth-Century Fiction*, 29 (1974): 257–72; and Sydney J. Krause, "*Clara Howard* and *Jane Talbot*: Godwin on Trial," in *Critical Essays on Charles Brockden Brown*, ed. Rosenthal, pp. 212–23.
69. [Charles Brockden Brown], *An Address to the Government of the United States, on the Cession of Louisiana to the French; and on the Late Breach of Treaty by the Spaniards: Including the Translation of a Memorial, on the War of St. Domingo, and Cession of the Mississippi to France, Drawn by a French Counsellor of State* (Philadelphia: Conrad, 1803), pp. 69, 14, 46. In his *Monroe's Embassy, or, the Conduct of the Government, in Relation to our Claims to the Navigation of the Missisippi [sic], Considered by the Author of An Address to the Government of the United States, on the Cession of Louisiana* (Philadelphia: Conrad, 1803), Brown called for military action to secure Louisiana for America. Useful studies of Brown's politics in the early 1800s are Charles C. Cole, Jr., "Brockden Brown and the Jefferson Administration," *Pennsylvania Magazine of History and Biography*, 72 (1948): 253–63; Friedman, *Inventors of the Promised Land*, pp. 79–105; and Charles E. Bennett, "Charles Brockden Brown: Man of Letters," *Critical Essays on Charles Brockden Brown*, ed. Rosenthal, pp. 212–23.

2. "Soulless Corporation"

Epigraphs: J. Hector St. Jean de Crèvecoeur, *Letters from an American Farmer*, ed. Albert E. Stone (New York: Penguin, 1981), p. 67; James Fenimore Cooper, *Gleanings in Europe: France*, ed. Thomas Philbrick and Constance Ayers Denne (Albany: State University of New York Press, 1983), p. 177.

1. James Fenimore Cooper, *Notions of the Americans: Picked up by a Travelling Bachelor*, 2 vols. (London: Colburn, 1828), 1:98. Cooper's Bachelor fondly recalls reading Brown's *Wieland* in his youth; see *Notions*, 2: 145–6.
2. *The Letters and Journals of James Fenimore Cooper*, ed. James Franklin Beard, 6 vols. (Cambridge, Mass.: Harvard University Press, 1960–8), 1:287, 421; 2:23; James Fenimore Cooper, *Gleanings in Europe: England*, ed. Donald A. Ringe, Kenneth W. Staggs, James P. Elliott, and R. D. Madison (Albany:

State University of New York Press, 1982), pp. 287, 290; Cooper, *Letters and Journals,* 4:25.

3. Cooper, *Gleanings in Europe: England,* pp. 288–9.

4. My understanding of the 1820s as a simultaneously celebratory and anxious postheroic moment is indebted to Fred Somkin's excellent *Unquiet Eagle: Memory and Desire in the Idea of American Freedom, 1815–1860* (Ithaca, N.Y.: Cornell University Press, 1967). On the postheroic tensions of the 1820s and 1830s, see also George B. Forgie, *Patricide in the House Divided: A Psychological Interpretation of Lincoln and His Age* (New York: Norton, 1979), pp. 13–54.

5. Indeed, most commentators on the Monroe Doctrine have observed that America in the 1820s faced no imminent dangers from foreign military powers. See, for example, Dexter Perkins, *The Monroe Doctrine: 1823–1826* (Cambridge, Mass.: Harvard University Press, 1932), pp. 141–52; and Ernest R. May, *The Making of the Monroe Doctrine* (Cambridge, Mass.: Harvard University Press, 1975), pp. 251–62.

6. Michael Rogin, *Fathers and Children: Andrew Jackson and the Subjugation of the American Indian* (New York: Vintage, 1976), p. 256. On the "corrupt bargain" see Robert V. Remini, *The Election of Andrew Jackson* (New York: Lippincott, 1963), pp. 11–121. For a shrewd analysis of the antiaristocratic and anticorporation rhetoric of the period, see Rush Welter, *The Mind of America: 1820–1860* (New York: Columbia University Press, 1975), esp. pp. 77–84. The image of the corporation as impersonal institution had its legal origins in Sir Edward Coke's 1612 ruling that a corporation has no conscience.

7. On American Antimasonry see Dixon Ryan Fox, *The Decline of Aristocracy in the Politics of New York, 1801–1840* (1919; rpt. New York: Harper Torchbooks, 1965), pp. 326–351; Whitney R. Cross, *The Burned-over District: The Social and Intellectual History of Enthusiastic Religion in Western New York, 1800–1850* (1950; rpt. New York: Harper Torchbooks, 1965), pp. 113–25; Ronald P. Formisano and Kathleen Smith Kutolowski, "Antimasonry and Masonry: The Genesis of Protest, 1826–1827," *American Quarterly,* 29 (1977): 139–65; Dorothy Ann Lipson, *Freemasonry in Federalist Connecticut, 1789–1835* (Princeton, N.J.: Princeton University Press, 1977); Kathleen Smith Kutolowski, "Freemasonry and Community in the Early Republic: The Case for Antimasonic Anxieties," *American Quarterly,* 34 (1982): 543–61; and William Preston Vaughn, *The Antimasonic Party in the United States: 1823–1843* (Lexington: University Press of Kentucky, 1983). Particularly useful is Michael F. Holt, "The Antimasonic and Know Nothing Parties," in *History of U.S. Political Parties,* ed. Arthur M. Schlesinger, Jr., 4 vols. (New York: Chelsea House, 1973), 1:575–740. Holt's Appendix collects key primary texts. See also *Antimasonry: The Crusade and the Party,* ed. Lorman Ratner (Englewood Cliffs, N.J.: Prentice-Hall, 1969).

8. "The Antimasonic National Platform of 1832," rpt. in Holt, "The Antimasonic and Know Nothing Parties," p. 662.

9. In *A Shopkeeper's Millennium: Society and Revivals in Rochester, New York, 1815–1837* (New York: Hill & Wang, 1978), Paul Johnson persuasively demonstrates, for example, that in Rochester, New York, Antimasonry

made perfect sense: "It was a skillfully directed assault upon wealthy and powerful men who had been the focus of resentment since the beginnings of settlement" (63). For a discussion of "the less than egalitarian reality" of the American 1820s and 1830s, see Edward Pessen, *Jacksonian America: Society, Personality, and Politics* (Homewood, Ill.: Dorsey, 1969), esp. pp. 39–58.

10. Reprinted in Elder David Bernard, *Light on Masonry: A Collection of All the Most Important Documents on the Subject of Speculative Free Masonry: Embracing the Reports of the Western Committees in Relation to the Abduction of William Morgan, Proceedings of the Conventions, Orations, Essays, &c.* (Utica, N.Y.: Williams, 1829), "Appendix," p. 34. Cited also in Thurlow Weed, "Report on the Progress of the Antimasonic Cause" (1829), in Holt, "The Antimasonic and Know Nothing Parties," p. 634.

11. Bernard, *Light on Masonry*, "Appendix," p. 34.

12. Cited in Lee Benson, *The Concept of Jacksonian Democracy: New York as a Test Case* (Princeton, N.J.: Princeton Paperback, 1970), pp. 19–20. Benson terms this speech "the best summary of the Antimasonic view of the struggle to preserve and enlarge the promise of American life" (19).

13. Cited in Benson, *The Concept of Jacksonian Democracy*, p. 20.

14. Thurlow Weed, "Report on the Progress of the Antimasonic Cause," reprinted in Holt, "The Antimasonic and Know Nothing Parties," p. 652.

15. Formisano and Kutolowski, "Antimasonry and Masonry," 162.

16. Bernard, *Light on Masonry*, p. x. For a discussion of the sensationalistic treatment of Masonic deviousness, see David Brion Davis, "Some Themes of Countersubversion: An Analysis of Anti-Masonic, Anti-Catholic, and Anti-Mormon Literature," *Mississippi Valley Historical Review*, 47 (1960): 205–24.

17. Marvin Meyers, *The Jacksonian Persuasion: Politics and Belief* (Stanford, Calif.: Stanford University Press, 1960), pp. 32, 11, 30.

18. Nathaniel Hawthorne, *The Blithedale Romance*, ed. Roy Harvey Pearce, Fredson Bowers, Matthew J. Bruccoli, and L. Neal Smith (Columbus: Ohio State University Press, 1964), p. 1. On Cooper's prefaces see Arvid Shulenberger, *Cooper's Theory of Fiction: His Prefaces and Their Relation to His Novels* (Lawrence: University of Kansas Publications, 1955). On Cooper's effort to engage and, in effect, to create a receptive reading public during the 1820s, see James D. Wallace, *Early Cooper and His Audience* (New York: Columbia University Press, 1986).

19. For an excellent discussion of Cooper's politics and art, see John P. McWilliams, Jr., *Political Justice in a Republic: James Fenimore Cooper's America* (Berkeley and Los Angeles: University of California Press, 1972). McWilliams makes a strong case that Cooper, at least to the time of *The Crater* (1847), was committed to the republican vision of *The Federalist*. See also Robert E. Spiller, *Fenimore Cooper: Critic of His Times* (1931; rpt. New York: Russell & Russell, 1963); Dorothy Waples, *The Whig Myth of James Fenimore Cooper* (New Haven, Conn.: Yale University Press, 1938); Marius Bewley, *The Eccentric Design: Form in the Classic American Novel* (New York: Columbia University Press, 1959), pp. 47–112; and George Dekker, *James Fenimore Cooper: The American Scott* (New York: Barnes & Noble, 1967).

20. Wayne Franklin proposes that many of Cooper's novels, even those addressing historical and political concerns, offer the reader "a vision of the chaotic
energies of [Cooper's] own creativity" (*The New World of James Fenimore
Cooper* [University of Chicago Press, 1982], p. 239). In "*The Last of the
Mohicans* and the Sounds of Discord," *American Literature*, 43 (1971): 25–41,
Thomas Philbrick similarly focuses on the play of Cooper's imaginative
energies and accordingly argues that *Mohicans* is characterized by an "ideological elusiveness" (25). Both Philbrick and Franklin wish to free Cooper
from the political intentionalists – Spiller, Bewley, McWilliams, and others
– who sometimes too strenuously link Cooper's novels to a specific political
agenda. See also D. H. Lawrence, *Studies in Classic American Literature* (1923;
rpt. New York: Viking, 1972), pp. 35–63; Leslie A. Fiedler, *Love and Death
in the American Novel* (1960; revised ed. New York: Stein & Day, 1966), pp.
162–214; and H. Daniel Peck's important revisionary study, *A World by
Itself: The Pastoral Moment in Cooper's Fiction* (New Haven, Conn.: Yale
University Press, 1977).

21. James Fenimore Cooper, *The Spy: A Tale of the Neutral Ground*, ed. J. E.
Morpurgo (New York: Oxford University Press, 1968), p. 1.

22. Cooper, *Notions of the Americans*, 1:293–4.

23. James Fenimore Cooper, *Lionel Lincoln: or, The Leaguer of Boston*, ed. Donald
A. Ringe and Lucy B. Ringe (Albany: State University of New York Press,
1984), p. 9. On the early nautical romances, see H. Daniel Peck, "A Re-
possession of America: The Revolution in Cooper's Trilogy of Nautical
Romances," *Studies in Romanticism*, 15 (1976): 589–606.

24. Dekker, *James Fenimore Cooper*, p. 33; Dekker's is the best study of Scott's
influence on Cooper. On historical conflict in Cooper's novels see also
Robert Clark, *History, Ideology and Myth in American Fiction, 1823–52* (London: Macmillan Press, 1984), pp. 48–50, 61–109; Philip Fisher, *Hard Facts:
Setting and Form in the American Novel* (New York: Oxford University Press,
1985), pp. 22–86; and Richard Slotkin, *The Fatal Environment: The Myth of
the Frontier in the Age of Industrialization, 1800–1890* (New York: Atheneum
Publishers, 1985), pp. 81–106.

25. Cooper, *Lionel Lincoln*, p. 63; Cooper, *The Wept of Wish-ton-Wish; a Tale*, 2
vols. (Philadelphia: Carey, Lea & Carey, 1829), 1:v. Even his seemingly
optimistic *Notions* is haunted by intimations of social disruption; see especially his comments on immigrants and slavery (*Notions*, 1:307; 2:336,
357–8, 453). On violence and historical conflict in *Mohicans*, see Robert
Milder, "*The Last of the Mohicans* and the New World Fall," *American Literature*, 52 (1980): 406–29.

26. William Kelly, *Plotting America's Past: Fenimore Cooper and the Leatherstocking
Tales* (Carbondale: Southern Illinois Press, 1983), p. 71. For fine analyses of
history and nature in Cooper, see Frank M. Collins, "Cooper and the Amer-
ican Dream," *PMLA*, 81 (1966): 79–94; and Joel Porte, *The Romance in
America: Studies in Cooper, Poe, Hawthorne, Melville, and James* (Middletown,
Conn.: Wesleyan University Press, 1969), esp. pp. 28–52.

27. James Fenimore Cooper, *The Prairie: A Tale*, ed. James P. Elliott (Albany:
State University of New York Press, 1985), pp. 9, 325. See also Henry Nash

Smith, *Virgin Land: The American West as Symbol and Myth* (New York: Random House, 1950), pp. 256–60; and Robert H. Zoellner, "Conceptual Ambivalence in Cooper's Leatherstocking," *American Literature*, 31 (1960): 397–420.

28. Cooper, *Letters and Journals*, 1:148.

29. Cooper, *Last of the Mohicans*, pp. 1, 350.

30. The draft of the appeal is reprinted in *Letters and Journals*, 2:127. In the draft Cooper used the word "one," which he later changed to "brother." Useful biographical information on Cooper's European residence of 1826–33 can be found in Spiller, *Fenimore Cooper;* James Grossman, *James Fenimore Cooper: A Biographical and Critical Study* (1949; rpt. Stanford, Calif.: Stanford University Press, 1967); and James Franklin Beard's excellent notes and commentary to *Letters and Journals*, Vols. 1 and 2. For a fine discussion of Cooper's republican commitments and political participations of the period, see Anne C. Loveland, "James Fenimore Cooper and the American Mission," *American Quarterly*, 21 (1969): 244–58.

31. Cooper, *Letters and Journals*, 1:419, 2:72, 77–8.

32. Ibid., 2:95, 107. Cooper was especially skeptical of the English Reform Bill, which, as he wrote Charles Wilkes in April 1831, "is framed with a view to popular appearance, but with a practical saving for the aristocracy" (*Letters and Journals*, 2:74).

33. The phrase is from Cooper's letter of 8 September 1830 to Peter Augustus Jay, *Letters and Journals*, 2:11.

34. In letters to Horatio Greenough in December 1829 and January 1830, Cooper responded enthusiastically to Jackson's first annual message to Congress (*Letters and Journals*, 1:402). In a letter of 20 September 1830 he conveyed his concerns to William Branford Shubrick about the Nullification crisis: "The present state of feeling in South Carolina is well known to me, and has given me much pain" (*Letters and Journals*, 2:19). Though the letters and journals do not directly address Antimasonry, it is apparent from the letters that he kept abreast of American political affairs; his references to Masons in his other works make it clear that he knew of the controversy.

35. James Fenimore Cooper, *The Red Rover*, ed. Warren S. Walker (Lincoln: University of Nebraska Press, 1963), p. 72.

36. James Fenimore Cooper, *The American Democrat*, ed. George Dekker and Larry Johnston (Baltimore, Md.: Penguin, 1969), pp. 81–2. Reflective of his distance from Antimasonic hysteria, however, Cooper that same year matter-of-factly took note of the Masonic presence in the Cooperstown of his youth: "The Free Masons opened a lodge in the village on the first Tuesday in March, 1799, and on the 27th December, they held a great religious festival in the Academy. They dined in the same place and in the evening had a ball." See "The Chronicles of Cooperstown" (1838), *A History of Cooperstown* (Cooperstown, N.Y.: Freeman's Journal Company, 1929), p. 23.

37. James Fenimore Cooper, *The Water-Witch; or, The Skimmer of the Seas*, 2 vols. (Philadelphia: Carey & Lea, 1831), 1:108. The English edition appeared in 1830.

38. As J. G. A. Pocock puts it in his invaluable *The Machiavellian Moment:*

Florentine Political Thought in the Atlantic Republican Tradition (Princeton, N.J.: Princeton University Press, 1975): "In the long run – at least as viewed in an Anglo-American perspective – the myth of Venice (at its most mythical) was to lie in the assertion that the Venetian commonwealth was an immortally serene, because perfectly balanced, combination of the three elements of monarchy, aristocracy, and democracy" (102). On the importance of Venice to republican political thought, see also pp. 83–113, 183–330.

39. *The Federalist,* ed. Jacob E. Cooke (Middletown, Conn.: Wesleyan University Press, 1961), pp. 250–1. The image of Venice as archetypal subverted republic would retain its currency at least to the time of the Civil War. For example, in Harriet Beecher Stowe's *Dred: A Tale of the Great Dismal Swamp,* 2 vols. (Boston: Philips, Sampson, 1856), a Virginian abolitionist remarks on the near lynching of his abolitionist companion: "The fact is that our republic, in these states, is like that of Venice; it's not a democracy, but an oligarchy, and the mob is its standing army. We are, all of us, under the 'Council of Ten,' which has its eyes everywhere. We are free enough as long as our actions please them; when they don't, we shall find their noose around our necks" (2:320).

40. Yvor Winters, *Maule's Curse: Seven Studies in the History of American Obscurantism* (1938), in *In Defense of Reason* (Chicago: Swallow, 1947), p. 198. In *Memorial of James Fenimore Cooper* (New York: Putnam, 1852), William Bryant took special note of *The Bravo:* "The work is written with all the vigour and spirit of his best novels" (56). In their introduction to *The American Democrat,* Dekker and Johnston contend that *The Bravo* is "probably his greatest political novel" (9).

41. The novel's relationship to a matrix of political activity has encouraged critics to center their readings of *The Bravo* on the problem of determining its precise political origins and intention. One group of interpreters, headed by Henry Walcott Boynton (*James Fenimore Cooper* [New York: Century, 1931], p. 230), maintains that *The Bravo* was inspired by what has come to be termed the Finance Controversy. Precipitating the controversy was an article in the June 1831 *Révue Britanique* by one Emile Saulnier, which sought to demonstrate the enormity of the costs required by a republican system of government. Lafayette brought the article to Cooper's attention in November of that year, and the result was Cooper's *Letter to General Lafayette* of November 25 and a series of articles in which he attempted to convince the French people of the cost-effectiveness of republicanism. But though Saulnier's June article clearly engaged his interest, Cooper reported to his publishers Colburn and Bentley in March of that year that *The Bravo* "is so far completed that it might easily be published on the 15th of June" (*Letters and Journals,* 2:63). Spiller too proposes that the Finance Controversy encouraged Cooper to celebrate American ideals in his European Trilogy (see esp. Spiller's "Fenimore Cooper and Lafayette: The Finance Controversy of 1831–1832," *American Literature,* 3 [1931]: 28–44), but basic chronology suggests that the Finance Controversy cannot be taken as the chief impulse behind *The Bravo.* Nor can Cooper's conflict with the Whig Party. Bewley

argues in *The Eccentric Design*, pp. 47–72, that Cooper knew all along of the transformations taking place in his country, that he anticipated Whig excesses, and that in *The Bravo* he intended to alert Americans to Whiggish duplicity and vulgarity. But the fact is that Cooper was not acutely disturbed by the Whigs until several years after his return to America in 1833. As with the Finance Controversy, Cooper's disenchantment with "Whiggism" came well after his composition of *The Bravo*.

The most plausible direct influences on composition and thematic intention, I believe, are the immediate European revolutionary events of 1830 and 1831. See Grossman, *James Fenimore Cooper*, pp. 75–103; Beard, *Letters and Journals*, 2:4; and Loveland, "James Fenimore Cooper and the American Mission."

42. McWilliams sensibly observes, "*The Bravo* is not, ultimately, a denunciation of France, Venice, Europe, or Whiggery. The government of Venice is rather the imaginative composite of all the political forces Cooper most detested" (*Political Justice in a Republic*, p. 165).

43. Cooper, *Letters and Journals*, 2:75; Cooper, *Gleanings in Europe: Italy*, ed. John Conron and Constance Ayers Denne (Albany: State University of New York Press, 1981), pp. 280–1, 289. Cooper visited Venice from 28 April 1830 to 7 May 1830. On Cooper and Italy, see Nathalia Wright, *American Novelists in Italy: The Discoverers: Allston to James* (Philadelphia: University of Pennsylvania Press, 1965), pp. 115–37; Constance Ayers Denne, "Cooper's Use of Setting in the European Trilogy," in *James Fenimore Cooper: His Country and His Art* (Papers from the 1980 Conference at State University College of New York), ed. George A. Test (Oneonta, New York, 1981), pp. 9–23; and Joy S. Kasson, *Artistic Voyagers: Europe and the American Imagination in the Works of Irving, Allston, Cole, Cooper and Hawthorne* (Westport, Conn.: Greenwood, 1982), pp. 137–64.

44. James Fenimore Cooper, *The Bravo: A Tale*, 2 vols. (Philadelphia: Carey & Lea, 1831), 1:9. All future parenthetical page references are to this edition, the first American printing. For a good modern edition, based on the 1831 Philadelphia text, see *The Bravo*, ed. Donald A. Ringe (New Haven, Conn.: College and University Press, 1963); and see Ringe's excellent "Introduction." My reading of *The Bravo* will pay close attention to the unfolding of plot. For an important defense of Cooper's art of plotting, see Jane Tompkins, *Sensational Designs: The Cultural Work of American Fiction, 1790–1860* (New York: Oxford University Press, 1985), pp. 94–121.

45. *Memorial of James Fenimore Cooper*, p. 56. For a discussion of the Hudson River school influence on *The Bravo*, see Donald Ringe, *The Pictorial Mode: Space and Time in the Art of Bryant, Irving & Cooper* (Lexingon: University Press of Kentucky, 1971), pp. 114–21.

46. Gordon S. Wood, "Conspiracy and the Paranoid Style: Causality and Deceit in the Eighteenth Century," *William and Mary Quarterly*, 39 (1982): 422. On Venice in the eighteenth century, see William H. McNeill, *Venice: The Hinge of Europe, 1081–1797* (University of Chicago Press, 1974), pp. 217–41; and John Julius Norwich, *A History of Venice* (New York: Knopf, 1982), pp. 583–631.

47. Terry Castle, "Eros and Liberty at the English Masquerade, 1711–1790," *Eighteenth-Century Studies,* 17 (1983–4), 159. Mikhail Bakhtin's comments on maskwearing in institutionalized forms of carnival seems particularly relevant to *The Bravo:* "In its Romantic form the mask is torn away from the oneness of the folk carnival concept. It is stripped of its original richness and acquires other meanings alien to its primitive nature: now the mask hides something, keeps a secret, deceives" *Rabelais and His World* [Cambridge, Mass.: MIT Press, 1968], p. 40.

48. The opening owes a good deal to Shakespearean drama, and the influence of Shakespeare on the overall text is unmistakable. Hosea the Jewish moneylender descends from *The Merchant of Venice*'s Shylock, the Don Camillo–Violetta love affair draws on *Romeo and Juliet,* and the repeated references to Venice's wars against the Turks recall *Othello.* In "A Second Glance Backward" (*Atlantic Monthly,* October 1887), Susan F. Cooper writes that, while Cooper was in Europe, his "small volumes of the 32° edition of Shakespeare [were] his constant traveling companions" (476). In addition to his firsthand observations, Cooper's principal source for Venetian history and landscape, as he notes in *The Bravo*'s preface (1:v), was Pierre Daru's multivolume *Histoire de la République de Venice* (1819). A distant and not particularly relevant source is M. G. Lewis, *The Bravo of Venice, a Romance: Translated from the German* (1805), which is a loose translation of Heinrich Zschokke's *Abaellino, der grosse Bandit* (1794). A popular stage adaptation of Lewis's text, *Rugantino; or the Bravo of Venice,* was published in Boston and New York in 1822. In a letter of 27 April 1831 to Charles Wilkes, Cooper implicitly denies Lewis's influence: "I have not yet decided on the name [of his novel in progress], but believe it will be 'Bravo.' I find Monk Lewis has a story called 'The Bravo of Venice,' which may induce me to choose another title" (*Letters and Journals,* 2:80).

49. Though *The Bravo* challenges oligarchical usurpation, it does not challenge Don Camillo's hierarchical authority over his servant Gino. For a good discussion of social hierarchy in Cooper, see Ross J. Pudaloff, "Cooper's Genres and American Problems," *ELH,* 40 (1983): 711–27.

50. Harry B. Henderson III, *Versions of the Past: The Historical Imagination in American Fiction* (New York: Oxford University Press, 1974), p. 62. Henderson's treatment of historical themes in Cooper is superb (see pp. 50–90). The early Cooper novel most informing *The Bravo* is *The Spy,* which Cooper revised while writing *The Bravo.* (He completed his new Introduction to *The Spy* on 4 April 1831, and the revised edition was published later that year by Colburn and Bentley.) Like the hero of *The Spy,* the bravo Jacopo finds himself misunderstood by the conflicting sides of the novel, and although a "patriot" in the mode of Harvey Birch, he must maintain the guise of a purely mercenary killer. And just as the New York citizenry of *The Spy,* fearful of declaring their political sympathies, "wore masks, which even to this day have not been thrown aside" (*The Spy,* p. 12), the citizenry of Venice remains masked, fearful of any form of openness.

51. James H. Huston writes, "In equating vigilance with jealousy, the eighteenth century frequently associated it with the eye" ("The Origins of 'The Para-

noid Style in American Politics': Public Jealousy from the Age of Walpole to the Age of Jackson," in *Saints and Revolutionaries: Essays on Early American History*, ed. David H. Hall, John M. Murrin, and Thad W. Tate [New York: Norton, 1984], p. 336).

52. J. F. Cooper, *The Heidenmauer; or, The Benedictines*, 2 vols., (Philadelphia: Carey & Lea, 1832), 1:186.

53. Though at times sentimentalized, the domestic and truly republican Violetta emerges as a rebel within the state. On the social significance of women in Cooper, see Nina Baym, "The Women of Cooper's Leatherstocking Tales," *American Quarterly*, 23 (1971): 696–709.

54. On marriage in eighteenth-century Venice, see Norwich, *A History of Venice*, pp. 594–7. For a wide-ranging discussion of the political significance of the marriage plot in early national and antebellum fiction, see Shirley Samuels, "The Family, the State, and the Novel in the Early Republic," *American Quarterly*, 38 (1986): 381–95.

55. M. M. Bakhtin, "Discourse in the Novel," in *The Dialogic Imagination: Four Essays by M. M. Bakhtin*, ed. Michael Holquist (Austin: University of Texas Press, 1981), p. 332.

56. Robyn R. Warhol, "Toward a Theory of the Engaging Narrator: Earnest Interventions in Gaskell, Stowe, and Eliot," *PMLA*, 101 (1986): 815, 812.

57. "The Antimasonic National Platform of 1832," rpt. in Holt, "The Antimasonic and Know Nothing Parties," pp. 662–3.

58. The centrality of the assassin figure, and even Jacopo's name, suggest Cooper's familiarity with Jacobean drama (as do the novel's chapter verses from Byron's *Marino Faliero*, a play much influenced by Jacobean "Italian" tragedies). At times Cooper's Venice seems less a city-state than a huge castle, its canals, "convenient graves for sudden deaths" (1:111), the passageways within.

59. Thurlow Weed, "Address to the People of Massachusetts" (1829), in Holt, "The Antimasonic and Know Nothing Parties," p. 652.

60. Ibid., p. 652.

61. Forgie, *Patricide in the House Divided*, p. 16.

62. Henry David Thoreau, *Walden and Civil Disobedience*, ed. Owen Thomas (New York: Norton, 1966), p. 233. The "just man" is also imprisoned in *The Spy* and *The Pioneers*. Cooper's attack on the Venetian oligarchy's self-avowed legal "objectivity" has an important precedent in his ironic representation of Judge Temple's "impartial" legal justice; see Brook Thomas, "*The Pioneers*, or the Sources of American Legal History: A Critical Tale," *American Quarterly*, 36 (1984): 86–111.

63. "The Cask of Amontillado," in *Edgar Allan Poe: Poetry and Tales*, ed. Patrick F. Quinn (New York: Library of America, 1984), p. 853; Herman Melville, *Israel Potter: His Fifty Years of Exile*, ed. Harrison Hayford, Hershel Parker, and G. Thomas Tanselle (Evanston, Ill.: Northwestern University Press; Chicago: The Newberry Library, 1982), pp. 70, 67.

64. Cooper, *Letters and Journals*, 1:380.

65. For Cooper, the Revolution of 1830 was a model revolution that, guided by the naturally noble Lafayette, was more reformatory than revolutionary, a

testament to the "moderation of the victors" (*Letters and Journals*, 2:7). The emergence of Louis Philippe, however, raised the possibility that a more violent revolutionism was in order, a revolutionism that Cooper feared would give rise to what he regarded as the anarchic revolutionism of 1793. Meditating on the guillotinings of the royal family, he remarked in an 1827 newspaper article: "Nations may be like *other* corporations, souless [*sic*]; but the individual who had committed one such act of madness, would be kept in wholesome restraint for the rest of his life" (*Letters and Journals*, 1:195). Arguably, then, Cooper's contempt for the "souless" mob of 1793 underlies his unsympathetic presentation of the revolutionary fishermen. For an excellent discussion of Cooper's conflicting attitudes toward revolution, see Mike Ewart, "Cooper and the American Revolution: the Non-fiction," *Journal of American Studies*, 11 (1977): 61–79. On Cooper's disdain for the tyrannous mob, see Nicolaus Mills, *The Crowd in American Literature* (Baton Rouge: Louisiana State University Press, 1986), pp. 41–5.

66. It would appear that, while Cooper the Jacksonian Democrat responded quite powerfully to the anticorporate and antioligarchical *republican* impulses of Antimasonry, he remained altogether suspicious of the movement's concomitant democratic insurgency, particularly, we may speculate, as it was exploited by demagogic Whigs such as Seward and Weed. My reading of Cooper as himself complicitous in "senatorial" forms of surveillance has been influenced by D. A. Miller's discussion of narrative omniscience as a kind of narrative policing; see "The Novel and the Police," *Glyph*, 8 (1981): 127–47.

67. Lord Byron, *Marino Faliero, Doge of Venice* (Philadelphia: Carey, 1821), p. 174.

68. Alan Axelrad, *History and Utopia: A Study of the World View of James Fenimore Cooper* (Norwood, Pa.: Norwood Editions, 1978), p. 19. Axelrad's insistence on Cooper's political and philosophical consistency over the course of thirty-two novels written over thirty some odd years ultimately condescends to Cooper by suggesting that immediate historical events had little impact on his thinking or writing. That said, Axelrad's little known study is an intellectually engaging work that should be better known. For Pudaloff the 1830s were "a turning point in Cooper's belief that America could possess both a social aristocracy and a political democracy" ("Cooper's Genres and American Problems," p. 713). Also responsive to Cooper's transformation in the 1830s is D. H. Lawrence, who observes in *Studies in Classic American Literature*, "It is perhaps easier to love America passionately, when you look at it through the wrong end of the telescope, across all the Atlantic water, as Cooper did so often, than when you are right there" (51).

69. J. Fenimore Cooper, *A Letter to His Countrymen* (New York: Wiley, 1834), pp. 14, 12.

70. John Patrick Diggins takes the argument one step farther and, noting Cooper's apparent belief in the impossibility of achieving virtue on a national scale, provocatively reads *The Bravo* as Cooper's farewell to classical republicanism; see *The Lost Soul of American Politics: Virtue, Self-interest, and the Foundations of Liberalism* (New York: Basic, 1984), pp. 180–91.

71. The "Cassio" review is cited in Cooper, *Letters and Journals*, 2:305. On *The Bravo*'s popularity, see Matthew J. Bruccoli, ed., *The Profession of Authorship in America, 1800–1870: The Papers of William Charvat* (Columbus: Ohio State University Press, 1968), pp. 291–2; and Grossman, *James Fenimore Cooper*, p. 68.
72. The phrase is from Meyers, *The Jacksonian Persuasion*, p. 57.
73. See Cooper, *A Letter to His Countrymen*, p. 59.
74. The reviews are reprinted in George Dekker and John McWilliams, eds., *Fenimore Cooper: The Critical Heritage*, (London: Routledge & Kegan Paul, 1973), pp. 174, 184.
75. Cooper, *Letters and Journals*, 2:237; Cooper, *Home as Found*, ed. Lewis Leary (New York: Capricorn, 1961), p. 190.
76. Cooper, *The American Democrat*, pp. 125, 93, 198, 199.
77. *Memorial of James Fenimore Cooper*, p. 36.
78. Franklin, *The New World of James Fenimore Cooper*, p. 191. On the anti-democratic politics of Cooper's later fiction, see Ross J. Pudaloff, "The Gaze of Power: Cooper's Revision of the Domestic Novel, 1835–1850," *Genre*, 17 (1984): 275–95; and Heinz Ickstadt, "Instructing the American Democrat: Cooper and the Concept of Popular Fiction in Jacksonian America," in *James Fenimore Cooper: New Critical Essays*, ed. Robert Clark (London: Vision; Totowa, N.J.: Barnes & Noble, 1985), pp. 15–37. See also Eric J. Sundquist's brilliant analysis (1–40) of Cooper's social-psychological effort to exert control in his later works through depictions of "aristocratic incest and inbreeding . . . the last, and most extreme, bulwark against the chaos of mob rule which Cooper found threatening himself and his country" (*Home as Found: Authority and Genealogy in Nineteenth-Century American Literature* [Baltimore, Md.: Johns Hopkins University Press, 1979], p. 3).
79. James Fenimore Cooper, *The Crater; or, Vulcan's Peak*, ed. Thomas Philbrick (Cambridge, Mass.: Harvard University Press, 1962), p. 325.
80. Rogin, *Fathers and Children*, p. 13.
81. James Fenimore Cooper, *The Redskins, or Indian and Injin* (New York: Townsend, 1861), p. 536. My discussion of Cooper and the American 1840s has been influenced by McWilliams, *Political Justice in a Republic*, pp. 238–402. I differ from McWilliams, however, in seeing Cooper increasingly uninterested in fusing "American" to "republicanism."

3. "A Confusion of Popish and Protestant Emblems"

Epigraphs: William Ellery Channing, *Letter on Catholicism* (1836), rpt. in *The Works of William E. Channing, D.D.* (Boston: American Unitarian Association, 1896), p. 471; *The Centenary Edition of the Works of Nathaniel Hawthorne*, ed. William Charvat, Roy Harvey Pearce, and Claude M. Simpson (Columbus: Ohio State University Press, 1962–), 4:267, 466. Future parenthetical references to Hawthorne's fiction and notebooks are to this edition.

1. James Fenimore Cooper, *Gleanings in Europe: Italy*, ed. John Conron and Constance Ayers Denne (Albany: State University of New York Press, 1981), pp. 3, 192, 245.

2. Ibid., pp. 232, 253. On Cooper's attitude to Catholicism during the early 1830s, see J. Gary Williams, "Cooper and European Catholicism: A Reading of *The Heidenmauer*," *ESQ*, 22 (1976): 149–58.

3. William Bradford, *Of Plymouth Plantation*, ed. Harvey Wish (New York: Capricorn, 1962), p. 26. On the colonial backgrounds of anti-Catholicism see Thomas More Brown, "The Image of the Beast: Anti-Papal Rhetoric in Colonial America," in *Conspiracy: The Fear of Subversion in American History*, ed. Richard O. Curry and Thomas M. Brown (New York: Holt, Rinehart & Winston, 1972), pp. 1–20; and Ann Kibbey, *The Interpretation of Material Shapes in Puritanism: A Study of Rhetoric, Prejudice, and Violence* (Cambridge University Press, 1986), pp. 121–48. The best introduction to political nativism is Ray Allen Billington, *The Protestant Crusade, 1800–1860: A Study of the Origins of American Nativism* (1938; rpt. New York: Quadrangle, 1964). See also Sydney E. Ahlstrom, *A Religious History of the American People* (New Haven, Conn.: Yale University Press, 1972), pp. 537–68; John Tracy Ellis, *American Catholicism* (University of Chicago Press, 1969); and Cushing Strout, *The New Heavens and New Earth: Political Religion in America* (New York: Harper & Row, 1974), pp. 71, 127–9, 255–6, et passim. For the dissenting view that anti-Catholicism has been overemphasized as a cultural phenomenon, see Lew O. Saum, *The Popular Mood of Pre–Civil War America* (Westport, Conn.: Greenwood, 1980), pp. 40–4.

4. See Bernard Bailyn, *The Ideological Origins of the American Revolution* (Cambridge, Mass.: Harvard University Press, 1967), pp. 98, 131, 133, 137, 207.

5. Adams to Jefferson, 3 February 1821, in *The Adams–Jefferson Letters: The Complete Correspondence between Thomas Jefferson and Abigail and John Adams*, ed. Lester J. Cappon (New York: Simon & Schuster, 1971), p. 571. On anti-Catholicism during the pre-Revolutionary and early national period, see Ruth H. Bloch, *Visionary Republic: Millennial Themes in American Thought, 1756–1800* (Cambridge University Press, 1985).

6. Ann Norton, *Alternative Americas: A Reading of Antebellum Political Culture* (University of Chicago Press, 1986), p. 66. The statistics are from Ahlstrom, *A Religious History of the American People*, p. 541; and Ellis, *American Catholicism*, pp. 50–1. E. R. Norman, *Anti-Catholicism in Victorian England* (New York: Barnes & Noble, 1968), provides a useful overview of anti-Catholic activity in England.

7. [Samuel F. B. Morse,] *Foreign Conspiracy Against the Liberties of the United States: The Numbers of Brutus, Originally Published in the New York-Observer, Revised and Corrected With Notes, by the Author* (1834; rpt. New York: Leavitt, Lord, 1835), pp. 14, 12, 47, 39.

8. Morse, *Foreign Conspiracy*, pp. 101, 124.

9. Lyman Beecher, *Plea for the West* (Cincinnati, Ohio: Truman & Smith, 1835), pp. 62, 85–6.

10. Morse, *Foreign Conspiracy*, pp. 47–8; Beecher, *Plea for the West*, pp. 60, 86. The Protestants' championing of the liberty to read was in part a response to the Catholics' decision, following their First Provincial Council's 1829 meeting in Baltimore, to oppose the use of the King James Bible in the public

schools. The reading controversy would become a major preoccupation of Catholic and Protestant leaders during the 1840s and 1850s, especially in New York City. See Billington, *The Protestant Crusade,* pp. 142–65.

11. Beecher, *Plea for the West,* p. 142. On Americans' interest in sensationalistic anti-Catholic novels, see David Brion Davis, "Some Themes of Countersubversion: An Analysis of Anti-Masonic, Anti-Catholic, and Anti-Mormon Literature," *Mississippi Valley Historical Review,* 47 (1960): 205–24. Also useful is David S. Reynolds, *Faith in Fiction: The Emergence of Religious Literature in America* (Cambridge, Mass.: Harvard University Press, 1981), pp. 180–6, et passim. On the relationship of the rise of modern printing to the Protestant Reformation, see Elizabeth L. Eisenstein, *The Printing Press as an Agent of Change: Communications and Cultural Transformations in Early-Modern Europe,* 2 vols. (Cambridge University Press, 1979). As Einsenstein observes, the "print shop and monastery were worlds apart" (1:378).

12. *Six Months in a Convent; or, The Narrative of Rebecca Theresa Reed, Who Was Under the Influence of the Roman Catholics About Two Years, and an Inmate of the Ursuline Convent on Mount Benedict, Charlestown, Mass., Nearly Six Months, in the Years 1831–32. With Some Preliminary Suggestions by the Committee of Publication* (Boston: Russell, Odiorne, 1835), pp. 115–16, 130, 100, 163. See also *Supplement to "Six Months in a Convent," Confirming the Narrative of Rebecca Theresa Reed, by the Testimony of More Than One Hundred Witnesses, Whose Statements Have Been Given to the Committee, Containing a Minute Account of the Elopement of Miss Harrison, with Some Further Explanations of the Narrative, by Miss Reed, and an Exposition of the System of Cloister Education, by the Committee of Publication* (Boston: Russell, Odiorne, 1835).

13. By alerting Americans to Canadian-based conspirators, Reed and Monk tapped into residual concerns that, sixty years earlier, had flared in response to the Quebec Act (1774) and played a central role in the American Revolution. Intended to ensure the loyalty of England's Canadian subjects, the Quebec Act seemed to Protestant Anglo-Americans part of a grand conspiracy to establish a Catholic nation on America's northern borders. As Peter Shaw observes, it "led to far greater actions in the streets than any political event for the rest of the decade, with the possible exception of the Declaration of Independence" (*American Patriots and the Rituals of Revolution* [Cambridge, Mass.: Harvard University Press, 1981], p. 68).

14. *Awful Disclosures of Maria Monk, as Exhibited in a Narrative of Her Sufferings During a Residence of Five Years as a Novice, and Two Years as a Black Nun, in the Hotel Dieu Nunnery at Montreal* (New York: Howe & Bates, 1836), pp. 115–16, 86, 56. A Reverend J. J. Slocum had ghostwritten most of the book, and by 1838 it was completely discredited. For a discussion of the publishing history and social backgrounds of Reed and Monk, see Billington, *Protestant Crusade,* pp. 85–117. In a letter of June 1836 to Horatio Greenough, Fenimore Cooper commented playfully, though with some concern too, on Samuel Morse's interest in the latest anti-Catholic novel: "I am very much afraid Morse is about to marry a certain Miss Monk, and when you see him I beg you will speak to him on the subject. I am afraid the

issue of such a celibate as himself and a regular Monk, who, by the way, has also been a *nun,* might prove to be a progeny fit only for the choir of the Sistine Chapel" (*The Letters and Journals of James Fenimore Cooper,* ed. James Franklin Beard, 6 vols. [Cambridge, Mass.: Harvard University Press, 1964], 3:220).

15. *Awful Disclosures,* p. 58. Some other examples of this popular genre include George Bourne, *Lorette: The History of Louise, Daughter of a Canadian Nun, Exhibiting the Interior of Female Convents* (New York: Mercein, 1833); Harry Hazel [Justin Jones], *The Nun of St. Ursula: or, The Burning of the Convent. A Romance of Mount Benedict* (Boston: Gleason, 1845); Charles Frothingham, *The Convent's Doom; A Tale of Charlestown in 1834* (Boston: Graves & Weston, 1854); and Josephine M. Bunkley, *Miss Bunkley's Book: The Testimony of an Escaped Novice from the Sisterhood of Charity in the United States* (New York: Harper & Brothers, 1855).

16. For a discussion of the impulses behind the Whigs' anti-Catholicism, see Daniel Walker Howe, *The Political Culture of the American Whigs* (University of Chicago Press, 1979), pp. 150–80.

17. As John Humphrey Noyes puts it in *History of American Socialisms* (1870; rpt. New York: Dover, 1966): "The Revivalists had for their great idea the regeneration of the soul. The great idea of the [communitarian] Socialists was the regeneration of society, which is the soul's society" (26). Excellent analyses of the social and religious backgrounds of reformism can be found in Whitney Cross, *The Burned-over District: The Social and Intellectual History of Enthusiastic Religion in Western New York, 1800–1850* (1950; rpt. New York: Harper Torchbooks, 1965); Timothy L. Smith, *Revivalism and Social Reform in Mid-Nineteenth-Century America* (New York: Abingdon, 1957); and John C. Thomas, "Romantic Reform in America, 1815–1865," *American Quarterly,* 7 (1965): 656–81. On American communitarianism see Noyes, *History of American Socialisms;* Constance Rourke, *Trumpets of Jubilee* (1927; rpt. New York: Harcourt Brace & World, 1963); Alice Felt Tyler, *Freedom's Ferment: Phases of American Social History from the Colonial Period to the Outbreak of the Civil War* (1944; rpt. New York: Harper Torchbooks, 1962), pp. 47–226; Arthur Eugene Bestor, Jr., *Backwoods Utopias: The Sectarian and Owenite Phases of Communitarian Socialism in America: 1663–1829* (Philadelphia: University of Pennsylvania Press, 1950); Russel Blaine Nye, *Society and Culture in America, 1830–1860* (New York: Harper Torchbooks, 1974), pp. 32–70; and Ronald Walters, *American Reformers: 1815–1860* (New York: Hill & Wang, 1978), pp. 39–76. For analyses of American utopianism in a larger Western context see Ernest Tuveson, *Millennium and Utopia: A Study in the Background of the Idea of Progress* (Berkeley and Los Angeles: University of California Press, 1949); and Frank E. Manuel and Fritzie P. Manuel, *Utopian Thought in the Western World* (Cambridge, Mass.: Harvard University Press, 1979), esp. pp. 641–93.

18. Albert Brisbane, *Social Destiny of Man: or, Association and Reorganization of Industry* (1840; rpt. New York: Franklin, 1968), p. 2. Elizabeth Palmer Peabody's "A Glimpse of Christ's Idea of Society" appeared in *Dial: A Magazine for Literature, Philosophy, and Religion,* 2 (1841): 214–28. Robert Owen's *A*

New View of Society had its first American publication in 1825. On the relation of communitarian reform to class conflict, see Sean Wilentz, *Chants Democratic: New York and the Rise of the American Working Class, 1788–1850* (New York: Oxford University Press, 1984), pp. 162–5, 176–83, 335–43. As opposed to the middle-class reformers at Brook Farm, the radical communitarians of New York's labor movement evinced a thoroughly anti-evangelical temper.

19. Brisbane, *Social Destiny of Man*, pp. 206, 22. Brisbane's text begins with an "explanation of terms," one of which is "subversive": "It signifies an overthrow or derangement of harmonic principles: it implies consequently a state of falseness and error, but supposes that a state of harmony may exist, or that the object to which it is applied is capable of harmony" (xiii). Brisbane would no doubt have agreed with Emerson's famous declaration in "Self-reliance" (1841): "Society everywhere is in conspiracy against the manhood of every one of its members" (*Emerson: Essays and Lectures*, ed. Joel Porte [New York: Library of America, 1983], p. 261).

20. Brisbane, *Social Destiny of Man*, pp. 33–4; Brisbane, "Association" (1842), cited in Michael Fellman, *The Unbounded Frame: Freedom and Community in Nineteenth Century American Utopianism* (Westport, Conn.: Greenwood, 1973), p. 13. On Brisbane and Fourier see also pp. 3–19. For an interesting discussion of Fourierist architectural design, see Dolores Hayden, *Seven American Utopias: The Architecture of Communitarian Socialism, 1790–1975* (Cambridge, Mass.: MIT Press, 1976), pp. 148–85.

21. Northrop Frye, "Varieties of Literary Utopias," in *Utopias and Utopian Thought*, ed. Frank E. Manuel (Boston: Beacon, 1967), p. 35.

22. Brisbane, *Social Destiny of Man*, pp. 123–4.

23. *National Intelligencer*, 30 April 1825, cited in Bestor, *Backwoods Utopias*, p. 126.

24. John F. C. Harrison, *Quest for the New Moral World: Robert Owen and the Owenites in Britain and America* (New York: Scribner, 1969), discusses the Owen community's decline to cultdom: "Owenism was essentially a sect which emerged round a leader whose teaching was accepted by followers, and which did not institutionally survive his death" (136).

25. Cited in Octavius Brooks Frothingham, *Transcendentalism in New England: A History* (1876; rpt. Philadelphia: University of Pennsylvania Press, 1972), p. 160.

26. Frothingham, *Transcendentalism in New England*, p. 157.

27. Charles Dana, "Association, in Its Connection with Religion" (1844), in Henry W. Sams, ed., *Autobiography of Brook Farm* (Englewood Cliffs, N.J.: Prentice-Hall, 1958), p. 110. Sams provides a superb collection of source materials. On the conversion of Brook Farm to Fourierism see Richard Francis, "The Ideology of Brook Farm," *Studies in the American Renaissance* (Boston: Twayne, 1977), pp. 1–48. In *The Burned-over District*, Cross notes that during 1844–5 Fourierism "quickly reached the proportions and acquired many of the characteristics of a religious revival" (328).

28. Reprinted in Sams, *Autobiography of Brook Farm*, p. 189.

29. [William Henry Channing,] "The Catholics and Associationists," *Harbinger*,

3 (1846): 102; see also pp. 103–4, 193–5. For a discussion of "the considerable interest in Catholicism" (196) at Brook Farm during the mid-1840s, see Anne C. Rose, *Transcendentalism as a Social Movement, 1830–1850* (New Haven, Conn.: Yale University Press, 1981), pp. 145, 185, 196–7, 210. Rose notes that Catholic conversions occurred at a number of reform communities, most notably at Brownson Alcott's Fruitlands.

30. For readings of the tale as Hawthorne's ethical attack on his unsophisticated reading public, see Michael J. Colacurcio, *The Province of Piety: Moral History in Hawthorne's Early Tales* (Cambridge, Mass.: Harvard University Press, 1984), pp. 78–93; and Tobin Siebers, *The Romantic Fantastic* (Ithaca, N.Y.: Cornell University Press, 1984), pp. 126–37. My reading draws somewhat on Dennis G. Coffey, "Hawthorne's 'Alice Doane's Appeal': The Artist Absolved," *ESQ*, 21 (1975): 230–40.

31. Hawthorne to Mathews and Duyckink, letter of 22 December 1841, in Nathaniel Hawthorne, *The Letters, 1813–1843*, ed. Thomas Woodson, L. Neal Smith, and Norman Holmes Pearson (Columbus: Ohio State University Press, 1984), p. 599; Hawthorne to Bridge, letter of 15 March 1851, in Hawthorne, *The Letters, 1843–1853*, ed. Woodson, Smith, and Pearson (Columbus: Ohio State University Press, 1984), p. 407; Hawthorne to Bridge, letter of 4 February 1850, *Letters, 1843–1853*, p. 311; Hawthorne to Ticknor, letter of 2 February 1855, in *Letters of Hawthorne to William D. Ticknor, 1851–1864*, 2 vols. (Newark, N.J.: Cateret Book Club, 1910), 1:75.

32. Useful discussions of Hawthorne's competing desires (literary and social) to engage and disengage can be found in Edgar A. Dryden, *Nathaniel Hawthorne: The Poetics of Enchantment* (Ithaca, N.Y.: Cornell University Press, 1977); and Kenneth Dauber, *Rediscovering Hawthorne* (Princeton, N.J.: Princeton University Press, 1977). On the American romancer's ambivalence toward his art and readers, see Michael Davitt Bell, *The Development of American Romance: The Sacrifice of Relation* (University of Chicago Press, 1980), esp. pp. 169–93; Evan Carton, "Hawthorne and the Province of Romance," *ELH*, 47 (1980): 331–54; and David Leverenz, "Mrs. Hawthorne's Headache: Reading *The Scarlet Letter*," *Nineteenth-Century Fiction*, 37 (1983): 552–75.

33. *Hawthorne as Editor: Selections from His Writings in the American Magazine of Useful and Entertaining Knowledge*, ed. Arlin Turner (1941; rpt. Folcroft, Penn.: Folcroft Library Editions, 1976), pp. 205, 203–4. "Churches and Cathedrals" appeared in the August 1836 issue.

34. Hawthorne to Elizabeth Hawthorne, letter of 5 May 1836, *Letters, 1813–1843*, p. 245; Hawthorne to Hillard, letter of 24 March 1844, *Letters, 1843–1853*, p. 23; Quentin Anderson, *The Imperial Self: An Essay in American Literary and Cultural History* (New York: Knopf, 1971), p. 60.

35. Michael Davitt Bell provides an excellent analysis of Hawthorne's historical typology in *Hawthorne and the Historical Romance of New England* (Princeton, N.J.: Princeton University Press, 1971); see esp. his discussion of Catholic villainy in contemporaneous historical romances, pp. 157–9. For a discussion of historical typology that focuses on Hawthorne's view of the American character, see John P. McWilliams, Jr., *Hawthorne, Melville, and the American*

Character: A Looking-glass Business (Cambridge University Press, 1984), pp. 23–129. On the romantic historians' anti-Catholicism, see David Levin, *History as Romantic Art: Bancroft, Prescott, Motley, and Parkman* (1959; rpt. New York: Harcourt Brace & World, 1963), pp. 93–125.

36. The central thrust of Colacurcio's brilliant, but at times one-sided *Province of Piety* is that Hawthorne was at a profound critical distance from consensual typological notions of American progress and that his fiction therefore served "to deconstruct, one by one, the various chapters of an emergent American mythology" (130). Colacurcio seems to believe that to betray a complicitous relationship to an unattractive prevailing ideology is to betray a damning complicity, and thus throughout his study he insists upon Hawthorne's untainted ironic vision. As he explains in an especially revealing passage on the "narrator" in Hawthorne's tales (in this case the narrator of "The Gray Champion"): "There is, of course, no perfect litmus test for detecting irony on the tongue of the speaker; it always exists (or not) pretty much in the ear of the listener. But in the end most of us will think better of Hawthorne's intelligence if he doesn't quite mean *all* that his 'narrator' says – if 'Hawthorne' is merely invoking the given and conventional definition of all American history as 'libertarian' (though often *malgré lui*), and of everything 'anti-American' as evil in the extreme. This is how we always decide the question of irony: how plausible – and how admirable – is the literary result?" (209). Colacurcio's generous inclinations, and his emphasis on the always problematizing presence of Hawthorne's sources ("pre-texts"), allow him to claim irony in tales that rhetorically only hint at such irony. I do not mean to deny that the irony is there; Colacurcio's meticulous readings are convincing. As opposed to Colacurcio, however, I believe that irony tells only part of the story.

My understanding of Hawthorne's attitude toward his readers during the early stages of his career is indebted to Nina Baym, *The Shape of Hawthorne's Career* (Ithaca, N.Y.: Cornell University Press, 1976). Baym observes that "it was part of Hawthorne's strategy through this part of his career [1834–9] to accede to the presumed view of his readers, and never assert either his superiority or his disagreement. By such a strategy he hoped to gain the goodwill of those on whom his success as an author depended" (81); see also pp. 53–83. On Hawthorne's desire to find community with his reading public, see also J. Donald Crowley, "Introduction," *Hawthorne: The Critical Heritage* (London: Routledge & Kegan Paul, 1970), pp. 1–39; and Bertha Faust, *Hawthorne's Contemporaneous Reputation: A Study of Literary Opinion in America and England, 1828–1864* (1939; rpt. New York: Octagon, 1968), esp. pp. 7–66. In an excellent analysis of Hawthorne's desire "to have it both ways: to apotheosize the Puritans as founders and liberators while interjecting ironic notes" (148), George Dekker shows that such doubleness was characteristic of "Romantic" irony generally and Sir Walter Scott's historical romances specifically; see *The American Historical Romance* (Cambridge University Press, 1987), pp. 133–59. For a suggestive study of how "the conditions of production and exchange emergent under capitalism" (151) informed Hawthorne's "opposing impulses that prompted him both to defy his audience and to seek its approval" (84), see Michael T. Gilmore, *American Romanticism and the Marketplace* (University of Chicago Press, 1985), pp. 52–112.

37. Colacurcio, *Province of Piety*, p. 210. On irony in "The Gray Champion" see also Frederick C. Crews, *The Sins of the Fathers: Hawthorne's Psychological Themes* (New York: Oxford University Press, 1966), pp. 39–41; and Frederick Newberry, " 'The Gray Champion': Hawthorne's Ironic Criticism of Puritan Rebellion," *Studies in Short Fiction*, 13 (1976): 363–70. For a reading of this and several of the other early tales as generally unironic, consensual depictions of the Puritans as heroic protorevolutionaries, see Peter Shaw, "Hawthorne's Ritual Typology of the American Revolution," *Prospects*, 3 (1977): 483–98.

38. Frederick Newberry discusses Endicott's fearsome characteristics in "The Demonic in 'Endicott and the Red Cross,' " *Papers on Language and Literature*, 13 (1977): 251–9. In *Province of Piety*, Colacurcio emphatically argues for Hawthorne's disdainful portrayal of Endicott (221–38). In contrast, Sacvan Bercovitch, in an anticipation of Shaw's "Hawthorne's Ritual Typology," finds Hawthorne for the most part in sympathy with the Puritans as harbingers of the American Revolution ("Endicott's Breastplate: Symbolism and Typology in 'Endicott and the Red Cross,' " *Studies in Short Fiction*, 4 [1967]: 289–99). I find Michael Davitt Bell's treatment of the tale's irony most persuasive. He writes, "The point of the irony is not that Endicott's intolerance undercuts his independence, but that the two qualities are inextricably joined in a single representative individual" (*Hawthorne and the Historical Romance of New England*, p. 56). See also McWilliams, *Hawthorne, Melville, and the American Character*, pp. 46–8. For a reading of the tale that emphasizes its manifestly anti-Catholic temper, see Ursula Brumm, "American Writers and European History: Nathaniel Hawthorne and Mark Twain," in *Forms and Functions of History in American Literature: Essays in Honor of Ursula Brumm*, ed. Winfried Fluck, Jurgën Peper, and Willi Paul Adams (Berlin: Schmidt, 1981), pp. 182–4. See also John Franzosa's provocative psychosocial analysis, "Young Man Hawthorne: Scrutinizing the Discourse of History," *Bucknell Review*, 30 (1987): 72–94.

39. Hawthorne's desire to please the "publick" is expressed most openly in letters to his sisters. He wrote Louisa in August 1841: "I have made an engagement with J. Munroe & Co. to write and edit a series of juvenile books, partly original and partly English books, to be adapted to our market. The first number is to be a new edition of Grandfather's Chair. We expect to make a great deal of money" (*Letters, 1813–1843*, p. 555). In a May 1836 letter to Elizabeth, his collaborator on the *American Magazine*, he urged her to "finish your life of Jefferson, and see that it contains nothing heterodox" (*Letters, 1813–1843*, p. 245).

40. For an illuminating study of various authors' treatments of the confrontation at Merry Mount, see John P. McWilliams, Jr., "The Fictions of Merry Mount," *American Quarterly*, 29 (1977): 3–30; and Richard Clark Sterne, "Puritans at Merry Mount: Variations on a Theme," *American Quarterly*, 22 (1970); 846–58. In Catharine Sedgwick's *Hope Leslie* (1827), Thomas Morton and his Merry Mounters are depicted as Royalist Catholic Christopher Gar-

diner's coconspirators. In Hawthorne's version there is little trace of conspiracy, simply of conspiratorial fear. Colacurcio thus reads the tale as an indictment of Endicott's expediency and concludes that we should speak of "the victory which the Lord and Lady win over Endicott" (*Province of Piety*, p. 272).

41. Carla Gardina Pestana observes: "Puritans found suspicious similarities between Quakers and Catholics. The inner light was likened to papal infallibility, since both claimed to be above reason. Both Quakers and papists used Satan's assistance to perform miracles that they then held up as proof of the superiority of their own beliefs. That both groups sought to denigrate Scriptures and learning was not lost on orthodox Puritans" ("The City upon a Hill under Siege: The Puritan Perception of the Quaker Threat to Massachusetts Bay, 1656–1661," *New England Quarterly*, 56 [1983]: 338–9).

42. R. Lawrence Moore, "Insiders and Outsiders in American Historical Narratives and American History," *American Historical Review*, 87 (1982): 404. For an opposing view that emphasizes the Catholics' nonconfrontational efforts to demonstrate their compatibility with republicanism, see Patrick W. Carey, "Republicanism within American Catholicism," *Journal of the Early Republic*, 3 (1983): 413–37.

43. Seymour L. Gross, "Hawthorne's Revision of 'The Gentle Boy,'" *American Literature*, 26 (1954): 199–208, shows how the 1837 revision of the original 1832 *Token* publication emphasizes "the mutuality of guilt" (208) between Quakers and Puritans. Bell, too, in *Hawthorne and the Historical Romance*, discusses Puritan intolerance in relation to Quaker complicity (110–17). See also Roy R. Male, *Hawthorne's Tragic Vision* (1957; rpt. New York: Norton, 1964), pp. 38–53. In "Hawthorne and the Sense of the Past or, the Immortality of Major Molineux," *ELH*, 21 (1954): 327–49, Roy Harvey Pearce argues that the 1832 version more responsibly and ethically emphasizes the guilt of the Puritans. Colacurcio follows Pearce, arguing that the tale utterly demolishes the Puritans' claims to authority and power; see *Province of Piety*, pp. 160–202.

44. The standard historicist readings are David Levin, "Shadows of Doubt: Specter Evidence in Hawthorne's 'Young Goodman Brown,'" *American Literature*, 34 (1962): 344–52; and Michael J. Colacurcio, "Visible Sanctity and Specter Evidence: The Moral World of Hawthorne's 'Young Goodman Brown,'" *Essex Institute Historical Collections*, 110 (1974): 259–99. See also James W. Clark, Jr., "Hawthorne's Use of Evidence in 'Young Goodman Brown,'" *Essex Institute Historical Collections*, 111 (1975): 12–34; and E. Miller Budick, "The World as Specter: Hawthorne's Historical Art," *PMLA*, 101 (1986): 218–32. For an excellent discussion of Hawthorne's historicism, see Roy Harvey Pearce, "Romance and the Study of History," in *Hawthorne Centenary Essays*, ed. Pearce (Columbus: Ohio State University Press, 1964), pp. 221–44. On Hawthorne's historicist approach to conspiracy see also Colacurcio's masterly readings of "My Kinsman, Major Molineux" and "Legends of the Province House," *Province of Piety*, pp. 130–53, 389–482.

45. Frank Shuffleton, "Nathaniel Hawthorne and the Revival Movement," *American Transcendental Quarterly*, 44 (1979): 311–23.

46. On Hawthorne's wavering response to the Shakers, see Rita K. Gollin,

"Hawthorne Contemplates the Shakers: 1831–1851," *Nathaniel Hawthorne Journal 1978*, pp. 57–65. Hawthorne's 1831 letters to Louisa on the Shakers can be found in *Letters, 1813–1843*, pp. 213, 220.

47. Ralph Waldo Emerson, "Man the Reformer" (1841), in *Emerson: Essays and Lectures*, p. 136. Emerson proclaims at the beginning of the essay: "In the history of the world the doctrine of Reform had never such scope as at the present hour" (135). Though Hawthorne's letters to Sophia are usually marshaled to show his disillusionment with Brook Farm, we must keep in mind that nearly two months passed before he began to write the despairing letters that would suggest he had turned away from the community's "pictured windows." So wearing were the community's physical demands, Hawthorne wrote Sophia on 1 June 1841, that utopianism had lost its gleam: "It is my opinion, dearest, that a man's soul may be buried and perish under a dung-heap or in a furrow of the field, just as well as under a pile of money" (*Letters, 1813–1843*, p. 545). Hawthorne's avowed reasons for joining Brook Farm were threefold: to test whether the community could serve as a home for him and Sophia, to see if the community could provide him with a healthy mix of physical and literary labor, and to follow through on his financial investment in the community. For biographical information I have relied on James R. Mellow, *Nathaniel Hawthorne in His Times* (Boston: Houghton Mifflin, 1980); and Arlin Turner *Nathaniel Hawthorne: A Biography* (New York: Oxford University Press, 1980).

48. Hawthorne to (presumably) Horatio Bridge, letter of 21 February 1846, *Letters, 1843–1853*, p. 144. On Hawthorne's legal actions against Brook Farm, see Robert F. Metzdorf, "Hawthorne's Suit Against Ripley and Dana," *American Literature*, 12 (1940): 235–41. Despite the favorable court verdict, Hawthorne probably never did recover his investment from the bankrupt community.

49. Frothingham, *Transcendentalism in New England*, p. 171.

50. Hawthorne to William B. Pike, letter of 24 July 1851, *Letters, 1843–1853*, p. 465.

51. To avoid cluttering the page, future parenthetical references to *Blithedale* in this section will not include the volume number.

52. Valuable discussions of Coverdale's narrative role include William L. Hedges, "Hawthorne's *Blithedale*: The Function of the Narrator," *Nineteenth-Century Fiction*, 14 (1960): 303–16; Nina Baym, "*The Blithedale Romance*: A Radical Reading," *Journal of English and Germanic Philology*, 67 (1968): 545–69; James H. Justus, "Hawthorne's Coverdale: Character and Art in *The Blithedale Romance*," *American Literature*, 47 (1975): 21–36; and Keith Carabine, "'Bitter Honey': Miles Coverdale as Narrator in *The Blithedale Romance*," in *Nathaniel Hawthorne: New Critical Essays*, ed. A. Robert Lee (London: Vision, 1982), pp. 110–30. For an excellent reading of the similarities between Coverdale as communitarian participant and Coverdale as romancer, see Evan Carton, *The Rhetoric of American Romance: Dialectic and Identity in Emerson, Dickinson, Poe, and Hawthorne* (Baltimore, Md.: Johns Hopkins University Press, 1985), pp. 228–52. On *Blithedale*'s thematics of community see Irving Howe, *Politics and the Novel* (New York: Hori-

zon, 1957), pp. 163–75; A. N. Kaul, *The American Vision: Actual and Ideal Society in Nineteenth-Century Fiction* (New Haven, Conn.: Yale University Press, 1963), pp. 196–213; Leo B. Levy, "*The Blithedale Romance*: Hawthorne's 'Voyage Through Chaos,'" *Studies in Romanticism*, 8 (1968): 1–15; John C. Hirsh, "The Politics of Blithedale: The Dilemma of Self," *Studies in Romanticism*, 11 (1972): 138–46; Roy Harvey Pearce, "Day-dream and Fact: The Import of *The Blithedale Romance*," in *Individual and Community*, ed. Kenneth H. Baldwin and David K. Kirby (Durham, N.C.: Duke University Press, 1975), pp. 49–63; and James McIntosh, "The Instability of Belief in *The Blithedale Romance*," *Prospects*, 9 (1984): 71–114. Although he does not discuss *Blithedale*, Terence Doody, *Confession and Community in the Novel* (Baton Rouge: Louisiana State University Press, 1980), offers a pertinent analysis of confessional tactics and desires.

My reading of *Blithedale* pays close attention to the ways in which the plotting enacts the text's themes. See Nina Baym, "The Significance of Plot in Hawthorne's Romances," in *Ruined Eden of the Present: Critical Essays in Honor of Darrel Abel*, ed. G. R. Thompson and Virgil L. Locke (West Lafayette, Ind.: Purdue University Press, 1981), pp. 49–70.

53. In a journal entry of 1842, Emerson observed that the Brook Farmers exacerbated rather than alleviated economic competition in the surrounding community: "Mr. Clapp of Dorchester to whom I described the Fourier project thought it must not only succeed but that agricultural association must presently fix the price of bread, & drive single farmers into association in self defence, as the great commercial and manufacturing companies had done" (*The Journals and Miscellaneous Notebooks of Ralph Waldo Emerson*, ed. William H. Gilman et al., 16 vols. [Cambridge, Mass.: Harvard University Press, 1970], 8:232).

54. See esp. Howe, *Politics and the Novel*, p. 168.

55. On the master–slave theme in *Blithedale*, see John C. Stubbs, *The Pursuit of Form: A Study of Hawthorne and the Romance* (Urbana: University of Illinois Press, 1970), pp. 120–37; Maria M. Tatar, *Spellbound: Studies on Mesmerism and Literature* (Princeton, N.J.: Princeton University Press, 1978), pp. 189–229; and Taylor Stoehr, *Hawthorne's Mad Scientists; Pseudoscience and Social Science in Nineteenth-Century Life and Letters* (Hamden, Conn.: Archon, 1978).

56. The conception of "utopian" Blithedale as an imprisoning community parallels a similar conception of community in Herman Melville's *Typee* – a text Brook Farmer John Sullivan Dwight celebrated in the *Harbinger* (1846) as a utopianist account of "true social brotherhood." More responsive to the text's ambiguities was Nathaniel Hawthorne, the anonymous reviewer in the 25 March 1846 *Salem Advertiser*, who pointed to a critical tension in the text that but six years later would inform his own novel of ideal community: He asked whether Tommo among the Typee islanders was in fact "the guest, or captive." Dwight's and Hawthorne's reviews are reprinted in *Critical Essays on Herman Melville's Typee*, ed. Milton R. Stern (Boston: Hall, 1982), pp. 25, 34.

57. On the veil motif in *Blithedale* see Frank Davidson, "Towards a Re-evalua-

tion of *The Blithedale Romance*," *New England Quarterly*, 25 (1952): 374–83; Norris Yates, "Ritual and Reality: Mask and Dance Motifs in Hawthorne's Fiction," *Philological Quarterly*, 34 (1955): 56–70; Richard Harter Fogle, "Priscilla's Veil: A Study of Hawthorne's Veil-Imagery in *The Blithedale Romance*," *Nathaniel Hawthorne Journal 1972*, 59–65; and Allan Gardner Lloyd Smith, *Eve Tempted: Writing and Sexuality in Hawthorne's Fiction* (London: Croom Helm, 1984), pp. 77–81.

58. Hawthorne's treatment of sexual desire at Blithedale probably also responds to contemporaneous debate on the communitarians' supposed advocacy of "free love." On sexuality and communitarianism, see Louis J. Kern, *An Ordered Love: Sex Roles and Sexuality in Victorian Utopias – the Shakers, the Mormons, and the Oneida Community* (Chapel Hill: University of North Carolina Press, 1981); and Lawrence Foster, *Religion and Sexuality: Three American Communal Experiments of Nineteenth-Century America* (New York: Oxford University Press, 1981).

59. As a polygamist of sorts, Hollingsworth can also be regarded as a type of Mormon patriarch. See Leonard Arrington and Jon Haupt, "Intolerable Zion: The Image of Mormonism in Nineteenth Century American Literature," *Western Humanities Review*, 22 (1968): 243–60.

60. See Barbara F. Lefcowitz and Allan B. Lefcowitz, "Some Rents in the Veil: New Light on Priscilla and Zenobia," *Nineteenth-Century Fiction*, 21 (1966): 263–75. For a provocative analysis of the genteel image of the "innocent" prostitute, see Christine Stansell, *City of Women: Sex and Class in New York, 1789–1860* (1986; rpt. Urbana: University of Illinois Press, 1987), pp. 171–92.

61. According to Norton, Protestant Americans regularly associated the Roman Catholic church with "a lascivious and seductive sexuality" (*Alternative Americas*, p. 69).

62. Stoehr, *Hawthorne's Mad Scientists*, p. 54.

63. George Lippard, *The Monks of Monk Hall*, ed. Leslie A. Fiedler (New York: Odyssey, 1970), p. 501. On the tension between countersubversion and subversion in Lippard's art and politics, see Larzer Ziff, *Literary Democracy: The Declaration of Cultural Independence in America* (New York: Viking, 1981), pp. 87–107. For a useful overview of Lippard's career, see David S. Reynolds, *George Lippard* (Boston: Twayne, 1982).

64. "Secret Societies – The Know-Nothings," *Putnam's Monthly*, 5 (1855): 92, 93.

65. Coverdale also resembles a reader at the mercy of a storyteller (recall "Alice Doane's Appeal"), Sophia at the mercy of an invasive mesmerist (see Hawthorne's famous letter of 18 October 1841), and a Pyncheon lady at the mercy of the mesmerical wizardry of a Maule (see Holgrave's near seduction/conquest of Phoebe [2:211]).

66. As Crews nicely puts it, Coverdale in the city becomes a "literary snoop" (*The Sins of the Fathers*, p. 200). Millicent Bell similarly focuses on Coverdale's selfishness, arguing "that the artist's egotism is a fatal deformity which separates him from his brother men" (*Hawthorne's View of the Artist* [Albany: State University Press of New York, 1962], p. 158).

67. The tavern, a haven for the down-and-out (and in antebellum Boston a haven for Irish Catholics), is itself a kind of "monastic" order. In an 1850 notebook entry on Boston's Parker's Bar, Hawthorne comments on the tavern as community: "Nothing is so remarkable in these bar-rooms and drinking-places as the perfect order that prevails there; if a man gets drunk, it is no otherwise perceptible than by his going to sleep, or inability to walk" (8:495). In his excellent discussion of *Blithedale* in *Hawthorne, Melville, and the Novel* (University of Chicago Press, 1976), pp. 91–115, Richard Brodhead shows how the tavern's "insistent artifice" (98) discloses the artifice of *Blithedale*'s other "artificial paradises" (98).

68. Hawthorne raises the possibility that Moodie, living among the Irish, may have married a Catholic; however, the fact that Priscilla is mocked by the Irish children as a pale outsider would suggest otherwise.

69. Hawthorne's personal desire to please his restless readers is conveyed in a letter of 22 July 1851 to Horatio Bridge: "I don't know what I shall write next. Should it be a romance, I mean to put an extra touch of the devil into it; for I doubt whether the public will stand two quiet books in succession, without my losing ground" (*Letters, 1843–1853*, pp. 461–2).

70. Lippard, *The Monks of Monk Hall*, pp. 533–4.

71. Robert Darnton brilliantly explores the relation of mesmerism to the French Revolution in *Mesmerism and the End of the Enlightenment in France* (Cambridge, Mass.: Harvard University Press, 1968); on Fourier's interest in mesmerism see esp. pp. 143–5. On spiritualism and mesmerism in America, see Stoehr, *Hawthorne's Mad Scientists*; R. Lawrence Moore, *In Search of White Crows: Spiritualism, Parapsychology, and American Culture* (New York: Oxford University Press, 1977); and Howard Kerr, *Mediums, and Spirit-Rappers, and Roaring Radicals: Spiritualism in American Literature, 1850–1900* (Urbana: University of Illinois Press, 1972). Also useful are Fred Kaplan, *Dickens and Mesmerism: The Hidden Springs of Fiction* (Princeton, N.J.: Princeton University Press, 1975); and Tartar, *Spellbound*.

72. *Brownson's Quarterly Review*, NS, 6 (1852); 563, 562.

73. O. A. Brownson, *The Spirit-Rapper; an Autobiography* (1854; rpt. Detroit, Mich.: Nourse, 1884) pp. 96, 97, 126. For all its alarmism, *The Spirit-Rapper* anticipates, to be sure rather crudely, Darnton's interpretation of the relationship of pseudoscience to revolution.

74. Ibid., p. 15.

75. Historian Michael Walzer writes that one large result of the rise of Puritanism as a social and political force is that the "very word *reform* took on a new meaning in the course of the sixteenth and seventeenth centuries: it had once suggested renewal, restoration to some original form or state. . . . By the 1640s the word implied transformations of the sort associated today with revolution." Revolutionism emerged, Walzer concludes, because the "thrust of Puritan doctrine, for all the evasiveness of the ministers, was clear enough: it pointed toward the overthrow of the traditional order." See *The Revolution of the Saints: A Study in the Origins of Radical Politics* (1965; rpt. New York: Atheneum Publishers, 1968), pp. 11, 118.

76. Carton argues for the centrality of the mesmerism–romance analogy, and

thus he interprets the impressario's account of Westervelt's mesmerical talents as "one of the most violent indictments of his own art that Hawthorne ever conceived" (*Rhetoric of American Romance*, p. 242). And yet as opposed to Hawthorne's romance artistry, mesmerists, within the fictive world of *Blithedale*, do very "real" and hurtful things to the bodies of "real" people.

77. For a good discussion of *Blithedale*'s wine imagery, see Judy Schaaf Anhorn, " 'Gifted Simplicity of Vision': Pastoral Expectations in *The Blithedale Romance*," *ESQ*, 28 (1982): 135–53.

78. Ralph Waldo Emerson, "Historic Notes of Life and Letters in New England," in *Lectures and Biographical Sketches* (Boston: Houghton Mifflin, 1889), pp. 328, 334. Actually, as Jonathan Beecher points out in *Charles Fourier: The Visionary and His World* (Berkeley and Los Angeles: University of California Press, 1987), the Jacobin terror left Fourier himself profoundly suspicious of revolution.

79. Charles Brockden Brown, *Ormond; or The Secret Witness*, ed. Sydney J. Krause, S. W. Reid, and Russel B. Nye (Kent, Ohio: Kent State University Press, 1982), p. 160.

80. Norton, *Alternative Americas*, pp. 69, 71.

81. For a discussion of similar projections and "exorcisms" in England's anti-Catholic discourse of the period, see Rosemary Clark-Beattie, "Fable of Rebellion: Anti-Catholicism and the Structure of *Villette*," *ELH*, 53 (1986): 821–47. On exorcism and the marketplace in Hawthorne's *The House of the Seven Gables*, see Walter Benn Michaels, "Romance and Real Estate," in *The American Renaissance Reconsidered*, ed. Michaels and Donald E. Pease (Baltimore, Md.: Johns Hopkins University Press, 1985), pp. 156–82.

82. On Coverdale's complicity in Zenobia's death, see Beverly Hume, "Restructuring the Case Against Hawthorne's Coverdale," *Nineteenth-Century Fiction*, 40 (1986): 387–99. Challenging the traditional reading of Coverdale's and Hollingsworth's roles in Zenobia's "suicide," Mary Suzanne Schriber suggests that Coverdale's antifeminist preconceptions make him an unreliable reporter and that Zenobia may have accidentally drowned or killed herself out of a despair only tangentially related to her involvement with Hollingsworth ("Justice to Zenobia," *New England Quarterly*, 55 [1982]: 61–78).

83. Coverdale's desire for a revolution that does not impinge upon his body comes through in his self-parodic remarks on Lajos Kossuth: "If Kossuth . . . would pitch the battle-field of Hungarian rights within an easy ride of my abode, and choose a mild, sunny morning, after breakfast, for the conflict, Miles Coverdale would gladly be his man, for one brave rush upon the levelled bayonets. Farther than that, I should be loth to pledge myself" (3:247). Perhaps the most extreme (and projected) expression of Coverdale's "puritanical" unease with the body is his description of the pigs "buried alive, in their own corporeal substance" (3:144). On the ways in which Hawthorne's characters "attempt to banish the physical aspects of being from their self-definitions" (p. 155), see Jeffrey Steele, *The Representation of the Self in the American Renaissance* (Chapel Hill: University of North Carolina Press, 1987), pp. 155–9.

84. Letter of 26 March 1840, in Hawthorne, *Letters, 1813–1843*, pp. 427–8.

85. On Hawthorne's conception of imaginative energy as a form of deviant and threatening revolutionism, see Bell, *Development of American Romance*, esp. pp. 169–71.

86. Noyes, *History of American Socialisms*, p. 107.

87. William G. McGloughlin, *Revivals, Awakenings, and Reform: An Essay on Religion and Social Change in America* (University of Chicago Press, 1978), p. 114.

88. James Fenimore Cooper, *The Bravo: A Tale*, 2 vols. (Philadelphia: Carey & Lea, 1831), 1:35.

89. Valuable discussions of Hester's "Catholic" character include Frederick Newberry, "Tradition and Disinheritance in *The Scarlet Letter*," *ESQ*, 23 (1977): 1–26; and Ronald J. Gervais, "'A Papist Among the Puritans': Icon and Logos in *The Scarlet Letter*," *ESQ*, 25 (1979): 11–16. Robert Clark argues that by linking Hester to Catholicism, Hawthorne cannot help but "imply that Hester's sufferings may be read as an analogy of hostility to Catholicism in Hawthorne's own time" (*Ideology and Myth in American Fiction, 1832–52* [London: Macmillan Press, 1984], p. 115). On conspiratorial themes in the novel, see also the source materials on the murder of Sir Thomas Overbury, rpt. in *The Scarlet Letter*, ed. Sculley Bradley, Richard Croom Beatty, E. Hudson Long, and Seymour Gross (New York: Norton, 1978), pp. 197–204.

90. See Michael J. Colacurcio, "Footsteps of Ann Hutchinson: The Context of *The Scarlet Letter*," *ELH*, 39 (1972): 459–94; and Amy Schrager Lang, *Prophetic Woman: Anne Hutchinson and the Problem of Dissent in the Literature of New England* (Berkeley and Los Angeles: University of California Press, 1987), pp. 161–92.

91. Larry J. Reynolds argues, for instance, that Hawthorne's suspicion of the French Revolution contributes to "a strong reactionary spirit which underlies his work" ("*The Scarlet Letter* and Revolutions Abroad," *American Literature*, 57 [1985]: 48). Though Reynolds provides a useful analysis of Hawthorne's response to various conservative texts on the French Revolution, he fails to consider the competing evidence in the romances themselves of Hawthorne's imaginative identifications with revolutionaries.

92. Cited in Henry G. Fairbanks, "Hawthorne and Confession," *Catholic Historical Review*, 43 (1957): 40. See also Ernest W. Baughman, "Public Confession and *The Scarlet Letter*," *New England Quarterly*, 40 (1967): 532–50.

93. To a certain extent *The Marble Faun* expresses an attraction to Roman Catholic art similar to that which informed the Gothic Revival; see Dennis Berthold's excellent "Hawthorne, Ruskin, and the Gothic Revival: Transcendent Gothic in *The Marble Faun*," *ESQ*, 20 (1974): 15–32. And yet, as William L. Vance argues in "The Sidelong Glance: Victorian Americans and Baroque Rome," *New England Quarterly*, 58 (1985): 501–32, central to Protestant Americans' idealization of the Gothic was a pronounced "anti-papalism" (520). Hilda's decision to return to America thus may be taken as an echo of Hawthorne's friend George Stillman Hillard's conclusion to *Six Months in Italy* (London: Murray, 1853): "The American does not see Italy aright who does not find there fresh cause of gratitude for having been born

where he was, and who does not bring home from it a new sense of the worth of labour and the dignity of duty" (2:357). For a discussion of the novel as a celebration of the ideals of Protestant art, see Paul Brodtkorb, Jr., "Art Allegory in *The Marble Faun,*" *PMLA,* 77 (1962): 254–67. For a political reading, see Robert S. Levine, "'Antebellum Rome' in *The Marble Faun,*" *American Literary History* (forthcoming).

94. James Jackson Jarves, *Italian Sights and Papal Principles, Seen Through American Spectacles* (New York: Harper & Brothers, 1856), p. 271. For all his attraction to Rome, Jarves insisted that "Romanism and republicanism are antagonistic powers. When together, one or the other must succumb" (342).

95. For a discussion of the carnivalesque as a social ideal, see Mikhail Bakhtin, *Rabelais and His World* (Cambridge, Mass.: MIT Press, 1968). During carnival, Bakhtin writes, the citizenry "for a time entered the utopian realm of community, freedom, equality, and abundance" (9). Hawthorne's carnival in *The Marble Faun* enacts both revolutionary expression and counterrevolutionary repression. On the political context of the novel, see Arnold Goldman, "The Plot of Hawthorne's *The Marble Faun,*" *Journal of American Studies,* 18 (1984): 383–404.

4. "Follow Your Leader"

Epigraphs: William Harper, *Memoir on Slavery* (1838); rpt. in *The Proslavery Argument; as Maintained by the Most Distinguished Writers of the Southern States, Containing the Several Essays on the Subject, of Chancellor Harper, Governor Hammond, Dr. Simms, and Professor Dew* (1852; rpt. New York: Negro Universities Press, 1968), p. 82; Herman Melville, *Moby-Dick; or, The Whale,* ed. Harrison Hayford and Hershel Parker (New York: Norton, 1967), p. 15. Future page references to *Moby-Dick* (MD) and Melville's other writings will appear in the the text parenthetically. In addition to the Norton *Moby-Dick,* I will use the following editions: References to *Typee: A Peep at Polynesian Life* (T), *Omoo: A Narrative of Adventures in the South Seas* (O), *Mardi: and a Voyage Thither* (M), *Redburn: His First Voyage* (R), *White-Jacket: or the World in a Man-of-War* (WJ), *Pierre; or, The Ambiguities* (P), *Israel Potter: His Fifty Years of Exile* (IP), and *The Confidence-Man: His Masquerade* (CM) are to *The Writings of Herman Melville,* ed. Harrison Hayford, Hershel Parker, and G. Thomas Tanselle (Evanston, Ill.: Northwestern University Press; Chicago: Newberry Library, 1968–). References to *The Piazza Tales* (PT) and the uncollected prose (UP) are to *Melville: Pierre, Israel Potter, The Confidence-Man, Tales & Billy Budd,* ed. Harrison Hayford (New York: Library of America, 1984), which uses the forthcoming Northwestern–Newberry texts. References to *Battle-Pieces and Aspects of the War* (BP) are to the text edited by Sidney Kaplan (Gainesville, Fla.: Scholars' Facsimiles, 1960). And references to *Billy Budd, Sailor: (An Inside Narrative)* (BB) are to the text edited by Harrison Hayford and Merton M. Sealts, Jr. (University of Chicago Press, 1962).

1. *Putnam's Monthly Magazine,* 4 (1854): iv.

2. F. O. Matthiessen, *American Renaissance: Art and Expression in the Age of*

Emerson and Whitman (1941; rpt. New York: Oxford University Press, 1974), p. 508; Sidney Kaplan, "Herman Melville and the American National Sin," *Journal of Negro History,* 42 (1957): 20. The four reviews of *The Piazza Tales* reprinted in *The Recognition of Herman Helville: Selected Criticism Since 1846,* ed. Hershel Parker (Ann Arbor: University of Michigan Press, 1967), pp. 81–4, refer to *Benito Cereno,* if at all, only by title.

3. For a sampling of some of the best of this revisionary criticism, see Eleanor E. Simpson, "Melville and the Negro: From *Typee* to 'Benito Cereno,'" *American Literature,* 41 (1969): 19–38; Jean Fagin Yellin, "Black Masks: Melville's *Benito Cereno,*" *American Quarterly,* 22 (1970): 678–89; Joyce Adler, "Melville's *Benito Cereno:* Slavery and Violence in the Americas," *Science and Society,* 38 (1974): 19–48; Paul David Johnson, "American Innocence and Guilt: Black–White Destiny in 'Benito Cereno,'" *Phylon,* 36 (1975): 426–34; Edward Margolis, "Melville and Blacks," *CLA Journal,* 18 (1975): 364–73; Howard Welsh, "The Politics of Race in 'Benito Cereno,'" *American Literature,* 46 (1975): 556–65; Glenn C. Altshuler, "Whose Foot on Whose Throat? A Re-examination of Melville's *Benito Cereno,*" *CLA Journal,* 18 (1975): 283–92; Marvin Fisher, *Going Under: Melville's Short Fiction and the American 1850s* (Baton Rouge: Louisiana State University Press, 1977); and Joshua Leslie and Sterling Stuckey, "The Death of Benito Cereno: A Reading of Herman Melville on Slavery," *Journal of Negro History,* 67 (1982): 287–301. On the relationship of the civil rights movement to the renewed interest in Melville's treatment of slavery, see Carolyn L. Karcher, *Shadow over the Promised Land: Slavery, Race, and Violence in Melville's America* (Baton Rouge: Louisiana State University Press, 1980), pp. ix–xii.

4. Robert Lowell's *Benito Cereno* re-presented Melville's *Benito Cereno* during a time when Lowell was outraged by racial injustice on the home front and military escalation in Vietnam. The play, which premiered in 1964, forms part of the trilogy *The Old Glory* (New York: Noonday, 1965). See Robert Ilson, "*Benito Cereno* from Melville to Lowell," in *Robert Lowell: A Collection of Critical Essays,* ed. Thomas Parkinson (Englewood Cliffs, N.J.: Prentice-Hall, 1968), pp. 135–42.

5. For a discussion of similar desires and concerns in nineteenth-century England, see Walter E. Houghton, *The Victorian Frame of Mind, 1830–1870* (New Haven, Conn.: Yale University Press, 1957), pp. 54–89.

6. Influencing my reading of the structural similarities of ship, prison, factory, and plantation is Michel Foucault, *Discipline and Punish: The Birth of the Prison* (New York: Vintage, 1979). For a thoroughgoing Foucauldian analysis of the institutional issues addressed in this chapter, see Myra C. Glenn, *Campaigns against Corporal Punishment: Prisoners, Sailors, Women, and Children in Antebellum America* (Albany: State University of New York Press, 1984).

7. Edward Pessen, "How Different from Each Other Were Antebellum North and South?" *American Historical Review,* 85 (1980): 1147.

8. Bertram Wyatt-Brown, "Proslavery and Antislavery Intellectuals: Class Concepts and Polemical Struggle," in *Antislavery Reconsidered: New Perspectives on the Abolitionists,* ed. Lewis Perry and Michael Fellman (Baton Rouge:

Louisiana State University Press, 1979), p. 313. Relatedly, in "A Southern Stewardship: The Intellectual and the Proslavery Argument," *American Quarterly,* 31 (1979): 63–80, Drew Gilpin Faust argues that the proslavery argument "rested on intellectual values and moral-philosophical assumptions shared throughout mid-nineteenth-century America" (64). See also Faust, "Introduction," *The Ideology of Slavery: Proslavery Thought in the Antebellum South, 1830–1860* (Baton Rouge: Louisiana State University Press, 1981), pp. 1–20. Recent reassessments of proslavery writing owe a good deal to David Donald, "The Proslavery Argument Reconsidered," *Journal of Southern History,* 37 (1971): 3–18, which suggested that proslavery writers were not so abberant after all: "In this time of rapid social change and of overwhelming social disintegration, the proslavery writers longed, as did members of the Jacksonian persuasion, for a return to agrarian simplicity; they hoped, as did so many New England abolitionists, for a restoration of social order and hierarchy; they dreamed, as did the Know-Nothings, of the pure, calm days of the early Republic" (17). In a revisionary study of the period, *Alternative Americas: A Reading of Antebellum Political Culture* (University of Chicago Press, 1986), Ann Norton reemphasizes regional differences, contrasting the industrial North with the agrarian South. As subsequent notes will indicate, I have profited from her book, though I believe that in her zeal to criticize Northern industrial capitalism, she romanticizes the South and overstates regional differences. On important differences and similarities between the regions' institutions, see also Michael Stephen Hindus, *Prison and Plantation: Crime, Justice, and Authority in Massachusetts and South Carolina, 1767–1878* (Chapel Hill: University of North Carolina Press, 1980).

9. William Gilmore Simms, "The Morals of Slavery," rpt. in *The Pro-slavery Argument,* pp. 205–6. Simms's article first appeared in the 1837 volume of the *Southern Literary Messenger* and in 1838 was published separately as a pamphlet.

10. Thomas R. Dew, *Review of the Debate in the Virginia Legislature of 1831 and 1832* (Richmond, Va.: White, 1832), pp. 6, 101–2, 111. Southerners' fears of abolitionist meddling were exacerbated by the fact that Turner's rebellion occurred soon after the publication of the inaugural issue of Garrison's *The Liberator.* On the lingering impact of San Domingo on the Southern imagination, see Winthrop D. Jordan, *White over Black: American Attitudes toward the Negro, 1550–1812* (Chapel Hill: University of North Carolina Press, 1968), p. 380. The relatively small number of slave revolts in America testifies not to black docility but to what Eugene Genovese has shown to be the slaveholders' hegemonic control; see his masterly *Roll, Jordon, Roll: The World the Slaves Made* (New York: Pantheon, 1974); and Genovese, *From Rebellion to Revolution: Afro-American Slave Revolts in the Making of the Modern World* (Baton Rouge: Louisiana State University Press, 1979). On slave revolts see also Herbert Aptheker, *American Negro Slave Revolts* (1943; rpt. New York: International, 1969); Kenneth M. Stampp, *The Peculiar Institution: Slavery in the Ante-bellum South* (New York: Vintage, 1956), pp. 86–191; George M. Fredrickson and Christopher Lasch,

"Resistance to Slavery," *Civil War History*, 13 (1967): 315–29; Harvey Wish, "American Slave Insurrections before 1861," in *Justice Denied: The Black Man in White America*, ed. William M. Chace and Peter Collier (New York: Harcourt, Brace & World, 1970), pp. 81–93; and George M. Fredrickson, *The Black Image in the White Mind: The Debate on Afro-American Character and Destiny, 1817–1914* (New York: Harper Torchbooks, 1972), pp. 8–9, 52–4, 109.

11. Dew, *Review*, p. 13; *The Confessions of Nat Turner*, in *The Nat Turner Rebellion: The Historical Event and the Modern Controversy*, ed. John B. Duff and Peter M. Mitchell (New York: Harper & Row, 1971), p. 13. Surely Ann Norton overstates the case when she asserts that Southerners "steadfastly refused to ascribe to blacks the savagery which they granted the Indians" (*Alternative Americas*, p. 162).

12. Fredrickson, *The Black Image in the White Mind*, p. 54. On Dew's influence in the South, see Joseph Clarke Robert, *The Road from Monticello: A Study of the Virginia Debate of 1832* (1941; rpt. New York: Negro Universities Press, 1968), p. 289. Dew's *Review* achieved a renewed influence in the 1850s when reprinted in *The Pro-slavery Argument*.

13. William John Grayson, *Letters of Curtius*, cited in William Sumner Jenkins, *Pro-slavery Thought in the Old South* (1935; rpt. Gloucester, Mass.: Peter Smith, 1960), p. 303; George Fitzhugh, *Sociology for the South; or The Failure of Free Society*, in *Antebellum: Writings of George Fitzhugh and Hinton Roman Helper on Slavery*, ed. Harvey Wish (New York: Capricorn, 1960), pp. 58–9; 94.

14. Paul Boyer, *Urban Masses and Moral Order in America, 1820–1920* (Cambridge, Mass.: Harvard University Press, 1978), p. 69. See also David Grimsted, "Rioting in Its Jacksonian Setting," *American Historical Review*, 77 (1972): 361–97; and Christine Stansell, *City of Women: Sex and Class in New York, 1789–1860* (1986; rpt. Urbana: University of Illinois Press, 1987).

15. In the *Workingman's Gazette* of 3 May 1831, for example, an anonymous writer asked "Who Are Slaves?" and responded that the laboring classes – black and white – were enslaved to the rich, for "might makes right, and money makes power." The factory operatives, another worker wrote, "are in fact nothing more nor less than slaves in every sense of the word" (cited in Norton, *Alternative Americas*, p. 238). On workers' perceptions of their status as "wage slaves," see Edward Pessen, *Most Uncommon Jacksonians: The Radical Leaders of the Early Labor Movement* (Albany: State University of New York Press, 1967); Sean Wilentz, *Chants Democratic: New York City and the Rise of the American Working Class, 1789–1850* (New York: Oxford University Press, 1984); and Norton, *Alternative Americas*, esp. pp. 234–9. For a discussion of the worker–slave analogy in England's labor discourse, see Catherine Gallagher, *The Industrial Reformation of English Fiction: Social Discourse and Narrative Form, 1832–1867* (University of Chicago Press, 1985), pp. 3–35.

16. George Lippard, *The Monks of Monk Hall*, ed. Leslie A. Fiedler (New York: Odyssey, 1970), pp. 389, 388.

17. David Walker, *Appeal . . . to the Coloured Citizens of the World,* in *The Nat Turner Rebellion,* ed. Duff and Mitchell, p. 10.
18. Orestes A. Brownson, "The Laboring Classes," *Boston Quarterly Review* (1840), rpt. in *Ideology and Power in the Age of Jackson,* ed. Edwin C. Rozwenc (Garden City, N.Y.: Anchor, 1964), pp. 323, 325, 331.
19. The speeches are reprinted in George M. Fredrickson's excellent collection, *William Lloyd Garrison* (Englewood Cliffs, N.J.: Prentice-Hall, 1968), pp. 26, 28, 19. For a valuable discussion of the ways in which the fearsome specter of San Domingo, on the one hand, and the revolutionary ideals of the American Revolution, on the other, informed numerous texts of the period, see Eric J. Sundquist, "Slavery, Revolution, and the American Renaissance," in *The American Renaissance Reconsidered: Selected Papers from the English Institute, 1982–83,* ed. Walter Benn Michaels and Donald E. Pease (Baltimore, Md.: Johns Hopkins University Press, 1985), pp. 1–23.
20. See Richard B. Morris, "Criminal Conspiracy and Early Labor Combinations," *Political Science Quarterly,* 52 (1937): 51–85; and Pessen, *Most Uncommon Jacksonians,* p. 50.
21. Erving Goffman, *Asylums: Essays on the Social Situation of Mental Patients and Other Inmates* (Garden City, N.Y.: Anchor, 1961), p. xiii.
22. John F. Kasson, *Civilizing the Machine: Technology and Republican Values in America, 1776–1900* (Harmondsworth: Penguin Books, 1977), p. 64. On the rise of urban-reform institutions in America, see also David J. Rothman, *The Discovery of the Asylum: Social Order and Disorder in the New Republic* (Boston: Little, Brown, 1971). In addition to Rothman's fine study, see Stanley K. Schultz, *The Culture Factory: Boston Public Schools, 1789–1860* (New York: Oxford University Press, 1973); Thomas Bender, *Towards an Urban Vision: Ideas and Institutions in Nineteenth Century America* (1975; rpt. Baltimore, Md.: Johns Hopkins University Press, 1982), pp. 129–57; Ronald G. Walters, *American Reformers: 1815–1860* (New York: Hill & Wang, 1978), pp. 173–211. On parallel developments in England, see Michael Ignatieff, *A Just Measure of Pain: The Penitentiary in the Industrial Revolution, 1750–1850* (New York: Pantheon, 1978).
23. Rothman, *The Discovery of the Asylum,* p. 85. For a vigorous defense of the humanitarian aims of America's antebellum reformers, see Gerald N. Grob, *Mental Institutions in America: Social Policy to 1875* (New York: Free Press, 1973). On the reformers' ethnic fears and pursuit of social control, see Norton, *Alternative Americas,* esp. pp. 64–96.
24. William Ellery Channing, "Ministry for the Poor," in *The Works of William E. Channing, D.D.* (Boston: American Unitarian Association, 1896), p. 78; Horace Mann, *Tenth Annual Report* (1846), cited in Schultz, *The Culture Factory,* p. 233; and Dorothea Dix, *Remarks on Prisons and Prison Discipline in the United States* (Philadelphia: Kite, 1845), p. 13. On reformers' hesitations in embracing total abolition of flogging, see Glenn, *Campaigns against Corporal Punishment,* pp. 58–9.
25. For a discussion of the reformers' idealizations of the urban institution as familial and republican, see Rothman, *Discovery of the Asylum,* p. 66 et passim; and Kasson, *Civilizing the Machine,* pp. 55–106.

26. Cited in Boyer, *Urban Masses,* p. 93. Hartley headed the Association for Improving the Condition of the Poor (AICP).

27. [Henry Mercier,] *Life in a Man-of-War; or Scenes in "Old Ironsides" During Her Cruise in the Pacific* (1841; rpt. Boston: Houghton Mifflin, 1927), p. xxi; Charles Briggs, *Working a Passage; or, Life in a Liner (Published for the Benefit of Young Travellers)* (1844) (rev. ed., 1846; rpt. New York: Garrett, 1970), p. 5; *The Journal of Richard Henry Dana, Jr.,* ed. Robert F. Lucid, 3 vols. (Cambridge, Mass.: Harvard University Press, 1968), 1:27; letter of 1 March 1835, in James Allison, "Five Dana Letters," *American Neptune,* 13 (1953): 166. For an excellent overview of the sea fiction of the period, see Thomas Philbrick, *James Fenimore Cooper and the Development of American Sea Fiction* (Cambridge, Mass.: Harvard University Press, 1961). Also useful is Bernard Rosenthal, "The Oceans of America," *City of Nature: Journeys to Nature in the Age of American Romanticism* (Newark: University of Delaware Press, 1980), pp. 138–66. In addition to Cooper's early nautical romances, the travel writings of the period, particularly polar-exploration texts, contributed to the popularity of antebellum sea narratives.

28. Richard Henry Dana, Jr., *Two Years before the Mast: A Personal Narrative of Life at Sea,* ed. Thomas Philbrick (New York: Penguin American Library, 1981), p. 56. The text of this edition follows the 1840 first edition published by Harper and Brothers.

29. William McNally, *Evils and Abuses in the Naval and Merchant Service, Exposed; with Proposals for Their Remedy and Redress* (Boston: Cassady & March, 1839), pp. 128, 129. The flogging debate in Congress split along sectional lines – John P. Hall, the leader of the Liberty (and later of the Free Soil Party), headed the antiflogging coalition, whereas Charles G. Atherton, the author of the 1838 "gag" restriction, championed the continued right to flog. Flogging was eventually banned by Congress in 1850. For background on the flogging debate, see Harold D. Langley, *Social Reform in the United States Navy, 1798–1862* (Urbana: University of Illinois Press, 1967); and Myra C. Glenn, "The Naval Reform Campaign against Flogging: A Case Study on Changing Attitudes toward Corporal Punishment, 1830–1850," *American Quarterly,* 35 (1983): 408–25.

30. Dana, *Two Years before the Mast,* pp. 38, 120, 155, 156, 153, 154, 463. So suggestive was the analogy between ship and plantation that *Two Years* was regarded by Southerners as an abolitionist text. In the only strongly negative review of the book, an anonymous reviewer for the *Southern Literary Messenger* portrayed Dana as a hustling Yankee out to make a buck: "We apprehend our young attorney's narrative was an after-thought, and that the book was written as a Yankee expedient to identify himself with the interests of seamen, and obtain a moiety of the legal business which poor Jack brings to the bar" (*SLM,* 6 [1840]: 781). Despite its captaincy-oriented politics, Dana's text was appropriated by reformers for their antiflogging campaign; see Robert F. Lucid, "*Two Years Before the Mast* as Propaganda," *American Quarterly,* 12 (1960): 392–403. For an interesting discussion of the book's more conservative representation of "the initiate's acceptance and mastery of a corporate identity" (259), see Robert A. Ferguson, *Law and*

Letters in American Culture (Cambridge, Mass.: Harvard University Press, 1984), pp. 241–72.

31. Dana, *Two Years before the Mast*, pp. 58, 470, 53, 470–71, 464. D. H. Lawrence distilled this lesson from *Two Years*: "A master had to be master, or it was hell" (*Studies in Classic American Literature* [New York: Viking, 1972], p. 116).

32. Guert Gansevoort's justification was conveyed by his mother, Mary Ann Gansevoort, to Peter Gansevoort, letter of 2 January 1843, in *The Melville Log: A Documentary Life of Herman Melville, 1819–1891*, ed. Jay Leyda, 2 vols. (1951; rpt. with additional material, New York: Gordian, 1969), 1:161. For background on the *Somers* mutiny, see *The Somers Mutiny Affair*, ed. Harrison Hayford (Englewood Cliffs, N.J.: Prentice-Hall, 1959); and Philip McFarland, *Sea Dangers: The Affair of the Somers* (New York: Schocken, 1985). On domestic ideology and the *Somers* see Michael Paul Rogin, *Subversive Genealogy: The Politics and Art of Herman Melville* (New York: Knopf, 1983), pp. 94–6.

33. R. H. Dana, Jr., *The Seaman's Friend: Containing a Treatise on Practical Seamanship, with Plates; a Dictionary of Sea Terms; Customs and Usages of the Merchant Service; Laws Relating to the Practical Duties of Master and Mariners* (1841; rpt. Boston: Thomas Groom, 1845), pp. 192, 212. Even before publication of *Two Years*, Dana had gained a reputation as the "Seaman's Friend" as a result of his article protesting the light sentences meted out to a master and mate for beating a seaman to death; see "Cruelty to Seamen: – Case of Nichols and Couch," *American Jurist and Law Magazine*, 22 (1839): 92–107. In that essay, unlike in his defense of Mackenzie, Dana contended that character witnesses should be regarded as unreliable. Though a captain may seem trustworthy enough in court, Dana argued, it is sometimes the case that when he is "far from all restraints of friends and superiors and public opinion, possessed of despotic power, and with none to see him but those who stand to him in the relation of slaves, [a captain] may show himself a very fiend" (100).

34. See Charles Francis Adams, *Richard Henry Dana: A Biography*, 2 vols. (Boston: Houghton, Mifflin, 1891), 1:53. Adams prints the complete text of Dana's 1843 letter.

35. *Proceedings of the Naval Court Martial in the Case of Alexander Slidell Mackenzie, a Commander in the Navy of the United States, &c. Including the Charges and Specifications of Charges, Preferred against him by the Secretary of the Navy. To which is Annexed, an Elaborate Review by James Fenimore Cooper* (New York: Henry G. Langley, 1844), p. 334. In response to Mackenzie's attack on his *History of the Navy*, Cooper wrote his wife: "MacKenzie [*sic*] is superficial and jesuitical – He does not meet the question . . . fairly, cavil[s] at the plainest significations, and shows any thing but honesty or talent. . . . This review, alone, satisfies me as to the man's character. He wants candor, and a sense of right" (letter of 19 October 1839, in *The Letters and Journals of James Fenimore Cooper*, ed. James Franklin Beard, 6 vols. [Cambridge, Mass.: Harvard University Press, 1964], 3:437). In 1843 Cooper somewhat unfairly used the *Somers* incident to attack both Mac-

kenzie's *Life of Perry* (1840) and his negative review of Cooper's *History of the Navy; see The Battle of Lake Erie: or Answers to Messrs, Burges, Duer, and Mackenzie* (Cooperstown, N.Y.: Phinney, 1843). Additionally motivating Cooper to take on Mackenzie was the fact that Cooper's despised Whig newspaper editors rallied to Mackenzie's defense.

36. *Case of the Somers' Mutiny. Defence of Alexander Slidell Mackenzie, Commander of the U.S. Brig Somers, before the Court Martial, Held at the Navy Yard, Brooklyn* (New York: Tribune Office, 1843), p. 17; Adams, *Richard Henry Dana,* 1:52; Richard Henry Dana, *The Boston Courier,* 18 August 1843, p. 2; [Charles Sumner,] "The Mutiny of the Somers," *North American Review,* 57 (1843): 232, 237. For a discussion of Sumner's essay in its contemporaneous legal context, see Brook Thomas, *Cross-examinations of Law and Literature: Cooper, Hawthorne, Stowe and Melville* (Cambridge University Press, 1987), pp. 208–14, 238–9.

37. *Case of the Somers' Mutiny,* p. 16.

38. [Sumner,] "The Mutiny of the Somers," pp. 196, 195.

39. Letter of 26 November 1840, in Leyda, *Melville Log,* 1:110; letter of 12 August 1841, cited in Herbert Mitgang, "Scholars to Examine Melville Treasure," *New York Times,* December 1983, p. C17. Biographical information is drawn from Leyda, *Melville Log,* and Leon Howard, *Herman Melville: A Biography* (Berkeley and Los Angeles: University of California Press, 1951).

40. Redburn anticipates Ishmael's similarly vague confessional opening: "Some years ago – never mind how long precisely – having little or no money in my purse, and nothing particular to interest me on shore, I thought I would sail about a little and see the watery part of the world" (MD, 12). For a fine discussion of Melville's thematics of landedness and landlessness, see Larzer Ziff, *Literary Democracy: The Declaration of Cultural Independence in America* (New York: Viking Press, 1981), pp. 260–79. Ziff writes: "Since Melville's sailors go to sea principally to find the community denied them on land, they do not fear a loss of identity in becoming members of the ship's society and acceding to its regulations and rituals. Rather, they fear being locked into separateness even there" (264–5). For a reading of Melville's sea fiction that celebrates the "democratic ethos" of male friendship over the "hierarchical ethos" of captain and ship, see Robert K. Martin, *Hero, Captain, and Stranger: Male Friendship, Social Critique, and Literary Form in the Sea Novels of Herman Melville* (Chapel Hill: University of North Carolina Press, 1986). On fraternalism in Melville, see also Wilson Carey McWilliams, *The Idea of Fraternity in America* (Berkeley and Los Angeles: University of California Press, 1973), pp. 328–71.

41. William H. Gilman, *Melville's Early Life and Redburn* (New York: New York University Press, 1951), p. xxi.

42. Far more darkly, and presumptuously, the narrator of "Bartleby, the Scrivener: A Story of Wall-Street" suggests that the Tombs will provide Bartleby with an "indulgent confinement" (PT, 669)

43. On slavery and flogging in *White-Jacket* see Priscilla Allen Zirker, "Evidence of the Slavery Dilemma in *White-Jacket,*" *American Quarterly,* 18

(1966); 477–92; H. Bruce Franklin, *The Victim as Criminal and Artist: Literature from the American Prison* (New York: Oxford University Press, 1970), pp. 31–70; Ann Douglas, *The Feminization of American Culture* (1977; rpt. New York: Avon, 1978), pp. 358–67; H. Edward Stessel, "Melville's *White-Jacket*: A Case Against the 'Cat,'" *Clio*, 13 (1983): 35–55; and Rogin, *Subversive Genealogy*, pp. 90–7, 188–9. Melville was both influenced by and suspicious of Dana. Writing in the 6 March 1847 issue of the *Literary World*, Melville blamed Dana for taking the romance out of nautical romances: "At the present day the poetry of salt water is very much on the wane. The perusal of Dana's Two Years Before the Mast, for instance, somewhat impairs the relish with which we read Byron's spiritual address to the ocean" (UP, 1117). But in a 1 May 1850 letter to Dana, Melville writes of "those strange, congenial feelings, with which after my first voyage, I for the first time read 'Two Years Before the Mast,' and while so engaged was, as it were, tied & welded to you by a sort of Siamese link of affectionate sympathy" (*The Letters of Herman Melville*, ed. Merrell R. Davis and William H. Gilman [New Haven, Conn.: Yale University Press, 1960], p. 106). On Dana and Melville, see Robert F. Lucid, "The Influence of *Two Years before the Mast* on Herman Melville," *American Literature*, 31 (1959): 243–56. Also influencing *White-Jacket*'s politics and structure are McNally's *Evils and Abuses,* and Samuel Leech's *Thirty Years from Home, or A Voice from the Main Deck* (Boston: Tappan & Dennet, 1843), an account of a voyage aboard a man-of-war that presents life in the navy as a form of slavery. Leech remarks: "A casual visitor in a man of war, beholding the song, the dance, the revelry of the crew, might judge them to be happy. But I know that these things are often resorted to, because they feel miserable, just to drive away dull care. They do it on the same principle as the slave population in the South, to drown in sensual gratification the voice of misery that groans in the inner man" (74). For a discussion of the many textual sources of *White-Jacket* see Howard P. Vincent, *The Tailoring of Melville's White-Jacket* (Evanston, Ill.: Northwestern University Press, 1970).

44. Briggs, *Working a Passage,* p. 66. For Briggs, a Jacksonian countersubversive of sorts, the *Somers* case revealed that "in the midst of our boasted democracy" lurks "an absurd aristocracy" (66).

45. Rogin, *Subversive Genealogy,* p. 96.

46. Michael Davitt Bell, *The Development of American Romance: The Sacrifice of Relation* (University of Chicago Press, 1980), p. 213. In *Plot, Story, and the Novel: From Dickens and Poe to the Modern Period* (Princeton, N.J.: Princeton University Press, 1979), Robert L. Caserio argues persuasively for a relationship between Melville's resistance to representing mutiny and his antiformalist resistance to traditional plotting; see pp. 133–66.

47. Melville to Duyckinck, letter of 6 October 1850, in *The Letters of Herman Melville*, pp. 114–15. In *An Essay on Flogging in the Navy; Containing Strictures upon Existing Naval Laws and Suggesting Substitutes for the Discipline of the Lash* (New York: Pudney & Russell, 1849), John A. Lockwood called for the abolition of flogging, while making the standard concession that discipline must remain a top priority on board ship: "All admit that . . .

commanders, acting singly, should be, on their peopled deck, superior to everybody and everything – except the laws of God and of their country" (1). *White-Jacket* too concedes, "A sea-officer in command should be clothed with a degree of authority and discipline inadmissible in any master ashore" (WJ, 304). There are numerous other parallels between these texts. In an illuminating analysis, Wai-Chee S. Dimock suggests that *White-Jacket*'s dialogical structure reflects "a sociable but also a misanthropic spirit," one that is often at odds with the text's reformist and fraternal spirit; see "*White-Jacket:* Authors and Audiences," *Nineteenth-Century Fiction,* 36 (1981): 307. See also Larry J. Reynolds, "Antidemocratic Emphasis in *White-Jacket,*" *American Literature,* 48 (1976): 13–28. In *Omoo* the narrator bitterly concedes: "I do not wish to be understood as applauding the flogging system practiced in men-of-war. As long, however, as navies are needed, there is no substitute for it. War being the greatest of evils, all its accessories necessarily partake of the same character; and this is about all that can be said in defense of flogging" (O, 108).

48. McNally, *Evils and Abuses,* p. 71; Briggs, *Working a Passage,* p. 80.

49. Henry Wadsworth Longfellow, "The Building of the Ship," *The Poetical Works of Henry Wadsworth Longfellow* (Boston: Houghton, Mifflin, 1891), p. 130. On Longfellow and Mackenzie see Hans-Joachim Lang and Fritz Fleischmann, " 'All This Beauty, All This Grace': Longfellow's 'The Building of the Ship' and Alexander Slidell Mackenzie's 'Ship,' " *New England Quarterly,* 54 (1981): 104–18. As Lang and Fleischmann point out, Longfellow's "The Building of the Ship" drew on Mackenzie's 1831 *Encyclopedia Americana* entry "Ship." See also Robert S. Ward, "Longfellow and Melville: The Ship and the Whale," *Emerson Society Quarterly,* no. 22, (1961), 57–63; Robert A. Ferguson, "Longfellow's Political Fears: Civic Authority and the Role of the Artist in *Hiawatha* and *Miles Standish,*" *American Literature,* 50 (1978): 187–215; and Thomas, *Cross-examinations of Law and Literature,* pp. 151–61.

50. Longfellow "The Building of the Ship," p. 130; Theodore Parker, *The New Crime Against Humanity: A Sermon Preached at the Music Hall, in Boston, on Sunday, June 4, 1854* (Boston: Mussey, 1854), p. 70.

51. Karcher, *Shadow over the Promised Land,* p. 58.

52. Charles H. Foster, "Something in Emblems: A Reinterpretation of *Moby-Dick,*" *New England Quarterly,* 34 (1961): 281; Alan Heimert, "*Moby-Dick* and American Political Symbolism," *American Quarterly,* 15 (1963): 314. For a succinct and very helpful discussion of Melville as political allegorist, see Peter Nicholls, "Melville and Politics," *Journal of American Studies,* 21 (1987): 95–8.

53. Karcher, *Shadow over the Promised Land,* p. 55.

54. On the social dynamics of Ahab's marshaling of the crew, see Nicolaus Mills, *The Crowd in American Literature* (Baton Rouge: Louisiana State University Press, 1986), pp. 55–66.

55. John Winthrop, "A Modell of Christian Charity," in *The Puritans: A Sourcebook of Their Writings,* ed. Perry Miller and Thomas H. Johnson, 2 vols. (New York: Harper Torchbooks, 1963), 1:198. On ship-of-state im-

agery in Puritan writings see Michael Walzer, *The Revolution of the Saints: A Study in the Origins of Radical Politics* (1965; rpt. New York: Atheneum Publishers, 1968), pp. 171–83.

56. Henry David Thoreau, *Reform Papers,* ed. Wendell Glick (Princeton, N.J.: Princeton University Press, 1973), p. 98. Appealing to a "higher law," abolitionists increasingly were willing to advocate violence as part of their political program. See John Demos, "The Antislavery Movement and the Problem of Violent Means," *New England Quarterly,* 37 (1964): 501–26; Aileen S. Kraditor, *Means and Ends in American Abolitionism: Garrison and His Critics on Strategy and Tactics, 1834–1850* (New York: Vintage, 1970); Jane H. Pease and William H. Pease, "Confrontation and Abolition in the 1850s," *Journal of American History,* 58 (1971): 923–37; and James Bremer Stewart, *Holy Warriors: The Abolitionists and American Slavery* (New York: Hill & Wang, 1976).

57. Robert M. Cover, *Justice Accused: Antislavery and the Judicial Process* (New Haven, Conn.: Yale University Press, 1975), p. 251; see also pp. 249–56. For a useful overview of Shaw's legal career see Leonard W. Levy, *The Law of the Commonwealth and Chief Justice Shaw* (Cambridge, Mass.: Harvard University Press, 1957). On Shaw and Melville see Brook Thomas's excellent "The Legal Fictions of Herman Melville and Lemuel Shaw," *Critical Inquiry,* 11 (1984): 24–51.

58. Amasa Delano, *A Narrative of Voyages and Travels, in the Northern and Southern Hemispheres: Comprising Three Voyages Round the World; Together with a Voyage of Survey and Discovery, in the Pacific Ocean and Oriental Islands* (Boston: House, 1817), pp. 292, 146. It is interesting that just before aiding Cereno, Delano learned that seventeen of his seamen were malcontent ex-cons (320–1); thus he was on the alert to the prospect of mutiny and revolt aboard his own ship.

59. To avoid cluttering the page, future parenthetical page references to *Benito Cereno* in this section will not include the text abbreviation.

60. R. G. Collingwood, *The Idea of History* (1946; rpt. New York: Oxford University Press, 1970), p. 213. Georg Lukács, *The Historical Novel* (1962; rpt. Lincoln: University of Nebraska Press, 1983), makes a similar point on the relationship of past to present in historical fiction: "Without a felt relationship to the present, a portrayal of history is impossible. But this relationship, as in the case of really great historical art, does not consist in alluding to contemporary events, a practice which Pushkin cruelly ridiculed in the work of Scott's incompetent imitators, but in bringing the past to life as the prehistory of the present, in giving poetic life to those historical, social and human forces which, in the course of a long evolution, have made our present-day life what it is and as we experience it" (53).

61. Eric J. Sundquist, "Suspense and Tautology in *Benito Cereno*," *Glyph,* 8 (1981): 109. Sundquist's internal quotation is from John Seelye, *Melville: The Ironic Diagram* (Evanston, Ill.: Northwestern University Press, 1970), p. 91.

62. Collingwood, *The Idea of History,* p. 289.

63. In his earlier nautical narratives, Melville similarly conjoined physical and

social decay. In *Typee*, for example, the narrator writes of the oppressive *Dolly:* "Poor old ship! Her very looks denote her desires: how deplorably she appears! The paint on her sides, burnt up by the scorching sun, is puffed out and cracked. See the weeds she trails along with her . . . ; and every time she rises on a sea, she shows her copper torn away, or hanging in jagged strips" (T, 4–5). In *Omoo* the narrator writes that the captain of the oppressive *Julia* looks "like a sickly counting-house clerk" (O, 6) and that the ship itself is "in a miserable plight. The lower masts were said to be unsound; the standing rigging was much worn; and, in some places, even the bulwarks were quite rotten" (O, 9).

64. David Brion Davis, *The Slave Power Conspiracy and the Paranoid Style: Images of Conspiracy in the Slavery Controversy* (Baton Rouge: Louisiana State University Press, 1969). See also Eric Foner's excellent *Free Soil, Free Labor, Free Men: The Ideology of the Republican Party before the Civil War* (New York: Oxford University Press, 1970); David R. Potter, *The Impending Crisis, 1848–1861,* ed. and completed by Don E. Fehrenbacher (New York: Harper & Row, 1976), pp. 228–41, 288–9; and Michael F. Holt, *The Political Crisis of the 1850s* (New York: Wiley, 1978), pp. 28–90, 151–4, 191–258.

65. Theodore Parker, *The Nebraska Question: Some Thoughts on the New Assault upon Freedom in America, and the General State of the Country* (1854), in Parker, *Additional Speeches, Addresses, and Occasional Sermons* (Boston: Little, Brown, 1855), p. 300. In the mid-1850s, Parker became obsessed with the similarities between antirepublican imperial Spain and the American South. See the essays collected in Parker, *The Slave Power,* ed. James K. Hosmer (Boston: American Unitarian Association, 1907). For an example of a contemporaneous nativist text linking the Inquisition to Spain, see Edward Beecher, *The Papal Conspiracy Exposed: Protestantism Defended, in the Light of Reason, History, and Scripture* (New York: Dodd, 1855), which proclaimed, "We will, then, summon the bishop and our readers to a country eminently blessed with Romish influences; favored as the great head quarters of the Inquisition, which, by fire and sword and tortures ineffable, has thoroughly purged out the leaven of Protestantism. We need not say that this country is SPAIN" (174). According to the major historians of the period, Spain was an especially villainous, antirepublican power. As David Levin observes: "All the romantic historians regarded Spain and New France as grim historical exhibits of the Roman Church's influence on government and society" (*History as Romantic Art: Bancroft, Prescott, Motley, and Parkman* [New York: Harcourt, Brace & World, 1963], p. 93). Insightful readings of Spanish and Catholic themes in *Benito Cereno* can be found in John Bernstein, "*Benito Cereno* and the Spanish Inquisition," *Nineteenth-Century Fiction,* 16 (1962): 345–50; Michael T. Gilmore, *The Middle Way: Puritanism and Ideology in American Romantic Fiction* (New Brunswick, N.J.: Rutgers University Press, 1977), pp. 165–82; and Gloria Horsley-Meachim, "The Monastic Slaver: Images and Meaning in 'Benito Cereno,'" *New England Quarterly,* 56 (1983): 261–6. On the novel's thematics of expansionism and imperialism, see Allan Moore Emery, "'Benito Cereno' and Manifest Destiny," *Nineteenth-Century Fiction,* 39 (1984): 48–68.

66. The standard discussion of sectional stereotypes is William R. Taylor, *Cavalier and Yankee: The Old South and American National Character* (New York: Braziller, 1961).

67. On 1799 and San Domingo, see H. Bruce Franklin, *The Wake of the Gods: Melville's Mythology* (Stanford, Calif.: Stanford University Press, 1963), pp. 144–6; and Thomas, *Cross-examinations of Law and Literature*, pp. 105–6. Also useful is C. L. R. James, *The Black Jacobins: Toussaint L'Ouverture and the San Domingo Revolution* (New York: Vintage, 1963). Eric J. Sunquist provides an excellent analysis of the larger Caribbean revolutionary context; see his "*Benito Cereno* and New World Slavery," in *Reconstructing American Literary History,* ed. Sacvan Bercovitch (Cambridge, Mass.: Harvard University Press, 1986), pp. 93–122.

68. On reform institutionalism in the novella, see Rogin, *Subversive Genealogy,* pp. 208–20; and Sandra A. Zagarell, "Reenvisioning America: Melville's 'Benito Cereno,'" *ESQ,* 30 (1984): 249. During the 1840s and 1850s, narrative accounts of the "disorderly" urban ghetto came to constitute a new popular genre. As Stansell writes, with suggestive implications for a reading of *Benito Cereno,* reformists such as George Matsell and Charles Loring Brace presented themselves in their writings as "intrepid explorers [who] plunged into Corlears Hook as if it were a remote African settlement on the Congo, its 'mysteries' and 'horrors' tucked away from civilized knowledge" (*City of Women,* 201).

69. Delano's paternalism also resembles that of some antebellum abolitionists, such as Theodore Parker, who wrote, "The African is the most docile and pliant of all the races of men"; cited in Michael Fellman, "Theodore Parker and the Abolitionist Role in the 1850s," *Journal of American History,* 61 (1974): 680. On paternalism among Northern abolitionists, see Leon F. Litwack, *North of Slavery: The Negro in the Free States, 1790–1860* (University of Chicago Press, 1961), pp. 214–46.

70. Delano's anxious perception of "Freemasons" recalls Tommo's similar perception in *Typee.* "Although hardly a day passed while I remained on the island that I did not witness some religious ceremony or other," Tommo remarks, "it was very much like seeing a parcel of 'Freemasons' making secret signs to each other; I saw everything, but could comprehend nothing" (T, 177).

71. Melville presents Delano's confusions and racialist thinking as part of a dualistic portrayal of the captain as both the trusting good Samaritan reassured by his racist notions of white supremacy and as the scared and suspicious captain intimating mutiny and revolt. For a good discussion of this dualism, see Stewart Justman, "Repression and Self in 'Benito Cereno,'" *Studies in Short Fiction,* 15 (1978): 301–6. On *Benito Cereno* as a sort of con game in which "Melville's narrator seems bent on legitimizing Delano's errors" (168), see John Bryant, "Melville's Comic Debate: Geniality and the Aesthetic of Repose," *American Literature,* 55 (1983): esp. 164–8. Valuable discussions of Melville's narrative strategies in the novella can also be found in Warner Berthoff, *The Example of Melville* (Princeton, N.J.: Princeton University Press, 1962), pp. 150–7; William Dillingham, *Melville's*

Short Fiction, 1853–1856 (Athens: University of Georgia Press, 1977), pp. 227–70; and Sundquist, "Suspense and Tautology," 103–26.

72. Harper, *Memoir on Slavery*, pp. 76, 82. Throughout the novella, Delano's belief in the blacks' stupidity reflects the "wisdom" of the scientific racialism of the antebellum period; see William Stanton, *The Leopard's Spots: Scientific Attitudes toward Race in America* (University of Chicago Press, 1960); and Reginald Horsman, *Race and Manifest Destiny: The Origins of American Racial Anglo-Saxonism* (Cambridge, Mass.: Harvard University Press, 1981), esp. pp. 156–7. For an excellent discussion of Melville's "The 'Gees" as a parodic attack on scientific racialism, see Karcher, *Shadow over the Promised Land*, pp. 160–85.

73. To be sure, when Babo drapes Cereno in the apron of the Spanish flag, the historically aware reader may well reflect on Cereno's ties to the abuses of the Inquisition and to the institution of slavery and conclude, as Cereno squirms under Babo's razor, that the Spanish captain now gets just what he deserves (see Seeyle, *Melville, The Ironic Diagram*, p. 109). And arguably for the rereader Babo's close shave represents one of his great and revolutionary theatrical performances, one that, as with the novella's other Babo-directed scenes, offers a subversive and "artistic" challenge to the authority of slavery itself (see Rogin, *Subversive Genealogy*, pp. 215–16; and Anthony Channell Hilfer, "The Philosophy of Clothes in Melville's 'Benito Cereno,' " *Philological Quarterly*, 61 [1984]: 220–9).

But no matter how artistic, revolutionary, or properly vengeful is Babo's theatrical shaving, there is little in this disturbing scene that encourages even the experienced reader to find *sole* community with Babo. Rather, the scene powerfully suggests that Cereno too is a pitiable victim of the current situation, of his country's past abuses, of history. We need but recall Vivenza's wry observation in *Mardi*: "The soil decides the man. And, ere birth, man wills not to be born here or there" (M, 534). Of course Babo, uprooted from his soil, has far larger claims to victimization than Cereno. But his vengeful desire to perform such an extravagant piece of sadistic theater would seem to teach the Hegelian lesson (embodied at its most extreme by Oberlus, the slave turned tyrannous master of "The Encantadas") of the enslaving character of lordship; power brings with it a dependency upon the object of one's power (see G. W. F. Hegel, *The Phenomenology of Mind* [New York: Harper Torchbooks, 1967], pp. 228–40). "Ah, this slavery breeds ugly passions in man" (PT, 721), Delano muses when Cereno later nicks Babo in apparent retribution; and if that is the case, the shaving scene, more than any other scene in the novella, insists upon the outsidership of potential victims of such passions. For this reason, I believe, the figure of a black barber shaving a vulnerable white haunted even the radical abolitionist Thomas W. Higginson, a contributor to *Putnam's* during the 1850s and a probable reader of Melville's novella, who wrote in 1858, "I have wondered in times past, when I have been so weak-minded as to submit my chin to the razor of a colored brother, as his sharp steel grazed my skin, at the patience of the negro shaving the white man for many years, yet kept the razor outside of the throat" (cited in Tilden G. Edelstein,

Strange Enthusiasm: A Life of Thomas Wentworth Higginson [New Haven, Conn.: Yale University Press, 1968], p. 211). Melville's earlier references to shaving in *Redburn* and *White-Jacket* are suggestive of a similar sense of vulnerability, particularly when Redburn observes the malevolent Jackson in the process of examining a sailor's teeth: "I trembled for the poor fellow, just as if I had seen him under the hands of a crazy barber, making signs to cut his throat, and he all the while sitting stock still, with the lather on, to be shaved" (R, 60).

74. Melville's account of Delano's fraternal feelings represents a significant change from Delano's *Narrative,* for the historical Delano came to view Cereno as an ingrate who duplicitously sought to avoid paying Delano for his services.

75. James H. Kavanagh, "That Hive of Subtlety: 'Benito Cereno' and the Liberal Hero," in *Ideology and Classic American Literature,* ed. Sacvan Bercovitch and Myra Jehlen (Cambridge University Press, 1986), p. 360. Though my interpretive emphasis is different from Kavanagh's, I have profited from his Althusserian analysis of the novella's enactment of "internal distantiation."

76. Thomas, *Cross-examinations of Law and Literature,* p. 111; on the thematic implications of Melville's use of proslavery rhetoric, see also pp. 110–13.

77. T. Walter Herbert, *Marquesan Encounters: Melville and the Meaning of Civilization* (Cambridge, Mass.: Harvard University Press, 1980), p. 178.

78. Cited in Harold Beaver, "Introduction" to Edgar Allan Poe, *The Narrative of Arthur Gordon Pym of Nantucket* (Harmondsworth: Penguin Books, 1977), p. 15.

79. J. Fenimore Cooper, *The American Democrat,* ed. George Dekker and Larry Johnston (Harmondsworth: Penguin Books, 1969), pp. 223, 222. Thomas Jefferson had similarly warned in *Notes on the State of Virginia* (1785) (New York: Harper & Row, 1964) that emancipation would "divide us into parties, and produce convulsions, which will probably never end but in the extermination of the one or the other race" (132–3). For a discussion of the ideological uses of alarmist warnings of race war, see Slotkin, *The Fatal Environment,* pp. 227–41.

80. Harper, *Memoir on Slavery,* pp. 89–90.

81. Poe, *The Narrative of Arthur Gordon Pym,* pp. 192, 228, 205.

82. Beaver, "Introduction," p. 17. See also Bernard Rosenthal, "Poe, Slavery, and the *Southern Literary Messenger:* A Reexamination," *Poe Studies,* 7 (1974): 29–38.

83. J. Fenimore Cooper, *Afloat and Ashore: A Sea Tale* (New York: Garretson, Cox, n.d.), pp. 170, 183, 188. As Roy Harvey Pearce has shown, fears of "savage" blacks and Indians often overlapped; see *Savagism and Civilization: A Study of the Indian and the American Mind* (Baltimore, Md.: Johns Hopkins University Press, 1965). Cooper's conjoining of Indian and black resembles Robert Montgomery Bird's, who refers to Indians on the warpath as "red niggurs" (*sic*); see *Nick of the Woods* (1837), ed. Curtis Dahl (New Haven, Conn.: College and University Press, 1967), p. 48.

84. "About Niggers," *Putnam's,* 6 (1855): 612. The concluding section of *Benito*

Cereno begins on p. 633: "Before returning to his own vessel, Captain Delano had intended communicating to Don Benito the practical details of the proposed services to be rendered."

85. M. M. Bakhtin, *The Dialogic Imagination* (Austin: University of Texas Press, 1981), pp. 299–300.

86. See Ronald T. Takaki, *Iron Cages: Race and Culture in Nineteenth–Century America* (New York: Random House, 1979). Takaki writes, "The existence of both racial and class anxieties during the Jacksonian era may well be why the ideology of the black 'child/savage' and the 'discovery of the asylum' occurred at the same time in American society" (127). On the relationship of Delano's "blindness" to Melville's critique of the social processes of political and institutional legitimation, see also John Schaar, "The Uses of Literature for the Study of Politics: The Case of Melville's *Benito Cereno*," *Legitimacy and the Modern State* (New Brunswick, N.J.: Transaction Books, 1981), pp. 53–87.

87. Peter Berger and Thomas Luckmann, *The Social Construction of Reality: A Treatise in the Sociology of Knowledge* (New York: Doubleday, 1967), p. 98.

88. Rogin, *Subversive Genealogy*, pp. 225, 226.

89. Kavanagh, "That Hive of Subtlety," p. 362. On the black trickster, see Lawrence W. Levine, *Black Culture and Black Consciousness: Afro-American Folk Thought from Slavery to Freedom* (New York: Oxford University Press, 1977), pp. 102–32. On Babo as "mute" (mutinous) director and heroic "Jacobin" revolutionary, see Charles Swann, "Two Notes on *Benito Cereno*," *Journal of American Studies*, 19 (1985): 110–14. Bakhtin's discussion of the centrality of parody and saturnalia – "uncrowning, travesty, thrashing" (198) – to carnivalesque revolutionism sheds additional light on Babo's subversive artistry; see *Rabelais and His World* (Cambridge, Mass.: MIT Press, 1968), esp. pp. 4–81, 197–200.

90. *The Confessions of Nat Turner*, in Duff and Mitchell, *The Nat Turner Rebellion*, pp. 12, 28. The deposition in *Benito Cereno* resembles the affidavit used against the "mutineers" in *Omoo*: "Though artfully drawn up, so as to bear hard against every one of us, it was pretty correct in the details; excepting, that it was wholly silent as to the manifold derelictions of the mate himself" (O, 139).

91. There are clear indications that Aranda had been cannibalized. See John Harmon McElroy, "Cannibalism in Melville's *Benito Cereno*," *Essays in Literature*, 1 (1974): 206–18; and Barbara J. Baines, "Ritualized Cannibalism in 'Benito Cereno': Melville's 'Black-Letter' Texts," *ESQ*, 30 (1984): 161–9. For a discussion of the centrality of feasting to revolutionary carnival, see Bakhtin, *Rabelais and His World*, pp. 8–11.

92. Given that, as Don E. Fehrenbacher notes, the 1850s saw an "increasing formalism and casuistry in the public debate over slavery" (*The Dred Scott Case: Its Significance in American Law and Politics* [New York: Oxford University Press, 1978], p. 196), Melville no doubt believed that it was of crucial importance for Americans to learn how to read juridical narratives. And because the Spanish had imported slavery to the New World, their legal practices were especially relevant to American legal practices. On

Spain's obsession with the legal and bureaucratic aspects of sustaining slavery in the Americas, see Charles Gibson, *Spain in America* (New York: Harper Torchbook, 1967), pp. 110–11. On the ways in which the "deposition undercuts the authority it tries to assert" (99), see Thomas, *Cross-examinations of Law and Literature*, pp. 99–102.

93. Though the violence in the novella is horrible, equally ghastly is the violence in Delano's *Narrative*. After capturing the blacks, the Spanish torture them, and Cereno himself vengefully stabs one of the blacks. As in *Benito Cereno*, Delano acts to stop the carnage: "Thus I was obliged to be continually vigilant, to prevent them [the Spanish enslavers] from using violence towards these wretched creatures" (328). The grim irony, of course, is that Delano protects the blacks from a "savage" violence only to release them to the "civilized" Spanish courts, which order them tortured and executed.

94. Harriet Beecher Stowe, *Uncle Tom's Cabin or, Life Among the Lowly* (Harmondsworth: Penguin Books, 1981), p. 391. On the abolitionists' belief that power was an atavistic intoxicant, see Ronald Walters, "The Erotic South: Civilization and Sexuality in American Abolitionism," *American Quarterly*, 25 (1973): 177–201; and James B. Stewart, "Heroes, Villains, Liberty and License," in *Antislavery Reconsidered*, ed. Perry and Fellman, esp. pp. 169–70.

95. Bernard Rosenthal, "Melville's Island," *Studies in Short Fiction*, 11 (1974): 8. On historical themes in *Benito Cereno*, see also George Dekker, *The American Historical Romance* (Cambridge University Press, 1987), pp. 197–208.

96. Following the bloody battle between the *Bon Homme Richard* and the *Serapis* in *Israel Potter*, the narrator asks rhetorically: "In view of this battle one may well ask – What separates the enlightened man from the savage? Is civilization a thing distinct, or is it an advanced state of barbarism?" (IP, 130).

Walter Benjamin writes, "There is no document of civilization which is not at the same time a document of barbarism" (*Illuminations* [New York: Schocken, 1969], p. 256). *Benito Cereno*, I have been arguing, offers a pedagogy on this paradox. For an application of Benjamin's ideas to *The Scarlet Letter*, see Jonathan Arac, "The Politics of *The Scarlet Letter*," in *Ideology and Classic American Literature*, ed. Bercovitch and Jehlen, pp. 247–66.

97. George B. Forgie, *Patricide in the House Divided: A Psychological Interpretation of Lincoln and His Age* (New York: Norton, 1979), p. 191.

98. See Stephen E. Maizlish, "The Meaning of Nativism and the Crisis of the Union: The Know-Nothing Movement in the Antebellum North," in *Essays on American Politics, 1840–1860*, ed. Maizlish and John J. Kushman (College Station: Texas A&M University Press, 1982), pp. 166–98; and William E. Gienapp, "Nativism and the Creation of a Republican Majority in the North before the Civil War," *Journal of American History*, 72 (1985): 529–59.

99. Robert A. Ferguson, *Law and Letters in American Culture* (Cambridge, Mass.: Harvard University Press, 1984), p. 313; see also pp. 305–17.

100. Nathaniel Hawthorne, *The Life of Franklin Pierce* (1852; rpt. Cambridge, Mass.: Riverside Press, 1900), p. 166.

101. Abraham Lincoln, "Second Inaugural Address," in *Abraham Lincoln: Selected Speeches, Messages, and Letters,* ed. T. Harry Williams (New York: Holt, Rinehart & Winston, 1964), p. 283.

102. Lincoln, "First Inaugural Address, in *Abraham Lincoln,* ed. Williams, pp. 146, 148; Lincoln, "Second Inaugural Address," p. 283; Nathaniel Hawthorne, *Our Old Home: A Series of English Sketches* (1863), ed. Roy Harvey Pearce, Fredson Bowers, and L. Neal Smith (Columbus: Ohio State University Press, 1970), p. 4.

103. Ferguson, *Law and Letters,* p. 314.

104. For a good overview of the voluminous criticism on *Billy Budd,* see Merton M. Sealts, Jr., "Innocence and Infamy: *Billy Budd, Sailor,*" in *A Companion to Melville Studies,* ed. John Bryant (Westport, Conn.: Greenwood, 1986), pp. 407–30. Recent writings on *Budd* that have influenced my thinking include Barbara Johnson, "Melville's Fist: The Execution of *Billy Budd,*" *The Critical Difference: Essays in the Contemporary Rhetoric of Reading* (Baltimore, Md.: Johns Hopkins University Press, 1980), pp. 79–109; Rogin, *Subversive Genealogy,* pp. 288–316; Thomas, "The Legal Fictions of Herman Melville" and *Cross-examinations of Law and Literature,* pp. 201–50; Richard H. Weisberg, *The Failure of the Word: The Protagonist as Lawyer in Modern Fiction* (New Haven, Conn.: Yale University Press, 1984), pp. 133–76; John P. McWilliams, Jr., *Hawthorne, Melville, and the American Character: A Looking-glass Business* (Cambridge University Press, 1984), pp. 201–25; and William B. Dillingham, *Melville's Later Novels* (Athens: University of Georgia Press, 1986), pp. 365–99.

Epilogue

Epigraph: Josiah Strong, *Our Country: Its Possible Future and Its Present Crisis* (New York: American Home Missionary Society, 1885), p. 30.

1. Henry James, *Hawthorne* (1879; rpt. Ithaca, N.Y.: Cornell University Press, 1956), p. 114.

2. David Brion Davis, *The Fear of Conspiracy: Images of Un-American Subversion from the Revolution to the Present* (Ithaca, N.Y.: Cornell University Press, 1971), pp. 149, 205. On the politics of countersubversion in twentieth-century American culture, see Michael Paul Rogin, *Ronald Reagan, the Movie: and Other Episodes in Political Demonology* (Berkeley and Los Angeles: University of California Press, 1987), pp. 44–80.

3. See Mark Seltzer, "*The Princess Casamassima:* Realism and the Fantasy of Surveillance," in *American Realism: New Essays,* ed. Eric J. Sundquist (Baltimore, Md.: Johns Hopkins University Press, 1982), pp. 95–118; Amy Kaplan, " 'The Knowledge of the Line': Realism and the City in Howells's *A Hazard of New Fortunes,*" *PMLA,* 101 (1986): 69–81; and June Howard, *Form and History in American Literary Naturalism* (Chapel Hill: University of North Carolina Press, 1985).

4. John Higham, *Strangers in the Land: Patterns of American Nativism 1860–1925* (1955; rpt. New York: Atheneum Publishers, 1978), p. ii.

Index